The L
and Spirit
of Biblical
Interpretation

The Letter *and* Spirit of Biblical Interpretation

From the Early Church to Modern Practice

KEITH D. STANGLIN

B
Baker Academic
a division of Baker Publishing Group
Grand Rapids, Michigan

Published by Baker Academic
a division of Baker Publishing Group
PO Box 6287, Grand Rapids, MI 49516-6287
www.bakeracademic.com

Printed in the United States of America

Library of Congress Cataloging-in-Publication Data
Names: Stanglin, Keith D., author.
Title: The letter and spirit of biblical interpretation : from the early church to modern practice / Keith D. Stanglin.
Description: Grand Rapids : Baker Publishing Group, 2018. | Includes bibliographical references and index.
Identifiers: LCCN 2018005064 | ISBN 9780801049682 (pbk. : alk. paper)
Subjects: LCSH: Bible—Criticism, interpretation, etc.—History.
Classification: LCC BS500 .S73 2018 | DDC 220.609—dc23
LC record available at https://lccn.loc.gov/2018005064

In keeping with biblical principles of creation stewardship, Baker Publishing Group advocates the responsible use of our natural resources. As a member of the Green Press Initiative, our company uses recycled paper when possible. The text paper of this book is composed in part of post-consumer waste.

18 19 20 21 22 23 24   7 6 5 4 3 2 1

for Amanda,
two wonderful decades in

Contents

Preface

When people have asked me what I am reading about, or which course I am teaching, or what the subject of this book is, and my answer is the "history of interpretation," I have noticed a facial expression that, as a historical theologian, I have become accustomed to seeing. Their look, or sometimes their accompanying explanation of it, conveys the message that both history and interpretation are sufficiently boring on their own, and the combination of the two must be dreadful. To ask about the history of biblical interpretation, however, is to ponder very important questions for our own day. How has the church viewed the Bible? How have the perspectives of the past influenced the way we read the Bible? And, in light of the different ways that Christians have read the Bible, what is the proper method of interpreting the Bible, of "rightly handling the word of truth" (2 Tim. 2:15)? What are our goals in biblical interpretation? What questions do we—or should we—bring to Scripture?

In some respects, the present study is something like an extension of David Steinmetz's celebrated and often anthologized article "The Superiority of Pre-critical Exegesis," which I first read way back in graduate school and to which I owe a great debt for articulating plainly what I was already thinking at the time. It is, I believe, a model of accurate historical description of premodern exegesis coupled with a keen interest in what the past can teach us today. Such are the aims of my book.

This book, lying at the intersection of church history and biblical interpretation, is directed primarily to readers who are specialists in neither discipline but have some interest in both. At the risk of being too specific, perhaps the ideal reader is a student who has had about one course in each area. But the goal is to reach anyone interested in either one of these topics, including students, ministers, and scholars.

I have had the pleasure of lecturing on the history of biblical interpretation not only to my own students but also in a variety of settings in the classroom and beyond, including at Harding University and Pepperdine University. After I delivered one of those guest lectures to Danny Mathews's class at Pepperdine in 2011, he, never lacking for ideas, suggested to me that I should write a brief book surveying the topic. I had too many other projects going at the time and obviously did not get around to it immediately, but he deserves the credit (or the blame) for proposing it, though the final product is longer than either of us intended. Short little books about big ideas always seem to grow, but I have tried to keep it under control.

My writing became more serious (temporarily) in the summer of 2015, during a brief fellowship at the Wesleyan Center at Point Loma Nazarene University, San Diego. My thanks go to Mark Mann, director of the Wesleyan Center, for inviting me for that second stay and making arrangements for my summer scholar lecture, "How to Read the Bible: Then and Now." He also ensured that my family was accommodated once again with an unbeatable ocean view. Closer to the end of the project, my research and writing were aided by a sabbatical granted by the administration and faculty of Austin Graduate School of Theology in the spring of 2017, for which and to whom I am grateful.

In addition to informal conversations about this book with friends, family, and colleagues over the last few years, several people have interacted directly with earlier drafts of this manuscript. My colleagues at Austin Grad listened (mostly) patiently as I read through a couple of chapters and bounced different outlines off them. Others have likewise given generously of their time and effort by reading through drafts of chapters at various stages and offering valuable feedback: Mark Elliott, Michael Legaspi, Peter Leithart, David Wilhite, Robert Louis Wilken, John Wright, and Mike Young. I am in their debt.

Throughout the entire process, it has been a genuine privilege to work with Dave Nelson at Baker Academic. His recommendations (never demands), along with his patience, sincerity, encouragement, support, and humor—at a distance and in person—always struck the right chord at the right time. Providence must have known that I needed to work with an editor who would understand and appreciate my obscure references to classic rock. Dave, Brian Bolger, and all the editorial staff at Baker Academic have helped this book to be better than it otherwise would have been.

In this month of historically significant and recognizable anniversaries, I cannot help mentioning that Amanda has (been) stuck with me officially for twenty years this month. She, together with Paul, Isaac, and Rachel, as they all well know, are my joy and love. I am so proud of them, and they are a constant blessing from the Father above. They deserve the utmost thanks simply for putting up with me on a daily basis. As usual, they bore the brunt of the book storm and could always be trusted in the last weeks to ask me whether the book was finished. I needed that.

Keith Stanglin
Austin, Texas
October 2017

Abbreviations

ACCS	Ancient Christian Commentary on Scripture. Downers Grove, IL: Inter-Varsity, 1998–2010
ACW	Ancient Christian Writers. New York: Newman Press/Mahwah, NJ: Paulist Press, 1946–
ad	replies (by Thomas Aquinas) to objections
AD	anno Domini, in the year of our Lord
ANF	*Ante-Nicene Fathers*
BC	before Christ
BDAG	Danker, Frederick W., Walter Bauer, William F. Arndt, and F. Wilbur Gingrich. *Greek-English Lexicon of the New Testament and Other Early Christian Literature*. 3rd ed. Chicago: University of Chicago Press, 2000
ca.	circa
CC	Calvin's Commentaries. Reprint, Grand Rapids: Baker, 1979
cf.	*confer*, compare
Civ.	*De civitate Dei* (*The City of God*), by Augustine
co.	company
col.	column
CWE	*Collected Works of Erasmus*. Toronto: University of Toronto Press, 1974–
CWS	Classics of Western Spirituality. Mahwah, NJ: Paulist Press, 1978–
d.	died
ed(s).	edition, editor(s)
e.g.	*exempli gratia*, for example
ET	English translation
et al.	*et alii*, and others
FC	Fathers of the Church. Washington, DC: Catholic University of America Press, 1947–

fl.	flourished
fol(s).	folios
Haer.	*Adversus haereses* (*Elenchos*) (*Against Heresies*), by Irenaeus
Hist. eccl.	*Historia ecclesiastica* (*Ecclesiastical History*), by Eusebius
Inst.	*Institutes of the Christian Religion*, by John Calvin
LCL	Loeb Classical Library
LW	*Luther's Works*. American Edition. St. Louis: Concordia/Minneapolis: Fortress, 1955–86
LXX	Septuagint
n(n).	note(s)
NETS	*A New English Translation of the Septuagint* (see bibliography at Pietersma and Wright). http://ccat.sas.upenn.edu/nets/edition/
NIV	New International Version
no(s).	number(s)
NPNF[1]	*Nicene and Post-Nicene Fathers*, Series 1. Edited by P. Schaff. 14 vols. 1886–1889. Reprint, Grand Rapids: Eerdmans, 1979–
NPNF[2]	*Nicene and Post-Nicene Fathers*, Series 2. Edited by P. Schaff and H. Wace. 14 vols. 1890–1900. Reprint, Peabody, MA: Hendrickson, 1994
PG	Patrologia Graeca. Edited by J.-P. Migne. 161 vols. Paris, 1857–86
PL	Patrologia Latina. Edited by J.-P. Migne. 217 vols. Paris, 1844–55
Princ.	*De principiis* (*Peri archōn*) (*On First Principles*), by Origen
resp.	response (by Thomas Aquinas)
ST	*Summa theologiae*, by Thomas Aquinas
trans.	translated by
vol(s).	volume(s)
WSA	*Works of Saint Augustine*. Hyde Park, NY: New City Press, 1990–

1

Introduction to the History of Biblical Interpretation

If you prefer to be strong spiritually rather than clever in debate, if you seek sustenance for the soul rather than mere titillation of the intellect, read and reread the ancient commentators in preference to all others, since their piety is more proven, their learning more profuse and more experienced, their style neither jejune nor impoverished, and their interpretation more fitted to the sacred mysteries.

—Desiderius Erasmus of Rotterdam[1]

Church history as the history of the interpretation of Holy Scripture is thus the history of the continued living presence of that same Jesus Christ who was crucified under Pontius Pilate and rose again.

—Gerhard Ebeling[2]

For many educated Christians interested in the study of Scripture, including preachers and many professional scholars, it may never have occurred to them to ask how ancient or medieval Christians interpreted the Bible. If it has, then it may mean nothing more than mere historical interest in seeing how people long ago interpreted Scripture before they discovered a better,

1. Erasmus, *Handbook of the Christian Soldier* (CWE 66:35).
2. Ebeling, *The Word of God and Tradition*, 30.

more scientific way of approaching the text. But of what practical use to us is an ancient method of interpretation? Why should the church today look to the distant past for models of biblical interpretation? Why should we care?

Ressourcement and Exegesis

Let us begin an answer to this question with a psalm. The Psalter was the worship book of Israel and of the early church. For millennia, God's people have turned to its pages for inspiration and comfort. This collection contains some of the most affective texts in all of Scripture. Psalm 137, composed during the time of Judah's exile, is a poignant example of the emotion of the Psalter:

> [1]By the rivers of Babylon we sat and wept
>   when we remembered Zion.
> [2]There on the poplars
>   we hung our harps,
> [3]for there our captors asked us for songs,
>   our tormentors demanded songs of joy;
>   they said, "Sing us one of the songs of Zion!"
> [4]How can we sing the songs of the LORD
>   while in a foreign land?
> [5]If I forget you, Jerusalem,
>   may my right hand forget its skill.
> [6]May my tongue cling to the roof of my mouth
>   if I do not remember you,
> if I do not consider Jerusalem
>   my highest joy.
> [7]Remember, LORD, what the Edomites did
>   on the day Jerusalem fell.
> "Tear it down," they cried,
>   "tear it down to its foundations!"
> [8]Daughter Babylon, doomed to destruction,
>   happy is the one who repays you
>   according to what you have done to us.
> [9]Happy is the one who seizes your infants
>   and dashes them against the rocks. (NIV)

Imprecatory psalms, so named for their imprecations or curse language, are common in the Psalter. Psalm 137 is an imprecatory psalm at its best, or its worst.

Imagine that you are a student interested in studying Scripture, interpreting it, and applying it to your life. You are also a Christian, who considers

Scripture to be more than simply a historical document, but also your primary rule of faith and practice. What do you make of this passage? Yes, it tells us something about the conditions and emotions of exiled Israel, but how can we as Christians sing this? David Steinmetz imagines a medieval priest trying to relate to this difficult psalm.[3] It is no less difficult for us today. I don't know about you, but I have not been wronged by Babylon (Ps. 137:3). I would like to visit Jerusalem someday, but it is not "my highest joy" (137:6). I don't have a particular beef against the Edomites (137:7). And I have never expressed a desire, or even entertained the thought, of dashing babies against the rocks (137:9).

Imagine that you have just run across this or an equally challenging text in your personal study of Scripture. What do you do? Do you say, "Here's what *I* think it means. Here's how *I* will apply it." What is wrong with that picture?

The problem is the individualism, the presumed authority of the individual. One cannot plumb the depths of God's Word or of theology without discussing it with others in community. Christ called his disciples to be in community. Indeed, the very meaning of "church" (ἐκκλησία, *ekklēsia*) is gathering, or assembly. An old adage states that one Christian is no Christian (*unus Christianus, nullus Christianus*). An isolated, solitary Christian is not practicing the Christian faith as it was intended. Bible reading and study, like prayer, can be done individually, but not exclusively so. When you encounter a difficult passage, do you have peers who might have an insight? Do you consult teachers? Commentaries? What about a church community? Biblical interpretation was never meant to be done in isolation. It is a communal task. As iron sharpens iron, we challenge each other's interpretations and applications. I have perspective that you do not have, and vice versa. I have blinders that you do not have, and vice versa.

So biblical interpretation ought to be done in community. But there is a part of this community of interpretation that has not yet been mentioned. We usually neglect these members of the community because they are the easiest to ignore. They are easy to ignore because they are dead. And the longer they have been dead, the more we tend to ignore them. The longer they have been dead, the more out of touch they are with our language and our culture and our problems and our addictions and our needs. And I would argue that this is exactly why we need to hear them. We must listen precisely *because* their perspective and their blinders are so different from ours. When we listen to them, sometimes we see why we interpret some Scriptures the way we do, or

---

3. This paragraph is inspired by Steinmetz, "Superiority of Pre-critical Exegesis," 29, who imagines a medieval priest trying to read and apply Ps. 137.

sometimes we see a new and fresh path that is really quite old. More often than not, these are the people whose knowledge of Scripture, devotion, and piety, whose wisdom and trust in God, would put us all to shame. Why wouldn't we want to hear such people? Why would we have a preference only for the latest commentaries or for the opinions of the people "who happen to be walking around"? To study the history of exegesis is to give a voice to the most marginalized of all; it is, to borrow the famous words of G. K. Chesterton, "the democracy of the dead."[4]

The point here is that the community of interpretation extends to those who are not us and who are not like us. Believers throughout history make up an important part of our interpretive community and, through the study of what Everett Ferguson calls "historical foreground," they can provide helpful perspective on the interpretation of Scripture.[5] The discipline is similar to Hans-Georg Gadamer's concept of the history of effects (*Wirkungsgeschichte*), which asks, What effects has the text had on subsequent generations? There is much to commend the study of reception history, or the history of biblical interpretation, inasmuch as Christian history is full of people who have labored hard to understand Scripture. What did they say? How did they interpret and apply the hard texts of Scripture?

In recent decades, Roman Catholics and Protestants alike have shown increasing appreciation for the communion of the saints past and have witnessed a marked rise of interest in the history of the church for the sake of understanding theology in general. This *ressourcement* is a returning to the sources of the early church for the sake of renewal today.[6] Through increased ecumenical contact and attention to tradition, many churches have begun to rediscover and recover ancient liturgical forms and theological norms. This renewed interest in the Christian past has also included increased engagement with premodern—that is, patristic, medieval, and Reformation—methods of biblical interpretation. The interaction is unavoidable for anyone who reads older theology, for, with few exceptions, premodern theology is a constant interaction with Scripture.

The interest in ancient approaches to theology and exegesis also comes at a time when the historical-critical method of exegesis has come under fire. The limitations of the historical-critical method as a tool for the church (which never was its purpose anyway), along with its weaknesses as a means for providing

---

4. Chesterton, *Orthodoxy*, 207.

5. See Ferguson, "Using Historical Foreground in New Testament Interpretation," 254–63.

6. *Ressourcement* refers specifically to a movement in Roman Catholicism to retrieve the thought of the church fathers for theological enrichment today. The term is applied more broadly to any retrieval of older (usually premodern) theology and its sources.

objective textual meaning (which was its sole purpose), are now widely recognized. As a reactionary alternative that takes such limitations seriously, subjective methods of interpretation, including the variety of so-called postmodern perspectives, have been introduced but also have been met with widespread discontent. The inability of any one of these methods to "do it all" or to attract a majority of adherents in the church and academy has further strengthened the turn toward the theological, as opposed to narrowly historical, interpretation of Scripture as a viable option.[7] There exists now a plethora of literature on the theological interpretation of Scripture and a growing mound of commentaries that explicitly employ such an approach. Along with the growing popularity of theological interpretation comes the recognition that premodern interpreters are excellent models for theological interpretation.

In short, these two pursuits—*ressourcement* and theological interpretation of Scripture—are fueling interest in older, premodern approaches to Scripture. This interest implies a rejection of the individualistic approach to the Bible that has characterized much of evangelical Protestantism. It also implies a growing consensus that the history of interpretation can be a means to better exegesis today.

The Challenge of Premodern Exegesis

The first point, then, is to admit learned Christians of all times and places into the community of faith. This admission, however, raises a problem. As with other beliefs and practices of the ancient church, there is an initial strangeness also when we encounter the exegetical techniques of early Christians. When we compare the basic exegetical techniques of professional interpreters today to those of Christian antiquity, there seems to be a fairly wide chasm. What they did with the Bible is not what I was taught to do with the Bible. As a friend of mine puts it, "I'm a big enthusiast for patristic exegesis in theory, and I want to find their exegesis illuminating. But when I turn to actual examples of patristic interpretation, what am I to do with some of their allegorical interpretations?" I doubt that he is alone. The initial excitement for the endeavor is lost, as it appears from our modern perspective, in so many decontextualized and metaphysical discourses. The reason for the disenchantment may be summed up in one word: allegory.

7. Although it is generally recognized when it is seen, defining "theological interpretation" of Scripture is notoriously difficult. Stephen Fowl's description is useful: "In brief, I take the theological interpretation of scripture to be that practice whereby theological concerns and interests inform and are informed by a reading of scripture." Fowl, introduction to *Theological Interpretation of Scripture*, xiii.

Contempt for allegory as a biblical hermeneutic runs deep in Protestant blood. Beginning with Martin Luther and continuing through other sixteenth-century Reformers, the Protestant and humanist polemic against the Roman Church was frequently connected with the rejection of certain allegorical readings of Scripture. The popular conception that the Protestant Reformers totally abandoned allegory in favor of a historical-critical approach to the Bible is overly simplistic. Yet the gradual triumph of this putatively more objective method is due primarily to early modern Protestant efforts. The rejection of allegorical interpretation became one of the unquestioned doctrines that united the majority of late modern Protestants, from the self-described "fundamentalists," through evangelical and mainline groups, to the self-described "liberals."

To give merely one example of the common Protestant bias against premodern exegetical methods, one may note the comments made about allegory in a popular evangelical survey of church history by Earle Cairns. Speaking of the ancient Alexandrian school of interpretation, the author writes, "Instead of emphasizing a grammatico-historical interpretation of the Bible, they developed an allegorical system of interpretation that has plagued Christianity since that time. This type of interpretation is based on the supposition that Scripture has more than one meaning."[8] Although there was no "grammatico-historical" method, as he imagines it, that was followed in the ancient church, for Cairns, "allegory"—and the concomitant assumption of multiple senses in Scripture—is the bogeyman. He faults Origen and Ambrose for their allegorical method.[9] Cairns later contrasts Jacques Lefèvre d'Étaples's "literal and spiritual interpretation of the Bible" with "the study of the text of the Bible," as if they are mutually exclusive enterprises.[10] Cairns's confusion is further evident in his denigration of some Radical Reformers whose "*literal* interpretation . . . often led to mystical or chiliastic excesses."[11] His readers are not treated to the right way to interpret the Bible, but they are left with the distinct impression that few premodern interpreters did it well. Protestants (the theologically conservative and otherwise) have thus predominantly rejected allegory and advocated a grammatico-historical, or historical-critical, method of biblical exegesis.

Now that many Protestants have seen the value of, in Steinmetz's words, "taking the long view,"[12] perhaps Cairns's blunt dismissal of premodern exegesis is passé. To be sure, traditional Protestant and evangelical prejudice

8. Cairns, *Christianity through the Centuries*, 108.
9. Cairns, *Christianity through the Centuries*, 110, 138.
10. Cairns, *Christianity through the Centuries*, 256.
11. Cairns, *Christianity through the Centuries*, 299–300, emphasis added.
12. Steinmetz, *Taking the Long View*.

against premodern and allegorical exegetical methods is not as widespread or as strong as it once was. But the reason behind it still lingers. To chase another metaphor, we have made room at the table for these others and acknowledged the value of their input. The remaining problem, though, is that we don't quite understand that input. Once we have given these older saints a place at the table, how are we to understand them? What is it that they contribute? How are we to bridge the cultural gaps? Because of our own cultural predilections and training, we are not fluently bilingual. Interest alone has failed to provide a fair account and evaluation of these methods.

Publishers and translators have made tremendous progress in the initial step of bringing these voices to the table. A greater number of primary sources and of examples of premodern exegesis are available now than ever before. In addition to new translations of older commentaries, there are series of anthologies on each book of the Bible.[13] Like a standard commentary, these volumes go through each book of the Bible, but instead of offering the new comments of a living scholar, they collect remarks from premodern Christian theologians on those same biblical texts. They make the sources available, yet aside from introductory statements, they don't usually clarify what readers are to do with the material. Many important points frequently go unmentioned in the use and promotion of such books. What exactly were the interpretive methods of the early church that are being modeled? How do these approaches differ from modern methods of exegesis? What are today's readers to make of these differences, and how can premodern methods be appropriated with benefit today? Even when the prefatory material addresses such questions, most readers will inevitably do what consumers of commentaries typically do: turn to the passage in question, not the editorial introduction, to find help.

To offer one example from the popular Ancient Christian Commentary, the comment at Genesis 14:14 includes the following excerpt from Ambrose of Milan: "When Abraham learned of this, he counted his servants born in the house and with 318 men won a victory and liberated his nephew. . . . He chose, in fact, those whom he judged worthy to belong to the number of the faithful who were to believe in the passion of our Lord Jesus Christ. Indeed, the letter *T* in Greek means 'three hundred,' and the sum *IH*—ten plus eight— expresses the name of Jesus. So Abraham conquered in virtue of faith, not through the strength of a numerous army."[14]

---

13. See, e.g., Ancient Christian Commentary on Scripture (ACCS) (InterVarsity), Reformation Commentary on Scripture (IVP Academic), and The Church's Bible (Eerdmans).

14. Ambrose, *On Abraham* 1.3.15, quoted in Sheridan, *Genesis 12–50*, 23. For further discussion of a similar interpretation of this text, see below, in chap. 2 under the heading "*Epistle of Barnabas* and the New Testament."

What is a modern biblical interpreter, student, or preacher supposed to do with these early Christian comments, which in some ways are very different from what one would find in a modern commentary? Ambrose's remarks can be downright disorienting. The section's introduction is not entirely helpful in figuring out how Ambrose gets there. A concise footnote adds information about Greek numerals and explains that there is a tradition behind Ambrose's comments. But excerpts like these could very easily leave modern readers puzzled. It should be clear that I am not criticizing the commentary or its editor. A full explanation at every turn would expand each volume into a dozen. The first step has been accomplished: Ambrose has been brought to the table, but he is not speaking our language. More is needed by way of translation.

What is true of Ambrose's approach in particular is also true of premodern exegesis in general. In comparison with the notes in our most recent study Bibles, our ancient predecessors in the faith often have very different things to say about Scripture, and it is not always clear to the modern reader why they say such things. It is necessary, therefore, to learn their language and idiom in order to understand and engage their reading and application of Scripture. Only then can we move on to discover what it could mean for our own reading, interpretation, and preaching.

This Book

This book is a short history of biblical interpretation that describes the shift from premodern to modern exegesis and then assesses the implications of this shift for reading, interpreting, and applying Scripture. In other words, historically, this study is concerned not simply with premodern interpretation but also with the shift to modern exegesis and how and why it happened. The chief motivating question behind this study may be summarized thus: "How, then, do we learn from modern historical interpretations of Scripture while also drawing on the church's premodern traditions of biblical interpretation?"[15] In other words, what can we learn from both premodern and modern approaches to Scripture? In order to address this question, an entire set of preliminary questions must be asked and answered: What are the premodern and modern approaches? How and why do they differ from one another? How can we understand and appropriate some of the more foreign aspects of the premodern approaches? When and how did the transition from premodern to modern exegesis take place? What was at stake? Are the two approaches compatible? Only after these issues have been handled

15. Davis and Hays, "Nine Theses on the Interpretation of Scripture," 3.

can we return to the initial concern about employing aspects of premodern and modern interpretation.

To tell this story, it is necessary to describe both the premodern and the modern methods of exegesis and to provide analysis along the way. For readers who may be unfamiliar with the broad contours of the history of biblical interpretation, it may be helpful to briefly consider how the Bible has been interpreted throughout the majority of church history and contrast it with modern, historical-critical exegesis. It is good to have a general idea of where the story is headed.

For premodern Christians, the reading of Scripture was primarily a liturgical act done in a liturgical context. Readers felt guided by the Holy Spirit to acquire true meaning, but not necessarily the sole meaning. The most important thing to understand from Scripture is its spiritual or mystical meaning. They believed that Scripture is inspired and is the word of God to the church in every age. Historical context was important, and the narratives were usually taken at face value, but if God is also the author of Scripture, then the meaning of Scripture is not necessarily restricted to the intent of the human author. And above all, as a word to the church, Scripture must be edifying to the church. It must speak to us. In the historic church, when the plain sense of Scripture did not edify or nurture or instruct in the way expected, then Christians sought a deeper sense of Scripture. Patristic and medieval exegesis is often associated with allegory, but it is also much more than simple allegory. Church tradition and the teaching office of the church were often authoritative for interpretation.

In contrast, the primary context of modern exegesis—by which I mean what is often called the historical-critical method—was and is academic and scientific. With modern readings of Scripture, interpretation came to mean accessing the one true meaning. The modern, historical-critical method sought only the truth of authorial intent. Whatever the original human author meant is the only thing a text can mean. Historical and cultural contextualization of the text is of utmost importance. Authorial intent entails reconstructing the psychology of the author and, because of increased skepticism about the text, the full history and previous authors behind the text. Although it is an impossible, conjectural task, it became the only criterion of meaning in the text. As a result of the Enlightenment, objectivity and detachment became prerequisites for interpreting a text. But the more the Protestant church focused its attention on Scripture as not only the primary—but the sole—source of truth and the deposit of the faith (explicitly excluding the voice of tradition), the more it focused on the literal reading. Both liberals and fundamentalists were united in their rejection of a fuller, spiritual sense. Authority for interpretation was decentralized, leading to a proliferation of individualistic, diverse, and contradictory interpretations.

Throughout the book, more shape will be given to these broad strokes. The descriptions of the exegetical principles and approaches at work in each age will be illustrated in certain figures. The book's structure is roughly chronological. It first describes the primary features and ends of premodern interpretation, focusing on the aspects that contrast with those of modern interpretation. That is, how did early Christians read the Bible, and how is it so different from the way we tend to read it? Then the book summarizes how and why the shift occurred that led to a different way of interpreting the Bible.

The central idea that these episodes will reflect is that the modern emphasis on the literal sense of the Bible and its focus on human authorial intention supplanted the premodern emphasis on spiritual senses and the ongoing significance of Scripture to the faith and practice of the church. In other words, rather than a balance in what may be dubbed "literal-spiritual" interpretation, modern exegesis devalued the spiritual dimension of Scripture.

One of my primary goals as a teacher of church history is to help students develop a historical perspective of the faith. One implication of such a perspective is that, as a historian, one must be open to differences. Depending on the object of study, this often means openness to a different time period, a different language, a different culture, a different worldview, and a different set of beliefs and motivations than our own. If there is going to be any degree of understanding on the part of the historian, there must be a corresponding degree of sympathy or at least desire to walk a mile in another's moccasins. The historian must be, as it were, bilingual. This, of course, is not meant literally, although being literally bilingual certainly helps. As students of history, it is our task to get as close to that "other" context as possible, in order then to understand and communicate the similarities and differences relative to our own context. We must be good tourists, letting the others speak for themselves and trying to understand before dismissing.

A disposition of historical hermeneutical charity will be needed when confronting premodern interpreters who speak a different language, literally and figuratively. It means beginning with the assumption that the writers themselves were rational and seeking truth. As such, some attention will be devoted to examples of premodern interpretations that appear to be outlandish at first glance but, on closer investigation, make better sense in their context. In this way, this book is intended to be an aid to *ressourcement*, a manual for how and why one should use premodern commentaries and anthologies. Much progress has been made with the first step of bringing the voices of the past to the table. More remains to be done in making those voices comprehensible to nonspecialists. By introducing readers to premodern exegesis, this study is intended to help fill that gap.

This book will offer reflections on how contemporary readers can learn from both premodern and modern ways of reading Scripture. It is an exercise in retrieval theology—that is, not simply replicating or repristinating older theology, but taking the best of theology and, in this case, the best of biblical interpretation from the past and allowing it to inform our own theology and biblical interpretation today. At the same time, there is a caution to be observed. As we come to find out why we read the Bible the way we do, sometimes we find that we are mistaken. Seeing some mistaken interpretations from the past should give us humility about some of our own treasured interpretations that may be influenced too much by surrounding culture. The goal here is to provide critical understanding of and appreciation for both premodern and modern exegesis. The book will suggest a way forward that tries to take the best from both methods, seeking a balanced and fruitful interaction between the letter and the spirit.

It is appropriate to add some precautionary notes about the method pursued in this study. All writing of history is selective. Some monographs attempt to tell only a small part of the history of biblical interpretation, focusing on one figure or one period. Others attempt the more encyclopedic task of introducing every significant figure in the history. The more comprehensive they are in scope and detail, however, the less accessible and manageable they become to the nonspecialist.[16] Even these works do not cover every important exegete or exegetical work.

Unlike those books, the descriptive history in this book does survey the whole, but it is more episodic than exhaustive: by no means does it intend to treat every influential exegete in the history of the church. Any book that attempts to cover the whole of Christian history via a few names will be dogged by the problem of selection. This study offers a bird's-eye view of the region, zooming in on a few specific targets that epitomize the landscape. The narrow selection of targets reflects the intent to keep the history manageable. Some figures are simply indispensable for any examination of the history of interpretation. Such writers as Origen, Augustine, and Calvin were indisputably influential on subsequent generations. The treatment of others may come as more of a surprise. Such figures as Dionysius, Perkins, and Campbell, now

16. Perhaps the best one-volume chronological, encyclopedic treatment with analysis is Bray, *Biblical Interpretation*. See also the dictionary-entry format in McKim, *Historical Handbook of Major Biblical Interpreters*. Multivolume histories worth consulting that cover the whole history include Hauser and Watson, *A History of Biblical Interpretation*; Reventlow, *History of Biblical Interpretation*; Saebø, *Hebrew Bible/Old Testament*.

sometimes forgotten, were influential in their day and in their circles: they appear here because they are representative of the period in review in the sense that scores of their own contemporaries were saying similar things. They, instead of others among the many scores, were chosen because they deserve a hearing by scholars today and, frankly, because they pique my interest. In every case, the individuals are not the main focus but are manifestations of the principles of the particular period in view. Neither is the book an attempt to explain all the reasons why particular figures interpreted the way they did, an impossible task for the bird's-eye approach intended here. As may be expected, there is also a vast literature that deals with the topics and figures treated in this book. It would be easy to fill the pages with footnotes only. But this is not a bibliographical essay that summarizes every important statement ever made about these topics. The focus is not on secondary sources but is on primary sources as examples of exegetical principles; secondary sources are cited mainly to point to further reading or when it is especially important to engage them in conversation. The final bibliography also suggests additional reading.

The selection of targets is based also on the fact that a very specific story is being told—namely, about the shift from premodern to modern exegesis. For the most part, modern, historical-critical exegesis is a Western phenomenon in which other Western phenomena—scholasticism and especially the Renaissance and Reformations—were prominent factors. Thus, for instance, no Syriac theologians and no Eastern theologians after about the fifth century are examined here. To the degree that modern exegesis was heavily shaped by Protestant opposition to ecclesiastical models of interpretation, no Roman Catholic writers are featured after the early modern period. Such omissions are not unintentional lacunae. The focus is both on the figures who influenced or reflected the trajectory that leads to the modern, historical-critical method and on the ancient theologians whom they read and appreciated most. For better or worse, it is the history of Western Christian (and later, Protestant) exegesis that most people in the West (and in other places now shaped by the West) are influenced by and react against.

Related to the problem of selection is the concern about what is sometimes called teleological history. In short, a teleological approach researches and writes history with a goal in mind, thus skewing the past for the sake of the thesis in the present. This method abridges or truncates the past in such a way that it ineluctably leads to a conclusion supported by the historian. Herbert Butterfield famously censured the "Whig interpretation of history," in which the past is abridged and its complexities omitted.[17] Often, as in the case of

---

17. Butterfield, *Whig Interpretation*, 9–33.

Butterfield's Whigs, history is presented as progress toward the present; in other cases, it may be a story of decline toward the present. Either way, the lens of the present—its concerns, prejudices, heroes, and villains—distorts the whole picture.

This is a legitimate concern for any attempt to write history. Although the present study is selective, the goal is to let the past speak for itself. As Butterfield wrote, "Real historical understanding is not achieved by the subordination of the past to the present, but rather by our making the past our present and attempting to see life with the eyes of another century than our own."[18] As we engage anything in the past, it expands our present horizon. At the same time, as I have said, all history writing is selective, and one's selections are usually based on something deeper than randomness. Personal and ecclesiastical interest and even empathy may motivate the research. In this regard, Henri de Lubac wrote about the inadequacy of "a certain pretension to pure objectivity." In speaking of Origen's exegesis in particular, he said, "For we are not at all concerned with the work of one solitary thinker or with a problem that in no way affects us. This work fits into a tradition that touches us ourselves."[19] Interest or empathy need not impede correct understanding or the goal of objectivity in description.[20]

History tells the story of pendulum swings. One benefit of gaining historical perspective is that we can see where we are and, perhaps, the pendulum's present position. My assumption is that most (though not all) readers of this book will have a basic familiarity with and appreciation for the tools and techniques of modern, historical-critical exegesis, but that most (though not all) will be less acquainted with and sympathetic to premodern exegetical methods. Therefore, if I have a bias, it is toward highlighting the positive aspects of the less familiar methods of a more remote time and place. Although I will note the potential pitfalls of premodern exegesis and the advantages of the modern methods, those aspects will not occupy the lion's share of the book's content. The goal may be somewhat analogous to writing a short history of communications technology with a prescriptive end in mind. That is to say, there is no need to extol the glories of modern communications to a modern audience, but it may indeed be beneficial to recall how people used to communicate, to describe what has been lost in the progress, and then to exhort toward a balanced, healthy use of the technology. If I were writing primarily to people who have no knowledge

18. Butterfield, *Whig Interpretation*, 16.
19. Lubac, *History and Spirit*, 12–13.
20. For a succinct and reasonable statement on the issue of objectivity in historical study, see Bradley and Muller, *Church History*, 48–52.

of or interest in modern historical criticism (or cellular phones), then the emphasis may have been different, though I believe that the conclusion would have been the same.

Along with selection, another problem of historiography is periodization. The distinctions between epochs in history are constructs that are seldom valid below the surface: lines of demarcation that hold true for one dimension of culture are irrelevant to another. Change over time is marked by continuities and discontinuities. With these conventional caveats aside, this book is predicated on the indisputable fact that the style of biblical interpretation typically practiced before about 1500 is in many ways different from that typically practiced after about 1800. This study examines what exegesis looked like in the so-called premodern period and in the modern period, and it gives an account of the centuries-long transition from one to the other. Otherwise, divisions of chapters are based partly (and artificially) on the amount of manageable content, but also on shifts of disposition and approach that, admittedly, can be seen best, or perhaps only, in hindsight. As such, some chapters (4 and 6) begin earlier than where their preceding chapters ended.

The main part of the book (chaps. 2–6) is devoted primarily to historical understanding. Chapters 2 through 4 focus on premodern interpretation, which, though it was practiced by a wide variety of Christian believers and was by no means uniform, was united by one common conviction: the Bible is directly relevant to the faith and morals of the contemporary church, and it should be read and applied with these spiritual meanings in mind. These chapters summarize the methods of premodern exegesis, examining select figures or movements that illustrate those methods. Chapter 2 concentrates on the first century and a half of Christian biblical interpretation, from the New Testament through the end of the second century. Chapter 3 begins with Origen, whose writings on Scripture ushered in a new era of running commentaries and homilies on Scripture, as well as second-order thinking about its interpretation. It focuses on Greek-speaking theologians whose engagement with Scripture was influential in both the Eastern church and the Western church. Chapter 4 focuses on Latin-speaking theology and exegesis, first backing up a bit chronologically to examine Augustine's impact on later medieval biblical interpretation. It proceeds to describe the Western development of the medieval quadriga (fourfold sense of Scripture), based especially on Augustine's hermeneutical method, and later features that shaped exegesis in subsequent centuries. As noted above, these chapters on premodern exegesis will include some cases of interpretation that, by today's standards, would seem far-fetched. The purpose is to plunge directly into the difficulties and see if even these examples can be read with sympathy and understanding. Some biblical passages—chief among them, the parable of the good Samaritan—will serve as a touchstone and illustration of evolving exegetical approaches.

The next two chapters document some signposts on the gradual road from premodern to modern methods of interpretation. The increasing marginalization of the spiritual senses of Scripture, along with the search for human authorial intention, came to distinguish modern historical-critical exegesis from its predecessors. Chapter 5 shows how the Renaissance and the Protestant Reformation contributed to this shift. The impulse of the Renaissance to return to the original sources and to question venerable traditions expressed itself theologically in Reformation and post-Reformation exegesis. To the Reformers, rejecting the autonomy of the pope's biblical interpretation meant that unbridled allegory was to be reined in by the literal sense of the Scripture and the sole intention of its human authors, which could allegedly be understood apart from the Roman Church's interpretations. This was a period of transition in exegesis, marked by traditional dogmatic interpretations alongside increasingly historical and even skeptical methods. Figures such as Martin Luther and John Calvin illustrate these developments and tensions. Chapter 6 summarizes the development and goals of the so-called historical-critical method and its repercussions for the life of the church. The dominance of philology and the interminable search for the history behind the biblical text resulted in doubts about Scripture and undermined its ability to address matters of doctrine and morals.

The second main part of the book is more overtly prescriptive. The motivating question is, What can we retrieve from the premoderns in our approach to Scripture without ignoring the advances of historical criticism? It argues that extreme forms of premodern ("spiritual") and modern ("literal") interpretation are irreconcilable, but that a balanced, dual emphasis on letter and spirit overcomes the impasse. To this end, chapter 7 explores what can be done to ease the tension often felt between doctrinal and historical approaches to Scripture, and it identifies some of the advantages and disadvantages of each method. This chapter shows how each emphasis provides a check and balance to the other. Any given interpretation must be taught somewhere in the literal sense, it must adhere to the rule of faith, and it must be informed by other Scriptures. The final chapter suggests how Christians might proceed with responsible and faithful biblical interpretation, advocating and illustrating the use of premodern exegetical principles within a set of prescribed limits. Interpretations are "spiritual" in the sense that they are circumscribed by the Spirit-guided oral and written tradition of the early church.[21] At the same time, spiritual readings must take into account and benefit from the modest and most assured results of historical criticism. The church's Scripture and the academy's Bible need not be separated by perceived irreconcilable differences.

21. English standards of capitalization tend to remove the ambiguity of the word "spirit." Unless the reference is clearly to the Third Person of the Trinity, I will keep "spirit" and "spiritual" lowercased. This does not mean to exclude, however, the Holy Spirit's role in inspiration and in biblical interpretation. Instead, the possibility of Spirit-guided exegesis is assumed throughout the discussions of the spiritual sense. As de Lubac wrote about spirit, "Even the very imprecision of the word is, in certain respects, valuable." Lubac, *History and Spirit*, 445.

Part 1

Historical Survey

2

Earliest Christian Exegesis

Open my eyes that I may see wonderful things in your law.

—Ps. 119:18 NIV

He said to them, "This is what I told you while I was still with you: Everything must be fulfilled that is written about me in the Law of Moses, the Prophets and the Psalms." Then he opened their minds so they could understand the Scriptures.

—Luke 24:44–45 NIV

He has made us competent as ministers of a new covenant—not of the letter but of the Spirit; for the letter kills, but the Spirit gives life.

—2 Cor. 3:6 NIV

LOL. BTW. FWIW. In a culture that communicates in increasingly smaller doses of digital characters, these groups of letters and a host of other shorthand symbols mean something now that they did not mean just a couple of decades ago. Used primarily in the specific context of social media, one should not expect to see such abbreviations in more formal writing, such as an academic essay or even a newspaper article. Certain unwritten rules obtain for their proper use; breaking those rules, or using the shorthand improperly out of ignorance, can result in miscommunication or humiliation. With any

19

medium of communication come almost endless possibilities for conveying and interpreting subtle messages that are contextually specific but also adaptable to new contexts. Yet communication is not a free-for-all; otherwise, there would be no effective transmission of a message. Certain restrictions apply.

The newest form of communication in the ancient world was the written word. In ways that are difficult for us to appreciate today, much was lost in the slow transition away from exclusively oral communication toward literacy. Thinkers from Socrates and Plato to the early church fathers Ignatius and Papias held the oral word to be superior to the written.[1] In other ways, however, written communication opened up a world of new possibilities. Besides the more obvious advantages of accurate preservation of an account and the ability to disseminate that account to anyone who can read it or hear it read, the written word also introduced new dimensions and nuances of interpretation that are not as easily reproduced with the spoken word alone.

Epistle of Barnabas and the New Testament

The early Christian author of the *Epistle of Barnabas* was not a Platonist when it comes to written texts. Instead, this "Barnabas" seems to revel in the play made possible by the visual word. A case in point is Barnabas's treatment of Genesis 14, a chapter that records the story of Abram rescuing his nephew Lot from captivity. In Genesis 14:14, we read, "When Abram heard that his relative [Lot] had been taken captive, he called out the 318 trained men born in his household and went in pursuit as far as Dan" (NIV). The following verses then narrate the successful rescue of Lot by Abram. Barnabas, who wrote his epistle around AD 130, comments on the number in this verse, which he takes to be the number of men later circumcised by Abraham: "Observe that it mentions the 'ten and eight' first, and then . . . the 'three hundred.'"[2] As for the 'ten and eight,' the *I* [*iota*] is ten, the *H* [*eta*] is eight; you have 'Jesus.' And because the cross, in the *T* [*tau*], was going to possess grace, it says also

---

1. See Plato, *Phaedrus* 274C–277A; Ignatius of Antioch, *To the Philadelphians* 8.2, ed. Holmes, *Apostolic Fathers*, 242–43: "For I heard some people say, 'If I do not find it in the archives, I do not believe it in the gospel.' And when I said to them, 'It is written,' they answered me, 'That is precisely the question.' But for me, the 'archives' are Jesus Christ, the unalterable archives are his cross and death and his resurrection and the faith that comes through him"; and Eusebius, *Hist. eccl.* 3.39.4, quoting Papias: "For I did not suppose that information from books would help me so much as the word of a living and surviving voice."

2. *Epistle of Barnabas* (9.8) indeed places the numbers in this order: δεκαοκτὼ καὶ τριακοσίους (*dekaoktō kai triakosious*). But the LXX has three hundred ten and eight, and the Masoretic Text has eight and ten and three hundred. The text of the *Epistle of Barnabas* in this section is from *Apostolic Fathers*, 408–9, ed. Holmes. I have modified some translations based on the Greek text.

the 'three hundred.' So it reveals Jesus in the two letters, and the cross in the other one."[3] The modern reader who jumps from Genesis 14 to these comments in the *Epistle of Barnabas* is likely to experience some hermeneutical whiplash. What just happened? How does this early Christian writer see a reference to Jesus and the cross in "318"? I have had more than one student react with the following assessment of this exegetical move: "Crazy." It is a puzzle, to be sure.

This experience reflects just the sort of thing that many readers of premodern biblical interpretation find perplexing and therefore discouraging. To be fair, however, these same readers, if they also read the New Testament with care, must acknowledge that what Barnabas has done is not all that foreign to early Christian handling of the Old Testament. It was no less an authority than the apostle Paul who said that the rock that accompanied the Israelites in the desert "was Christ" (1 Cor. 10:4), and who also interpreted Sarah and Hagar as an "allegory" of two covenants (Gal. 4:24), both of which applications are not self-evident in their original contexts. We could easily expand the list of New Testament writers who read out of Old Testament documents something other than the original intent of their human authors. Why did they do this?

Without rehearsing all the ways that the New Testament writers read their Scriptures and why they did so, three points are worth noting. First, it is important to get the hermeneutical priority clear. Although the New Testament writers were already recipients of a scriptural tradition, they began their interpretation of Scripture with assumptions outside of Scripture—namely, the revelation of Christ, their witness of the Christ event. Then they used Scripture to support their experience and new understanding, rather than starting with a biblical passage and seeking to find an application in their experience. The messiahship and lordship of Jesus constitute the fundamental reality.

This priority is evident in the way the disciples later remembered and read the Old Testament in light of Jesus. It was especially after his resurrection that they recalled and understood the Scriptures anew (indicated in passages such as Luke 24:25–27, 32, 44–47; John 2:17, 22; 12:13–16; 14:26; 20:9; cf. Luke 18:34 with 24:8). The risen Jesus, between resurrection and ascension, is depicted especially in Luke 24 and Acts 1 as busy teaching the disciples how to interpret the Old Testament christologically. With Jesus's help, early Christian hindsight became twenty-twenty. Thus the experience of the Christ event was sufficient to lead the early church to see their Jewish Scriptures in a whole new light. It was already customary for Jewish exegetes to look for

3. *Barnabas* 9.8.

the fulfillment of biblical prophecies in a messianic figure (or in the case of Qumran, *figures*).[4] Thus the disciples never encountered Jesus as blank slates. But it was after Jesus's resurrection, which was the proof of his messianic identity, that the disciples began to view his words and deeds, as well as the God-inspired Scriptures, with new clarity. The Scriptures informed their interpretation of Jesus, and the experience of Jesus informed their interpretation of the Scriptures.

Sometimes, the connection was obvious. When Psalm 2:2 speaks of the "anointed one," it is indeed speaking of the "Messiah," or in the Greek of the Septuagint, "Christ." It is understandable that, according to Acts 4:26, early disciples of Jesus would associate this reference with Jesus, whom they called the "Christ" or "Messiah." At other times the connections were more subtle. In light of what God had done in Christ, and given that God is assumed to be the ultimate inspiration behind Scripture, it was only natural for Paul to compare the life-giving water that flowed from the rock in the desert to the spiritual, living water that flows from Christ (1 Cor. 10:4). It was only natural for early Christians to read the Psalter, Isaiah, and the rest of their received canon in a new light. There was no going back. Whatever the old Scriptures meant beyond their original, human authorial intent, at some level they also had to do with Christ. To be sure, Jesus entered into an Israel that was already a scriptural community, and he used titles and ways of speaking that were already laden with meaning. But it was his person and work that fulfilled those Scriptures and enabled new readings, often by overturning the customary interpretations.

Second, those very assumptions—namely, the Christian story, the recognition of the revelation of God in Christ—allowed for a variety of exegetical practices, all of which were put into the service of a prior reality. That is, rather than one systematic method yielding an exegetical result, the exegetical methods were flexible in light of the newly discovered scope of Scripture: Christ. The truth about Christ justified the exegetical methods, not the reverse.[5] Ways of reading that could see Christ in the Old Testament were a part of early Christian culture; by the time of the first century, there were plenty of Hellenistic and Jewish antecedents congenial to this type of interpretation. As far back as the sixth century BC, Greek authors allegorized Homer and Hesiod and the stories about the gods, largely for the purpose of removing the rampant immorality present in the pantheon and ensuring that nothing

---

4. E.g., see the discussions in Matt. 2:3–6; John 7:41–43.

5. In a similar vein, "The truth of things grounded in themselves justified a certain method of knowledge and not the reverse." Torjesen, *Hermeneutical Procedure and Theological Method*, 4, speaking here of Origen's exegesis and its lack of "method" by modern standards.

unworthy of the gods was believed.[6] Pre-rabbinic Jewish sources were also known to engage in allegorical interpretation. At the turn of the Christian era, Philo of Alexandria, a Hellenistic Jew, allegorized the Scriptures in an effort to reconcile them with Platonism and, like the Greek philosophers, to say nothing unworthy of God.[7] More proximate to the context of the apostles are the Jewish exegetical methods of pesher, midrash, and allegory, taken up by the writers of the New Testament.[8] In any case, the precise methods were subordinate to the truth about God, Christ, and the world.[9]

Third, in the New Testament's christological reading of the Old, all of these methods, whether Hellenistic-style allegory or rabbinic midrash, served the theme of "fulfillment." Fulfillment was understood in terms deeper than simply prophecy and explicit verification or reenactment. The revelation of God in the Old Testament points forward to Jesus, and it does so in many ways.[10] Thus, "to fulfill" (πληρόω, *pleroō*) was understood in its fuller meaning of filling up. In sum, the Old Testament, read in its fuller sense (*sensus plenior*), gave a voice to Christian understandings.

The hermeneutical lesson summarized in these three points was modeled, in oral proclamation and later in written word, by the apostles and their companions and then subsequently absorbed by the early church. "Spiritual" interpretations—a broad category that could include christological, figural, or allegorical interpretations[11]—employed by early Christian writers were not attempts to do something novel, nor were they merely reproducing Greek ways of reading a text. At their most basic level, they were seeking to imitate the hermeneutic of the New Testament's use of the Old, reading the Old Testament with a christological lens.

This brief aside on the New Testament's use of the Old Testament brings us back to Barnabas, whose apparently bizarre treatment of Abram's 318 servants leaves most modern readers dismayed. Because this association between the number and Jesus and his cross seems so far-fetched, it serves as a good indication of the assumptions at work that are foreign to today's readers. First of all, ancient culture was much more attuned to the symbolism and meaning of numbers than ours generally is, although "thirteen" still bears immediate and pervasive connotations of misfortune, especially if it is a date

6. See the discussion in Sheridan, *Language for God*, 45–59.
7. See the survey in Sheridan, *Language for God*, 61–77.
8. See, e.g., Longenecker, *Biblical Exegesis*; Kugel and Greer, *Early Biblical Interpretation*, 128–36.
9. Cf. the discussion in Kugel and Greer, *Early Biblical Interpretation*, 127–28.
10. See Longenecker, *Biblical Exegesis*, xxvii, 190.
11. Ἐν πνεύματι, as in Rev. 11:8 and *Barnabas* 10.2 and 10.9.

and it falls on a Friday. Think of the New Testament book of Revelation and its prevalent use of number symbolism. One particularly common use of number symbolism was the Jewish interpretive method of gematria—that is, the computation of the numeric value of letters. Since each letter in the Hebrew or Greek alphabet also doubled as a numeral, letters in a word could be added together to form a number. Richard Longenecker counts gematria among the "most fanciful" of the rabbinic interpretive devices.[12] But it was apparently used in Revelation as well. For example, in Hebrew transliteration "Nero Caesar" yields the infamous number of the beast, 666.[13] With regard to the 318 servants in Genesis 14, Jewish rabbis were inclined to see the number as a reference to Abram's servant, Eliezer, a name whose numerical value adds up to 318.[14]

Modern readers do not notice this symbolism as readily because we now use Arabic numerals, which are distinct from the alphabet, and thus our letters do not have numerical value. The closest analogy in modern Western society is the numerical value given to letters on a telephone keypad, enabling a business to embed its name in its phone number.[15] But before the introduction of these Arabic numerals to the West in the late medieval period, a word could always add up to a number, or as in the case of Barnabas's reading of Genesis 14, a number always had the potential to spell out or remind one of a word. Combine this number symbolism with a vast array of abbreviations, and the possibilities for interpretation are wide open. For example, as many Americans now immediately know what "LOL" means, most literate early Christians would have known that IH (or eighteen) is a common abbreviation for "Jesus" (ΙΗΣΟΥΣ) and that T (or three hundred) is the shape of the cross.[16] When Barnabas read Genesis 14:14 and saw (not simply heard) 318, or IHT, it did not take much imagination—or at least not as much imagination as it initially seems—to find Jesus and the cross.

12. Longenecker, *Biblical Exegesis*, 21.

13. Aune, *Revelation 6–16*, 770–71.

14. See Hamilton, *Book of Genesis*, 406–7. Philo, commenting on Genesis (*De Abrahamo* 41.236–44), spends quite some time allegorizing the number of kings mentioned in Gen. 14, though he does not deal with the number of servants (318).

15. This symbolism also survives in the occasional use of Roman numerals, which, of course, are letters. Since only a few letters (and not the entire alphabet) are used, however, it is more difficult to make an intelligible word out of a number. Since MM equals 2,000, leading up to the turn of this millennium, M&M's marketed their product as the official candy of the new millennium.

16. Hurtado, *Earliest Christian Artifacts*, 114–15: "IH seems to have been a way of representing Jesus' name that was reasonably well known and very early in origin, and that must have arisen among Christians familiar with Jewish exegetical techniques." On the abbreviation *IH* and the so-called *nomina sacra*, see Hurtado, *Earliest Christian Artifacts*, 95–134.

In addition to appreciating the ubiquity of number symbolism in antiquity, Barnabas's interpretive move makes even more sense when his own literary context is considered. It would be unfair for modern readers to wrest this small passage away from its surroundings; after all, it is this sort of alleged decontextualization that modern interpreters generally despise about premodern exegesis. Barnabas's exercise in number symbolism comes in the context of his discussion of the Jewish practice of circumcision. Barnabas intends to emphasize the Christian abolition of physical circumcision in favor of spiritual circumcision of the heart. In so doing, though, he must acknowledge Abraham, who introduced the physical practice by literally circumcising his servants, presumably these same 318 men (Gen. 14:14; 17:23). In circumcising this precise number, Barnabas seems to be saying, Abraham's very act pointed forward to Christ and to the eventual obsolescence of physical circumcision in favor of true, spiritual circumcision of the heart and ears. Given the context and his theological goal of explaining the abrogation of the necessity of the sign of physical circumcision, one can see how a discussion of Jesus is not completely unexpected in this context. One important lesson learned so far is not to dismiss as crazy some idea from history that has not yet been fully understood. There may be more going on than meets the eye.

To take things a little further than Barnabas explicitly did, there are two other "messianic" connections in Genesis 14 that may reinforce Barnabas's christological interpretation of "318." First, it is also in Genesis 14 where a famous type, or foreshadowing model, of Christ appears: Melchizedek (cf. Gen. 14:18–20; Ps. 110:4; Heb. 7:1–28). The mysterious figure of Melchizedek and the superiority of Jesus Christ's priesthood over Aaron's converge in the Epistle to the Hebrews, a book in which the theme of the obsolescence of Old Testament types is prominent. Second, the whole story of Lot's rescue by Abram is a story of grace, of a savior delivering a helpless captive from the clutches of the enemy. In more ways than one, then, christological significance is present in Genesis 14, and at least one such interpretation (Hebrews) precedes Barnabas. Although Barnabas does not elaborate on these themes, they may not have been far from his mind when he read about the 318 servants and saw the "name" of this number—IHT.

Following the lead of Barnabas, later Christians found significance in this same number. When Clement of Alexandria discusses the mystical meaning of numbers, he begins by making the same christological point as Barnabas from Genesis 14, and he then extends it soteriologically, noting how Abram's servants "were in salvation."[17] Ambrose treats the number similarly, making the

---

17. Clement of Alexandria, *Stromata* 6.11 (*ANF* 2:499).

christological point and observing that the servants were "elect" or chosen, a word that has soteriological connotations of its own.[18] Athanasius—looking back on the pivotal Council of Nicaea (AD 325), when Arius, the enemy of Nicene orthodoxy, was excommunicated—recalled the number of bishops at the council as 318, different from his earlier estimate of 300,[19] but now the precise number of Abram's servants victorious in battle against the foe. These examples indicate that Barnabas's interpretations were not unique or necessarily marginal within early Christianity.

How could such meanings be legitimately imposed on Genesis, whose author had no concept of Jesus or Nicaea? Consider an analogy. Suppose at a book sale you find a small tome written in 1978 on the history of slang in North America. Suppose further that, as you pick it up and randomly read through pages of a chapter that describes humorous etymologies and obsolete usage, you look down to find numerous footnotes that read simply "*Lol.*" Since the book itself has an ironic or even comedic undertone, you indeed "laugh out loud" when you read this. Puzzled, you turn to the book's front matter, where you discover that the reference is to a classic text in the field: "*Lollygagging*" *and Other Colloquialisms*, written in 1949. You know that both books were written long before "LOL" became common internet slang, and that it was not the original intention of the author or copy editor (of either book) to cause the reader to laugh out loud, at least not at each footnote. Nevertheless, you can hardly suppress your laughter, and it is difficult to ignore the new meaning that this abbreviation has developed. What's more, though it was completely unintended by the original author, it is hard to imagine that the writer of a humorous book about slang would take exception to this new meaning and application, but might rather revel in the situation. Although this analogy breaks down at several points, Barnabas may feel a similar, irrepressible urge when he runs across the number 318 (*IHT*), which at first glance is an insignificant detail, but after a double take, actually comes to mean something more to him as a Christian reader. Words can play and gain new meaning.[20]

Beyond this small excerpt, the whole *Epistle of Barnabas* is a fascinating example of early Christian spiritual interpretation of Scripture. Barnabas goes on, for instance, to discuss the true meanings of Israelite food laws.[21] God did not intend the Israelites literally to abstain from such food; rather,

18. Ambrose, *On Abraham* 1.3.15, quoted in Sheridan, *Genesis 12–50*, 23.
19. Athanasius, *Epistola ad Afros* 2 (NPNF[2] 4:489). Cf. Williams, *Arius*, 67.
20. The multivalence of language, an assumed feature of literature in the ancient world, is a point stressed throughout Leithart, *Deep Exegesis*.
21. *Barnabas* 10.

these ordinances were intended to be understood figuratively or "spiritually" (ἐν πνεύματι, en pneumati).[22] The command to abstain from swine, to take one example, actually means to refrain from associating with people who behave like pigs.[23] Barnabas wonders aloud why the Jews failed to understand or perceive such applications.[24] Once again, it looks to the modern reader as if Barnabas's interpretation is arbitrary and his charges unfair to Jews. But Barnabas was not the first to spiritualize the kosher food laws. Long before Barnabas, Jewish interpreters such as the writer of the *Letter of Aristeas* used the same exegetical technique in applying the Torah's dietary restrictions,[25] and this spiritual explanation of the same laws would reappear in later Christian interpreters.[26] To be clear, the *Letter of Aristeas* does not claim that the dietary laws were merely symbolic; in contrast with Barnabas, the spiritual significance does not nullify the literal command. The Old Testament prophets set the precedent for applying what had been regarded merely as literal laws in a spiritual fashion, whether it was animal sacrifices (Hos. 6:6) or circumcision (Jer. 4:4), but without negating the literal command. Jesus himself spiritualized the food laws (Mark 7:15–23), and Acts connects the food and cleanliness laws to the question of the acceptance of Gentiles (Acts 10:9–16, 34). Even the prohibition against muzzling the working ox (Deut. 25:4) is not about the ox, according to Paul, but about the human worker (1 Cor. 9:9–10). We might like to add, not about the ox "only." At any rate, Jesus and Paul seem to have taken the spiritualizing tendencies of the Hebrew prophets and the *Letter of Aristeas* to the next level.

Were Jesus and Paul intending to give a brand-new interpretation or to use the interpretation that was meant all along? It is not clear, but Barnabas and many early Christians believed the latter. That is, following Jesus's lead on food and the apostolic teaching on circumcision, Barnabas not only favors the spiritual meaning of these laws but also rejects the obligation of their literal application. Incidentally, Barnabas excoriates the Jews for not grasping the true point of the Mosaic law, all the while using good Jewish interpretive methods such as gematria and spiritual applications. In a qualified way, then, we may agree with Henri de Lubac's suggestion that there is "at the heart of the doctrine of the spiritual sense . . . a certain tendency to depreciate the Jewish Scriptures. It generally points out the *modus judaicus intelligendi* (Jewish way of understanding) only in order to reject it

---

22. *Barnabas* 10.2.
23. *Barnabas* 10.3.
24. *Barnabas* 10.11–12.
25. *Letter of Aristeas* 128–71 (Charlesworth 2:21–24).
26. E.g., Clement of Alexandria, *Paedagogus* 10.

with disdain."[27] If this is a fair description, then it should be qualified by observing that this "depreciation" of the Jewish Scriptures and "rejection" of Jewish understanding began with the Jews themselves. Christian interpreters were simply following the example of Jewish prophets, rabbis, and apostles who sought to reveal the true intent of the sacred writings. Whether or not depreciation is an appropriate description, the point is clear: Jesus and his early followers interpreted and applied these laws not on the literal level, but on the spiritual level. One cannot easily read the New Testament without noticing its spiritual interpretation of the Old.

In one sense, Barnabas is indicative of the fact that the earliest Gentile Christians did not know exactly what to do with the Old Testament. The ubiquitous, apostolic use of the Old Testament seemed a sufficient ground for its acceptance. One option, therefore, was to accept it as Scripture by obeying literally and precisely the whole Mosaic law. Some Jewish Christians (also known as Ebionites) sought this option, though they, like non-Christian Jews, were obliged to spiritualize the sacrificial commands in the wake of the second temple's destruction in AD 70. For this and various other reasons, this option of literal obedience was neither theologically desirable nor physically possible for either Jews or Christians.

At the same time, one could imagine good reasons for Christians to refuse the Old Testament at every interpretive level. In addition to the fact that pagan outsiders derided Christians for their Jewish connection, many if not most of the laws found in its pages appeared prima facie irrelevant to Christians. Another option, therefore, was to reject the Old Testament altogether as Christian Scripture. Marcion of Sinope chose this option, taking the Old Testament's laws only literally and failing to see their relevance to Christian faith and life.[28] Ultimately, finding no room for what he considered to be nonsense or room for the deity who inspired it, Marcion chose an abridged Gospel according to Luke and ten Letters of Paul for his authoritative documents.

Both of these extreme options of dealing with the Old Testament—literal obedience or total rejection—were predicated on taking its laws merely literally and, as such, were rather quickly rejected by the Great Church. One could not dismiss the same Hebrew Scriptures that Jesus and Paul received as authoritative. At the same time, one had to ask how Jesus and Paul received and applied those Scriptures. In light of these live options at the time, one must admire Barnabas's attempt to make the Old Testament relevant,

27. Lubac, *History and Spirit*, 454–55.
28. See Tertullian, *Against Marcion* 3.5 (ANF 3:324). Cf. the comments in Pelikan, *Emergence of the Catholic Tradition*, 77.

rather than abrogating or ignoring it altogether. Barnabas, like the church at large, sought to balance the continuity and discontinuity, taking on the burden of spiritualizing the so-called ceremonial laws of the Old Testament on the basis of the Old Testament itself and after the model of Jesus and the apostles. It was spiritual and christological interpretation that allowed Christians to receive Israel's Scriptures as canon and to continue to regard them as normative.

In an important sense, then, Barnabas is not grasping at straws as much as he is following the lead of Jewish exegetes, Paul, the Gospel writers, and other first-century Christians in handling Scripture, and Barnabas is arguably no more or less supersessionist than much of the New Testament. Exegetically, there is nothing "crazier" (to borrow the term from my students) in Barnabas and in the church fathers than there is in the New Testament. Like the New Testament writers, Barnabas and the vast majority of second-century Christians could not help but read the Old Testament in light of Christ.

Irenaeus of Lyons

After Marcion's sojourn in Rome and departure from its church around 144, and perhaps in response to this event, Christian leaders began to highlight their use of the Old Testament. Justin Martyr exemplifies the copious, Christian use of the Old Testament during this period. In his *Dialogue with Trypho the Jew*, Justin answers the objections of a non-Christian Jew who does not see Jesus as the Messiah anticipated in the Old Testament. If Trypho is a literary creation of Justin, then the character is likely a cipher not only for the majority of Jews but perhaps also for Gentile believers such as Marcion, who denigrated the Old Testament or simply did not understand its Christian significance.[29] In his proof that Jesus is the Messiah, Justin stresses not the miracles of Jesus as much as his fulfillment of Old Testament prophecy, an apologetic trend that becomes dominant after Justin. Throughout the *Dialogue with Trypho* as well as in the *First Apology*, Justin shows that Jesus Christ is the fulfiller of prophecy as well as the interpreter of obscure prophecies. The "divine Logos" (θεῖος λόγος, *theios logos*) and the "prophetic Spirit" (προφητικὸν Πνεῦμα, *prophētikon Pneuma*) spoke through the inspired prophets.[30] Justin is confident that these prophecies are sufficient to prove to open-minded

29. Although it is certainly possible that Justin had similar conversations with Jews in and around his native Nablus, many scholars think Trypho is a literary creation. For the suggestion that Justin's interlocutor represents Marcion or Marcionism, see Barton, *Holy Writings, Sacred Text*, 56–58.

30. Justin, *First Apology* 32–53 (PG 6:377–408).

people of reason (λόγος, *logos*) the inspiration of the Old Testament and its fulfillment in Christ.[31]

Christian interpretation of the Old Testament was advanced by Irenaeus (d. ca. 200), whose writings reflect the central doctrinal beliefs and exegetical practices of the early church. As bishop in Lyons, Irenaeus struggled to keep the church in Gaul pure from Marcionite and Valentinian or gnostic influences. In so doing, he is certainly not the first Christian to offer christological interpretations of the Old Testament, nor is he the first to cite apostolic writings as authoritative "Scripture." In his debate with gnostics, however, the way Irenaeus, first, reads each Testament in light of the other and, second, reads both in light of a grand scheme of the history of salvation—that appears to be his contribution to the history of exegesis. These two points are worth fleshing out in more detail.

First, whereas Marcion simply severed the Old Testament from the New, and the *Epistle of Barnabas* simply assembled a collection of types and figurative interpretations, Irenaeus goes beyond his predecessors by exemplifying the positive relationship between the Testaments in his comprehensive use of typology. Indeed, it is Irenaeus who introduces the language of Old and New Testament (*testamentum*) with reference to written documents.[32] Irenaeus's "New Testament" canon was not yet the definite list it would be two centuries later, but he was explicitly working with a group of authoritative writings that, even if it is not yet an authoritatively closed list, has some clearly marked boundaries as to inclusion and exclusion.[33] He is therefore reading and interpreting two collections of sacred literature that are drawn together in fundamental unity and ought to be interpreted in light of one another. The Old and New Testaments are one corpus. The content of this Scripture is one because its divine author is one, as opposed to the Marcionites and gnostics, who posited a different god behind the Old Testament. What Scripture proclaims is the unified plan of the God who both created and redeemed (or better, recapitulated and divinized) creation for the goal of eternal fellowship. As with earlier interpreters, this unity is reflected in the fulfillment of prophecies, which become clear only after their fulfillment.[34] It is also reflected in Irenaeus's typological interpretation, which begins with and expands on similar interpretations in the New Testament.

31. Justin, *First Apology* 1–2, 53 (PG 6:329, 408B–C).
32. Irenaeus, *Haer.* 4.15.2 (PG 7:1014A). Although Irenaeus wrote in Greek, *Adversus haereses* survives in toto only in Latin, and partially in Greek.
33. On the four Gospels, see Irenaeus, *Haer.* 3.1.1; 3.11.8. See also the summary by Denis Farkasfalvy in Farmer and Farkasfalvy, *Formation of the New Testament Canon*, 143–48.
34. Irenaeus, *Haer.* 4.26.1.

Although the term "typology" is modern, the language of a "type" that foreshadows the "antitype," or fulfilled reality, is present in the New Testament, as in 1 Peter 3:18–21, which compares the salvation wrought in the floodwaters with the salvation appropriated in the waters of baptism, the antitype or corresponding reality. Examples of typological fulfillment in the New Testament invited second-century Christians like Barnabas and Irenaeus to make similar connections between persons, things, and events in the two Testaments. Again, it was hindsight that opened the door to seeing the full range of possibilities.

Irenaeus uses this same language of type (τύπος, *typos* = *praefiguratio*) to show that the whole of Scripture is an account of Christ. Christ is hidden in the Scriptures like a treasure in a field, inviting the reader to contrast the things of secondary importance with those of primary, the temporal with the eternal, the earthly with the heavenly.[35] In this way, Christ is the key to the Scriptures. One instance of such christological typology is Irenaeus's expansion of the parallel Paul draws between Adam and Christ (Rom. 5:12–21; 1 Cor. 15:21–22), who are points of contrast rather than of strict comparison. For Irenaeus, as for Paul, Christ undoes what Adam did, and the eternal Logos, by becoming flesh, recapitulates humanity and restores human nature to the image and likeness of God. The sin of the first created man was corrected by the first begotten. Irenaeus goes on, though, to draw a parallel typology, not found in Paul, between Eve and Mary. "The knot of Eve's disobedience was loosed by the obedience of Mary. For what the virgin Eve had bound fast through unbelief, this did the virgin Mary set free through faith."[36] Later in the work, Irenaeus writes that just as Eve was led astray by the word of a fallen angel, Mary received news through an angel of her role in redemption. "As the human race fell into bondage to death by means of a virgin, so is it rescued by a virgin; virginal disobedience having been balanced in the opposite scale by virginal obedience."[37]

For Irenaeus, the Scriptures display a fundamental unity that allows this kind of typological and intertextual play within the bounds of this grand story of redemption. Such unity of Scripture is also an aid when interpretation becomes difficult. Irenaeus acknowledges the clarity, or perspicuity, of Scripture—that is, that these writings "can be clearly, unambiguously, and harmoniously understood by all."[38] At the same time, he admits of some obscurities in Scripture, some of which, by God's grace, can be explained,

35. Irenaeus, *Haer.* 4.14.3 (PG 7:1012A–B); 4.26.1 (PG 7:1052A–B).
36. Irenaeus, *Haer.* 3.22.4.
37. Irenaeus, *Haer.* 5.19.1.
38. Irenaeus, *Haer.* 2.27.2.

but others of which must be left "in God's hands." In such cases, the unity of Scripture provides a hermeneutical aid by serving as a commentary on itself. Irenaeus writes:

> If, therefore, according to the rule which I have stated, we leave some questions in the hands of God, we shall both preserve our faith uninjured, and shall continue without danger; and all Scripture, which has been given to us by God, shall be found by us perfectly consistent; and the parables shall harmonize with those passages which are perfectly plain; and those statements the meaning of which is clear, shall serve to explain the parables; and through the many diversified utterances [of Scripture] there shall be heard one harmonious melody in us, praising in hymns that God who created all things.[39]

In other words, obscure passages of Scripture should be illuminated by the clearer passages of Scripture. This principle was common in rabbinic exegesis.[40] Known later as the "analogy of Scripture" (*analogia scripturae*), this exegetical rule of Irenaeus will endure throughout the subsequent history of exegesis as long as Scripture is seen as a unified whole whose parts, despite their diversity, all testify to the same God and the same plan of redemption.

A second important feature of Irenaeus's exegesis has to do with the relationship between Scripture and the Christian account of God's nature and human salvation, summed up in the rule of faith. In order to grasp this point, it first is necessary to understand what is meant by the rule of faith. The rule of faith—or as Irenaeus usually calls it, the rule of truth—refers to the oral tradition representing the apostolic preaching, received from the apostles themselves and passed down through their successors (bishops) in the second-century church. This rule or standard (κανών, *kanōn* = *regula*) was passed on at baptism, received as one was ushered into the new community of believers. In its fuller accounts, this rule included three main points: belief in the Father, the Son, and the Holy Spirit. Irenaeus provides a clear summary of these three points:

> This then is the order of the rule of our faith, and the foundation of the building, and the stability of our conversation: God, the Father, not made, not material, invisible; one God, the creator of all things: this is the first point of our faith. The second point is: The Word of God, Son of God, Christ Jesus our Lord, who was manifested to the prophets according to the form of their prophesying and according to the method of the dispensation of the Father: through whom all things were made; who also at the end of the times, to complete and gather up

39. Irenaeus, *Haer.* 2.28.3.
40. See the various articulations of this general principle in Longenecker, *Biblical Exegesis*, 20.

all things, was made man among men, visible and tangible, in order to abolish death and show forth life and produce a community of union between God and man. And the third point is: The Holy Spirit, through whom the prophets prophesied, and the fathers learned the things of God, and the righteous were led forth into the way of righteousness; and who in the end of the times was poured out in a new way upon mankind in all the earth, renewing man unto God.[41]

This oral tradition, the content of which happens to have been written down in this and several other instances, reflects the doctrine that unified the second-century church against the heresies of the day, especially gnosticism.[42] The rule of faith gave the church its identity, and it belonged to the church.

Among its many functions, this oral rule of faith, which is centered on what God has done in Christ, served as a guide for reading and interpreting Scripture. It was as well known in the second century as it is in the twenty-first that Scripture can be interpreted in many different and even contradictory ways. The author of 2 Peter complains that false teachers twist the wrong meaning out of the same scriptural letters of Paul (2 Pet. 3:15–16). In comparison with Irenaeus and what would become orthodox Christianity, gnostics held vastly different beliefs about the identity of God, the nature of Jesus Christ, and the material world. Yet these gnostics were able to connect their unorthodox beliefs to the same corpus of Scripture revered by Irenaeus. The gnostics held, as it were, to a different rule of faith, though their Scriptures overlapped with that of the Great Church. Thus, for Irenaeus, the only proper interpretations of Scripture are those in agreement with the apostolic rule of faith that belongs to the church. Consequently, the proper interpretation of Scripture takes place within the church. This rule, as opposed to the gnostic account, is proved to be authentic because of its public presence in the churches known to be apostolic and led by direct successors of the apostles.

Irenaeus offers an illustration of how the rule of faith aids in the correct interpretation of Scripture. Imagine a beautiful and intricate mosaic whose various gems are brought together to depict a majestic king. Now imagine that those same stones are taken up and scrambled together, and out of them someone now forms a picture of an ugly dog or a fox, all the while supposing this new picture of a dirty animal to be what was intended.[43] This scenario is

---

41. Irenaeus, *Demonstration of Apostolic Preaching* 6.

42. For earlier, truncated versions of the rule of faith in its polemical context, see Ignatius of Antioch, *To the Trallians* 9; Ignatius, *To the Smyrnaeans* 1. For a later, fuller version of the rule of faith, see Origen, *Princ.* 1.preface.4–10. For more on the rule of faith and its functions in the early church, see Blowers, "The *Regula Fidei* and the Narrative"; Ferguson, *Rule of Faith*.

43. Irenaeus, *Haer.* 1.8.1. Dogs and foxes were not considered majestic animals. One is reminded of the king (Herod Antipas) whom Jesus called a fox (Luke 13:32).

similar to what the heretics do with Scripture. Just as the individual stones of
the mosaic can likewise be manipulated to yield a new and repulsive portrait,
individual texts of Scripture can be manipulated to mean whatever someone
wants them to mean. By way of example, Irenaeus summarizes what some
gnostics do with the prologue of the Gospel of John. Rather than simply
identifying the Logos who became flesh with the Only-begotten, the gnostics
distinguish not only these two figures but also six additional names in order
to arrive at eight distinct deities or Aeons (the "ogdoad"). Such an interpretation of John 1 is possible only because these readers bring to the text their
own *hypothesis* (ὑπόθεσις, *hypothesis*)—that is, their own assumption or
principle or narrative.[44] As a further example of mistreating a text, Irenaeus
observes that one could do the same thing with the works of Homer, and he
constructs a cento, taking verses of Homer out of their respective contexts
and assorting them at random to make them say something new.[45]

Irenaeus's younger contemporary Tertullian of Carthage battled a similarly
broad range of heresies. In agreement with Irenaeus, Tertullian, who had no
patience for Marcion's brash editing of the scriptural volumes, acknowledges
that what Valentinus the gnostic does with Scripture is more subtle but, for
that reason, far worse:

> One man perverts the Scriptures with his hand, another their meaning by his
> exposition. For although Valentinus seems to use the entire volume, he has none
> the less laid violent hands on the truth, only with a more cunning mind and skill
> than Marcion. Marcion expressly and openly used the knife, not the pen, since
> he made such an excision of the Scriptures as suited his own subject-matter.
> Valentinus, however, abstained from such excision, because he did not invent
> Scriptures to square with his own subject-matter, but adapted his matter to
> the Scriptures; and yet he took away more, and added more, by removing the
> proper meaning of every particular word, and adding fantastic arrangements
> of things which have no real existence.[46]

Tertullian likewise notes how some poets pillage Homer to make their own
points, and he further comments that the divine Scriptures are even more
fruitful for this kind of use, or abuse, "being arranged by the will of God in
such a manner as to furnish materials for heretics."[47] Tertullian, like other
early Christian thinkers, believes that heresies are in a sense necessary within
the church (an assumption based on 1 Cor. 11:18–19), and thus it can be that

44. Irenaeus, *Haer.* 1.9.2–3 (PG 7:540–44).
45. Irenaeus, *Haer.* 1.9.4.
46. Tertullian, *Prescription against Heretics* 38 (ANF 3:262).
47. Tertullian, *Prescription against Heretics* 39 (ANF 3:262).

even Scripture may serve as a source for heresy. Like 2 Peter, Tertullian exhibits not a little pessimism when it comes to the potential for false teachers to twist Scripture.

> Our appeal, therefore, must not be made to the Scriptures; nor must controversy be admitted on points in which victory will either be impossible, or uncertain, or not certain enough. But even if a discussion from the Scriptures should not turn out in such a way as to place both sides on a par, (yet) the natural order of things would require that this point should be first proposed, which is now the only one which we must discuss: "With whom lies that very faith to which the Scriptures belong. From what and through whom, and when, and to whom, has been handed down that rule, by which men become Christians?" For wherever it shall be manifest that the true Christian rule and faith shall be, there will likewise be the true Scriptures and expositions thereof, and all the Christian traditions.[48]

In order to prevent such wild—albeit possible—misinterpretations of the text, the rule of faith serves as a pattern and guide for interpretation. Upon encountering a gnostic interpretation, according to Irenaeus, anyone who retains the "rule of truth, which he received through baptism," will recognize the words and names from Scripture but not the "blasphemous hypothesis" of the heretics. To illustrate again, one may recognize the individual precious gems, but not the deformed image that they have been made to depict.[49] In this illustration, the hypothesis functions as a pattern for the mosaic. Valentinian gnostics approached Scripture with an erroneous pattern, a narrative about the Pleroma and thirty Aeons, and about an ignorant Demiurge who created the evil, material world out of which the human spirit must escape. For Irenaeus, though, the rule of faith is analogous to the correct pattern on the box of a jigsaw puzzle, and Scripture is composed of the various puzzle pieces. Anyone who knows and sees the true pattern or rule will be able to judge whether the constructed picture in fact resembles the pattern.

Along with the *analogia scripturae* (analogy of Scripture), then, these comments from Irenaeus and Tertullian indicate another hermeneutical key: the Christian doctrine contained in the rule of faith functions as a lens for interpretation. This key is later called the "analogy of faith" (*analogia fidei*). This phrase is used by Paul in Romans 12:6 when he encourages the gift of "prophecy according to the analogy of the faith" (ἀναλογία τῆς πίστεως, *analogia tēs pisteōs*), that is, prophecy in agreement with the faith.

48. Tertullian, *Prescription against Heretics* 19 (ANF 3:251–52).
49. Irenaeus, *Haer.* 1.9.4 (PG 7:545B–548A).

In considering the relationship between these two authoritative sources—Scripture and the rule of faith—it is important not to succumb to the temptation of driving a wedge between them. Indeed, while the rule of faith serves as the lens for reading Scripture, at the same time Scripture informs and ultimately determines what the rule is. For Irenaeus, even without the rule of faith, one can arrive at something congruent to that rule by the "natural" reading of Scripture. The gnostics, by contrast, partake in an unnatural reading of Scripture. To elicit the kind of picture that the gnostics get out of Scripture, not only must they reorder and decontextualize the Scriptures, but they also must bring in elements from outside the Scriptures.[50] In Irenaeus's estimation, the gnostic interpretation is not the natural interpretation.[51] For Tertullian, the four Gospels all begin with the same "rules of faith."[52] To carry the illustration further still, the jigsaw puzzle comes already assembled, or sufficiently assembled so that, even without access to the pattern on the box, one can readily see, from the arranged pieces alone, what the picture should be. Even without the pictorial pattern, though it would be more difficult, one could still piece it together correctly. In other words, Scripture determines the content of the rule. Gnostic heretics do not start from scratch, but they take the correctly assembled puzzle, pull it apart piece by piece, and then must force and twist pieces together unnaturally (cf. 2 Pet. 3:16) and bring in pieces from other puzzles to corroborate their hypothesis or pattern.

Therefore, the written rule or canon (Scripture) and the oral canon (rule of faith), though distinct, inform each other and are like two sides of the same coin, or like two siblings whose features clearly link them together with the same set of parents. On the one hand the rule of faith confirms what is the natural reading of Scripture, and on the other hand it clarifies and sets boundaries on occasions when Scripture is obscure or when contrary interpretations are proposed. Returning to John 1, though it is possible to read several different deities into the text, on a natural reading one can see that the Logos and the Only-begotten are the same, the one who became flesh. And just in case it is not perspicuous, whatever John 1 means, it does not contradict what the rule of faith—that is, the apostolic proclamation and tradition—teaches about the nature of God and Jesus Christ.[53] For Irenaeus, the Christ proclaimed in the rule of faith is the key to the Scriptures.

50. Irenaeus, *Haer.* 1.8.1.
51. Irenaeus, *Haer.* 1.9.4. For a summary of Irenaeus on the unity of Scripture and its *hypothesis*, see Behr, *Asceticism and Anthropology*, 28–33.
52. Tertullian, *Against Marcion* 4.2.
53. A similar articulation of this point may be found in Gavrilyuk, "Scripture and the *Regula Fidei*," 33–38.

Canon and Text

By the end of the second century, the canon of the New Testament had assumed a more definite shape than it had at the beginning of the same century. This development was due in part to the fact that the apostles and their contemporaries ("apostolic men") were now long dead, the subsequent generation that was entrusted with their words was passing away, and thus the living memory of Jesus and the authoritative application of the gospel needed to be preserved. In addition, the collection and use of a written canon was already natural to the Jewish faith, and the impulse to collect and read apostolic writings is discernible already in the New Testament itself (see Col. 4:16; 2 Pet. 3:15–16). That this canon would be defined—that is, limited in some way—is a necessary corollary to having a canon. The defining of the canon was not initiated by the second-century church's debates related directly to the canon, but such definition was most likely hastened by those debates. As mentioned above, Marcionism defined the canon too narrowly. The schismatic movement of Montanism, which emphasized the role of new, authoritative teaching through its prophets and prophetesses, left the definition of the canon too broad, implicitly questioning the criterion of apostolicity and perhaps the need for a written canon at all. Thus, alongside the organic process of canon formation that was already at work, the church's development of the New Testament canon in the second half of the second century was, in part, a response to movements that challenged the emerging consensus.[54]

When that emerging and almost tacit consensus on the canon was challenged, it was natural for the church to think more carefully about its canon, which is why lists of the New Testament books began to emerge. The most famous such catalog from the late second century is the Muratorian Fragment.[55] Along with this list, Irenaeus's writings indicate the functional shape of the New Testament canon in the late second century. As Rowan Greer notes, Irenaeus uses the four Gospels, most of Paul's Letters, Acts, Revelation, 1 Peter, and 1–2 John. He does not explicitly cite James, Jude, or 2 Peter, and he

---

54. *Pace* Barton, *Holy Writings, Sacred Text*, 35–62, who, against this standard account and for reasons I do not find ultimately convincing, downplays the significance of these movements in the canonization process.

55. Debate continues on the date of this document, with the options ranging between the late second century and the fourth century. The best attempts to place the document in the fourth century argue that it is a later imitation of a second-century author in order to secure early authority for a fourth-century list. Due to its distinctively second-century flavor, however, the result is probably too well done for anyone after the third century. See an argument for the early date in Ferguson, "The Muratorian Fragment."

excludes Hebrews.[56] When the larger scope of authors is taken into account, the vast majority of the contents of the present New Testament—except for the disputed or hardly used books of James, 2 Peter, 2–3 John, Jude, and Revelation—were in wide usage by the turn of the third century, along with the Old Testament canon.[57]

Although the early church gave no systematic examination to the books in question, one criterion for canonicity came to dominate: apostolicity. In short, three questions could be asked of a book that would help reveal its apostolicity and therefore canonical authority. First, was it composed by an apostle or apostolic man (such as Matthew or Mark, respectively)? Second, does the book conform to the apostolic doctrine handed down in the rule of faith? And third, is the book in wide use in apostolic churches (such as Jerusalem and Rome)? It is interesting that, although inspiration was an assumed minimal qualification, it was not one of the exclusive criteria employed for canonicity. In general, a work that was orthodox and especially useful for teaching the faith was regarded as inspired.

The New Testament canon's mostly definite shape, with somewhat fluid borders, is given expression by Eusebius of Caesarea in his *Ecclesiastical History* (ca. 323). He distinguishes four types of books: (1) the undisputed, accepted books (*homologoumena*), (2) the disputed books (*antilegomena*) that are recognized (*gnorima*) by many, (3) the rejected books (*notha*) that are mostly orthodox but simply not canonical because not apostolic, and (4) the books rejected because of being heretical, "absurd, and impious."[58] In Eusebius's first category are twenty-two undisputed books: the four Gospels, Acts, fourteen Letters of Paul (including Hebrews), 1 Peter, 1 John, and Revelation.[59] In the second category are five disputed books: James, 2 Peter, 2–3 John, and Jude. Eusebius's classification well reflects the situation as it had stood for over a century. More important, his first two categories combined include the exact twenty-seven books that Athanasius would list as canonical in 367, calling these writings the "springs of salvation" that alone contain the "doctrine of piety." Athanasius goes on to mention a few intertestamental books and two Christian documents (*Didache* and *Shepherd of Hermas*) that

56. Kugel and Greer, *Early Biblical Interpretation*, 109–10. It is more difficult to identify allusions, but Irenaeus may use all but Philemon and 3 John. See the discussions and notes in Farkasfalvy, "Theology of Scripture in St. Irenaeus," 330–31; and Peckham, "Epistemological Authority," 51–54.

57. For more on the early development of the New Testament canon, see Farmer and Farkasfalvy, *Formation of the New Testament Canon*; L. McDonald and Sanders, *The Canon Debate*.

58. Eusebius, *Hist. eccl.* 3.25.1–7.

59. Eusebius acknowledges that some would rather place Revelation in the third category, under rejected books.

are not canonical but still worth reading.[60] Significantly, Athanasius's canon consists of the same twenty-seven books that were codified in subsequent, local councils and make up the New Testament.

Although Athanasius's list did not distinguish between accepted and disputed books as did Eusebius's, the assumption continued of a somewhat fluid boundary to the canon. This fluidity is evident, for example, in the great New Testament codices of the fourth and fifth centuries, which include such Christian books as *1–2 Clement, Epistle of Barnabas*, and *Shepherd of Hermas*.[61] At the risk of some confusion, the acknowledgment of marginal books within the canon—and, functionally speaking, in a codex—implies central books that can be called "the canon within the canon." It is not that the books on the margins are seen as noncanonical or uninspired. Rather, the concept simply recognizes that some books (or passages) are more central than others. Specifically, these books are perceived as including the most important doctrines and therefore also serve as a lens through which to read the rest of the canon.

As natural as the idea of a canon was to early Christians, so also was the idea of the canon within the canon. Jewish interpreters universally acknowledged the centrality of the Torah within the Tanak, the Sadducees going so far as to reject everything but those five books.[62] Like other rabbis, Jesus repeatedly used the language of summary and did not hesitate to name the greatest commands and weightier matters within the whole canon (Matt. 7:12; 22:37–40; 23:23). Therefore, it should be no surprise that the church took to summarizing their faith with select passages and using some books more than others.

Besides the obvious relevance of the canon's development and its conclusion to the present discussion of biblical interpretation—namely, that these are the books to be interpreted alongside the Old Testament—there are also three less obvious implications of the canon's fluidity. First, as Irenaeus has already observed and others after him will say, Scripture clarifies Scripture (the *analogia scripturae*). With the common recognition of a canon within the canon, there would come also a common recognition of the biblical lens, the clearer and more central passages, through which obscure passages would be clarified. Second, the fact that the church recognized central books will explain why some books are used more and commented on more than others, as well as why figures throughout church history will eagerly and unapologetically rank books of the Bible and advise readers where to start. In other words, even those who do not use the language of accepted and disputed books functionally

60. Athanasius, *Festal Letter* 39 (*NPNF*[2] 4:551–52).

61. L. McDonald, "Lists and Catalogs," 597.

62. Flavius Josephus, *Antiquities of the Jews* 13.10.6; 18.1.4, trans. Whiston, 327, 438; Ferguson, *Backgrounds of Early Christianity*, 486–87.

marginalize the same books in Eusebius's second category by neglecting them (as is often the case today). Third, the fact that there is an indistinct boundary to the canon means not only that the intertestamental books will continue to be read and appreciated, as all Christians have agreed, but also that many interpreters will include these books in their functional canons.

Related to the matter of canon, a brief word should be said about the textual basis for Old Testament interpretation. The Septuagint (LXX) was the Greek translation of the Hebrew and Aramaic Old Testament, begun in the third century BC in Alexandria under Ptolemy II Philadelphus and thought to be divinely approved. This Greek version, in all its complexity and diversity of manuscripts, became the Bible of the apostolic and early church.[63] As Justin Martyr said to Trypho the Jew, they are not your Scriptures, but ours.[64] So thorough was the Christian appropriation of the LXX that non-Christian Jews proceeded to make new and improved translations for their own use, and they began to interpret their common Scripture in ways that excluded Christian interpretations. With the exception of Origen, there was very little desire in the early church to read the Hebrew originals at all. The wide use of the LXX affected biblical interpretation in at least two profound ways. First, the fact that many Jewish intertestamental books came to be included in the LXX aided their continued use among Christians, as noted above. Second, the text of the LXX differs in some subtle and other not-so-subtle ways from the Hebrew Masoretic Text of the Old Testament, and some translations are idiosyncratic. The most famous of these instances is the translation of עַלְמָה (*almah*, young maiden) as the more specific παρθένος (*parthenos*, virgin) in Isaiah 7:14, quoted as such in Matthew 1:23. The result is that interpretations of the Old Testament by Greek writers (from the New Testament onward) should always be compared with the LXX.[65] Not until Jerome (ca. 347–420) would a Christian return to the Hebrew as the basis for an Old Testament translation.

Principles of Earliest Christian Exegesis

Biblical interpretation in the early church was a conscious continuation of the hermeneutical principles practiced by Jesus Christ and his apostles. The

63. See Hengel and Deines, *The Septuagint as Christian Scripture*; Lamarche, "The Septuagint: Bible of the Earliest Christians." On the quality of the translation, see Wevers, "Interpretative Character."

64. Justin Martyr, *Dialogue with Trypho 29*, in *Writings of Saint Justin Martyr*, trans. Falls, 191.

65. Such comparison is also possible for those limited to English. E.g., see Pietersma and Wright, *A New English Translation of the Septuagint*.

assumption was not, as many modern Protestants have presumed, that because the apostles were inspired they were therefore able to make what would otherwise be considered illegitimate exegetical leaps, and thus the exegetical practices enabled by unique inspiration could not and should not be carried out by subsequent generations of disciples. No one in the early church understood exegesis in this way. Instead, Jesus and his apostles modeled how biblical exegesis ought to be done within the church.

Since we now have looked at these significant representative documents and issues in early patristic biblical interpretation, it is appropriate to summarize the most important features that have surfaced. It has often been observed that the distinction between ancient and modern exegesis is less about "methods" than about different worldviews and presuppositions—a different "set of attitudes"—regarding Scripture.[66] Thus the following summary, in line with summaries in subsequent chapters, is less a list of methods than it is a catalog of principles or assumptions that the early church shared about Scripture. All of these principles have been illustrated or implied in this chapter.

1. *Divine inspiration.* Early Christians all concurred that Scripture is divinely inspired. Divine inspiration may not have been a sufficient criterion for canonical authority, but it was a necessary one. The belief that Scripture is inspired changes everything about one's disposition toward it. For instance, as a divine word, there is no superfluous or trivial passage of Scripture. Thus the numeral 318 in Genesis 14 was not an inconsequential matter to Barnabas or his fellow believers. Early readers and hearers of Scripture were not less attentive to details than their modern counterparts; rather, they sought and found a different significance in the details. Everything was written for a purpose and for us, so the importance of every word is upheld. Scripture is human but not merely human. Likewise, many of the assumptions and techniques that follow in this list are predicated on or related to the belief that Scripture is divinely inspired.

2. *Twofold sense.* In contrast to moderns, the ancients approached their religious and otherwise great literature with the expectation of finding deeper meanings, a fuller sense (*sensus plenior*). One does not simply read an Old Testament narrative, note the interesting data in the story, and then put it away. Scripture was usually taken at face value, but never merely at face value.

---

66. Kugel and Greer, *Early Biblical Interpretation*, 200–201; F. Young, *Biblical Exegesis*, 207. Frances Young goes on to argue that the ancient and modern methods are, in the grand scheme of things, quite similar. Put negatively, it is a difference in what interpreters find to be principally problematic in a text: doctrinal issues (premodern) versus historical issues (modern).

In addition to the literal sense, there is always more beneath the surface.[67] It is analogous to the way we are trained to read Aesop's fables: with this genre and corpus, we know to look for something deeper. Parents who read such fables to their children may not know all the meanings or even the original contexts, but they know that they ought to look for significance deeper than the surface and that merely reporting the story on the literal level would be to interpret it incorrectly. Similarly, second-century Christians approached Scripture with ears to hear what the Spirit says to the church.

Furthermore, all commentary really is based on the presence of problems of some sort, a question raised by the text whose solution may not be self-evident to every reader. The problems often include an unclear word or a contradiction. Additionally, the problems may present larger hermeneutical issues, such as how an Old Testament dietary restriction or the narrative about Adam applies to Christians. Taken literally—and this is the chief hermeneutical problem—the Old Testament is not a Christian book. If Scripture indeed has to do ultimately with Jesus Christ, then one must account for the fact that the Old Testament, with the exception of a few fairly overt messianic prophecies, is silent about him. Such silence, said early Christians, only applies to the literal sense of the text. But because Scripture is inspired by the divine author, it possesses a sense that need not destroy but does go beyond the letter and, in many cases, beyond the intent and knowledge of the human author.

For many cultural, textual, and even exegetical reasons, then, Scripture was seen to have a twofold sense—the letter and the spirit. The spiritual sense itself can be multivalent, not limited to only one meaning or application. And it is this spiritual sense beyond the letter that allows Christian application of otherwise puzzling food laws, irrelevant historical narratives, and unfulfilled prophecies. This spiritual sense also extended to other revered Christian texts. As catechumens heard the exposition of the creed, for example, the bishop would explain it both literally and spiritually.[68] As such, there is a wide openness to the orthodox, spiritual interpretations and applications that an inspired or orthodox text can yield.

3. *Christological interpretation.* Ultimately, that fuller, spiritual sense points to Christ. The theologians of the early church, with the occasional exceptions

---

67. On the literal sense and its development in the second century, see Ayres, "'There's Fire in That Rain.'"

68. As in Jerusalem, reported by the pilgrim in *Egeria's Travels* 46: "[The bishop] explains the meaning of each of the phrases of the Creed in the same way he explained Holy Scripture, expounding first the literal and then the spiritual sense. In this fashion the Creed is taught." *Egeria: Diary of a Pilgrimage*, trans. Gingras, 123. See also Ferguson, "Irenaeus' *Proof of the Apostolic Preaching*," 128, who argues that Irenaeus's catechetical manual, *Demonstration of Apostolic Preaching*, has a literal-spiritual outline.

of some gnostics and the heretic Marcion, agreed that Jesus Christ is the scope and center of the whole of Scripture, including the Old Testament. Along with the assumption of divine inspiration, exegesis was governed by christological interpretation. Finding Christ in the New Testament is natural enough. But, following New Testament writers such as Paul, who said that the life-giving rock in the desert was Christ (see Exod. 17:6; Num. 20:11; 1 Cor. 10:3–4), early Christians also found their Messiah throughout the Old Testament. As the New Testament implied and Irenaeus acknowledged, the meaning of prophecy was now clear in light of the ultimate fulfillment in Christ.[69] This recognition has many implications for what is now possible in reading the Old Testament in light of the New. There is no book of the Old Testament, no matter how intimately tied to its ancient Near Eastern context, that is not finally about Christ. Such readings are not Christocentric to the exclusion of the Father and the Holy Spirit or to the subversion of the narrative at hand. But the narratives, laws, psalms, wisdom, and prophecies all point to the revelation of God in Christ and testify to the reconciliation that God brings his people in Christ. When the earliest Christians speak about Christ, they do so in the biblical idiom, repurposing Old Testament language of God's love and salvation, so that Christ is seen as fulfilling the ancient words in a new way.

4. *Variety of approaches and terms.* The approaches to the fuller sense were not fixed, and the fluid terminology for describing the approaches reflects the unsystematic nature of the enterprise. A text and its interpretation could variously be described as spiritual, mystical, allegorical, parabolic, typological, figurative, theoretical, scholarly, tropological, or anagogical, and the differences among them were occasionally ambiguous or obscured. These approaches were inclusive of christological interpretation, but broader in their application to other spiritual realities. The early flexibility of the categories would give way to sharper distinctions down the road. For instance, the appeal to types and antitypes, present in the New Testament, would come to refer specifically to connections between antecedent figures and consequent realities.

5. *Unity of Scripture.* Because Scripture is divinely inspired by the same Holy Spirit and is meant to draw its readers to God in Christ, and based as it is on the doctrinal unity of the apostles and prophets, the early church presupposed the unity of Scripture. By the late second century, the Old Testament canon had been received by all but the Marcionites, and the center of the New Testament canon had taken distinct shape. The presence of diversity between the Testaments and among the many human authors does not supplant the overarching unity of the whole, the christological thread that runs

69. See also F. Young, *Biblical Exegesis*, 286–87.

from Genesis through the Apocalypse, the one story of redemption. Against some gnostics and Marcion, who sought to drive a wedge between the Testaments, Irenaeus and others emphasized the unity of this written revelation. The presupposition of biblical unity enables the christological and typological connections that were made. It also grounds the method of *analogia scripturae*, seen at least as early as Irenaeus, in which one clear Scripture may be used to illumine another obscurer passage, even if they were written by different human authors in different contexts.

6. *Rule of faith*. The only way for the early church to ensure that Scripture would not be employed in support of heresy was to interpret it through the lens of the rule of faith. Without that hermeneutical lens of the *analogia fidei* (analogy of faith), the Scriptures could be wrested to support anything that one desired. Therefore, the rule of faith, the summary of apostolic teaching handed along in the church, provided a pattern for interpretation as well as limits to interpretive possibilities. The Bible was not to be read just like any other book.

7. *Reading as worship*. Most of the features of early Christian interpretation mentioned above relate to the observation that reading Scripture in the early church is intimately connected with worship. The gathering of God's people to worship was the primary context of Bible reading and interpretation, whether in the synagogue (Luke 4:16–21) or the early Christian assemblies.[70] Like worship itself, which is meant to engage both the spirit and the intellect (1 Cor. 14:1–19), the reading of Scripture in the early church never excluded the use of reason, and it was never to be read apart from faith. Bible reading was certainly not a primarily scientific or scholarly activity. Texts function differently in a congregational, liturgical gathering than they do in a university classroom. "Think how differently a verse from the Scriptures touches us when it is sung or spoken in the Liturgy."[71] The act of reading Scripture is prayer, communication with the divine, and therefore an act of worship. Like language itself, Scripture is sacramental.[72] Scripture was a sacred text for a sacred setting. It is the church's book, and its proper interpretation can only happen in conversation with the church.

Early patristic exegesis was not monolithic in its approach, but there are common themes. All these foregoing assumptions shaped biblical interpretation in profound ways. Early biblical interpretation was also much more

---

70. See the description in Justin, *First Apology* 67.
71. Wilken, *Spirit of Early Christian Thought*, 74.
72. This point is made in F. Young, *Biblical Exegesis*, 140–60; and Boersma, *Scripture as Real Presence*.

than can be contained in this list, more than the sum of these parts. But these principles illustrate the contrast to modern exegesis, and they begin to show why exegesis appears to be such a very different enterprise in the patristic period than it is today. In light of these presuppositions about Scripture, for example, phrases and words from one book of the Bible would frequently be employed to explain or apply similar phrases in another book. Although attention would be given to the literal sense, equal or much more space on the commentator's page would be devoted to spiritual interpretation and moral application. No interpretation was considered correct that offended against the rule of faith. At the same time, many interpretations of the same text could be true if they were in accord with that apostolic doctrine.

3

Later Patristic Exegesis

We maintain that the law has a twofold interpretation, one literal and the other spiritual, as was also taught by some of our predecessors. . . . It is consistent with this when Paul also says that "the letter kills," which is equivalent to the literal interpretation; whereas "the spirit gives life," which means the same as the spiritual interpretation.

—Origen[1]

For he is the best student who does not read his thoughts into the book, but lets it reveal its own; who draws from it its sense, and does not import his own into it, nor force upon its words a meaning which he had determined was the right one before he opened its pages. Since then we are to discourse of the things of God, let us assume that God has full knowledge of himself, and bow with humble reverence to his words. For he whom we can only know through his own utterances is the fitting witness concerning himself.

—Hilary of Poitiers[2]

But here some one perhaps will ask, Since the canon of Scripture is complete, and sufficient of itself for everything, and more than sufficient, what need is there to join with it the authority of the Church's

1. Origen, *Contra Celsum* 7.20.
2. Hilary of Poitiers, *De Trinitate* 1.18 (NPNF[2] 9:45).

interpretation? For this reason—because, owing to the depth of Holy
Scripture, all do not accept it in one and the same sense, but one un-
derstands its words in one way, another in another; so that it seems
to be capable of as many interpretations as there are interpreters.

—Vincent of Lérins[3]

By the turn of the third century, the Great Church, which for a long time
had been an overwhelmingly Gentile movement, accepted the Jewish
Scriptures by interpreting them spiritually and supplemented them with a
canon of apostolic writings. At this point, however, though many had practiced
spiritual interpretation, no one had yet articulated its principles very clearly.
It was left to Origen, a teacher of the church, a catechist in Alexandria, to
elaborate on the doctrine of Scripture passed down as part of the rule of faith.
His exegetical principles and practices would have a profound impact on the
later development of patristic exegesis, especially in the Greek-speaking East.

Origen

Origen (ca. 185–254) was born and raised in Alexandria, where at a young
age he became head of its catechetical school. He later moved to Caesarea in
232. Origen is one of the most learned minds and most prolific writers in the
history of the church, composing, according to the church father Epiphanius,
around six thousand works, the vast majority of which are now lost.[4] His
many contributions to biblical interpretation include the *Hexapla*, in which
he engaged in textual criticism that was ahead of his time. He is also the first
Christian to write scholarly commentaries on biblical books, and he produced
a commentary on nearly every one of those books.[5]

The interpretive approach for which Origen has become justly famous—and
to his opponents, infamous—is allegory. The charge that Origen introduced

3. Vincent of Lérins, *Commonitory* 2.5 (NPNF[2] 11:132).
4. For this citation and a helpful list of Origen's major extant works, including which ones
survive in the original Greek or only in Latin translation, see introduction to Origen, *Homilies
on Genesis and Exodus*, trans. Heine, 25–27. See also Crouzel, *Origen*, 37–49.
5. Among the many treatments of Origen's exegesis, Martens, *Origen and Scripture*, provides
an excellent overview of all the major topics. In addition, see Lubac, *History and Spirit*; Hanson,
Allegory and Event; Crouzel, *Origen*, 61–84; Torjesen, *Hermeneutical Procedure and Theological Method*; Lauro, *Soul and Spirit of Scripture*; Heine, "Reading the Bible with Origen";
Heine, *Origen: Scholarship*, which makes a clear distinction between the early Alexandrian
works and the later Caesarean works.

allegory into Christian biblical interpretation, a view associated now mostly with Protestants, did not originate with Protestants. Rather, the charge goes back to Origen's own contemporaries. Porphyry, the Neoplatonic philosopher, scandalized by the Christian treatment of the Old Testament as a divine book, complains thus about Christian exegesis:

> Some . . . had recourse to interpretations [ἐξηγήσεις, *exēgēseis*] that are incompatible and do not harmonize with what has been written. . . . For they boast that the things said plainly by Moses are riddles, treating them as divine oracles full of hidden mysteries . . . ; and so they put forward their interpretations [ἐξηγήσεις]. . . . This kind of absurdity must be traced to a man whom I met when I was still young, who had a great reputation, and still holds it, because of the writings he has left behind, I mean Origen, whose fame has been widespread among the teachers of this kind of learning.[6]

Christians soon joined in the criticism. Porphyry's contemporary, Methodius of Olympus, opposed Origen's interpretation of the dry bones story in Ezekiel 37. Methodius insisted that the story is about the future, bodily resurrection of the dead, and he accused Origen of "allegorizing" (ἀλληγοροῦντος, *allēgorountos*) the text.[7] Origen's allegedly allegorical interpretation, by the way, took the story to be about the restoration of Israel from exile, which, ironically, happens to be the "literal" interpretation now preferred by modern commentators. After Methodius, the Antiochene exegetes began to focus their critique of Alexandrian allegory on Origen.[8] Because he has been such a controversial figure in the history of exegesis, rather than dismissing Origen's exegetical methods or taking the polemic at face value, it is necessary to take some time to examine what Origen actually wrote and how he arrived at and employed his allegorical method.

As a means to examining Origen's exegetical approach, we begin, therefore, with a typical example, a lengthy passage that, to most modern readers, is puzzling. In a homily about the departure of the Israelites from Egyptian slavery, Origen says:

> The children of Israel "departed," the text says, "from Ramesse and came to Socoth. And they departed from Socoth and came to Etham" [Exod. 12:37; 13:20]. If there is anyone who is about to depart from Egypt, if there is anyone who desires to forsake the dark deeds of this world and the darkness of errors,

---

6. Eusebius, *Hist. eccl.* 6.19.4–5. For more on Porphyry's views of the Old Testament and its allegorization, see Cook, *Interpretation of the New Testament*, 128–33.

7. Methodius of Olympus, *On the Resurrection* 3.18 (PG 18:324A).

8. See the discussion of the school of Antioch below.

he must first of all depart "from Ramesse." *Ramesse* means "the commotion of a moth." Depart from Ramesse, therefore, if you wish to come to this place that the Lord may be your leader and precede you "in the column of the cloud" [Exod. 13:21] and "the rock" may follow you, which offers you "spiritual food" and "spiritual drink" [1 Cor. 10:3–4] no less. Nor should you store treasure "there where the moth destroys and thieves dig through and steal" [Matt. 6:20].

"They came," the text says, "to Socoth." The etymologists teach that *Socoth* is understood as "tents" among the Hebrews. When, therefore, leaving Egypt, you have dispelled the moths of all corruption from yourself and have cast aside the inducements of vices, you will dwell in tents. For we dwell in tents of which "we do not wish to be unclothed but to be further clothed" [2 Cor. 5:4]. Dwelling in tents, however, indicates that he who hastens to God is free and has no impediments. . . .

Etham, they say, is translated in our language as "signs for them," and rightly so, for here you will hear it said: "God was preceding them by day in a column of cloud and by night in a column of fire." You do not find this done at Ramesse nor at Socoth, which is called the second encampment for those departing. It is the third encampment in which divine signs occur.[9]

This passage, characteristic of Origen's exegesis, is a puzzle because he seems to make so much of such a simple travel narrative. The Israelites' journey from A to B to C is a detail that most modern readers pass over, regarding it as significant, at most, at the level of historical curiosity, but not at the level of theological or moral significance. How, then, does Origen start with this detail about Israelite pit stops and arrive at Jesus's words of moral instruction and the moral symbolism of camping in tents? Let us return to these questions about this passage later. For now we should examine Origen's general approach to Scripture for some background.

Scripture is no ordinary collection of writings. Because he considered it to be "divine" and "inspired,"[10] Origen had a dynamic view of Scripture, regarding the Bible as a living word, not dead (cf. Heb. 4:12). The divine Logos is incarnate in the words of Scripture, whether or not the reader recognizes it.[11] As God has accommodated himself to humanity in the incarnation of his Son, fully divine and fully human, likewise the words of Scripture, fully divine and fully human, are another form of God's accommodation to his people. As Henri Crouzel explains Origen's thought, "Scripture and the Logos constitute a single Word. Scripture is, in a way, an incarnation of the Word

9. Origen, *Homilies on Exodus* 5.2, in *Homilies on Genesis and Exodus*, trans. Heine, 277–78.
10. Origen, *Princ.* 4.1.1; 4.2.1. In *Princ.* 4.2.6, Origen calls the inspired writer Paul a "divine man."
11. Origen, *Princ.* 4.1.7.

into the letter analogous to the other incarnation into the flesh: not, however, a second incarnation for it relates entirely to the Unique Incarnation, preparing it in the Old Testament or expressing it in the New." [12] Building on the language of the incarnational analogy, Origen regards it as imperative to search Scripture for the spiritual meaning enfleshed in its literal words. Thus Scripture must be not only read but also studied, explored, discovered—in short, interpreted.

Like many before and after him, Origen had to deal with the relationship between the Old and New Testaments. Since the Logos is present throughout Scripture, Origen finds Christ throughout the Old Testament. Indeed, allegorical interpretation simply is, for Origen, christological interpretation. He was convinced that the Old Testament illumines the New, and vice versa. He states that the divine character of the Old Testament can be affirmed only in light of its fulfillment in the New Testament. [13]

Furthermore, as already reported, Origen did not originate the practice of spiritual interpretation. The Greeks and Jews had all engaged in allegorical readings of their sacred texts. In fact, in the ancient world it was expected that sacred literature was to be interpreted and applied in ways that transcend the literal meaning. [14] This assumption may be one reason why Porphyry criticizes Origen, as cited above; it is not that Porphyry finds allegorical readings of sacred literature to be illegitimate, but that he does not regard the Christian Scriptures as sacred. [15] Yet for those who did regard the Old Testament and the emerging New Testament canon as sacred, some manner of spiritual interpretation and even allegory was normal. As we have seen, the first- and second-century Christian writers before Origen shared this interpretive assumption about their canon of Scripture. More proximate to Origen, a generation earlier Clement of Alexandria had introduced Philonic exegesis into Christian interpretation. With Philo, Clement, and now Origen, a definite Alexandrian school of exegesis was developing in continuity with broader practices, but also, thanks to Origen, with an increasingly systematic basis and implementation.

Like his Christian predecessors, Origen would also claim the apostle Paul as the precedent for his biblical hermeneutic. It was Paul who introduced the language of "allegory" into Christian exegesis. The verb Paul used in

12. Crouzel, *Origen*, 70.

13. Origen, *Princ.* 4.1.6.

14. Cf. Barton, *Holy Writings, Sacred Text*, 53–54; and Froehlich, introduction to *Biblical Interpretation in the Early Church*, 17.

15. But Origen notes at least one instance of a pagan, Numenius the Pythagorean, who interpreted the Old Testament allegorically. See Origen, *Contra Celsum* 1.15.

Galatians 4:24, ἀλληγορέω (*allēgoreō*), means to speak or imply something other than what is said. It was Paul, Origen said, who taught the Gentiles how to interpret the Old Testament rightly. In the introduction to the homily on Exodus quoted above, Origen explains that Paul's interpretations of the Old Testament, found throughout his letters to Gentile Christians, were meant to provide examples for these newcomers to the faith. They should strive to understand the books of the Law "spiritually," avoiding the mistakes of the Jews who rejected Christ. Having received these examples, says Origen, we should follow Paul's lead and interpret other passages accordingly. "Let us cultivate, therefore, the seeds of spiritual understanding received from the blessed apostle Paul."[16] Origen simply wants to interpret in the footsteps of Paul.[17] In fact, throughout Scripture there is self-conscious acknowledgment of its deeper meaning. Biblical history was written "with an eye to an allegorical meaning," and "the very authors of the doctrines themselves and the writers interpreted these narratives allegorically."[18] For Origen, in other words, allegorical interpretation by the reader was the intent of the authors.

By the way, here one cannot find any hint of the explanation that later became common fare among Protestants who rejected "allegory." Paul and other New Testament writers, so that explanation goes, were uniquely inspired to produce their select christological and allegorical interpretations of the Old Testament. Those particular, inspired interpretations can be repeated, but they cannot serve as models for the allegorical interpretation of other texts that are not so handled in the New Testament. In short, writers of New Testament books were justified in such off-the-wall interpretations because of their special inspiration. On the contrary, Origen and every other premodern interpreter would have regarded this understanding as an inconsistent and impoverished way to interpret Scripture. The New Testament does not provide an exhaustive reading of every Old Testament text. Instead, Paul's exegesis and application of the Old Testament provide illustrative models for Christians, inviting readers to do the same with other passages.

Though implicitly approved by apostolic example, the trouble is that Paul—and for that matter, the *Epistle of Barnabas*, Irenaeus, and others who interpreted spiritually—did not provide any set of rules for interpreting figuratively. Origen thus stands out as the first Christian to systematize an exegetical approach. To be sure, Christian authors before him had all interpreted Scripture.

16. Origen, *Homilies on Exodus* 5.1, in *Homilies on Genesis and Exodus*, trans. Heine, 275–77.
17. Origen, *Contra Celsum* 4.44.
18. Origen, *Contra Celsum* 4.49–50.

But Origen was the first to consider the second-order question of method and articulate principles for how interpretation, including allegory, ought to be done.[19]

Origen provides this hermeneutical account in his treatise *On First Principles* (*De principiis*). In this book he takes the rule of faith, the oral summary of apostolic doctrine reflected in the writings of Irenaeus and others, and as we would expect from a teacher of catechumens, he expands on each of its main points. In his systematic exposition of Christian teaching, Origen is the first writer to include the doctrine of Scripture in his discussion of the rule of faith. That he includes the doctrine implies its antiquity and place in the apostolic tradition. He connects the spiritual sense of Scripture to the doctrine of inspiration: the Spirit gives Scripture its spirit, so to speak. He expressly states that the affirmation of Scripture's spiritual sense is "unanimous" in the church, though such interpretive work should be carried out by those who are "gifted with the grace of the Holy Spirit in the word of wisdom and knowledge."[20] It is in this context that Origen reveals his theology of biblical interpretation. Because so many erroneous interpretations have arisen among the Jews and gnostics, Origen emphasizes the importance of articulating and following the right method.[21] The errors of both groups—the Jewish rejection of the Messiah and the heretical ascription of the Old Testament to an evil Demiurge—are the result of their following the letter to the exclusion of the spirit.[22]

Like most interpreters before him, especially in his native Alexandria, Origen distinguished between the literal and spiritual meanings of Scripture. He went beyond his predecessors, however, in delineating a "threefold way" of reading. Seeking to show how his method, or way of reading, is reflected in the Scripture itself, Origen finds the key in Proverbs 22:20–21, which in the Septuagint reads: "Now then, copy them [the words of the wise] for yourself three times over, for counsel and knowledge." Based on this instruction, Origen writes:

> One must therefore portray the meaning of the sacred writings in a threefold way upon one's soul, so that the simple man may be edified by what we may call the flesh of the scripture, this name being given to the obvious interpretation;

19. A possible exception would be the gnostic Ptolemy, who expressed his method of interpreting the Old Testament in his letter to Flora. See Epiphanius, *Panarion* 33, in *Panarion: Book I*, 198–204. See also the discussion in Kugel and Greer, *Early Biblical Interpretation*, 151–53.

20. Origen, *Princ.* 1.preface.8.

21. Origen, *Princ.* 4.2.1.

22. Origen, *Princ.* 4.2.2.

while the man who has made some progress may be edified by its soul, as it were; and the man who is perfect . . . may be edified by the spiritual law, which has "a shadow of the good things to come." For just as man consists of body, soul and spirit, so in the same way does the scripture, which has been prepared by God to be given for man's salvation.[23]

Origen held to a Platonic, tripartite anthropology of body, soul, and spirit, with the spirit representing the rational part of the animate soul. This same tripartite anthropology is corroborated by Paul in 1 Thessalonians 5:23. Using this analogy, Origen distinguishes a threefold meaning of Scripture, corresponding to body, soul, and spirit. In this anthropological analogy, the somatic or corporeal (that is, bodily) sense of Scripture stands for the literal, historical meaning. The second level is the psychic or animal (that is, soul-ish) sense, which represents the moral or typological meaning of the passage. The third sense of Scripture is the pneumatic or spiritual, corresponding to the highest, mystical meaning. The threefold mode is simply an expansion of the twofold. Origen's body of the text corresponds to the letter. Origen's soul and spirit amplify the spirit.

Figure 3.1

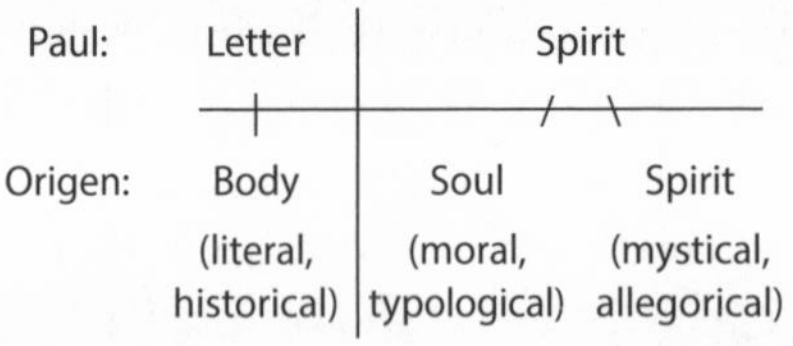

Paul's twofold approach evolved into a threefold approach in Origen.

Any given passage of Scripture may or may not include all three senses. All passages will have a spiritual sense, but some passages, Origen claims, "have no bodily sense at all," in which case the reader "must seek only for the soul and the spirit, as it were, of the passage."[24] The first, bodily sense, when present, serves to benefit the genuine believer whose faith and knowledge are simple. Whether or not that first sense is present, however, the goal is to be drawn upward to the higher senses. Once again, Origen finds his model in Pauline exegesis, quoting 1 Corinthians 9:9–10, in which the apostle cites the law forbidding the muzzling of the ox that is treading grain. Paul claims that this law is not about oxen but about us. Likewise,

23. Origen, *Princ.* 4.2.4.
24. Origen, *Princ.* 4.2.5. Cf. *Princ.* 4.3.5: "For with regard to divine Scripture as a whole we are of the opinion that all of it has a spiritual sense, but not all of it has a bodily sense."

Origen sees precedent here for the second sense: moral application beyond the letter of the text.[25]

Origen then discusses the third sense, the pneumatic, or spiritual, exegesis. It is interesting to observe, first of all, that he reserves pursuit of the highest spiritual meaning for those with sufficient insight to identify "heavenly things." It is not a task for everyone, but only for "those who are gifted with the grace of the Holy Spirit in the word of wisdom and knowledge."[26] As a prime example of the spiritual interpretation of the Old Testament, Origen cites Paul's use of Exodus and Numbers in 1 Corinthians 10. There the apostle refers to the literal food, drink, and rock as τύποι (*typoi*) and then interprets them as "spiritual food" and "spiritual drink" from the "spiritual rock" (1 Cor. 10:1–6). Among other passages, Origen goes on to cite Paul's allegory in Galatians 4:24 as an example of what he means by the spiritual sense.[27]

Why has God inspired Scripture with these distinct senses? According to Origen, the Holy Spirit's primary scope or goal (σκοπός, *skopos*) in the inspiration of Scripture was to communicate what is necessary for human salvation in the literal sense, so that all believers may search the mysteries and share in spiritual doctrine.[28] In short, the first goal of the Spirit is to reveal. The second goal of inspiration was to hide the deeper mysteries of the faith underneath the literal sense, just as the human spirit is hidden unseen in the external body.[29] In other words, the second goal of the Spirit is to conceal, but not so deeply that the mysteries cannot be discovered. The result is that Scripture is beneficial proportionate to the capacity of every reader. Even on the literal level, Scripture is usually edifying and profitable for those who cannot understand its deeper, spiritual sense, but there is something also for the more mature believer to uncover.

Given that a spiritual meaning is always the intended goal, how is one to know when the literal should be bypassed? One should take the text literally whenever possible, when it is meant to be taken literally, or when it is already spiritually edifying on the literal level. This does not mean that Origen gave the literal sense as much attention as we would today; he often neglected it on his way to what he and all ancient interpreters regarded as the more important meanings. After all, for Origen one question is always central: To what spiritual meaning are these incarnate words pointing?

25. Origen, *Princ*. 1.2.6.
26. Origen, *Princ*. 1.preface.8. Origen's emphasis on spiritual maturity for exegesis is addressed in Martens, *Origen and Scripture*, 168–78, et passim.
27. Origen, *Princ*. 4.2.6.
28. Origen, *Princ*. 4.2.7.
29. Origen, *Princ*. 4.2.8.

On the way to that spiritual meaning, indeed the literal sense at times may be sidestepped. For instance, Origen claims that Scripture sometimes documents events on the literal level that are meant only to convey spiritual realities. Occasionally there is nonhistorical narrative, particularly in the Old Testament. Origen's first example comes from the opening chapters of Genesis:

> Now what man of intelligence will believe that the first and the second and third day, and the evening and the morning existed without the sun and moon and stars? And that the first day, if we may so call it, was even without a heaven? And who is so silly as to believe that God, after the manner of a farmer, "planted a paradise eastward in Eden," and set in it a visible and palpable "tree of life," of such a sort that anyone who tasted its fruit with his bodily teeth would gain life; and again that one could partake of "good and evil" by masticating the fruit taken from the tree of that name?[30]

Origen claims that there are innumerable such examples that are "recorded as actual events, but which did not happen literally."[31] Although most of Origen's examples come from the Old Testament, he occasionally finds nonhistorical narrations also in the New Testament. He singles out as patently impossible the description of the devil taking Jesus to a high mountain from which could be seen all the kingdoms of the world (Matt. 4:8).[32] These are instances in which one is presumably better off not spending too much time contemplating the bodily, or literal, sense.

Just as there is the occasional nonhistorical narrative, there are also some irrational or impossible laws. Origen mentions the prohibition against eating vultures, for no one would want to eat one anyway, and against eating a griffin, for no one has ever caught one; the decree to sacrifice a goatstag, for this animal does not exist; and the command to stay seated in one's home on the Sabbath, for no one can stay in a seated position all day long.[33] His occasionally ad hominem tone notwithstanding, Origen's point is that the many difficulties that follow from taking these narratives literally serve as clues that there is a spiritual message to be teased out of the text.

Other examples of unintelligible passages on the literal level are those that speak about God in improper ways. Origen points out the biblical descriptions of God walking in the garden and of Cain going out "from the face of the

---

30. Origen, *Princ.* 4.3.1.
31. Origen, *Princ.* 4.3.1.
32. Origen, *Princ.* 4.3.1.
33. Origen, *Princ.* 4.3.2. It should go without saying that it is Origen who misunderstands the fauna.

LORD" (Gen. 4:16).[34] To paraphrase a bit, unless one is willing to depict God as embodied and ignorant, no one takes everything narrated in Genesis 1–11 literally. A governing principle for Origen and other early Christians is that "everything recorded about God, even if it may be immediately unsuitable, must be understood [as] worthy of a good God."[35] For instance, "It is obvious that the statements about God's wrath are to be interpreted allegorically from what is also recorded of His sleep."[36] The rationale is that, when God speaks to humans through Scripture, he accommodates the words, "just as when we are talking with little children we do not aim to speak in the finest language possible to us, but say what is appropriate to the weakness of those whom we are addressing."[37] Scripture is akin to baby talk for the immature. This principle of accommodation or adaptability is pervasive throughout patristic exegesis, especially John Chrysostom, and prominent in later exegetes, such as John Calvin.[38]

When such unreasonable or impossible passages are encountered in Scripture, the reader can know that those passages are there for a reason: to challenge and stretch the reader to consider the spiritual lesson hidden in the mystery. In other cases, a difficulty in the text may be explained on the literal level, though the allegorical meaning is not thereby ruled out.[39] That is, Origen is not so quick to ignore the historical meaning even when an allegorical meaning is ready at hand.

A reader does not encounter difficulties such as these on every page of the Bible. But Origen's method is a step ahead of the *Epistle of Barnabas*, whose author seems more than willing to jettison the literal sense of the Old Testament. Origen's approach also contrasts with the assertion of Justin, who declared that no Scriptures are contradictory.[40] Origen is closer to the opinion of his older contemporary Tertullian, who, while acknowledging contradictions in the chronology of the Gospels, focuses instead on the main points of each narrative.[41]

---

34. Origen, *Princ.* 4.3.1.

35. Origen, *Homilies on Jeremiah*, homily 20, in *Homilies on Jeremiah; Homily on 1 Kings 28*, trans. J. Smith, 221.

36. Origen, *Contra Celsum* 4.72; for other examples, see 6.61–63; 7.27.

37. Origen, *Contra Celsum* 4.71.

38. See Sheridan, *Language for God*, 224–26. For the prominence of accommodation or adaptability in John Chrysostom, see Rylaarsdam, *John Chrysostom on Divine Pedagogy*. Cf. John Calvin, *Inst.* 1.13.1.

39. Origen, *Contra Celsum* 4.45, 47; 5.56.

40. Justin, *Dialogue with Trypho* 65. This opinion is expressed in earlier writers as well; e.g., 1 Clement 45.2–3.

41. Tertullian, *Against Marcion* 4.2.

Most of Origen's opponents, long past and more recent, fail to read him, and, if they do, they stop with these points and make no further effort to understand him. But he writes on, as if anticipating the caricatures that will be applied to him and to his method. He says that no one should suspect him of generalizing and saying that because one particular story did not happen, therefore nothing in the Bible happened as reported, or that, because one law cannot be taken literally, no law should be followed literally. When the factual truth of historical narrative is presented plainly, there is no need to doubt its reliability. In regard to thousands of facts, "we are clearly aware that the historical fact is true." Rufinus's ancient translation captures the sense: "For the passages which are historically true are far more numerous than those which contain a purely spiritual meaning."[42] Origen respects the historical sense unless it is patently absurd or false. Straightforward moral laws, such as those found in the Decalogue, are to be followed literally.

Whether or not a given story or law can be interpreted literally is generally clear. But what should an interpreter do if it is not clear whether this story actually happened or whether that law is to be literally obeyed? Citing Jesus, Origen writes, "Search the Scriptures" (John 5:39). One should look throughout Scripture for similar expressions and themes in order to gain clarity regarding the ambiguous passage.[43] Origen advocates the *analogia scripturae*, explaining obscure passages "from the scriptures themselves by comparing them with one another."[44] He recommends a kind of mental concordance search, which, for him and other church fathers who had memorized most or all of the New Testament, could be quite effective. As observed with Irenaeus, this practice of using Scripture as its own commentary assumes the fundamental unity of Scripture.

An example of a possible ambiguity would be the Old Testament promises referring to Israel, many of which were never literally fulfilled. Origen notes that Paul's reference to "Israel according to the flesh" (1 Cor. 10:18) implies that there is also an Israel according to the spirit. His inference is confirmed elsewhere in Paul's distinction between the inward and outward Jew (Rom. 2:28–29) and the declaration that "not all who are descended from Israel are Israel" (Rom. 9:6 NIV). Those prophecies concerning Israel, then, as well as any mention of Israel, may be interpreted spiritually as God's people,

42. Origen, *Princ.* 4.3.4. Hans Boersma observes that most examples that scholars provide of Origen's dismissal of historicity come from Gen. 1–2 or Revelation. Boersma, *Scripture as Real Presence*, 29–30.
43. Origen, *Princ.* 4.3.5.
44. Origen, *Contra Celsum* 4.72; 7.11.

regardless of their physical pedigree, just as the declarations about Egypt or Babylon may refer to the enemies of God, even if literal descendants of Jacob are among them.[45] The same spiritual interpretation is possible for the city of Jerusalem, for the apostle Paul declares that "the Jerusalem above is free; she is our mother" (Gal. 4:26).[46] Once a referent is identified, the intertextual search for similar referents opens the door for spiritual interpretations and applications. As Frances Young indicates, the search for and identification of referents is just as important as any distinction between the literal and the spiritual senses.[47]

Origen himself practiced this apparently rigid threefold theory of interpretation that he lays out in *De principiis* (*On First Principles*) rather loosely, often blurring the distinction between the psychic (soulish) and pneumatic (spiritual) senses. The method of a threefold sense would frequently collapse back into a twofold sense, only distinguishing letter from spirit. Origen anticipates this simplification already in *De principiis* itself. After his initial explanation of his tripartite interpretation, Origen essentially shuffles between letter and spirit in his subsequent discussion. One of Origen's favorite texts supporting this distinction was 2 Corinthians 3:6: "The letter kills, but the Spirit brings to life." As he explains in his *Commentary on John*, "Now the person who is enslaved to the letter that kills and has not partaken of the spirit that makes alive, and who does not follow the spiritual meanings of the law would be the one who is not a true worshipper and does not worship the Father in spirit."[48]

Origen describes the twofold hermeneutic, which he claims to have inherited from those before him, even more simply in *Against Celsus* (*Contra Celsum*, written about two decades after *De principiis*). To the pagan Celsus's charge that there are contradictions in Scripture, Origen responds, "We maintain that the law has a twofold interpretation, one literal and the other spiritual, as was also taught by some of our predecessors. . . . It is consistent with this when Paul also says that 'the letter kills,' which is equivalent to the literal interpretation; whereas 'the spirit gives life,' which means the same as the spiritual interpretation."[49] Origen, following traditional Christian exegetical principles, does not deny that there are contradictions—that is,

45. Origen, *Princ.* 4.3.6–9.
46. Origen, *Princ.* 4.3.8.
47. F. Young, *Biblical Exegesis*, 119–39.
48. Origen, *Commentary on the Gospel according to John* 13.110, trans. Heine, 90–91, commenting on John 4:23–24.
49. Origen, *Contra Celsum* 7.20; cf. 4.21; 5.31; and 6.70, trans. Chadwick: "[Paul] calls the sensible interpretation of the divine scriptures 'the letter' and the intelligible interpretation 'the spirit.'"

if Scripture is read incorrectly.[50] He then points out an example of Celsus's mistake: "If, then, the letter of the law promises wealth to the righteous, Celsus may follow the letter that kills and think that the promise is speaking of blind wealth. But we regard it as the riches that have keen sight, according as a person is rich 'in all utterance and all knowledge.'"[51] This transition from a theoretically triple to a functionally double hermeneutic is reflected throughout Origen's extant homilies and commentaries.[52] To mention just one example that is indicative of the whole, in his opening homily on Genesis, a constant refrain is the juxtaposition between, on the one hand, what the text says "according to the letter" in its "historical meaning" and, on the other hand, what it signifies "according to the spiritual meaning" or "allegorically."[53] What Origen, ever the catechetical teacher at heart, intends to do in going beyond the letter to the spiritual meaning is to "relate the meaning to ourselves."[54] This "attention to the text" is both for doctrinal instruction and for moral edification, so that the hearers may be instructed in holiness and may receive the mind of Christ.[55]

With these principles in mind, we may now return to the homily quoted above about the Israelites' departure from Egypt. Recall that Origen begins his exposition of the text by saying, "If there is anyone who is about to depart from Egypt, if there is anyone who desires to forsake the dark deeds of this world and the darkness of errors, he must first of all depart 'from Ramesse.'" Why does Origen immediately equate Egypt with the dark deeds of the world? In short, along with the aid of popular etymologies, he takes the physical journey out of Egypt, from Ramesse to Socoth to Etham, to be a metaphor for the spiritual journey. Everything that he says thereafter in the homily follows from this assumption. But from where does this assumption come?

Origen builds his exegesis on what is surely the most enduring and detailed typology in Christian history: the exodus story as a foreshadowing of and metaphor for salvation through Christ. The exodus is the central and

50. In *Contra Celsum* 2.32, Origen notes that Christians are more aware than their critics of the discrepancies.

51. Origen, *Contra Celsum* 7.21, trans. Chadwick; cf. 1.17–18; 2.37. Like Porphyry, Celsus found fault with those who interpret the Mosaic history "figuratively and allegorically." *Contra Celsum* 7.18.

52. Frances Young, "Alexandrian and Antiochene Exegesis," 338, notes that *De principiis* is neither the best nor the only place to see Origen's actual exegetical practice.

53. Origen, *Homilies on Genesis* 1.1, 15, 17, in *Homilies on Genesis and Exodus*, trans. Heine, 48, 68–70, et passim.

54. Origen, *Homilies on Genesis* 1.3, in *Homilies on Genesis and Exodus*, trans. Heine, 52.

55. Origen, *Homilies on Genesis* 1.17, in *Homilies on Genesis and Exodus*, trans. Heine, 71.

foundational story of Israel's redemption. Already in the Old Testament, the exodus story is symbolic of salvation, and subsequent rescues, such as deliverance and return from Babylonian exile, are couched in terms of a new exodus.

This exodus typology is given new life through the lens of the New Testament, which often depicts Jesus in the role of a new, spiritual Moses who came out of Egypt (Matt. 2:15), passed through the water and endured forty days of testing in the wilderness (Matt. 3:16–4:11), delivered his torah from the mount (Matt. 5:1), and more than once fed the hungry multitudes with bread. Jesus, in fact, supersedes Moses in his teaching, gifts of grace, and provision of spiritual nourishment (Mark 9:7; John 1:17; 6:35). The typology is expanded in 1 Corinthians, where Paul takes further details in the story and likens them to Christian realities. The cloud and sea are baptism, the manna and water are spiritual food and drink (Eucharist), and the rock is a spiritual rock—that is, Christ (1 Cor. 10:1–4).

Therefore, it is not with Origen, but with the New Testament and especially Paul, that one sees the beginning of Christian allegorical or typological interpretation of the individual details of the exodus story. In his homily, Origen quotes from this passage in Paul to show the biblical connection to his own interpretation. The logic is simple. If the crossing of the Red Sea is baptism, then the journey toward the sea is one from darkness to light. Egypt is the darkness before salvation; it is slavery to sin. The New Testament does not say this in so many words, but how can this be an illegitimate interpretation for one who takes Paul's interpretation seriously? If one wishes to flee the life of sin that is Egypt, then indeed, as Origen says, one must begin by departing from Ramesse (Egypt). Furthermore, if Ramesse was thought to be related etymologically to "a moth's commotion," then it is natural to gravitate toward Jesus's negative statement about worldly pleasures and the moth's destructive power. All of these readings are natural to someone who reads the Old Testament christologically and assumes an overarching unity to all of Scripture.

It does not take much creativity, by the way, to envision the journey from the sea to the promised land as the journey from baptism, when one is initiated into the people of God, to final salvation. The Christian life of sanctification is, indeed, Paul's concern when he warns the baptized Corinthians not to fall away as the once-rescued Israelites did (1 Cor. 10:5–13). It is this enduring typology that has inspired Christian interpretations throughout the ages, as evident in hymns such as "Guide Me, O Thou Great Jehovah" and all language about "Jordan's stormy banks" and "Canaan's land."

After seeing how Origen spelled out his approach and put it into practice, the following observations are worth recapitulating, particularly since they counter some of the popular notions about Origen.

First, Origen was occupied with the literal sense. He often found the biblical text to be historically reliable, morally edifying, and doctrinally sound on the literal level. It was the basis for the spiritual meaning. Origen, one of the few Greek church fathers who could read Hebrew, was an expert interpreter of the literal sense. In Crouzel's estimation, Origen, along with Jerome, was the greatest literal and critical exegete of Christian antiquity.[56] It is true that he would always look for the deeper meaning, but for him, examining the literal sense is the means for discerning the spiritual sense. For this reason, Origen stresses the importance of entering "into the intent [βούλημα, *boulēma*] of the writers" of the Gospels in order to find the true spiritual meaning.[57]

Second, Origen's exegetical methods were not unique to him: despite the claims of later detractors, he was not the inventor of allegory. The particular techniques from which he drew were commonly found in pagan exegesis, especially in the interpretations of Homer's corpus.[58] What's more, it was common to Christian exegesis of the Old Testament as well, and Origen acknowledges that he is following the tradition of his predecessors. When he found types in Old Testament referents, employed number symbolism, used clear passages of Scripture to clarify the obscure passages, or dismissed the literal meaning of a law in favor of its moral significance, Origen was following and contributing to a Christian and even Jewish tradition seen, among others, in the *Letter of Aristeas*, Philo, *Epistle of Barnabas*, Irenaeus, and Clement of Alexandria before him. Indeed, these and other methods are attested in the New Testament itself, and they were simply common ways for people to read sacred texts. Doctrinal instruction and moral edification were there to be found, even if not on the literal level.

Third, to appreciate Origen's exegesis, it is important to see the centrality of Jesus Christ in Origen's hermeneutic. The simple fact is that Christ is the unifying thread throughout his Old Testament exegesis. As he states in the preface to *De principiis*, "By the words of Christ we do not mean only those which formed his teaching when he was made man and dwelt in the flesh, since even before that Christ the Word of God was in Moses and the prophets."[59] The centrality of Christ can also be seen by contrasting Origen's motivation

56. Crouzel, *Origen*, 61. For more on the literal sense in Origen, see Lubac, *History and Spirit*, 103–58; Boles, "Allegory as Embodiment."

57. Origen, *Contra Celsum* 1.42 (PG 11:737B–C); 3.74.

58. F. Young, *Biblical Exegesis*, 76–96.

59. Origen, *Princ.* 1.preface.1.

for allegorizing with that of the pagans. Allegorical interpretations of Homer were generally motivated by the many philosophical and moral problems raised in Homer's depictions of the gods. Although the methods may have looked very similar, Origen's motivation was not to solve a problem as much as to disclose the subject matter, the scope. The resolution of doctrinal and moral tension between the two Testaments will become a factor, but this task is logically subsequent and therefore subordinate to the fact that Christ is the scope of the one Scripture. A difficulty in the text may occasion a spiritual interpretation, but it is not the sole factor motivating allegory. For Origen, most biblical passages do not present such problems on the literal level, but they do all testify to Christ. In other words, a text need not have insurmountable problems to prompt spiritual interpretation. Origen's allegorical interpretation of the Old Testament simply is christological interpretation. The prior assumption is that, as the incarnate Christ's divinity lay hidden to the carnal eye, so there is a divine meaning to every word of Scripture.

Finally, despite what later medieval figures or even Origen may have sometimes practiced, Origen himself acknowledged certain boundaries to allegorical interpretation. For instance, as noted above, when there is ambiguity in the text, "search the Scriptures." Origen, like most of the figures examined in this book, was a master of intertextual comparisons of expressions. He assumed a canonical unity in which the part must fit the whole. This principle reflects nothing other than the *analogia scripturae*.

In sum, Origen's interpretations are both richly imaginative and profoundly biblical. Such a hermeneutic allows him to see, in an otherwise dull travelogue, a christological, moral, and spiritual use that instructs and edifies the hearer. There are no dispensable passages of Scripture. The study of Scripture is, for Origen, a spiritual offering to God, and those who devote their lives to it are our "Levites and priests."[60] With Origen there is an exuberance and joy in allegorical, christological readings of Scripture that can hardly be contained, a limitless potential to discover anew God's message to the church in every age.

Antiochene Interpretation

Less than a century after Origen, in the environs of Syria there arose a certain discontent with Origen's exegesis. The only surviving document of Eustathius, who was bishop of Antioch from about 324 to 327, was a work against Origen's way of reading Scripture. Eustathius was the first representative of what

---

60. Origen, *Commentary on the Gospel according to John* 1.10, trans. Heine, 33.

would become known as the Antiochene school of exegesis, whose most prominent figures were the Antioch native Diodore of Tarsus (d. ca. 390) and his students, Theodore of Mopsuestia (350–428) and John Chrysostom (354–407). The Antiochene school[61] is famous for its emphasis on historical interpretation of the literal sense of Scripture and its tendency to reject allegory, though exactly what that means needs to be qualified.

One classic way of understanding the chief difference of emphasis between the Alexandrians and Antiochenes is to consider their respective approaches to Christology, with a view toward Origen's analogy between the incarnate Word and the written word. On the one hand, the Alexandrians tended to prioritize the divine Logos above the humanity of Jesus (the so-called "Word-flesh" Christology), with the divine nature threatening to efface the human nature. The extreme manifestation of this emphasis was defended later by Eutyches and the later so-called Monophysites, who argued that there was one (divine) nature in Jesus Christ. This articulation was condemned at the Council of Chalcedon (451) and subsequent councils. On the other hand, the Antiochenes tended to emphasize the humanity of Jesus Christ and dichotomize his two natures (the so-called "Word-man" Christology), in order to protect, among other things, the impassibility of the divine nature. The extreme manifestation of this emphasis came when Nestorius, bishop of Constantinople, denied the title Theotokos (God-bearer) to the virgin Mary, a view that was condemned at the Councils of Ephesus (431) and Chalcedon. (Diodore of Tarsus and Theodore of Mopsuestia were later condemned as proto-Nestorians, although modern scholars have observed that their and even Nestorius's actual "Nestorianism" was overstated.[62]) At any rate, the Antiochenes wanted to balance Mary's role as Theotokos (God-bearer) and *anthrōpotokos* (human-bearer), sometimes settling on *Christotokos* (Christ-bearer), thus exceeding the Alexandrians in their attention to Christ's humanity. Analogous to the Christology of each, as this understanding goes, Origen of Alexandria emphasized the hidden, spiritual (divine) nature of Scripture, whereas the Antiochenes highlighted the historical and literal (human) sense. As Diodore said, contrasting his approach with Origen's, "We far prefer the historical [τὸ ἱστορικόν, *to historikon*] to the allegorical [τὸ ἀλληγορικόν, *to allēgorikon*]."[63]

---

61. Although Diodore did instruct students, the broader Antiochene school is not so much a place with a concrete curriculum as a way of thinking influenced by the cultural climate and a few leading thinkers.

62. See J. N. D. Kelly, *Early Christian Doctrines*, 306–9.

63. This is a fragment from Diodore's commentary on the Octateuch, cited in Hill, "Introduction," 10–11.

In the preface to his only surviving work, a commentary on Psalms, Diodore briefly describes his method of interpretation. Pointing to the importance of the text's literal sense, he writes:

> We shall treat of [the text] historically and literally and not stand in the way of a spiritual and more elevated insight [θεωρία, theōria]. The historical sense, in fact, is not in opposition to the more elevated sense [θεωρία]; on the contrary, it proves to be the basis and foundation of the more elevated meanings. One thing alone is to be guarded against, however, never to let the discernment process [θεωρία] be seen as an overthrow of the underlying sense, since this would no longer be discernment [θεωρία] but allegory; what is arrived at in defiance of the content is not discernment [θεωρία] but allegory. The apostle, in fact, never overturned the historical sense by introducing discernment despite calling discernment allegory.[64]

Several observations are worth noting from Diodore's comments. First, although Diodore lays stress on the historical and literal sense of the text, this sort of interpretation is not opposed to a spiritual interpretation, which he calls *theoria* (Latin = Greek *theōria*). Second, any spiritual interpretation, he claims, must be based on and flow from the literal sense. Already one can see that Diodore, as the paragon of the Antiochene school, intended to guard the respective integrity of the literal sense and the spiritual sense. Consistent with a Christology that does not undermine the human Jesus of Nazareth, any interpretation of Scripture should not undermine or contradict the historical sense, or body. *Historia* (ἱστορία, *historia*) is the foundation of the higher senses, and both should be apprehended together, not separately. Third, Diodore distinguishes between *theoria* and what is commonly called allegory. Whereas the spiritual insight of *theoria* can be added to the literal sense without destroying the latter, allegory—as he conceives it—does indeed overthrow the history, and so he cautions against this kind of interpretation. Fourth, faced with the fact that the apostle Paul appeals explicitly to allegory, Diodore claims that what Paul calls allegory is not the sort of allegory that undermines the history, but is in fact the same as what Diodore means by *theoria*.

Later in the commentary, just before his discussion of Psalm 118, Diodore reiterates the difference between *theoria* and what the Greeks generally mean by allegory. Scripture knows the term "allegory" but does not acknowledge its application in the way understood by Greeks.[65] Diodore does not feel obliged

---

64. Diodore of Tarsus, *Commentary on Psalms 1–51*, trans. Hill, 4.
65. Diodore, *Commentary on Psalm 118*, in Froehlich, *Biblical Interpretation in the Early Church*, 87.

to regard episodes that are extraneous to the narrative or fictitious speeches (such as those in the book of Job) as historical, but *theoria* always respects the history—that is, the "pure account of an actual event of the past."[66] Diodore declares that the original occasion of Psalm 118 has to do with the exiled Israelites who are longing for Jerusalem, but he also allows for spiritual application to all saints who long for the general resurrection. His commentary focuses on the historical sense, but, by means of *theoria*, a Christian can see that this psalm applies to God's people everywhere. Such *theoria*, he says, "must be left to those endowed with a fuller charism."[67]

Theodore of Mopsuestia is the greatest of the Antiochene exegetes. Along with Diodore, he is often considered a forerunner of modern historical-critical exegesis.[68] The commentary on Galatians 4:21–31, the passage in which Paul uses the term "allegory," is perhaps the best place to find Theodore's opinion on allegory.[69] Like his teacher Diodore before him, Theodore emphasizes the difference between what Paul means by "allegory" and what later interpreters mean, who take from this term "the right to dismiss the entire meaning of divine scripture."[70] The apostle, however, "does not do away with the history (*historiam*), nor does he get rid of what happened long ago. Instead, he put it down as what had actually taken place at that time, but in such a way that he also used the history of what had actually happened for his own interpretation."[71] As for these other interpreters, Theodore observes that their desire to interpret Scripture "spiritually" (*spiritaliter*) means that Adam, paradise, and the serpent did not actually exist as they are narrated. This mode of "spiritual interpretation," according to Theodore, breaks up or separates off the history so that they no longer have a history. Moreover, once those narrated events of the fall have been dismissed on the literal or historical level, Theodore wonders if it means anything to say that Christ came to undo Adam's disobedience.[72] Pauline allegory, Theodore insists, is the comparison made between the *actual* past and the present.[73] This relation between events or

66. Diodore, *Commentary on Psalm 118*, in Froehlich, *Biblical Interpretation in the Early Church*, 91.

67. Diodore, *Commentary on Psalm 118*, in Froehlich, *Biblical Interpretation in the Early Church*, 93.

68. These and other scholarly assessments are reported in Hill, "Introduction," 9–10. For a survey of Theodore's Old Testament exegetical practice, see Zaharopoulos, *Theodore of Mopsuestia on the Bible*.

69. Greer, "Introduction," xiii–xiv.

70. Theodore of Mopsuestia, *Galatians*, in *Minor Epistles*, trans. Greer, 112–13.

71. Theodore of Mopsuestia, *Galatians*, in *Minor Epistles*, trans. Greer, 112–15, translation modified.

72. Theodore of Mopsuestia, *Galatians*, in *Minor Epistles*, trans. Greer, 114–15.

73. Theodore of Mopsuestia, *Galatians*, in *Minor Epistles*, trans. Greer, 120–21.

persons of the past with later events or persons, what Theodore here regards as Pauline allegory, is now referred to as typology.

It ought to be clear that the differences between the Alexandrian and Antiochene approaches to exegesis are real but, in the grand scheme of things, negligible. The most noticeable difference between Alexandrian and Antiochene exegesis, much of which can be attributed to the difference between philosophical and rhetorical schools of late antiquity,[74] is that the Antiochenes attended more to the literal and historical sense of the text. This point of difference requires a bit of qualification, since the terms "literal" and "historical" were not as narrow then as they tend to be now. The letter, or literal sense, attends to the words, but it also includes attention to genre, so passages that are meant figuratively are read "literally" (that is, rightly as intended) when they are interpreted figuratively. Taking a text literally could simply mean taking it at face value or following the intention of the narrative. *Historia* sometimes means narrative, without regard to what moderns would call historicity. At other times, however, it is clear that the Antiochenes often mean to emphasize that the narrative under consideration actually happened, and they use the word *historia* and its related terms accordingly. Granting the difficulties of translating these concepts into English, it is generally true that the Antiochenes took the historical narrative of Scripture more seriously than did the Alexandrians. As a result, the Antiochenes were generally less likely to acknowledge impossible narratives and more hard-pressed to resolve contradictions. For example, in the preface to his work on the Octateuch, the Antiochene exegete Theodoret of Cyrus declares that his task is to clarify "apparent" problems in Scripture and to demonstrate its consistency (συμφωνία, *symphōnia*), even on the literal level.[75]

Yet, even if the Antiochenes spent a little more time on the literal sense than did Origen, they did not stop with the literal sense. That is, though striving to keep the ἱστορία (*historia*) intact, they also found spiritual interpretation to be indispensable. The favorite Antiochene term for going beyond the letter was *theoria* (insight), which was used earlier by the Alexandrians Clement and Origen to describe their own practice of allegory. These passages cited above from Diodore and Theodore also reflect their common assumption that Pauline allegory is very different from Origen's allegory. By contrast, the Antiochenes preferred the term *theoria*, which included moral application as well as what would now be called typology and double-fulfillment prophecies. Given their predilection for *theoria* that goes beyond the letter, it is clear that

74. F. Young, "Alexandrian and Antiochene Exegesis," 344.
75. Theodoret of Cyrus, *Questions on the Octateuch*, trans. Hill, 1:2–5.

the Antiochenes cannot be regarded as the forerunners of the historical-critical exegesis that is free from fuller meanings and spiritual applications.

This point leads to a consideration of important similarities between Origen and the Antiochenes. According to both approaches, not every narrative in Scripture can or must be taken as a historical account. The Antiochenes agree that more history is preserved than Origen seems to think, but Diodore still dismisses the historicity of the speeches in Job, for reasons not unlike those given by Origen in his rejection of other narratives. Furthermore, both approaches attend to both the literal and spiritual dimensions of Scripture. Although each school of thought differs in the amount of attention given to each dimension, and the Antiochenes preferred the word *theoria* to describe the spiritual sense, neither approach thinks that biblical interpretation can be done with attention only to the letter or to the spirit; it requires both. Alexandrian and Antiochene is not spiritual versus literal, for both schools knew that "the wording of the Bible carried deeper meanings and that the immediate sense or reference pointed beyond itself."[76] Finally, not only do both schools of thought acknowledge the importance of spiritual interpretation, they also agree that it is best left to those who possess that gift.

To summarize the common bond between these two supposedly competing schools of thought: they both believed that Scripture is a living word for all Christians. The Holy Spirit inspired Scripture as a source of teaching for all times and situations, and that same Spirit is thus the source of true exegetical insight (*theoria*) that leads the reader upward. What John Chrysostom said concerning the Sermon on the Mount applies to Scripture as a whole and could have been said by any Christian from this period: "For though it was spoken to them, it was written for the sake also of all people afterwards."[77] According to Frances Young, "The most important thing these so-called schools had in common was a desire to foster the life of faith."[78] In these assumptions, as well as in actual practice, the Antiochene school of interpretation has more in common with Origen than it does with modern, historical-critical exegesis.

Gregory of Nyssa

The future of Eastern Orthodox exegesis is foreshadowed in the writings of Gregory of Nyssa (ca. 332–395). Gregory—along with the other two Cappadocian Fathers, his older brother Basil of Caesarea (330–379) and their

---

76. F. Young, "Alexandrian and Antiochene Exegesis," 352.
77. John Chrysostom, *Gospel of St. Matthew* 15.2 (*NPNF*[1] 10:91, translation modified).
78. F. Young, *Biblical Exegesis*, 185.

friend Gregory of Nazianzus (ca. 329–390)—was an admirer of Origen and of Origen's student Gregory Thaumaturgus (ca. 210–260). Thus Gregory of Nyssa can be fairly placed in conceptual proximity to the Alexandrian school of thought.

Gregory's book *The Life of Moses* well represents his exegetical approach. Working under the assumption that the story of Moses is recorded for the moral benefit of its readers, in the book's prologue Gregory makes the case that one must go beyond the mere letter if one is to imitate the virtue of the story's characters.[79] Thus Gregory treats the life of Moses in two parts: First, he simply describes the narrative (ἱστορία, *historia*), and later he moves to the spiritual understanding (θεωρία, *theōria*) "in order to obtain suggestions of virtue."[80] In other words, he follows the same literal-spiritual (ἱστορία, θεωρία) approach that was seen especially in Origen.[81]

Because the virtuous life of Moses cannot be literally imitated or replicated— that is, because one cannot obey by literally following in the steps of Moses— Gregory recommends passing over anything in the historical sense that is not profitable for teaching virtue.[82] When he encounters the description of the priestly garments, for instance, the application of the spiritual sense is to clothe the soul with the virtues.[83] Occasionally, when the narrative raises a moral problem, he is overtly critical of the historical sense. At the death of Egypt's firstborn, he sees a contradiction between this narrative (ἱστορία) and what is "worthy of God." How, he asks, "can the history [ἱστορία] so contradict reason [λόγῳ, *logō*]?"[84] In such cases, readers must look for the true spiritual meaning (ἀναγωγή, *anagōgē*) and determine whether the events took place typologically (τυπικῶς, *typikos*).[85] Gregory finds a similar moral problem in the command to plunder the Egyptians, which would involve robbery and wrongdoing. Instead, he concludes that the loftier meaning commands the virtuous to "equip themselves with the wealth of pagan learning," bringing it to the church as a gift to God.[86] This figurative interpretation of the spoiling

79. Gregory of Nyssa, *Life of Moses* 1.12, 14; 2.48–49, trans. Ferguson and Malherbe. I have modified some translations based on the Greek text. For a reliable summary of Gregory's "mystical" thought, see Louth, *Christian Mystical Tradition*, 78–94.

80. Gregory of Nyssa, *Life of Moses* 1.15 (PG 44:304C, 328A).

81. See Ferguson and Malherbe, introduction to Gregory of Nyssa, *Life of Moses*, 1–9.

82. Gregory of Nyssa, *Life of Moses* 2.50.

83. Gregory of Nyssa, *Life of Moses* 2.190.

84. Gregory of Nyssa, *Life of Moses* 2.91 (PG 44:352C–D).

85. Gregory of Nyssa, *Life of Moses* 2.92 (PG 44:352D–53A).

86. Gregory of Nyssa, *Life of Moses* 2.113–16. The problem raised by Israel's spoliation of Egypt is a perennial issue for later theologians. See, e.g., Peter Lombard, *Sentences* 3.142.4, trans. Silano, 155–56; Nicholas of Lyra, "Commentary on Exodus 3," in Fowl, *Theological Interpretation of Scripture*, 124.

of the Egyptians, seen as early as Origen,[87] became a widespread metaphor for the Christian use of the best of pagan culture, which in many cases was seen as originating from God's people in the first place.

In addition to these moral problems, at other times the biblical narrative could present some doctrinal problems if interpreted merely on the literal level. For instance, Moses asks to see the face of God, but instead God reveals his back to Moses. Taken "according to the letter" (κατὰ τὸ γράμμα, *kata to gramma*), the narrative speaks of the face, front, and back of God, all of which implies the absurd notion that God has a physical body.[88] In such cases, when the literal sense is incoherent, the interpreter must read the narrative spiritually.

With the examples of the plague on the firstborn and the plundering of the Egyptians, it is not clear whether Gregory of Nyssa thinks that these events happened as narrated. Neither is it clear, based on his spiritual interpretation of the vestments, exactly what he thinks the Israelite priests wore. He certainly does not dismiss the historicity as explicitly as Origen did with the opening chapters of Genesis. But because he sees theological or moral problems on the literal level, Gregory does quickly move to what he regards as the true moral instruction to be taken from each story, paying little attention to the question of historicity.

Besides the basic literal-spiritual pattern of exegesis, several other aspects of Gregory's exegesis should be underscored. These features, fundamentally consistent with Origen's exegesis, could easily be overlooked. First, as much as Gregory labors to move beyond the literal sense to the spiritual, the places are few and far between where he finds the literal sense to be incoherent. As with Origen, the fact that Gregory finds one narrative description or command to be impossible does not mean that he dispenses with the historicity of the whole story.

Second, the importance of the literal sense is reflected in the fact that it is always the necessary point of departure for any spiritual meaning. Gregory's attention to the historical narrative is prior to the spiritual understanding that he draws from it. As he writes at one point, "The *theoria* according to the higher spiritual sense [ἀναγωγήν, *anagōgēn*] agrees with the narrative [ἱστορία, *historia*]."[89] The spiritual senses flow from and are in harmony with the literal sense. "Anagogy," one of Gregory's favorite words for the spiritual sense, will become an important word in later, medieval exegesis.

87. Origen, "Letter of Origen to Gregory Thaumaturgus," 1–2, trans. Slusser, 190–91. According to Lubac, *History and Spirit*, 87, Origen did not invent this metaphor.

88. Gregory of Nyssa, *Life of Moses* 2.221–22 (PG 44:400B).

89. Gregory of Nyssa, *Life of Moses* 2.217 (PG 44:397C).

Third, the spiritual interpretations that Gregory provides, though based to some degree on the narrative, are not the only possible or true readings. In one passage he acknowledges that some of his interpretations are conjectural and should be evaluated by his readers.[90] Furthermore, the priestly vestments, which Gregory here interprets as virtues, not only are interpreted differently by other early church fathers, but also are interpreted differently in another writing of Gregory.[91] A passage need not have only one spiritual meaning but may have many true meanings. If a given interpretation is doctrinally sound and it encourages virtue, then it is a true interpretation.[92] Like Origen, Gregory recommends leaving spiritual interpretations to those readers who have from the Holy Spirit the insight to speak about mysterious things.[93]

Finally, the goal of reading Scripture is to bring the reader closer to God. As with all good literature, the narrative about Moses is meant to instruct morally. Gregory's assumption is simple: the historical life of Moses is a model of virtue for all God's people, but it must be interpreted in a spiritual sense if it is to be applicable.[94] The goal is eternal progress in virtue, to transfer to one's own life "what is contemplated [θεωρηθέντα, theōrēthenta] through spiritual interpretation [ἀναγωγῆς, anagōgēs] of the things spoken literally [ἱστορικῶς, historikōs]."[95] In fact, the primary criterion of interpretation is that it leads to Christian virtue, which itself has no limit.[96] Reading about Moses comes with the moral obligation of becoming what Moses was: a friend of God.[97] Just as Moses ascended the mountain and entered into the darkness, where God is, so also Scripture, rightly interpreted, leads the understanding upward to the knowledge of God.[98] The spiritual sense in Gregory's treatise is rarely anything other than moral application.

Dionysius the Areopagite

The tradition of biblical interpretation and theology that Gregory of Nyssa exemplifies was carried forward, with variations, in the Greek-speaking East.

90. Gregory of Nyssa, *Life of Moses* 2.173.
91. This observation is according to Ferguson and Malherbe, notes to Gregory of Nyssa, *Life of Moses*, 182n256.
92. Gregory of Nyssa, *Life of Moses* 2.191; cf. Ferguson and Malherbe, introduction to Gregory of Nyssa, *Life of Moses*, 8.
93. Gregory of Nyssa, *Life of Moses* 2.173.
94. Gregory of Nyssa, *Life of Moses* 2.153.
95. Gregory of Nyssa, *Life of Moses* 2.320 (PG 44:429C).
96. Ferguson and Malherbe, introduction to Gregory of Nyssa, *Life of Moses*, 8.
97. Gregory of Nyssa, *Life of Moses* 2.319–20.
98. Gregory of Nyssa, *Life of Moses* 2.152.

One representative of this exegetical tradition, fascinating for his influence both in the East and later in the Latin-speaking West, is (Pseudo-)Dionysius the Areopagite (fl. ca. 500). The works of Dionysius, written in the person of the apostle Paul's convert in Athens (Acts 17:34), are not overtly exegetical works, and indeed he has been criticized by later writers for his extrabiblical speculation. Yet it is clear that the Dionysian corpus can be characterized as a theological interpretation of Scripture that is influenced by earlier exegetes such as Gregory of Nyssa and is indicative of the direction of Eastern Christian biblical interpretation.

In *The Divine Names*, Dionysius's aim is to consider the names and descriptions of God in order to contemplate what they reveal about the divine nature. He is careful, though, to ground his thoughts in Scripture. Because God's essence is ultimately unknowable, "we must not dare to resort to words or conceptions concerning that hidden divinity which transcends being, apart from what the sacred scriptures have divinely revealed."[99] Throughout his writings, Dionysius reiterates the principle that "we can only use what scripture has disclosed."[100] This principle, however, does not mean that the theologian is limited to the literal meaning of the words in Scripture. Words by themselves cannot approach the inexpressible Good, but they can draw seekers upward toward the divine.

In his attempt to elaborate the nature of God, Dionysius later admits that some of his language goes beyond that of Scripture, which seems to contradict his principle of sticking closely to biblical terminology. He explains, however, that one should not look merely at the words without paying attention to the power of their meanings. "The truth we have to understand is that we use letters, syllables, phrases, written terms and words because of the senses. But when our souls are moved by intelligent energies in the direction of the things of the intellect then our senses and all that go with them are no longer needed."[101] That is, the words of Scripture, necessary as they may be as a starting point in theology, are an accommodation to humanity's embodied finitude. Just as the bodily senses point the intellect to contemplation of the divine, the words point to greater realities that can be expressed in other ways and, ultimately, that cannot be expressed at all. When they concern God, words are analogical. Words reveal the deeper meanings that go beyond words. As Dionysius puts

99. Dionysius, *Divine Names* 1.1, in *Complete Works*, trans. Luibheid, 49. Subsequent references in English are to this edition. For a summary of Dionysius's thought and writings, see Rorem, *Pseudo-Dionysius: A Commentary*; Louth, *Christian Mystical Tradition*, 154–73; Rocca, *Speaking the Incomprehensible God*, 15–25.
100. Dionysius, *Divine Names* 1.2, trans. Luibheid, 50.
101. Dionysius, *Divine Names* 4.11, trans. Luibheid, 80.

it in *The Mystical Theology*, in the flight upward to God, "we find ourselves not simply running short of words but actually speechless and unknowing."[102] The higher one climbs, the more language falters.

Dionysius reiterates similar points throughout his works. Scripture, like the visible realm in general, reflects and reveals the invisible things of God. Dionysius observes that the authors of Scripture, whom he calls "theologians," write from different contexts and perspectives, speaking about matters sometimes on a merely human level and at other times in a transcendent mode of perfection. Echoing his many predecessors, biblical discourse, he claims, is not totally on the level of "bare history" (ἱστορία ψιλή, *historia psilē*), but instead has to do with "life-giving perfection."[103]

Since Dionysius sees Scripture as a means to drawing the reader higher, using words as the means for going beyond words, it should not be surprising that his theological exegesis of Scripture is done in a liturgical context. "We must begin with a prayer before everything we do, but especially when we are about to talk of God."[104] Throughout his treatises, it is not uncommon for Dionysius to exhort his readers to praise God or to view his own writing in a doxological mode.[105] Scripture and the "hierarchical traditions" are part of the same liturgy that draws the senses up to God.[106] In Greek, since the words "mystery" and "mystical" refer to the sacraments, "mystical" theology and the "mystical" interpretation of Scripture are connected to the liturgy and are to be pursued in a liturgical context.[107] Just as we noted in the previous chapter, Scripture is sacramental.

As an interpreter of Scripture, Dionysius is not an innovator but sees himself as part of a tradition and indeed is typical of his time and place. Even when he uses nonbiblical words to describe biblical concepts, he does so with an appeal to other orthodox Christian figures.[108] He reads Scripture not as an exercise in historical curiosity, but as an act of prayer and worship. Scripture is the means by which God draws his people into the brilliant darkness, the deepest shadow, overwhelming light—that is, his presence.[109]

---

102. Dionysius, *Mystical Theology* 3, trans. Luibheid, 139.

103. Dionysius, *Epistle* 9.2, trans. Luibheid, 284 (PG 3:1108B–C).

104. Dionysius, *Divine Names* 3.1, trans. Luibheid, 68.

105. E.g., Dionysius, *Divine Names* 12.1, trans. Luibheid, 126; Dionysius, *Ecclesiastical Hierarchy* 1.2, trans. Luibheid, 196.

106. Dionysius, *Divine Names* 1.4, trans. Luibheid, 52.

107. "Mystery" (μυστήριον, *mystērion*) is the Greek term for Latin *sacramentum*. On the liturgical function of Dionysius's entire corpus, see Louth, *Christian Mystical Tradition*, 160–61, 206–8.

108. E.g., Dionysius, *Divine Names* 4.12, trans. Luibheid, 81.

109. Dionysius, *Mystical Theology* 1.1, trans. Luibheid, 135.

Principles of Later Patristic Exegesis

The same assumptions and approaches that characterized second-century exegesis also hold true for the later Greek church fathers. While surveying the exegesis from the New Testament and apostolic fathers to fourth- and fifth-century Eastern fathers, one can see movement from an unsystematic method to the more orderly articulation and practice of the same earlier principles. Building on the earlier principles articulated in the previous chapter, the following additional features help summarize the development.

1. *More systematic*. Beginning with Origen, a more systematic approach was articulated for biblical interpretation. He was the first of many writers in the history of Christianity to lament the diversity of interpretation and attempt to rectify it with a method. To be sure, the method is not systematic by modern standards, it may raise more questions than it answers, and Origen himself did not follow it consistently. But he is the one who initiates the conversation about exegesis. And the debate ensued. Almost immediately, Origen had his admirers and his critics.

2. *Threefold sense*. Part of Origen's method was the distinction between the body, soul, and spirit of Scripture, corresponding to the literal, moral, and doctrinal senses. This schema is consistent with and expands on the twofold sense, which remains the fundamental distinction. Although it was not followed consistently, even by Origen, it is evidence of the increasing nuance that was applied to the spiritual sense. This more precise categorization is the beginning of the process whereby the different words and ideas that describe the spiritual sense were classified and given more specific meanings. The threefold sense also clarified the kinds of questions that readers should be putting to the biblical text. It anticipated the further systematizing of the spiritual senses that would take place in the medieval West.

3. *Scripture as literature*. As the postapostolic generations of Christians lost the living memory of Jesus and came to rely exclusively on the "memoirs of the apostles,"[110] and as the shape of the canon was further defined, attention invariably shifted to Scripture and its interpretation. Textual evidence and arguments slowly but surely replaced the purely oral and miraculous. And, although Christians continued to preserve and plunder the best of pagan literature, the Christian Scriptures, despite their low literary quality and mean style, eventually became preeminent and superseded the pagan literature. To treat a corpus as great literature demanded commentary on it. Thus, in the third and following centuries, commentaries and homi-

---

110. Justin Martyr, *First Apology* 66–67.

lies that run through books of the Old and New Testaments became more commonplace.[111]

4. *Purpose.* An assumption of most readers in the ancient world is that literature is for the purpose of moral formation. As Frances Young puts it, "Plato's classic attack on the poets as morally subversive, echoed by Plutarch, who could speak of poetry as a seductive form of deception, stimulated the school tradition that literature should be read as morally edificatory."[112] Factual narratives may be recorded, but if there is no practical application, the data are pointless. Even among ancient pagans, there was a fairly common understanding that one is not to read for historical or intellectual curiosity alone. For instance, Livy makes abundantly clear that the primary purpose in his *History of Rome* is moral instruction.[113] Moreover, such literature may be both morally formative and entertaining, but if a work is intended solely for entertainment, amusement, or distraction, then that very literature is also pointless or even immoral.

The same goes for Scripture as literature. Notwithstanding the human origin and occasional nature of Scripture, the claim that Scripture is inspired means that it is an authoritative word from God for his people of all times and places. The various biblical documents may not have been written to us, but they were written for us. As such, the Bible continues to be useful and profitable for the church (2 Tim. 3:16). It must speak to the present. This need to make Scripture relevant to the interpreter's own time is what James Kugel calls the "actualizing" quality of Scripture.[114]

In the case of Scripture, the assumption of early Christians is that it must be edifying to the church morally and spiritually. One reads Scripture for moral and spiritual transformation, to draw nearer to God. For Christians, then, Scripture instructs in love and morals, but it also instructs in the faith and doctrine. This doctrinal and moral purpose of Scripture, certainly evident in second-century writers, comes out more clearly in the running commentaries and homilies of the later fathers. Whether one reads Origen's commentaries or Gregory of Nyssa's *Life of Moses*, their task is the same: to apply the ancient Old Testament narrative to contemporary Christian faith and life.

5. *Character of the interpreter.* Correct interpretation requires a virtuous interpreter. An unbeliever, almost by definition, fails to see and believe the

---

111. For more on this entire point, see F. Young, *Biblical Exegesis*, especially 47–116.

112. F. Young, "Alexandrian and Antiochene Exegesis," 340.

113. Titus Livius, *History of Rome*, preface. Cf. the similar purpose stated in Bede, *Ecclesiastical History of the English People*, 3.

114. Kugel and Greer, *Early Biblical Interpretation*, 80; cf. Sheridan, *Language for God*, 226–29.

basic assumptions grounding biblical interpretation: that Scripture is inspired and Christ is its scope. Biblical interpretation calls for humility, a desire to be formed morally, willingness to listen, and openness to spiritual illumination and understanding. The greater the character, virtue, and holiness of the interpreter, the further the interpreter can progress in spiritual interpretation. Again, this assumption is also present in earlier writers, but it was perhaps more important to articulate, as Scripture was becoming more widely available to a greater number of believers. As Origen, Diodore, Gregory of Nyssa, and others agreed, spiritual interpretation is for the spiritually mature.

Origen's way of reading Scripture, which owed so much to his forebears, influenced later exegetes, including both the ones who admired him and the ones who opposed some of his hermeneutical and theological speculations. As de Lubac reports, in the Latin Middle Ages, Origen was "the most read of all the ancient Greek authors, in all areas of endeavor."[115] It is a somewhat chastened form of Origen's method, combined with the influences of Jerome and Augustine, that would become the dominant form of exegesis in the medieval period.

115. Lubac, *Medieval Exegesis*, 1:165, citing Jean Leclercq. On the mixed reception of the "Latin Origen" in the medieval West, see 1:161–224.

4

Medieval Exegesis

The words of your holy scripture have knocked at the door of my heart, O Lord, and, in this poverty-stricken life of mine, my heart is busy about many things concerning them.

—Augustine of Hippo[1]

Perhaps I might say it [the Word of God] is like a river both shallow and deep, in which a lamb walks and an elephant swims.

—Gregory the Great[2]

We ought also to add that there is no doubt that anyone who wishes to search the scriptures in the way we have described will surely find that Christ is hidden in them. . . . No one can be thought to understand the scriptures who does not know how to find its hidden marrow—Christ, the Truth. Hidden under the parables we are speaking of are very many of the properties that belong to God alone, the First Principle, and that point to his nature.

—Meister Eckhart[3]

1. Augustine, *Confessions* 12.1.1.
2. Gregory I, the Great, "Letter to Leander" 4, trans. Kerns, 53.
3. Meister Eckhart, *Parables of Genesis* 3, in *Meister Eckhart*, trans. Colledge and McGinn, 94.

Medieval exegetes, like their patristic forerunners, assumed many of the same basic principles that affect biblical interpretation: the divine inspiration, unity, and transformative purpose of Scripture; the necessity of a spiritual and virtuous interpreter; and the church's rule of faith as the key to proper interpretation. In this and similar ways, medieval exegesis is simply a continuation of patristic exegesis. In other respects, Western medieval exegesis is more than a continuation of patristic interpretation: it develops the patristic contribution to the degree that biblical interpretation is increasingly systematized and becomes centered in the setting not only of churches and monasteries but also of schools. In addition, as a source of religious authority, the late medieval Roman Church had to wrestle with Scripture's relationship to the church's teaching magisterium.

At the risk of oversimplification, it may be said that the history of biblical interpretation in the medieval West begins and ends with Augustine— well, two Augustines, to be more precise. The first Augustine (354–430) is the famous bishop of Hippo Regius, who flourished at the dawn of the Middle Ages. He is the most influential theologian and one of the most prolific writers in church history. As Gerald Bonner observes, "The influence of Augustine on the later biblical exegesis of the Latin Middle Ages was enormous."[4]

Augustine's influence on medieval exegesis, however, has not always been seen as a salutary influence. In his influential Bampton Lectures from 1885, F. W. Farrar, who was no fan of premodern exegesis anyway, begins his discussion of Augustine's biblical interpretation by claiming that "nothing, indeed, can be theoretically better than some of the rules which he lays down."[5] Farrar's criticism is that Augustine lays down good rules but fails to follow them. "In the writings of St. Augustine we see the constant flashes of genius, and the rich results of insight and experience, which have given them their power over the minds of many generations. But these merits cannot save his exegetic writings from the charge of being radically unsound."[6] Farrar excuses earlier Christian exegesis in the days of Justin Martyr and Origen because, in the attempt to distinguish Christian interpretation from Jewish and heretical exegesis, it "had been driven to allegory by an imperious necessity." In the days of Augustine, Farrar continues, the allegorical method "had degenerated into an artistic method of displaying ingenuity and supporting ecclesiasticism."[7] Farrar's qualified generosity toward second- and third-century exegetes apparently

4. Bonner, "Augustine as Biblical Scholar," 561.
5. Farrar, *History of Interpretation*, 234.
6. Farrar, *History of Interpretation*, 237.
7. Farrar, *History of Interpretation*, 239.

does not extend to those of the fourth and fifth centuries. As a result, Augustine becomes the epitome of allegorical excess, the harbinger of the worst of medieval biblical interpretation.

As an introductory glimpse of Augustine's exegetical style, we may take a sample from his book titled *Questions on the Gospels*, in which he interprets Jesus's parable of the good Samaritan.

> *A certain man was going down from Jerusalem to Jericho* ([Luke] 10:30). He is understood to be Adam himself, representing the human race. *Jerusalem* is that city of peace from whose blessedness he fell. *Jericho* is translated as "moon" and signifies our mortality, because it begins, increases, grows old, and sets. The robbers are the devil and his angels, *who stripped him* of immortality, *and having beat [him] with blows*, by persuading him to sinfulness, *left him half alive* ([Luke] 10:30), because the man was alive in the part by which he could understand and know God, and he was dead in the part in which he was wasting away and weighed down by sins. And for this reason he is said to be half alive. But the priest and the Levite who saw him and passed by signify the priesthood and ministry of the Old Testament, which could not be of benefit toward salvation. *Samaritan* is translated as "guardian," and for this reason the Lord himself is signified by this name. The binding of the wounds is the holding of sins in check. The oil is the consolation of good hope because of the forgiveness given for the reconciliation of peace. The wine is an exhortation to work with fervent spirit. His beast of burden is the flesh in which he deigned to come to us. To be placed on the beast of burden is to believe in Christ's incarnation. The stable [inn] is the Church where travelers are refreshed from the journey as they return to the eternal fatherland. The following day is after the resurrection of the Lord. The two denarii are the two commandments of love that the apostles received through the Holy Spirit in order to bring the Gospel to others, or they are the promise of the present and future life. . . . The innkeeper, then, is the Apostle [Paul].[8]

With these words, Augustine offers his interpretation of the famous parable of the good Samaritan (Luke 10:25–37). And with these words, the worst fears of those who disparage "allegory" have been realized. Indeed, C. H. Dodd began his book *The Parables of the Kingdom* (1935) by quoting this same passage and then stated that "to the ordinary person of intelligence, . . . this mystification must appear quite perverse."[9] After the publication of Dodd's study of the parables, this example of Augustinian interpretation

8. Augustine, *Questions on the Gospels* 2.19, trans. Teske (WSA I/15–16):388.
9. Dodd, *Parables of the Kingdom*, 11–13.

became rather notorious in some well-known exegetical handbooks. Robert Stein refers to Augustine's reading as an instance of "eisegesis" that should be rejected, for it makes the parable "say something other than what Jesus and the Gospel writers intended."[10] G. B. Caird calls it a "farrago [that] bears no relationship to the real meaning of the parable."[11] Gordon Fee and Douglas Stuart feature it as an example of how not to interpret a parable, asserting that "it is not what Jesus intended."[12]

Augustine's interpretation of this parable has apparently become a locus classicus to illustrate how exegesis is not to be done. What exactly is motivating Augustine's allegorical reading of this parable, and what are the exegetical principles that he intends to follow? We will return to this parable and its interpretation below.

The second Augustine (d. 1282) is the much less famous monk of Dacia, who flourished toward the latter part of the Middle Ages. This monk is known primarily for the sole surviving work from his pen, the *Rotulus pugillaris*. In this summary of theology for Dominicans under his watch, he composed a short couplet about what to look for in Bible reading, later passed down as follows:

The letter teaches what happened, the allegory what you should believe,

The moral sense what you should do, the anagogy what you should hope.[13]

These lines, often repeated in subsequent centuries, provide a succinct summary of exegesis as it was taught and practiced at the end of the medieval period. This method calls for a fourfold interpretation of Scripture. Eventually it became known as the quadriga, named after the four-horse chariot of ancient Rome.[14] The poem may be a thirteenth-century creation, but the way of reading that it describes is much older. What, then, are the sources for this method? How did Origen's threefold method of body, soul, and spirit—which, as we saw in chapter 3, tended to collapse into a twofold method of letter and spirit—develop into a fourfold method? Moreover, how do the theology and hermeneutical principles of the earlier Augustine relate to and anticipate the verse of his later, obscurer namesake?

10. Stein, *Method and Message of Jesus' Teachings*, 47–48.
11. Caird, *Language and Imagery of the Bible*, 165.
12. Fee and Stuart, *How to Read the Bible*, 150.
13. The Latin text from Nicholas of Lyra is cited in Lubac, *Medieval Exegesis*, 1:271n1; see 272n9 for Augustine of Dacia's earlier version.
14. On the origin of this image from Song of Songs 6:12 (LXX and Vulgate), see Froehlich, *Sensing the Scriptures*, 5–7.

Augustine of Hippo

In 380 the Roman emperor Theodosius declared that Christianity, as it was believed and practiced in Rome, would be the official religion of the empire.[15] In many ways, this official joining of Christian church and Roman state represents the end of the beginning, a further step in the gradual transition from the patristic era to what would become, in the West, the medieval church. And the figure who would come to personify this transition is Augustine of Hippo, who, like the empire itself, turned to the Christian faith as an adult. Augustine lived to see not only Theodosius's edict but also the sack of Rome by Alaric and the Visigoths in 410 and, just before his own death, the siege of Hippo by the Vandals in 430. The church was now fully institutionalized in a world that was facing the new reality of "barbarian" invasion. Hence, although Augustine should be considered a figure of the patristic era (and he does antedate Dionysius of the preceding chapter), his impact on the medieval church warrants his placement at the head of this chapter on medieval exegesis.

Augustine's thought—doctrinal, moral, philosophical, psychological, political, and otherwise—as distilled and dispersed by subsequent generations of admirers, set the tone for the Western medieval church. It is not surprising, then, that Augustine's influence can also be seen in medieval biblical interpretation. Throughout all of Augustine's writings, and especially in his biblical commentaries and sermons, medieval readers found an exegetical method that was both accessible and imitable. But his hermeneutical theory was most succinctly articulated in what was perhaps his most frequently read volume in the Middle Ages: *On Christian Teaching* (*De doctrina Christiana*).[16]

Although it is no comprehensive hermeneutical handbook, in *De doctrina Christiana* Augustine sets out to teach the fundamentals of biblical interpretation.[17] He opens his treatise with a reflection on semiotics, the study of signs and their meanings. He distinguishes between a sign (*signum*) and the thing signified (*res significata*); this "thing" (*res*) is a substantial "reality" (from *res*) to which the sign points.[18] Signs are means to the ends, which are things. These things, as only proximate ends, can then function as signs that point to more ultimate realities.

---

15. For the relevant text in the edict, see Stevenson, *Creeds, Councils, and Controversies*, 174.

16. For summaries of Augustine's exegetical principles and practice, see Van Fleteren, "Principles of Augustine's Hermeneutic." On *De doctrina Christiana*, see Cameron, *Christ Meets Me Everywhere*, 215–40.

17. Augustine, *De doctrina Christiana* preface to *On Christian Teaching*, trans. Green, 4. Subsequent references are to this edition.

18. Augustine, *De doctrina Christiana* 1.2.2, trans. Green, 8–9.

Once this initial distinction is introduced, Augustine immediately launches into an exposition of "things" as the objects of love. In doing so, he distinguishes between the enjoyment (*frui/fruitio*) and the use (*uti/usus*) of things. "To enjoy something is to hold fast to it in love for its own sake. To use something is to apply whatever it may be to the purpose of obtaining what you love."[19] Use is the means to the end of enjoyment. One can use the things of this world in a rightly ordered way. By contrast, sin, as the privation and disordering of good, involves taking the things of this world and *using* (or better, abusing) them for the creature's end.

This distinction can be applied to biblical interpretation. As with the right use of anything in creation, Scripture rightly used always and everywhere must point to God and the creature's ultimate *enjoyment* of God for God's own sake.[20] The words of Scripture are penultimate things that lead the reader to the one ultimate reality, God. "The things which are to be enjoyed, then, are the Father and the Son and the Holy Spirit, and the Trinity that consists of them, which is a kind of single, supreme thing, shared by all who enjoy it."[21] This affirmation does not imply that vestiges of the Trinity can be found in each jot and tittle of Scripture, but that knowledge of the whole of Scripture helps one understand the nature of the God who is to be loved and worshiped above all else.

Pure, rightly ordered love, as expressed by Christ in the love commands, is the key hermeneutical category for Augustine. Everything in Scripture, if interpreted correctly, should lead to the twofold love for God and neighbor. Augustine writes, "So anyone who thinks that he has understood the divine scriptures or any part of them, but cannot by his understanding build up this double love of God and neighbor, has not yet succeeded in understanding them. Anyone who derives from them an idea which is useful for supporting this love but fails to say what the writer demonstrably meant in the passage has not made a fatal error, and is certainly not a liar."[22] Just as the failure to find divine love in Scripture indicates that something is amiss in one's interpretation, so the hermeneutic of love, it seems, covers a multitude of exegetical sins.

With reference to 1 Corinthians 13, Augustine then associates "all knowledge and prophecy" with Scripture. This knowledge and prophecy, which the apostle predicts will pass away, are means that are subordinate to and ought to lead to faith, hope, and love (1 Cor. 13:13).[23] In fact, Augustine claims that

19. Augustine, *De doctrina Christiana* 1.4.4, trans. Green, 9; the discussion of *uti* and *frui* continues throughout book 1.
20. Augustine, *De doctrina Christiana* 1.27.28, trans. Green, 21.
21. Augustine, *De doctrina Christiana*, 1.5.5, trans. Green, 10.
22. Augustine, *De doctrina Christiana* 1.36.40, trans. Green, 27.
23. Augustine, *De doctrina Christiana* 1.37.41, trans. Green, 28.

anyone who is mature in faith, hope, and love no longer has need of Scripture except in order to instruct others.[24] When one learns that the aim of every commandment is love, then one "will be ready to relate every interpretation of the holy scriptures to these three things and may approach the task of handling these books with confidence."[25] This relation of Scripture to the three so-called theological virtues is an important point that will resurface later.

Having examined realities, or things, in the first book, in the second book Augustine returns to his discussion of signs. In most cases, the thing to which a sign points is itself another sign pointing ultimately to an ideal form. The hermeneutical import has to do with the meaning of words, which are themselves signs pointing to something.[26]

Because signs may be either unknown or ambiguous, Augustine acknowledges that Scripture itself can often be ambiguous and mislead readers.[27] Yet some positive results may come from the ambiguity. For example, this ambiguity can awaken readers and plunge them into more profound interpretations.[28] In his later book *The City of God* (*De civitate Dei*), Augustine admits that obscure passages can lead to multiple interpretations; but this situation is not deleterious.

> The obscurity of the divine word is beneficial in this respect: that it causes many views of the truth to appear and to be brought into the light of knowledge, as one reader understands a passage in one way and another in another. Any interpretation of an obscure passage should, however, be confirmed by the testimony of manifest facts or by other passages where the meaning is not in the least open to doubt. In this way we shall, by the investigation of several views, either arrive at the meaning intended by whoever wrote the passage, or, failing this, the examination of a profoundly obscure passage will lead to the statement of a number of other truths.[29]

He finds great benefit in multiple interpretations, for a couple of things may happen. First, out of the many hypotheses may arise the meaning intended by the document's author. This comment demonstrates, by the way, that the issue of authorial intent was on Augustine's radar, as it was for most premodern interpreters. Second, if the author's intended meaning cannot

24. Augustine, *De doctrina Christiana* 1.39.43, trans. Green, 28–29.
25. Augustine, *De doctrina Christiana* 1.40.44, trans. Green, 29.
26. Augustine, *De doctrina Christiana* 2.1.1–4.5, trans. Green, 30–32; cf. 1.2.2, trans. Green, 8–9.
27. Augustine, *De doctrina Christiana* 2.6.7, trans. Green, 32; 1.10.15, trans. Green, 37–38.
28. Augustine, *De doctrina Christiana* 2.6.7–8, trans. Green, 32–33.
29. Augustine, *Civ.* 11.19, in *City of God against the Pagans*, trans. Dyson, 472–73. Subsequent references are to this edition.

be discerned, at least "a number of other truths" may be discerned in the process of interpretation. Thus, although he is interested in authorial intent, Augustine does not find the reading and the interpretation of Scripture to be vain pursuits if the authorial intent remains uncertain. Later he states, with reference to a difficult passage in Genesis 1, "Let each interpret these words as he will, then. For they are so profound that they can give rise to many different opinions which are not at odds with the rule of faith."[30] Like church fathers before him, Augustine allows many truths to emerge from obscure passages, but he uses the rule of faith as a boundary for those interpretations.

What procedure does Augustine recommend for clarifying the ambiguities? "One should proceed to explore and analyse the obscure passages, by taking examples from the more obvious parts to illuminate obscure expressions and by using the evidence of indisputable passages to remove the uncertainty of ambiguous ones."[31] It is therefore a fundamental assumption of Augustine, as it was of Irenaeus and others, that clearer passages of Scripture should help explain passages that are less clear. "Virtually nothing is unearthed from these obscurities which cannot be found quite plainly expressed somewhere else."[32] Elsewhere, after observing the occasional obscurity of Scripture, he says that any interpretation of an obscure passage should "be confirmed by the testimony of manifest facts or by other passages where the meaning is not in the least open to doubt."[33]

In addition to the use of other Scriptures, one must learn to recognize when signs are being used literally or metaphorically.[34] In the case of literal signs, the knowledge of the original languages and comparison of different translations can be helpful.[35] In other cases, such investigation of texts can lead to more obscurity. For instance, an obscurity occurs when the Hebrew and the LXX are compared at Jonah 3:4. In the former, Jonah proclaims that Nineveh will be destroyed in forty days, but the LXX has him saying three days. Augustine advises the interpreter to "raise himself above mere history and to seek out the meanings which the historical narrative was intended to convey." He goes on to draw a symbolic meaning out of both numbers in the context of the book of Jonah, without worrying to resolve which one Jonah might have spoken. Just as both the Hebrew and Greek versions of the Old

30. Augustine, *Civ.* 11.32, trans. Dyson, 493.
31. Augustine, *De doctrina Christiana* 2.9.14, trans. Green, 37.
32. Augustine, *De doctrina Christiana* 2.6.8, trans. Green, 33.
33. Augustine, *Civ.* 11.19, trans. Dyson, 472–73.
34. Augustine, *De doctrina Christiana*, 2.10.15, trans. Green, 37–38.
35. Augustine, *De doctrina Christiana* 2.11.16–15.22, trans. Green, 38–43.

Testament were quoted by the apostles as divine and authoritative, both of the numbers in Jonah are inspired and convey truth.[36]

In the case of metaphorical or figurative signs, Augustine generally advocates a wide-ranging education as beneficial to interpretation. He provides examples of how the knowledge of natural science, music, and mathematics can aid the biblical interpreter.[37] For example, he elsewhere reads the six-day creation story in light of his observation that six is a perfect number.[38] In general, Augustine praises the best of pagan learning as a means to understanding Scripture. Like Origen before him, he compares the Christian use of pre- or non-Christian truth to Israel's plundering of the Egyptians.[39]

Augustine also gives attention to the virtue of the interpreter. Love, which builds up, is superior to knowledge, which puffs up (cf. 1 Cor. 8:1). Though informed by the best of pagan learning, the interpretation of Scripture will still be hampered if the moral and spiritual character of the interpreter is found wanting. "Even if they leave Egypt well provided for, they realize that without first observing the Passover they cannot be saved. . ∴. Hyssop also has a cleansing power, so that nobody should boast, with his head inflated by a knowledge of the wealth he has taken from Egypt."[40]

In the midst of a number of helpful principles and illustrations throughout his book, Augustine distinguishes between the literal and figurative senses of Scripture. Sometimes the literal level already contains the highest spiritual meaning possible, as, for example, with the two greatest love commands in Matthew 22:37–40. It is not necessary to search for any higher spiritual meaning than to love God and neighbor. At other times, if the literal level of a divine discourse does not relate "to good morals or to the true faith," then it should be taken figuratively.[41] Augustine is dogged in his insistence on the hermeneutic of love: "Therefore in dealing with figurative expressions we will observe a rule of this kind: the passage being read should be studied with careful consideration until its interpretation can be connected with the realm of love. If this point is made literally, then no kind of figurative expression need be considered."[42]

Augustine does not seem as ready as Origen to find a symbolic reference in every detail. Some details of historical narration in Scripture have no symbolic

---

36. Augustine, *Civ.* 18.44, trans. Dyson, 886–87. For Augustine's thoughts on the LXX, see Augustine, *De doctrina Christiana* 2.15.22, trans. Green, 42–43; *Civ.* 18.42–43, trans. Dyson, 883–86.

37. Augustine, *De doctrina Christiana* 2.16.23–18.28, trans. Green, 43–47.

38. Augustine, *Civ.* 11.30, trans. Dyson, 490–91.

39. Augustine, *De doctrina Christiana* 2.40.60, trans. Green, 64–65. Cf. *Confessions* 7.9.15.

40. Augustine, *De doctrina Christiana* 2.41.62, trans. Green, 66–67.

41. Augustine, *De doctrina Christiana* 3.10.14, trans. Green, 75–76.

42. Augustine, *De doctrina Christiana* 3.15.23, trans. Green, 80.

significance. They are not, however, details without purpose. Although they may not have significance of their own, they point to other matters or details that do have significance. The words of Scripture either testify directly about God and his people, or they illustrate or otherwise point to the words that so testify.[43]

In light of this brief survey, let me summarize what seem to be the most important principles of Augustine's hermeneutics.

First, for Augustine, Scripture has a mediating function. That is, it has the essential but subordinate role of a sign pointing to the reality signified—namely, God. Scripture is a means to the enjoyment of God. As with Origen, who saw the words of Scripture pointing to deeper truths, and Dionysius, who, after Augustine, spoke of moving beyond the words of Scripture to the ineffable contemplation of God, Augustine believes that the sanctified Christian who is mature in faith, hope, and love no longer has a personal need for Scripture. This is not meant to demote Scripture, but to clarify its role in Christian theology. Scripture is not the incarnate Word himself as the proper object of worship, but a pointer to that object of worship.

Second, when there is ambiguity in the text, the rule of faith and plainer passages of Scripture, *analogia fidei* and *analogia scripturae*, clarify obscurities. "Once close consideration has revealed that it is uncertain how a passage should be punctuated and articulated, we must consult the rule of faith, as it is perceived through the plainer passages of the scriptures and the authority of the church."[44]

Third, many truths can be found in Scripture, as long as they inspire love for God and neighbor. There may be many wrong interpretations of a text, but there may also be more than one right interpretation. As long as an interpretation leads to love and is consistent with sound doctrine, it can be true.

With these basic principles in mind, we may now return to Augustine's allegorical treatment of Jesus's parable of the good Samaritan. To identify the Samaritan as Christ, rather than simply any good neighbor, goes against what every modern churchgoer knows. Furthermore, to take the parable as a complex allegory, rather than as a simple story with only one or two main points, contradicts what every biblical scholar knows. Isn't a simple "moral" application intended by the words "Go and do likewise"? Surely Jesus, the original speaker, and Luke, the original writer, did not have these hidden meanings in mind. How did Augustine arrive at an interpretation that, to most modern readers, seems so utterly bizarre? And how could a modern

43. Augustine, *Civ.* 16.2, trans. Dyson, 697–98.
44. Augustine, *De doctrina Christiana* 3.2.2, trans. Green, 68.

reader interpret the parable, with good conscience, in a similar way? Let me
offer three points or contextual clues that may help.

First, it should be observed that Augustine did not invent the main contours
of this interpretation. Rather, this reading goes back to the earliest surviving
Christian comment on the parable. It was Irenaeus who, in the late second
century, likened the Samaritan to the Lord, who had compassion on the man
who fell among the thieves, binding his wounds, granting two denarii, which
are the Father and the Son.[45] In the third century, Origen gave a similar interpretation, attributing it to "one of the elders":

> The man who was going down is Adam. Jerusalem is paradise, and Jericho is
> the world. The robbers are hostile powers. The priest is the Law, the Levite is
> the prophets, and the Samaritan is Christ. The wounds are disobedience, the
> beast is the Lord's body, the *pandochium* (that is, the stable), which accepts
> all who wish to enter, is the Church. And further, the two *denarii* mean the
> Father and the Son. The manager of the stable is the head of the Church, to
> whom its care has been entrusted. And the fact that the Samaritan promises
> he will return represents the Savior's second coming. All of this has been said
> reasonably and beautifully.[46]

The similarity of Origen's interpretation to Irenaeus's before him and Augustine's after him is striking. This reading is not properly the *Augustinian*
interpretation, but the *patristic* interpretation.[47] It would remain the standard
interpretation throughout the medieval period.[48]

The fact that Augustine's interpretation is traditionary does not per se
make the interpretation correct. It does, however, mitigate the initial feeling that Augustine is trying too hard to be novel in his reading. If nothing
else, it presents a challenge to Farrar's view, quoted at the beginning of this
chapter, that Augustine's use of allegory "had degenerated into an artistic
method of displaying ingenuity and supporting ecclesiasticism."[49] If there
is any "degeneration" in the case before us, Augustine is not to blame;
it had happened already in the second century. Slight expansion may be
discernible, but the difference is quantitative, not qualitative. Augustine is

45. Irenaeus, *Haer.* 3.17.3.

46. Origen, *Homilies on Luke* 34.3–4, trans. Lienhard, 138.

47. For further comment on this common, early Christian interpretation, see Roukema,
"Good Samaritan."

48. E.g., Peter Lombard, *Sentences* 4.1.1, trans. Silano, 4:3, compares the half-dead man's
wounds to sin and the bindings provided by the Samaritan to the sacraments; see also 2.159.1,
trans. Silano, 2:119; 2.234.2, trans. Silano, 2:179; 3.prologue, trans. Silano, 3:3; and 3.106.3,
trans. Silano, 3:120.

49. Farrar, *History of Interpretation*, 239.

simply repeating what appears to have been the unanimous interpretation of the church.

Second, although Jesus could have illustrated the command of neighbor love in a number of ways, the parable that he presented is clearly a rescue story, a story about salvation. This choice carries significant consequences for interpretation. In a day when all Christian interpreters agreed that the scope of Scripture is Christ, it would not require a great hermeneutical leap to imagine the rescuer, the *savior*, in this story as Christ. Once this christological point is recognized, then the main contours of the common patristic reading follow.[50] Since this is a rescue story, then who are we in the story? Clearly, at least to premodern Christians, the half-dead man represents those who are in need of saving, who have fallen into sin. Here is a rescuer who does not just *happen* to find the man, but is sufficiently prepared and goes out in search of people in need. Why else is he equipped with a first-aid kit? As Origen suggests, there may be many other people in similar straits that he will rescue.[51] On this reading, the inn to which rescued humanity is brought can be nothing other than the church. The two coins are undeserved gifts that become the means of caretaking (whether they are knowledge of the Father and Son, or the sacraments, or the like). Other details may vary since they are subordinate to these principal elements of the story.[52]

This allegorical interpretation does not preclude seeing the parable as an exhortation to Christian action. To the half-dead ones out there, "Go and do likewise" could mean, "Be rescued by the loving Savior." Alternatively, "Go and do likewise" is a mandate to God's people to be the Samaritan, to show their love by finding people in need, binding up their wounds, and bearing their burdens. Indeed, Augustine also applied the parable in this way, declaring that our neighbor is anyone to whom we are bound to show mercy, which is to say, every person.[53] But, as Origen also affirmed, when one imitates the Samaritan of the parable by loving one's neighbors, such a one is simply imitating

50. As Richard Lischer puts it, "Once the christological coordinate is established, the details of the story fall into place." Lischer, *Reading the Parables*, 152.

51. Origen, *Homilies on Luke* 34, trans. Lienhard, 140: "I do not think that the Samaritan carried these things with him only on behalf of that one, half-dead man, but also on behalf of others who, for various reasons, had been wounded and needed bandages, oil, and wine."

52. Cf. Teske, "Good Samaritan," 351: "Given this basic identification of the Samaritan as Christ, the other elements of the parable do not constitute distinct interpretations, but rather complement the christological interpretation." In addition to a summary of the story of salvation, the detailed interpretations that Augustine suggests are based on intertextual connections and etymologies, many of which are laid out by Teske, "Good Samaritan," 349–57.

53. Augustine, *De doctrina Christiana* 1.30.31–32, trans. Green, 22–23. So also Peter Lombard, *Sentences* 3.106, trans. Silano, 3:120.

Christ.[54] In either case, whether we see ourselves as the half-dead man or as the Samaritan, the traditional patristic interpretation of the Samaritan as Christ still illustrates neighbor love and is applicable to Christians.

Third, as we have already observed directly from Augustine, true meaning is not bound to or limited by human authorial intent or, more precisely, our hypothesis regarding that intent. In other words, *a* true interpretation is not necessarily the *only* true meaning. For Augustine's interpretation to be "true," it was not necessary for Jesus and the original audience to have in mind every detail of the story as Augustine laid it out. Although he thinks it is a correct interpretation, Augustine does not claim to be giving the one true interpretation of the story that excludes all others and that Jesus had in mind. In fact, on at least five other occasions, Augustine interprets the parable as a simple moral story whose intent is to show that every person is a neighbor to be loved, which corresponds with the straightforward interpretation given by most modern scholars.[55] As recognized above, this "moral" interpretation is not incompatible with the "allegorical." But there is not just one interpretation. Thus the allegorical interpretation is not *the* Augustinian interpretation, but *an* Augustinian interpretation. Augustine does not seem overly concerned with which precise meaning Jesus or Luke had in mind.

It is this freedom to interpret beyond the confines of original authorial intent that has made Augustine's reading of this parable so scandalous to the champions of modern exegesis. Stein, Caird, and Fee and Stuart, as cited at the beginning of this chapter, all denounce Augustine's interpretation for one primary reason: it does not reflect authorial intent. After noting Augustine's interpretation, Craig Blomberg summarizes what he sees as the problem with the allegorical interpretation of parables: "Some of the meanings attributed to details in the parables were clearly anachronistic. . . . No one in his [Jesus's] original audience, for example, could ever have been expected to associate the Samaritan's innkeeper with the apostle Paul!"[56]

For Augustine, however, if an interpretation says something doctrinally true and abides within the rule of faith, and if the interpretation promotes the love of God and neighbor, then authorial intent, especially if it cannot easily be determined, becomes a subordinate matter. It is of comparatively little consequence if Jesus, Luke, or the original audience(s) did not consider the inn to be the church. Confining the story's significance to human

54. Origen, *Homilies on Luke* 34.9, trans. Lienhard, 141.

55. These passages are cited and briefly analyzed in Teske, "Good Samaritan," 348–49.

56. Blomberg, *Interpreting the Parables*, 31–32; to be fair, on 229–33. Blomberg does go on to acknowledge the complexity of the parable, challenging the older scholarly consensus that parables had only one main point.

authorial intent would limit its capability to speak to the church of later generations.

At the same time, it was not Augustine's desire to ignore either human or divine authorial intent.[57] Within the biblical text itself are hints that the author may be inviting further interpretation along the christological lines suggested by Irenaeus, Origen, and Augustine. First of all, the very genre of narrative invites the hearer to interpret with some imagination. After all, Jesus easily could have replied to the lawyer's question, "Who is my neighbor?" (Luke 10:29), with an unambiguous, straightforward answer: "Everyone, even Samaritans." But the story is an ambiguous answer that in turn poses a question. Notice first that, in the command to love neighbor, "neighbor" means the one being shown mercy. Thus the lawyer's question "Who is my neighbor?" means, in effect, "To whom should I show mercy?" After the story, however, Jesus asks the question, "Who was a neighbor to the man who fell among robbers?" (Luke 10:36), which is to say, "Who showed mercy?" Jesus shifts the focus of the story, or at least the referent of the question, from the one who receives mercy to the one who shows it. In other words, in the love command, the "neighbor" who is the object of love becomes, in the narrative response, the Samaritan, the one showing love, not the one receiving it. That ambiguity alone invites imaginative interpretation beyond a one-word answer. Perhaps the story simply *is* the author's invitation to imagine.

Moreover, Jesus himself engaged in such imaginative, or allegorical, interpretation of his own parables, as is shown following the parable of the sower (Mark 4:13–20; parallels in Matt. 13:18–23; Luke 8:11–15) and of the wheat and tares (Matt. 13:36–43). Significantly, he seems to invite his hearers to do the same. Before he gives his extended, allegorical interpretation of the parable of the sower, he says, "Do you not know this parable? And how will you know all the parables?" (Mark 4:13). Based on this statement, one can see the possibility of similar principles of interpretation at work in "all the parables." After the same interpretation by Jesus, he goes on to say, "For nothing is hidden, except that it might be made manifest" (Mark 4:22). The parables contain hidden gems, which Jesus explains to his disciples (Mark 4:34). Since the door is open in the text itself to imaginative interpretation of parables, perhaps authorial intent is not as narrowly limited as some modern

57. Cf. Teske, "Good Samaritan," 356: "Augustine would at very least argue that the christological sense of the parable of the Good Samaritan was providentially intended by God under whose inspiration Luke wrote his gospel. Moreover, he would argue that the content of the parable interpreted in the christological sense is true, even if Luke did not intend that sense. In any case, Augustine is quite convinced that Jesus Christ taught us that he was that Samaritan."

scholars have assumed. As Origen earlier perceived, the writers themselves expected further spiritual interpretation. In a case such as this, the otherwise helpful distinction that Froehlich draws between "rhetorical allegory" (when the speaker or writer intends a hidden or other meaning) and "interpretive allegory" (when a later reader finds a new hidden meaning in an old text) breaks down.[58] The authors (Jesus and Luke) seem to open the door for hidden meaning but without specifying or limiting its content.

An additional feature within the biblical text opens the door to imaginative application. Once again, it is the genre itself, a story, that invites the listeners to find themselves in the story and to identify with the characters. Take another well-known Lukan parable, the story of the prodigal son, in Luke 15:11–32. The chapter begins by reporting that two different groups were present to hear this famous set of three parables in Luke 15—tax collectors and sinners on the one hand, and Pharisees and scribes on the other, with the latter grumbling about the former (Luke 15:1–2). Then, in the parable of the prodigal son, there are two sons of the father: the sinner who abandons and later returns to the father, and the envious one who is always with the father but grumbles and refuses to rejoice over the rescued sinner. The parable does not specify or close with any particular interpretation, but it would be a gross misinterpretation to *fail* to identify the characters with the two groups of hearers, the sinners and the Pharisees. Similarly, given the distinction between narrated time (when Jesus spoke it) and the time of narration (when Luke wrote it), and given the context of Luke's second volume, Acts, which is concerned with the inclusion of Gentiles, it is very difficult not to imagine that Luke is identifying the two sons with Gentiles and Jews, respectively, something perhaps not meant by Jesus or understood by his original audience. Who is the younger son? Is he the tax collectors (in Jesus's time) or the Gentiles (in Luke's time)? Who is the elder son, the Pharisees or the Jews? To both questions, Luke would say, "Yes." The sons are types that, within their own literary context, beg to be applied in new settings. Thus a modern audience cannot hear this parable aright without also imagining whom these sons represent today. Based on the literal sense, it is equally legitimate to interpret the younger son as a group of modern "sinners" loved by God. This interpretive move is not an additional application but is the meaning inherent in the text.

So it is with the good Samaritan. The story invites the hearer to identify with the characters and to ask, "Who am I in the story?" or "Who is the half-dead man?" Again, once the theme of rescue becomes evident, the patristic interpretation becomes more or less clear.

---

58. Froehlich, *Sensing the Scriptures*, 47–48.

Now we may return to the criticism of Stein and others—namely, that Augustine makes the parables "say something other than what Jesus and the Gospel writers intended."[59] But what if Jesus and the Gospel writers intended this and other stories to inspire imaginative interpretation and broad application? After all, regardless of their specific faith, what united the ancient authors of literature was their common goal for the moral transformation of the hearer. What if Jesus and the Gospel writers, like their contemporaries, intended such stories to apply to potential readers in ways beyond what they intended at the moment? In short, what if their intent was to let it transcend their intent? There is good reason to think that this is the case. Even if only the possibility of this intent is granted, then Augustine's interpretation is not the flagrant violation of authorial intent that is often alleged.

Augustine certainly had his faults as an interpreter. Linguistic limitation was one of them. Even if older accounts of his ignorance of Greek are exaggerated, it is true that he often did not bother to consult the Greek New Testament. Furthermore, at times his allegorical points do not seem connected to the literal sense. But he read Scripture looking for true doctrine, for moral edification, for the love of God and neighbor, for eschatological hope, for a word to the church. These goals are all in accord with earlier patristic exegesis and, combined with his reliance on Latin translations and his penchant for the occasional, overwrought allegory, Augustine anticipates the features of Western medieval exegetical practice.

John Cassian

The monk John Cassian (ca. 360–ca. 435), later known in the West as a "semi-Pelagian" for his opposition to Augustine's doctrine of irrevocable grace, was revered in both the East and the West for his wisdom regarding the spiritual life. In the late 420s, he wrote the *Conferences*, which summarize his conversations with a number of Egyptian monks, but surely also reflect Cassian's own thoughts.[60]

In a conference with Abba (Father) Nesteros, Cassian deals with the topic of spiritual knowledge. Cassian, through Nesteros, claims that theoretical knowledge is divided into two parts: historical interpretation and the spiritual sense. He then observes that the spiritual sense may be further divided into

---

59. Stein, *Method and Message of Jesus' Teachings*, 47–48.
60. On Cassian and issues pertaining to the *Conferences*, see Stewart, *Cassian the Monk*; and Ramsey, introduction to Cassian, *The Conferences*, trans. Ramsey. References to the *Conferences* are based on this edition.

three: tropological, allegorical, and anagogical.[61] Cassian then explains these various interpretive senses, and he employs the famous allegorical passage from Galatians 4 to illustrate each sense. The history, or historical interpretation, embraces the knowledge of what is past and visible, as in the description of Abraham's begetting a son by his wife, a free woman, and another son through her handmaid, a slave (Gal. 4:22). Cassian then moves on to the spiritual senses. The allegorical sense is the "mystery" prefigured in the history. As Paul, who calls this interpretation "allegory," says, they "are two covenants," and the slave represents the "Jerusalem that now is" and is in bondage (Gal. 4:24–25).[62] Next, the anagogical sense rises above the spiritual mysteries to the more sublime and sacred secrets of heaven. In this regard, Paul speaks of the Jerusalem that is above and is free, our mother (Gal. 4:26). Finally, the tropological sense is the moral sense that provides practical instruction for the improvement of life. Cassian here appeals to a psalm to illustrate how Jerusalem can symbolize the individual soul (Ps. 147:12).[63]

Cassian sums up these interpretations by showing how the word "Jerusalem" can be taken in four distinct senses: "According to history it is the city of the Jews. According to allegory it is the Church of Christ. According to anagogy it is that heavenly city of God 'which is the mother of us all.' According to tropology it is the soul of the human being, which under this name is frequently either reproached or praised by the Lord."[64] This multilayered use of "Jerusalem" would later become the classic illustration of multiple meanings in Scripture. In this way, Cassian systematically summarizes what would come to be the dominant exegetical guide for the next millennium: the quadriga, the fourfold sense of Scripture.

It is tempting to note this first clear description of the fourfold sense and ignore the context in which it appears. Although these senses can be applied to Scripture, the *Conferences* as a whole and *Conference* 14 in particular should not be thought of as a treatise on biblical interpretation.[65] The application of historical and spiritual knowledge to Scripture is but one facet of the spiritual life of the monk. The more important point is that spiritual maturity and understanding are prerequisites for the right interpretation and application of Scripture. Without the training and virtue emphasized throughout the *Conferences*, the interpretation of Scripture will be hampered no less than the spiritual life in general.

61. Cassian, *Conferences* 14.8.1, trans. Ramsey, 509.
62. Cassian, *Conferences* 14.8.2, trans. Ramsey, 509–10.
63. Cassian, *Conferences* 14.8.3, trans. Ramsey, 510.
64. Cassian, *Conferences* 14.8.4, trans. Ramsey, 510.
65. On this point, see Stewart, *Cassian the Monk*, 90–95.

Gregory the Great

In the wake of the dissolution of the Western Roman Empire, two more or less stable forces provided continuity during a time of transition and social and political chaos: Scripture and the church. First of all, when we say "Scripture" in the medieval West, we mean, with very few exceptions, the Latin Vulgate. Jerome, the greatest translator and one of the most prolific exegetes of the early church, was responsible for the Vulgate Bible. He is notable for his decision to translate the Old Testament from the original Hebrew and Aramaic rather than from the hallowed Greek translation (LXX), which gradually fell out of use in the West. Jerome's Vulgate gradually replaced the Old Latin versions and became the Bible of the medieval West and, later, of the Roman Catholic Church.[66] The gradual shift from the Old Latin to the Vulgate's predominance can be seen in the writings of Gregory the Great,[67] who, as head of the greatest church in the western Mediterranean, was another stabilizing factor in the West.

Gregory I, the Great (ca. 540–604), bishop of Rome from 590 until his death in 604, was an able administrator and energetic pastor who extended the influence of the papacy in the West. He was a brilliant popularizer of Augustinianism through his many writings, including his homilies and commentaries on Scripture. Later medieval figures praised him for his writing style and content.[68] The most celebrated exegetical effort of Gregory, and one of the longest works of late antiquity, is the *Moral Reflections on Job* (*Moralia in Job*), which is a running commentary on the book of Job with emphasis, as the title indicates, on moral reflections. The book's preface is addressed to Leander, bishop in Seville. In it, Gregory offers valuable insights into the assumptions that drive his biblical interpretation.

In his prefatory letter, Gregory declares that he is going to expound the book of Job by paying attention to three senses: literal, allegorical, and moral.[69] Although Gregory finds it important to keep the three senses in mind, he does

66. For a brief history of the Vulgate from Jerome through the medieval period, see Van Liere, *Medieval Bible*, 80–109. On Jerome as translator and biblical interpreter, see D. Brown, "Jerome and the Vulgate."

67. Houghton, *Latin New Testament*, 60.

68. See the accolades reported in Lubac, *Medieval Exegesis*, 2:117–21. Contra Farrar, *History of Interpretation*, 240, who describes Gregory's writing style as "interminable tedium," further demonstrating Farrar's inability to read through a bias other than his own. De Lubac also contextualizes and explains Gregory's apparently negative assessment of the study of grammar, cited in Farrar, *History of Interpretation*, 246. See Lubac, *Medieval Exegesis*, 3:36–54.

69. Gregory I, "Letter to Leander" 1–3, in *Moral Reflections* [= *Moralia*], trans. Kerns, 1:48–51. Subsequent references will be to this edition. For a survey of Gregory the Great's exegetical approach, interacting also with the letter to Leander, see Zinn, "Exegesis and Spirituality."

not emphasize each sense equally with every passage in Job. He admits that not everything in Job easily conduces to moral instruction. Thus, when the opportunity for moral edification arises, the interpreter should pursue it by going beyond the letter.[70] Indeed, there are occasions when attending to the literal sense alone can produce error or simply contradict other passages of Scripture. Such cases of difficulty provide the reader hints for going beyond the letter.[71] At the same time, the literal sense should not for this reason be neglected. If, as a rule, the literal sense were to be bypassed, the reader could miss a spiritual truth conveyed directly through it.[72] Gregory summarizes the significance of the three senses working together: "First and foremost we base ourselves on the sacred history, then we elevate the mind's construction into an edifice of faith through the typical meaning, and finally we adorn the building with exterior color through the charm of moral action."[73]

In the opening book of *Moralia* (*Moral Reflections*), Gregory stays true to the plan outlined in the letter. He covers the first five verses of Job in three discrete sections. In the first section, he explains the historical context and words, though doctrinal and moral instructions are never far from view, along with his unceasing fondness for illustrative analogies.[74] After the literal exposition, he turns to a discussion of the "secret allegories" contained in those same five verses.[75] Allegory, according to Gregory, prefigures both Christ and the church and teaches "what we should believe."[76] Finally comes the section on moral teaching, which explains "how we should live."[77]

Back to the prefatory letter, whose principles are followed throughout the massive commentary, several points about Gregory's exegesis become clear. First, Gregory explains Scripture according to three senses, not the four mentioned by Cassian. It is not that Gregory was unaware of the anagogical sense or never used it. De Lubac in fact calls Gregory an "expert" in the four senses, "one of the principal initiators and one of the greatest patrons of the medieval doctrine of the fourfold sense."[78] Gregory's practice here reflects the fluidity of the quadriga (the fourfold sense) as an exegetical guideline at this

70. Gregory I, "Letter to Leander" 2, trans. Kerns, 50–51.
71. Gregory I, "Letter to Leander" 3, trans. Kerns, 51–52.
72. Gregory I, "Letter to Leander" 4, trans. Kerns, 53.
73. Gregory I, "Letter to Leander" 3, trans. Kerns, 51.
74. Gregory I, *Moralia* 1.1.1–1.10.14, trans. Kerns, 77–85.
75. Gregory I, *Moralia* 1.10.14, trans. Kerns, 85. This second sense is handled in 1.11.15–1.24.33, trans. Kerns, 85–98.
76. Gregory I, *Moralia* 1.24.33, trans. Kerns, 98.
77. Gregory I, *Moralia* 1.24.33, trans. Kerns, 98. This third section is treated in 1.25.34–1.37.57, trans. Kerns, 98–116.
78. Lubac, *Medieval Exegesis*, 2:118; 1:134.

stage in its history. Origen's threefold sense, the precursor to the quadriga, was still dominant. The anagogical sense, as an expansion and development of the allegorical, was not always treated distinctly by Gregory.

Second, one should not fail to see the importance that Gregory places in understanding the literal sense as the first step toward accurate interpretation. It is true that the ultimate focus of Gregory's commentary is the moral sense, and in later books of this work he even tends to focus less on the literal sense in order to leave more room for discussing the spiritual sense.[79] Yet the literal sense, as the basis for the spiritual, should never be abandoned. As Gregory puts it, "We have spoken these commentaries according to three senses. . . . We earnestly beg you, however, that in raising your minds to spiritual understanding you not abandon your respect for history."[80]

Third, Scripture accommodates itself to the reader's level of understanding and, as an instrument of God's Spirit, gives believers what they need. Gregory says that the Word of God "is like a river both shallow and deep, in which a lamb walks and an elephant swims."[81] In other words, novices in the faith can wade with benefit in the river of Scripture without being overwhelmed. In the same river, those who are mature in faith and understanding will find in Scripture an inexhaustible fount so profound that their feet will never reach the bottom. Implied in this statement is the recognition that not everyone is an elephant, and lambs should not haphazardly plunge themselves into the deep waters.

Quadriga

In the early church, there was flexibility in the use of the terms "allegory," "tropology," and "anagogy." Some writers, for example, used "allegory" interchangeably with "anagogy." In other cases, early Christians used one or another of these terms to encompass the whole range of the one spiritual sense.[82] As described above, John Cassian distinguishes these terms and, as a result, summarizes more clearly than anyone before him what has come to be known as the quadriga, or fourfold interpretation of Scripture, used implicitly also by Gregory the Great. Gradually, in the following centuries, each of these three terms denoting spiritual interpretation became more firmly connected to their respective spiritual senses. Because of its importance in the history of

79. According to DelCogliano, introduction to *Moralia*, 18–19.
80. Gregory I, *Moralia* 1.37.57, trans. Kerns, 116.
81. Gregory I, "Letter to Leander" 4, trans. Kerns, 53.
82. See Lubac, *Medieval Exegesis*, 2:33–39, 129.

exegesis and its special importance in this book, the quadriga deserves some further description in its more developed stage.

The first sense is the historical. To the early church fathers the Greek word *historia*, borrowed by Latin, denoted more than historicity or historical reliability, although it could include that idea as well. It referred primarily to the narrative and its straightforward interpretation. It is the letter (*littera*), the description of "what happened." This level concerns what the text actually reports. The literal sense also takes into consideration a document's genre and figures of speech, and thus it does not intend to interpret figures of speech "literally." In this case, the "literal," straightforward interpretation of a figure is figurative.

The spiritual sense comes after and indeed flows from the literal sense. It is properly juxtaposed with the literal as another sense. In the quadriga, the one spiritual sense itself is distinguished into three senses. Augustine did not spell out these three senses as clearly as Cassian did, but his emphasis on pursuing the three theological virtues of faith, hope, and love reflects the point well. Augustine said that these virtues are the guiding principles of religion, and seeking the proper objects of our faith, hope, and love—what one should believe, hope for, and do—is therefore the most important quest.[83] Even if Augustine is not the proper origin of the quadriga, he specifically linked the theological virtues to the interpretation of Scripture. Scripture was given for the edification of the church and the nurturing of the three theological virtues. He said that the biblical interpreter ought to be able to relate every passage of Scripture to faith, hope, and love.[84] As if to meet this challenge, the following three spiritual senses relate to faith, love, and hope, respectively.[85]

The second sense is the allegorical. Allegory comes from a Greek verb that means to speak or imply something other than what is expressly said or written. From Paul's Greek, Tertullian coined the Latin verb (*allegorizare*) that forms the basis of the English verb "allegorize."[86] As Paul used the category of allegory to teach about the two covenants, the allegorical sense came to symbolize doctrinal interpretation (*doctrina*). Allegory encompassed types that link the Old and New Testaments together. The object of allegorical

83. Augustine, *Enchiridion* 1.3–4, in WSA I/8:274.

84. Augustine, *De doctrina Christiana* 1.40.44, trans. Green, 29.

85. Just as the three spiritual senses correspond to the three theological virtues, they also correspond to three advents, or comings, of Christ. According to de Lubac, the first advent of Christ on earth, the incarnation, is by faith extended in the church and its sacraments. The second presence of Christ takes place within the individual soul and is pursued in love. The final coming of Christ will be his appearance in glory, the object of hope. See Lubac, *Medieval Exegesis*, 2:179.

86. Lubac, *Medieval Exegesis*, 2:4; see 2:83–125 for the fuller discussion of the allegorical sense.

instruction usually focuses on Christ or his body, the church, or both. It corresponds to the theological virtue of faith, for it pursues what one is to believe.

The third sense is the tropological. *Tropos* denotes a turning—that is, a figure or a turn of phrase. It eventually was distinguished from allegory and anagogy to signify the moral sense or meaning of Scripture.[87] The moral instruction in Scripture could apply to the corporate church or to the individual soul. The tropological sense relates to the theological virtue of love, for it reveals what one is to do.

With the tropological sense one finds a common point of contact with other ancient literature. As noted especially in the conclusion to chapter 3, all premodern writers and readers acknowledged the moral importance of literature. Frances Young observes that, in ancient times, "literature was expected to be morally edificatory."[88] Furthermore, she writes, "It might be said that paraenetic exegesis had primacy of place. . . . The common assumption of the surrounding culture was that literature was read for the sake of moral improvement."[89] Reading literature not only for information but also for transformation was applied no less to the Bible.

The fourth sense is the anagogical. The meaning of anagogy changed with use, and it came to mean a climbing or ascent in the sense of leading or going up.[90] The term "anagogy" was used by Origen, Gregory of Nyssa, and others to describe the spiritual sense in general. By the time of Cassian's discussion, as seen above, it was distinguished from the other senses. The "going up" referred to the heavenly destination and its realities. It came to symbolize the eschatological sense in particular. As such, the anagogical sense relates to the virtue of hope, for it points forward to the fulfilled eschaton, the eternal kingdom to which God's people are headed.

The final three senses are all expansions of the one spiritual or mystical sense. They flow out of the historical or literal sense but also go beyond it in their direct applications to the current reader of Scripture. The idea here is that these spiritual senses are not just subordinate, homiletical points with no connection to the text. Rather, they are all divinely intended and legitimate meanings of the text. As long as the primary setting of biblical interpretation is the same as it has always been—namely, the church—then interpretation within the church's rule of faith and application to the church's doctrine and practice are legitimate.

87. Lubac, *Medieval Exegesis*, 2:129; see 2:127–77 for the fuller discussion of the tropological sense.

88. F. Young, *Biblical Exegesis*, 81.

89. F. Young, *Biblical Exegesis*, 248.

90. Lubac, *Medieval Exegesis*, 2:179–80; see 2:179–97 for the fuller discussion of the anagogical sense.

How does this fourfold way of interpretation relate to other ways of read-ing that came before? Although the quadriga may look like an alternative way that supersedes Origen's method, it is better understood as a development and slight expansion of the threefold interpretation.

First of all, the threefold method, as noted in the previous chapter, was based on the more basic twofold distinction between letter (or historical sense) and spirit (or mystical sense). In practice, this fundamental distinction between letter and spirit is the one most prevalent in Origen's sermons and commentaries. Origen's second and third senses, the soul and spirit, are an expansion of the one mystical sense. Likewise, as Cassian explains, knowledge is essentially divided between the historical sense and the spiritual or mystical sense. The three spiritual senses of the quadriga are subdivisions of the single spiritual sense. Some later writers even spoke of seven senses,[91] but it was the quadriga's four senses that would be more commonly used.

Second, just as Origen expanded the mystical sense into two distinct senses, it is Origen's third sense in particular that the quadriga expands into two distinct senses. That is, both Origen and Cassian begin with the historical or literal sense. They also both include a moral sense: Origen's "soul" and Cas-sian's tropological sense. Origen's highest "spiritual" sense is now represented by the quadriga's allegory and anagogy. It is not a departure or a significant modification, and indeed, anagogy is frequently subsumed under allegory, and the fourfold mode easily becomes threefold again in some authors.[92]

Figure 4.1

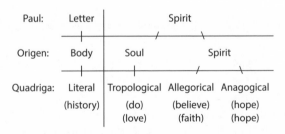

The quadriga maintained the basic twofold approach, but it
expanded Origen's two spiritual senses into three.

A final observation about the quadriga concerns the order of the four senses, for they are listed sometimes with slight variation. The literal sense

91. See Lubac, *Medieval Exegesis*, 1:84–86.
92. See Lubac, *Medieval Exegesis*, 1:90–94, 142.

always comes first, and the anagogical sense is nearly always in the fourth position. The allegorical and tropological senses, however, are not as fixed, but shift between the second and third positions. The order in which tropology precedes allegory may be considered Origenist, for it is directly tied to Origen's threefold way, keeping allegory and anagogy together as an expansion of Origen's third sense, the "spiritual."[93]

The other order, in which tropology follows allegory, was codified especially in the exegesis of Gregory the Great and the Venerable Bede.[94] It underscores the distinction between the allegorical and anagogical senses. By placing the tropological sense between the two, it made it slightly more difficult to collapse the two senses back into one spiritual, or pneumatic, sense. De Lubac also observes that this order reflects a more explicitly Christian way than the Origenist order. In the Origenist order of the quadriga, tropology precedes allegory: morality comes before faith. In other words, what one should do is considered before what one should believe. With the Gregorian order, however, doctrine precedes ethics. The idea is that it is belief that motivates action. Specifically Christian faith, which motivates all spiritual senses in the first place, is by definition absent from pagan and Jewish ways of reading and the ethics they inspire.[95]

Figure 4.2

Alternative order:	Literal	Allegorical	Tropological	Anagogical
		(faith)	(love)	(hope)

At any rate, whatever the order, even if tropology was discussed first among the spiritual senses, medieval commentators interpreted Scripture within a Christian context that acknowledged the central teachings summed up in the rule of faith and the ancient creeds. Furthermore, regardless of the order, these spiritual senses were meant to plunge the interpreter of Scripture ever deeper into spiritual insight as they draw the reader upward into union with God. Taken as a whole, the quadriga reflects a hermeneutic of spiritual ascent.[96]

93. Cassian's description also kept allegory and anagogy together, bumping tropology to the final position.

94. This order is evident in Gregory's *Moralia* and is noted in Froehlich, *Sensing the Scriptures*, 73, 123.

95. See Lubac, *Medieval Exegesis*, 1:94–96, 142–48.

96. I owe this way of putting it to Froehlich, *Sensing the Scriptures*, 78: "The fourfold sense explicates a dynamics of ascent."

Scholasticism and the *Glossa Ordinaria*

A significant development in the history of the Western church concerns the rise of scholasticism as a method for the study of theology, which in turn shaped the interpretation of Scripture. Scholasticism flourished in the newly established universities of the high and late Middle Ages. Centers devoted to higher learning were not new in the Christian West. In the medieval period, education was promoted primarily in the monasteries, which, along with the cathedral schools, were the precursors of the universities. In these monastic schools, especially since the fourth century, Scripture and other ancient texts were preserved, copied, recited, and studied. It is only natural that they were centers of biblical interpretation, and they remained so throughout the medieval period.

At places such as Saint-Victor, the art of commentary flourished under such masters as Hugh and his students, Richard and Andrew.[97] The Victorine tradition of literal biblical interpretation was highly influential on later exegetes. But spiritual interpretations were just as prominent. In particular, the cloister was a perfect place for the laity, and especially women, to express their thoughts outside of the more carefully regulated ecclesiastical orders.[98] So-called mysticism and the spiritual interpretation of Scripture that is often associated with these movements thrived in the writings of influential women such as Hildegard of Bingen (1098–1179), Julian of Norwich (1342–ca. 1416), Catherine of Siena (ca. 1347–80), and Teresa of Ávila (1515–82).[99] It should be noted, however, that mysticism is a modern classification used to describe something experiential as opposed to content that is doctrinal or even strictly rational, a use quite different from its Greek patristic meaning.[100]

As heirs to the monastic- and cathedral-school models, there was much that was old about the new universities. The university was a collection of teachers and students gathered for the purpose of specialized instruction in the arts, law, medicine, or theology.[101] A characteristic method of instruction in the university was the lecture (*lectio*)—that is, the reading of an authoritative text and running commentary on it. The primary text for theological study was, of course, the Bible. As a teacher read and commented, questions

97. On the Victorines and Andrew in particular, see Smalley, *Bible in the Middle Ages*, 83–195.

98. On the monastic context of biblical interpretation, see Leclercq, *Learning and the Desire for God*, 71–88.

99. On mysticism and the interpretation of Scripture, see McGinn, *Presence of God*.

100. See the discussion on the history of the term in Louth, *Christian Mystical Tradition*, 200–214.

101. For an old but thoroughly informative study of the medieval universities, see Rashdall, *Universities of Europe*. For a more recent, brief summary, see Madigan, *Medieval Christianity*, 266–74.

(*quaestiones*) about the text naturally arose. Some of these questions related directly to the passage; others were not as specific to the text at hand but were related to theology more generally. Such disputed questions, based on Scripture but not tied to or determined by any one passage, tended to be set aside and collected for the purpose of separate treatment in a disputation (*disputatio*) devoted to doctrinal topics. Distinct from the running commentary, the disputation would deal with the contested question and any apparently contradicting authorities—for example, among the church fathers and various passages of Scripture. The resolution would involve making logical and linguistic distinctions, as well as delineating the causes of the doctrine being discussed. Possible objections would be raised and answered. All these features were part of scholasticism, which functioned as a heuristic method for investigating a topic in any university discipline.[102]

With the rise of the disputation came the increasing tendency to discuss doctrinal questions apart from the running biblical commentary. Reading the Bible and dealing with theological questions had always gone hand in hand, but in the university there was now emerging a distinction between the sacred page (*sacra pagina*) of Scripture and the church's sacred teaching (*sacra doctrina*) as discrete fields of inquiry and disciplines of study. It is not that they were separated from or placed in tension with one another. An intimate connection was still taken for granted: Scripture was the primary source for doctrine, and the rule of faith still informed the interpretation of Scripture. But, like the texts of philosophy, medicine, the church fathers, canon law, and the church's doctrine in general, Scripture also became the object of intense classroom study in a new and unprecedented way. The university thus attracted scholars who were devoted in a new way to such scientific questions in all fields of inquiry, including biblical exegesis.[103]

This new reality had simple but far-reaching effects, such as in the practice of referring to chapters in the Bible, which became increasingly common in the latter half of the twelfth century. The introduction and standardization of chapter divisions facilitated the study of Scripture in the classroom and the writing of commentaries, and chapter divisions have shaped the way people read the Bible to this day.[104]

---

102. For a fuller description of the university curriculum and the disputation in particular, but with emphasis on the early modern context, see Stanglin, *Public Disputations of Jacobus Arminius*, 7–28; cf. Smalley, *Bible in the Middle Ages*, 196–213.

103. See Smalley, *Bible in the Middle Ages*, 72–76, 275–76; Lubac, *Medieval Exegesis*, 1:55–66. For a summary of the gradual, high medieval distinction between *sacra pagina* and *sacra doctrina*, along with a summary of the quadriga, see Leinsle, *Introduction to Scholastic Theology*, 43–54.

104. Smalley, *Bible in the Middle Ages*, 222; cf. Van Liere, *Medieval Bible*, 43–45.

Around this same time arose the most well-known and widely used medieval commentary on the sacred page: the Ordinary Gloss (*Glossa ordinaria*). The rise of the *Glossa* (Gloss) reflects the gradual shift from predominantly oral education to a written medium in which books were more widely available (yet still scarce compared to the era of print). The *Glossa* denotes medieval manuscripts and early modern printings of the Latin Bible, thousands of which survive, that include a set of comments running continuously alongside the biblical text.[105] These comments appeared on the page in the margins and between the lines of the biblical text, giving the *Glossa* a fairly standardized and distinct form by the end of the twelfth century. Any individual comment on a particular passage, from brief definitions to long explanations, came to be called a "gloss." The comments were derived from patristic sources, supplemented with early medieval contributions, and redacted and passed on orally by scholastic masters. That the *Glossa* is *ordinaria* (standard) signifies that the comments themselves also became somewhat consistent in its various editions, lending to the *Glossa* a standardized content. This standardization does not mean that there was one single text, however, for the *Glossa* in its many editions remained a living book, with variations in the comments.[106]

Thomas Aquinas

The separate categorization of monk, mystic, and scholastic breaks down in figures who were all of the above, such as Thomas Aquinas. Thomas Aquinas (1225–74) is, in the Western church, the most influential theologian after Augustine. He is best known for his long works of theology, especially *Summary against the Pagans* (*Summa contra Gentiles*) and *Summary of Theology* (*Summa theologiae*). Paragons of scholasticism, these volumes investigate theological topics by appealing to authorities, providing precise definitions and distinctions, and raising and answering objections. Because of his stature and continued influence in the Western tradition, even to the present, Thomas is worth consulting as a reflection of high medieval thought on biblical interpretation.

105. Other texts than the Bible also had their own *Glossa* for their respective fields of inquiry, such as civil law and canon law. Smalley, *Bible in the Middle Ages*, 52.

106. For an excellent introduction to the origin, authorship, purpose, and use of the *Glossa* and all its complexities, see L. Smith, *Glossa Ordinaria*. See also Matter, "Church Fathers and the *Glossa Ordinaria*"; Salomon, "*Glossa Ordinaria*" as Medieval Hypertext. For a brief description of the *Glossa*, see Van Liere, *Medieval Bible*, 151–56. In addition, seven informative essays on the *Glossa* by Froehlich are in his *Interpretation from the Church Fathers to the Reformation*.

In the *Summa theologiae*, Thomas discusses his views on the senses of Scripture, which are reflected in his many biblical commentaries. To the question of whether a word can have multiple senses in Scripture, Thomas's reply is in line with the long tradition before him: Indeed, there can be multiple senses. He begins by observing that the author of Holy Scripture is God. Thus, although it is correct to say that Thomas is concerned with authorial intent, it is not the sort of authorial intent that excludes divine authorship and intention, which could presumably transcend the intent of the human author. Thomas first notes the traditional distinction between the literal and the spiritual senses. The literal sense corresponds to the first level of words, pointing to things (*res*).[107] Here Thomas is channeling Augustine's discussion in *De doctrina Christiana* of signs and things signified. Thomas goes on to clarify that the literal sense is broad enough to include history and interpretive techniques such as the analogy of Scripture.[108] The literal sense also embraces figures and parables that are proper to the genre in question. For example, when Scripture speaks of God's arm, the literal sense is not that God has a physical arm. The literal sense is whatever is plainly signified by the metaphor—in this case, God's operative power.[109] In other words, the literal sense is the plain meaning of Scripture in its historical and literary context. It is what the author intends.

The spiritual sense, Thomas says, is based on and presupposes the literal sense. The thing signified by the literal sense can itself point to another reality or truth. Once again, Thomas is following Augustine's semiotics. This further truth or reality is the spiritual sense, which Thomas distinguishes into three: allegorical, moral, and anagogical.[110] He therefore endorses the full quadriga, though he also acknowledges that some commentators continue to follow the threefold sense by subsuming the anagogical under the allegorical.[111] The acknowledgment of multiple senses also allowed Thomas, on rare occasion, to forego the apparent literal sense if it proved to be false. Later, in the context of his discussion of the days of creation (from Gen. 1), he writes: "One should adhere to a particular explanation, only in such measure as to be ready to abandon it, if it be proved with certainty to be false; lest Holy Scripture be exposed to the ridicule of unbelievers, and obstacles be placed to their believing."[112]

Thomas raises the objection, which probably reflects the concern of some of his contemporaries, that allowing multiple senses would produce interpretive

107. *ST* Ia.i.10 resp.
108. *ST* Ia.i.10 ad 2.
109. *ST* Ia.i.10 ad 3.
110. *ST* Ia.i.10 resp.
111. Such as Hugh of Saint-Victor; *ST* Ia.i.10 ad 2.
112. *ST* Ia.lxviii.1 resp.

confusion and "destroy the force of argument."[113] This objection also sums up the concerns of many modern biblical interpreters. As Farrar would put it, the presence of multiple senses is "subversive of all exactitude."[114] In reply, Thomas reiterates that the spiritual senses flow from what is signified by the literal sense; that is, the spiritual senses are an extension of the literal sense. To a certain degree, Thomas seems to agree with the objection that arguments drawn from multiple, disparate senses would cause confusion. As with all spiritual senses, so also all arguments to support doctrine can only be drawn from the literal sense. He then adds: "Nothing necessary to faith is contained under the spiritual sense that Scripture does not pass on elsewhere manifestly through the literal sense."[115]

This limitation of basing necessary doctrines on the literal sense is an important control on interpretation and doctrinal application. On the one hand, as Beryl Smalley has shown, Thomas is in a long line of high medieval commentators who gave increasing attention to the literal sense, essentially equating it with human authorial intent. Her description of Albert the Great's pursuit of the literal sense is indicative of Thomas and the era in general: "The 'literal truth' takes on a new meaning. It is not an easy preliminary but a difficult goal."[116] On the other hand, recall that when Thomas emphasizes that the literal sense is the basis for the spiritual sense and for necessary doctrine, he is not saying anything qualitatively different from what the early church fathers said, who also based their interpretations and applications on the literal sense. In fact, he reflects the mainstream of patristic and medieval interpreters, who admitted that interpretation should begin with the literal sense before moving beyond it. In medieval practice it may have sometimes proved otherwise, when spiritual interpretations might be hardly traceable to the literal sense, a situation that motivated the objection and Thomas's stress on the literal sense. For Thomas and other medieval theologians, however, it is clear that the occasional or even frequent abuse of spiritual senses does not invalidate their proper use.

Nicholas of Lyra

As the *Glossa* was evolving into a standard form and content, new comments were added alongside the biblical text by interpreters and teachers. These additional comments came to be known as postils (*postillae*), a neologism

---

113. *ST* Ia.i.10 obj. 1.
114. Farrar, *History of Interpretation*, 296.
115. *ST* Ia.i.10 ad 1.
116. Smalley, *Bible in the Middle Ages*, 299; see 292–308. Cf. Van Liere, *Medieval Bible*, 135: "For the scholastic theologians such as Thomas Aquinas, . . . the literal sense had achieved a primacy that it had not possessed for the Church fathers."

probably from the Latin phrase for "after those" (*post illa*). That is, after these words of the biblical text and of the *Glossa* follows more commentary. *Glossa* came to mean the abridged or more restricted marginal and interlinear comments. Postil seems to indicate the longer exposition that supplements the *Glossa*. The first great "postillator" was Hugh of Saint-Cher, whose postils were read and respected throughout the thirteenth and fourteenth centuries.[117]

A century after Hugh, the postillator par excellence was Nicholas of Lyra (ca. 1270–ca. 1349). Whereas Hugh dealt with the Latin Bible and cited Latin commentators, Nicholas, who read Hebrew, was interested in updating the *Glossa* with the comments and opinions of Jewish interpreters. Nicholas's literal and moral postils would come to accompany many editions of the *Glossa ordinaria*, even in early modern printings.[118]

Like Thomas Aquinas, Nicholas agrees that, although there may be a number of mystical, or spiritual, meanings in a text, they all presuppose the literal sense as the foundation (*fundamentum*). As a building that separates from its foundation is likely to collapse, so a mystical exposition that strays from the literal sense is, in the words of Nicholas, "indecent and inappropriate, or at least less decent and less appropriate." Therefore, those who wish to study Holy Scripture "must begin from an understanding of the literal sense."[119]

Nicholas notes that the literal sense, which ought to be the beginning of interpretation, has been "much obscured in modern days." Among the several reasons for this obscuring, he points to a common way of handling Scripture, "passed down by others," that simply neglects the literal sense in favor of spiritual senses. Nicholas does not identify these "others." Such interpreters provide many good spiritual interpretations, but the result of this abundance is that "the literal sense is cut off, partly suffocated, among so many mystical expositions." As a correction to this common error, in his comments Nicholas intends to emphasize the literal sense and only occasionally to offer spiritual interpretations.[120]

Nicholas's stress on the literal sense, however, does not mean that he has no legitimate place for anything beyond the human author's intent and context. In actual practice, Nicholas introduces what he calls the "double literal sense," which allows him to read Old Testament prophecies in a messianic

117. On the postils, see Smalley, *Bible in the Middle Ages*, 264–81; Van Liere, *Medieval Bible*, 165–68.

118. For a brief introduction to Nicholas's life and thought, especially with respect to his biblical exegesis, see Krey and L. Smith, *Nicholas of Lyra*, 1–18.

119. Nicholas of Lyra, "Prologus secundus" (PL 113:29C). Cf. Nicholas of Lyra et al., *Biblia sacra cum glossa ordinaria primum quidem*, vol. 1. For ET of excerpts from Nicholas's "Prologus secundus" and "Prologus in moralitates," see Yarchin, *History of Biblical Interpretation*, 99–102.

120. Nicholas of Lyra, "Prologus secundus" (PL 113:30C).

way, something he was generally reluctant to do.[121] The double literal sense seems to be Nicholas's way of emphasizing that the spiritual senses must be based on the literal sense. With the double literal sense, the letter of Scripture contains many senses. "The reason for this is because the principal author of this book is God himself, in whose power it lies not only to use words to signify something, . . . but also he uses the things signified through words to signify other things."[122] Nicholas is clearly influenced by Augustine's discussion of semiotics in *De doctrina Christiana*. The first level of meaning, the literal, points to the spiritual meanings. As Nicholas writes elsewhere, "One thing subjectively sometimes signifies many and diverse things mystically."[123] Nicholas associates the first signification through the words as the "literal or historical sense." The second signification is the "mystical or spiritual sense, which is threefold in general." What is to be believed (*credenda*) in the new law is the allegorical sense; what is to be done (*agenda*) is the moral or tropological sense; what is to be hoped for (*speranda*) in the future state of beatitude is the anagogical sense.[124] Nicholas then quotes, and thus helps to make famous, a version of the poem that originated with Augustine of Dacia around 1260, cited at the beginning of this chapter.

> The letter teaches what happened, the allegory what you should believe,
> The moral sense what you should do, the anagogy what you should hope.[125]

Nicholas then illustrates the fourfold sense with the famous example of Jerusalem, cited earlier by John Cassian, which can signify at least four distinct things.[126]

While he advocates the fourfold sense of Scripture, Nicholas is also quick to observe that not every portion of Scripture has all four meanings. First of all, some passages, such as the command to love God, have only a straightforward,

---

121. See Krey, "Apocalypse Commentary of 1329," 284–88. For the use of the double literal sense in John Wyclif and Jean Gerson, see Levy, *Holy Scripture and the Quest*, 68–69, 211. Froehlich, *Sensing the Scriptures*, 41–42, sees the double literal sense of Nicholas as an example of exegetical "confusion if not chaos," calling it, among other things, "tortured."

122. Nicholas of Lyra, "Incipit prologus" (PL 113:28C).

123. Nicholas of Lyra, "Prologus in moralitates" (PL 113:34D).

124. Nicholas of Lyra, "Incipit prologus"(PL 113:28C).

125. Nicholas of Lyra, "Incipit prologus" (PL 113:28D).

126. Nicholas of Lyra, "Incipit prologus" (PL 113:28D–29A). Much of this discussion, including the quotation of the brief poem, is paralleled in Nicholas's "Prologus in moralitates" (PL 113:33–36).

literal sense.[127] In this instance, there is no need to seek a further, spiritual meaning beyond this greatest love command. Second, Nicholas then claims that, in other passages, there may be no literal sense, such as the Lord's command to cut off one's hand to avoid sin. He acknowledges that some interpreters would still call an intentional metaphor or figure of speech the "literal sense," as he admits to doing in some of his own commentaries.[128] In a book such as Song of Songs, for example, Nicholas's literal sense really is the traditional literal sense—that is, what scholars today would call allegorical.[129] In effect, like Origen and other predecessors, Nicholas is saying that the difficulty or nonsense of the literal meaning points the reader beyond that surface meaning to something deeper. Finally, in other passages, "sacred Scripture has [both] the literal and the mystical sense."[130]

In light of these features of Scripture, Nicholas promises that his comments will expound Scripture "according to the literal sense," and then he will expound "according to the mystical sense, where it must be mystically expounded." His intention is not to record all the mystical senses, and he asks his readers not to be surprised if he omits "many mystical things." Such omission is for the sake of "brevity" and because previous expositors have given mystical interpretations.[131] Nicholas clearly feels the need to counterbalance the abundance of mystical expositions of Scripture by emphasizing the literal sense. He does it intentionally, but without neglecting the legitimacy of the spiritual sense, as long as it is based on and flows from the literal.

These features of biblical interpretation that Nicholas explains are consistent with what he assumes to be the goal of Scripture. Interpreted correctly, Scripture contains nothing false, but rather the "perfections of practical and theoretical knowledge." It is an "instrument" whose purpose is to lead its readers to the blessed life and to eternal happiness.[132]

Principles of Medieval Exegesis

The features of early Christian exegesis, based as they are on a set of shared assumptions about Scripture, anticipate the direction of Western medieval biblical interpretation. The most prominent characteristics of patristic interpretation remain present throughout the millennium or so that we have treated

127. Nicholas of Lyra, "Prologus in moralitates" (PL 113:33D–34B).
128. Nicholas of Lyra, "Prologus in moralitates" (PL 113:34C–D).
129. See the discussion in Dove, "Literal Senses in the Song of Songs."
130. Nicholas of Lyra, "Prologus in moralitates" (PL 113:34D).
131. Nicholas of Lyra, "Prologus in moralitates" (PL 113:35–36).
132. Nicholas of Lyra, "Incipit prologus" (PL 113:29–30).

as the Middle Ages. The imaginative allegories and spiritual interpretations of medieval exegetes continue what was seen as the apostolic method of interpretation. Such interpretation is possible because of the ongoing assumption that Christ is the center or scope of Scripture. Scripture is the revelation of what God has done for his people in Christ and is thus a testimony to the story of salvation. The Old Testament must be read in light of this christological and salvific scope; the New Testament is already fundamentally christological.

The transition from patristic to Western medieval biblical interpretation can be described as a history dominated by continuities. When it comes to assumptions about Scripture and how one should read and interpret it, much more unites these fourteen centuries of interpreters than divides them. However, a few notable developments, or discontinuities, should be mentioned.

1. *Further systematizing.* Medieval exegetes, from Augustine of Hippo to Augustine of Dacia and beyond, may be said to further systematize what was already implicit and practiced in the ancient church. This standardization is an entirely expected phenomenon and, it should be emphasized, is a standardization mostly of continuities. Nevertheless, this natural process is still a development. One example of this evolution is Augustine of Hippo, who did his part in systematizing Christian hermeneutical theory with his discussion of semiotics in *De doctrina Christiana*, which had a profound influence throughout the medieval period.[133] His distinction between signs and things signified lent clear theoretical language to what had long been understood and practiced by Christian interpreters. Scripture has not merely one sense, but many true meanings, and the skilled interpreter is enabled by God to explore its depths.

2. *Quadriga and its controls.* The process of systematizing is reflected in Cassian's fourfold interpretation, later known as the quadriga. Cassian builds on the same twofold method of literal-spiritual interpretation that was assumed and practiced by the earliest Christian exegetes and was given expression in a threefold manner by Origen. The quadriga's three expressions of the one spiritual sense—allegorical, tropological, and anagogical—came to be associated with the three theological virtues—faith, love, and hope—that Augustine connected also with biblical interpretation. The point is not to struggle to find four distinct meanings in each text of Scripture or, for that matter, to limit it to four. Instead, the point is simply that Scripture still instructs the church in doctrine and morals, and that such instruction should

133. In addition to the examples of Thomas Aquinas and Nicholas of Lyra cited above, note that Peter Lombard begins his *Sentences*, which would be the most influential theology text of the high medieval period, with a lengthy discussion of Augustine's semiotics. Peter Lombard, *Sentences* 1.1–3, trans. Silano, 5–11.

be sought and discovered. By the high and late medieval period, the quadriga became the standard way for theologians to think about and practice biblical interpretation.

The more standardized spiritual interpretation was not without its controls. As in the early church, in the medieval period there continued to be a recognition of the primacy of the *analogia fidei*, the use of the content of Christian teaching summarized especially in the ancient creeds and councils. Scripture must not be interpreted apart from or in contradiction to the one faith that is reflected in Scripture itself. Similarly, the *analogia scripturae* continued to serve as a hermeneutical lens, enabling exegetes to interpret obscure passages in light of clearer ones. The ongoing belief in the fundamental unity of Scripture and received Christian doctrine is what makes these distinct but interrelated methods possible.

The literal sense provides another limit to spiritual interpretation. The necessary relationship of the literal sense to the spiritual sense is a recurring theme throughout the patristic and medieval eras. The literal sense is understood to be the foundation of the spiritual. This ubiquitous acknowledgment does not mean that this or any other controls were consistently followed by a person, or even throughout all the writings of any one individual. Thus one can find allegory run amok. Such abuses of the spiritual sense prompt reactions by figures such as the Victorines, Thomas Aquinas, and Nicholas of Lyra.[134] They perceived that many of their contemporaries were putting forward spiritual meanings with little or no prior consideration of the literal sense.

3. *Emphasis on the literal sense.* The literal sense's limiting of the spiritual sense leads to another development from early to medieval exegesis: the increased privilege of the literal-grammatical sense. As Moisés Silva writes, "We would not be exaggerating greatly if we described the [historical] progress of biblical exegesis as the gradual abandonment of allegorical interpretation."[135] This shift is especially apparent toward the end of the medieval era. It is not that spiritual interpretations languished across the board; in many cases, they continued to flourish, sometimes to the detriment of the literal sense. It was against the abuses of some spiritual interpretation that focus shifted toward the literal sense, especially in the schools.

4. *Academic setting.* The literal sense, always understood to be the starting point of exegesis, received renewed attention in the setting of the university lecture. New tools were put to use. It is not that there were no commentaries before the scholastic period. But commentaries and postils focusing on the

---

134. See Van Liere, "Literal Sense."
135. Silva, *Has the Church Misread the Bible?*, 52.

literal sense, such as those of Nicholas of Lyra, multiplied, as did the word-study tools used for expounding the literal sense.[136] Lengthy commentaries proliferated, and it was the academic and so-called secular theologians, not the monks, who produced most of the late medieval commentaries.[137] In the academic setting, worship was no longer the primary context for the reading and interpretation of Scripture. Different questions were asked of the text.

5. *Exegesis and theology*. Attention increasingly shifted to the interpretation of a written text as distinct from tangential theological questions. But by setting aside disputed questions more suited to the study of doctrine, the precedent was set for a reading of Scripture that was narrower in scope and was less burdened by theological inquiry. The new academic context encouraged scholastic theologians to react against interpretations that they perceived as negligent of the literal sense, even as, it should be added, others reacted against the perceived overemphasis on the literal sense. This marks the early stage of a tension that would eventually work to drive a wedge between the literal and the spiritual senses, between exegesis and dogmatic theology.

But it is still early in that gradual process of division between the literal and spiritual senses. At this point in the history, the occasional abuse of spiritual interpretation does not imply to any interpreters that spiritual exposition should be abandoned altogether. Rather, it should be tied more carefully to the literal sense. At any rate, it seems clear that the literal sense was enjoying something of a renaissance on the eve of the Reformation. The stage was set for early modern theologians to question the legitimacy of some doctrinal traditions and of the spiritual sense that seemed to convey them.

136. Van Liere, "Literal Sense," 68.
137. See Courtenay, "Bible in the Fourteenth Century."

5

Early Modern Exegesis

I think the principal reason why we see that monastic piety is everywhere so cold, languid, and almost extinct is that they are growing
old in the letter and never take pains to learn the spiritual sense
of the Scriptures.

—Erasmus of Rotterdam[1]

I often asked the few monks who tried to find nourishment in
Sacred Scriptures what sweetness they experienced and savored.
Most of them answered that as often as they fell into—I do not
know what—literal sense, especially when they tried to understand the divine Psalms, they became utterly sad and downcast
from their reading.

—Jacques Lefèvre d'Étaples[2]

It is also useful for the student to receive some sort of brief catechetical instruction, which Scripture provides for us. . . . All understanding and exposition of Scripture takes place according to the
analogy of faith, which is, as it were, a sort of norm of healthy
faith or a barrier whereby, whether through an external storm or
an inner impetuousness, we are kept from being dragged outside
the fence (Rom. 12:6). Everything, therefore, that is said about or

1. Erasmus, *Handbook of the Christian Soldier* (CWE 66:35).
2. Lefèvre d'Étaples, "Introduction to Commentary on the Psalms," 298.

from Scripture ought to be harmonious with this aforementioned
catechetical summary, or articles of faith.

—Matthias Flacius Illyricus[3]

Lorenzo (Laurentius) Valla (1407–57) was a gifted writer, philologist,
and lay theologian. Despite all his achievements, he is well known to
later generations primarily for one reason: his critical work on the *Donation of Constantine*. This purportedly was the text of a decree of Emperor
Constantine the Great, who, when he moved the Roman Empire's capital
eastward to Byzantium (Constantinople), granted civil rule in the West to
the bishop of Rome. The document was put to effective use by a number of
medieval popes, beginning with Urban II in 1098,[4] in support of their claims
of supreme authority over the church and of civil jurisdiction. In the perennial
struggle between church and state in the medieval West, such a decree from
the first Christian emperor himself became a handy tool. The *Donation* was
later appended to Gratian's twelfth-century *Decretum*, the magnum opus of
canon law in the West. Needless to say, the *Donation of Constantine* was an
important text, at least to many Western clergy.

The problem is that Constantine and his court never composed such a
document. Valla demonstrated what others had asserted before him: the
Donation was not a fourth-century document, but a forgery from a later
hand, probably during the mid-eighth century, as scholars now believe. Valla's
scathing critique, titled *On the Donation of Constantine*, is a mélange of
satirical rhetoric and serious philology. The rhetoric, from the beginning
of the work until the end, intends to accentuate the utter implausibility of
such a "donation" and of the whole scenario. The more objective philological and historical observations are devastating to the forged decree. Valla
proceeds through the text of the *Donation* and identifies the barbaric style
that is more typical of the postclassical, medieval period than of the early
fourth century. He points also to numerous anachronisms, such as the document's famous use of "satraps" to refer to high officials in Rome, a title not
used in Rome until the mid-eighth century.[5] The document has Constantine
referring to Constantinople as one of the four patriarchal sees in the East,
an anachronism that Valla ridicules.[6] Further proof of the forgery, and of

3. Flacius Illyricus, *Sacred Scriptures*, 77, 79.
4. Fried, *Middle Ages*, 147–48.
5. Valla, *On the Donation*, 33–34, 100n47.
6. Valla, *On the Donation*, 36–37.

the forger's lack of talent, is provided by a host of historical inaccuracies regarding everything from diadems to patricians to the pages of a codex.[7] He chides the pseudonymous author: "You fail to explain what is unclear, and you explain what is altogether clear."[8]

In the West there had been a long tradition of literary criticism, and as long as there had been literary forgeries, there had also been methods for detecting forgeries, methods honed first by ancient scholars from Alexandria.[9] Valla further sharpened the received tools and, from within a Christian context, directed them toward a Christian document that enjoyed official status in the church. Above all, he was shocked at the gullibility with which its advocates had defended the authenticity of this document without any corroborating attestation in contemporary histories. If it had been the ancient Greeks or barbarians passing down such a story, Valla speculates, then people would ask critical questions about the author and the written text. But since this is a famous book written in their own language—and, I would add, because it is a book with religious implications—they either "make no inquiry about such an unbelievable item" or they "show such headlong credulity" that they accept it as it is written and as true.[10] Valla is encouraging a little healthy skepticism about this received, written tradition. Although he does not expose the Bible to the same degree of criticism, he implies the propriety of subjecting it to the same inquiries: "When I was a boy, I remember asking someone who had written the Book of Job. When he answered, 'Job himself,' I asked the further question of how therefore he managed to mention his own death. This can be said of many other books, although it is not appropriate to discuss them here. For how can something that has not yet taken place be accurately told?"[11]

Valla's work and the questions that he asked reflected the values of Renaissance humanism, which would have a profound impact on the church and its reading of Scripture, contributing to a gradual but unmistakable shift of emphasis in the assumptions and practice of biblical interpretation. By the end of the early modern period, the same techniques of historical and literary criticism, with increasing doses of skepticism, would be commonly applied to the books of the Bible, a process hinted at and anticipated by Valla. The shift would not happen overnight, but steadily over the course of a couple of centuries.

7. Valla, *On the Donation*, 43, 46, 56.
8. Valla, *On the Donation*, 43–44.
9. See Grafton, *Forgers and Critics*.
10. Valla, *On the Donation*, 31.
11. Valla, *On the Donation*, 56.

To the Sources

The movement of Renaissance humanism, as Johan Huizinga put it, "got its start by nothing more dramatic than that a learned circle took more care than usual to observe a pure Latin and classical sentence structure."[12] This description, of course, omits both the important causal factors that made such study possible and the extent to which the humanistic spirit shaped culture. Since the Crusades (begun in 1096), Western Europeans had increasing awareness of and contact with the Eastern world and the ancient culture that it more naturally preserved. With this contact came greater access to the texts of pagan antiquity, as evident in the West's discovery and use of influential treatises by Aristotle, such as his *Physics*, *Metaphysics*, and *Ethics*. The rise and proliferation of universities also contributed to the study of such texts and the desire to recover the past that these texts reflect. Humanism, moreover, would go beyond the study of languages and texts, quickly spreading to other fields such as philosophy, theology, art, and natural science.[13]

At the same time, Huizinga's insight about the initial core of the Renaissance is accurate, and humanism never abandoned its roots in scholarly attention to the pursuit of classical texts combined with earlier traditions of medieval rhetoric. The learned late medieval and early modern figures of the Renaissance wanted to return "to the sources" (*ad fontes*)—that is, to the classical texts of Greece and Rome in their original languages. In order to be a competent humanist and truly return *ad fontes*, it was necessary to know ancient history and to master classical Greek and Latin. If one desired to apply humanist methods to the Bible, it was necessary to add Hebrew to one's arsenal. Whereas Greek and especially Hebrew were rarely known and much less mastered in the medieval West, later, as the Renaissance flourished in northern and western Europe, being "trilingual" became an ideal and, by the end of the sixteenth century, a common feature of the serious student of Scripture.

Key outcomes for biblical interpretation follow from the humanistic return *ad fontes*, results that can be seen throughout the early modern period (ca. 1450–ca. 1650). Careful textual studies led to the gathering, collating, correcting, and publishing of critical editions of classical literature. The philological enterprise came to include greater attention to literary context and historical details, which led to increased literary and historical skepticism, as well as the questioning of textual traditions on the basis of earlier, more

12. Huizinga, *Autumn of the Middle Ages*, 383.
13. Kristeller, *Renaissance Thought*, 92–119; Turner, *Philology*; Witt, "Humanist Movement." For a sound introduction to biblical interpretation in the Renaissance, Erasmus, and Luther, see George, *Reading Scripture with the Reformers*.

reliable manuscripts. It was only natural that these same tools and practices would be applied not only to classical texts but also to ecclesiastical texts (as Valla did) and eventually to Scripture itself. As with secular books, the Renaissance methods initiated the process that would eventually ensure a "nondoctrinal, historical approach to the Bible."[14] The increased attention to historical context would lead to greater emphasis on human authorial intention as central to the exegetical task, and thus also to a de-emphasis on spiritual interpretations not obviously present to the human author. As these humanistic approaches came to dominate, the Sacred Scripture inspired by the Holy Spirit would gradually be treated more like a text to be scientifically dissected than a divine revelation to be contemplated and heeded.

Along with the increased skepticism concerning the state of received texts, there was new skepticism about all received traditions, including doctrinal traditions of the church. Printed Bibles were stripped of the glossed commentaries that once seemed an inseparable part of Scripture, thus freeing the text and its interpreter from traditional and doctrinal interpretations.[15] It would not take long, however, for new notes and comments to make their way into the margins of the page.

The most significant aid in the return to the sources and the spread of humanistic scholarship was the arrival of the printing press in the mid-fifteenth century, which for the first time in history enabled the mass production of a uniform text. It is hard to exaggerate the revolution initiated by Johann Gutenberg's invention—perhaps the advent of the internet is analogous—which made books less expensive and more widely available, eventually leading to an increase in literacy levels. By the end of the sixteenth century, thanks to the press, a printed Bible would be 1 percent of the price of a manuscript Bible written on vellum a century and a half earlier.[16] Thus vernacular translations of Scripture would be affordable for and legible to more people than ever before, enabling as many as could own and read a copy also to interpret it for themselves.

Erasmus of Rotterdam

Of the many humanist scholars whom Valla inspired, the most notable was Desiderius Erasmus of Rotterdam (1466–1536), who represents the pinnacle

14. Turner, *Philology*, 45.
15. Turner, *Philology*, 46.
16. Marcus Zueris van Boxhorn (1612–53) claims that the price went from "four [hundred] or 500 crowns" down to "4 or 5." See his *Nederlandsche historie*, 266–67.

of humanist learning and its application as it relates to biblical interpretation. James Turner characterizes Erasmus as the "synthesizer of philological craft built up since Petrarch."[17] Erasmus's synthesis of actually millennia-old techniques marks the beginning of modern textual criticism—that is, the establishing of the original text, a science that has been central to modern biblical exegesis ever since. Erasmus was an admirer of the text critic Valla, whom he called simply "Laurentius," and whose annotations on the New Testament he had discovered and published in 1505. Erasmus's own textual skill is on full display in his most famous contribution to textual criticism, the Greek New Testament, published first as *Novum instrumentum* in 1516. Although the Complutensian Polyglot included an earlier printing of the Greek text of the New Testament (1514), it was not widely published until 1522,[18] making Erasmus's text the first publicized printing of the Greek New Testament. He did for the New Testament what Renaissance scholars had long been doing with secular texts: comparing and emending the text.

Several features of Erasmus's New Testament are noteworthy. First of all, the presentation of the text is significant. Each page is laid out in two columns, with the Greek on the left and a new, revised Latin translation on the right. In fact, his primary purpose for this publication was to produce a fresh, readable Latin translation of the New Testament, with the Greek text appearing next to it so that readers could see the basis of his Latin translation. It is the Greek text, however, that ended up making this book famous. Although Erasmus added his own annotations in the second part of the book, the New Testament itself is presented as a simple text, free of all commentary and apparatus. The only interruptions to the text are the chapter numbers that appear in the margin.[19] Lack of commentary alongside the text was notable, particularly since the *Glossa* and postils had become the expected companions of many late medieval biblical texts. This lack of commentary is one reason why Erasmus's New Testament, in this and its subsequent editions, became the New Testament of the Reformers. It allowed, even invited, new interpretation.

Another striking feature of Erasmus's New Testament text is that it is eclectic. As an eclectic text, it is not simply a reproduction of any single manuscript. Rather, it is based on a comparison of the best manuscripts available and, in cases with textual variants, it reflects what he, the editor, considered to be the original reading. The number of manuscripts available to him is minimal by today's standards. But in the process of evaluating textual

17. Turner, *Philology*, 43.
18. Turner, *Philology*, 42.
19. See Erasmus, *Novum instrumentum omne*. Chapter numbers became commonplace in the high medieval period. Verse numbers would be introduced later, in the mid-sixteenth century.

variants, Erasmus helped to develop principles that would become central to modern textual criticism, such as the preference for "the more difficult reading" (*lectio difficilior*).

The most famous result of his textual criticism is his Greek New Testament's omission of the words here italicized in 1 John 5:7–8, now called the Johannine clause or comma (*comma Johanneum*): "For there are three who testify *in heaven, the Father, the Word, and the Holy Spirit, and these three are one. And there are three that testify on earth*: the Spirit and the water and the blood, and these three are one." With this omission, Erasmus was simply following the evidence of the manuscripts and the logic of his own observation that it is "much easier . . . to corrupt a sound text than to correct a corrupted one."[20] This *comma Johanneum*, for which he found no textual evidence in the available Greek manuscripts, was clearly added to 1 John later in the Western Latin textual tradition. The trouble for Erasmus is that these pious words had in recent centuries become the favorite and clearest biblical proof of the doctrine of the Trinity. For his integrity in following the Greek manuscripts, he met stiff opposition from those who accused him of deception and Arian, anti-trinitarian sympathies. It did not seem to matter that the early church and the Greek church had held to the centrality of the Trinity in the absence of any such clause in 1 John. In the nineteenth century a myth grew, now often repeated, that Erasmus rashly vowed to add the debated text if a Greek manuscript could be found with it. He never made such a promise, yet after a late Greek manuscript was found with the clause, Erasmus indeed added it to his third (1522) and later editions, noting, however, that the manuscript in question was recent and that the phrase was reverse translated from Latin. He wanted to avoid unnecessary controversy so that his book would be used and so that neither it nor its editor would be suspected of heresy.[21] This incident surrounding the *comma Johanneum* reflects just how controversial textual criticism could become when it challenged cherished traditions and doctrines. The same goes for other results of the emerging methods of exegesis.[22]

In addition to his groundbreaking work on the Greek text of the New Testament, Erasmus also commented on Scripture. Some of these commentaries, especially his *Paraphrases* of the New Testament books, were widely

20. Erasmus, "To the Reader" (*CWE* 3:199). This general letter appears after the biblical text and before the annotations in the 1516 edition of *Novum instrumentum*.

21. De Jonge, "Erasmus and the Comma Johanneum"; Whitford, "Yielding to the Prejudices of His Times"; G. McDonald, *Biblical Criticism in Early Modern Europe*.

22. A survey of the importance and reception of Erasmus's Greek New Testament may be found in Nellen and Bloemendal, "Erasmus's Biblical Project," in part of an entire journal issue (*Church History and Religious Culture* 96/4) devoted to Erasmus's *Novum instrumentum* on its five hundredth anniversary.

read and respected. In general, Erasmus's principles of interpretation are characteristic of the period. He emphasizes the importance of returning to the original languages of Scripture and the classics: "Those who venture to write, not merely on the Scriptures, but on any ancient books at all, are devoid of both intelligence and modesty if they do not possess a reasonable command of both Greek and Latin."[23] His expert proficiency in Greek surpassed his grasp of Hebrew; recognizing this as a deficiency, he sought assistance from better Hebraists.[24] In short, Erasmus's biblical interpretation epitomizes the methods of Renaissance textual scholarship.

At the same time, Also typical of late medieval interpretation, Erasmus likewise reacted against what he perceived to be overzealous allegory. Following the majority of his Christian predecessors, he insists that the literal sense should be the basis for the spiritual. "It is the least part of Scripture, what they call the letter; but this is the foundation on which rests the mystic meaning. This is only rubble; but rubble carries the august weight of the whole marvelous edifice." Erasmus then endorses Jerome's criticism of those who "despise the historical sense and prefer to indulge in allegory as their fancy leads them."[25] He is also reluctant to find hidden allegorical meanings in the details of the parables. Erasmus finds the "best key" toward the understanding of any passage of Scripture to be a consideration of its main theme.[26]

At the same time, Erasmus is far from rejecting spiritual meanings in Scripture. His support for the spiritual sense comes out clearly in his *Enchiridion*, or *The Handbook of the Christian Soldier* (1503, revised 1518). In the midst of this devotional work, he offers twenty-two rules for Christian living, the fifth of which is to pursue the spirit, not the flesh, a principle that he applies to biblical interpretation. He encourages readers to rise to the level of spiritual things and despise what is visible in favor of that which is invisible. This principle of seeking what is spiritual applies to all literary works, whose words include body and soul—that is, a literal and a mystical sense—but it applies especially to Sacred Scripture.[27] If one were to read the biblical creation narratives without the aid of allegorical interpretation, then one could do just as well reading other creation myths. In fact, Erasmus claims, reading the pagan poetic fables as allegory is better than reading the biblical accounts

23. Erasmus, "Letter 182" (*CWE* 2:96).

24. In checking New Testament quotations based on the Hebrew Old Testament, Erasmus was helped by Johannes Oecolampadius (1482–1531), later a reformer in Basel. Erasmus, "To the Reader," 200.

25. Erasmus, "To the Reader," 201.

26. Erasmus, *De libero arbitrio*, 82–83.

27. Erasmus, *Handbook of the Christian Soldier* (*CWE* 66:67).

without penetrating the surface. Erasmus writes, "If you read unallegorically of the infants struggling within the womb, the right of primogeniture sold for a mess of pottage, the fraudulent seizing of a father's blessing ahead of time, David's slaying of Goliath with a sling, and the shaving off of Samson's locks, then it is of no more importance than if you were to read the fiction of the poets."[28] Erasmus proceeds to cite biblical stories that, on their surface, would undermine good morals. One must, therefore, uncover the spiritual sense of Scripture, and especially of the Old Testament.[29]

As an aid to finding the spiritual sense, Erasmus recommends the approach reflected in the works of Dionysius the Areopagite (*On Divine Names*) and Augustine (*De doctrina Christiana*). He also credits Paul and Origen as model allegorical interpreters.[30] Earlier in the same book, he writes, "Of the interpreters of divine Scripture choose those especially who depart as much as possible from the literal sense, such as, after Paul, Origen, Ambrose, Jerome, and Augustine. I notice that modern theologians are too willing to stick to the letter and give their attention to sophistic subtleties rather than to the elucidation of the mysteries, as if Paul were not right in saying that our law is spiritual."[31] But, Erasmus complains, "theologians of the present day either practically despise allegory or treat it very coolly." He attributes this shortcoming to the current lack of rhetorical sensibility among interpreters and the dominance of Aristotle to the exclusion of Platonism and Pythagoreanism. In these latter schools of thought were the figures who excelled in the kind of exegesis of the poets and of the philosophers that is necessary for the interpretation of Scripture. He warns his readers not to be content with "the letter that kills," for "it is the spirit that gives life" (2 Cor. 3:6; John 6:63). According to Paul, Erasmus claims, the letter "is fatal unless it is referred to the spirit."[32] In his recognition of the mystical sense and the necessity of moving beyond the literal sense, especially when it is unedifying or contrary to Christian doctrine or morals, Erasmus is a conscious and appreciative disciple of Origen.

In addition to Erasmus's philological acuity and admiration for the spiritual sense, it is important to point out his views on the authority of Scripture and the right of interpretation. Writing as he did at the beginning of the Protestant Reformations (and there were several), Erasmus witnessed enough of these movements to express alarm at the jettisoning of traditional interpretations. He observed among many Reformers a lack of regard for earlier interpreters

28. Erasmus, *Handbook of the Christian Soldier* (CWE 66:68).
29. Erasmus, *Handbook of the Christian Soldier* (CWE 66:68–69).
30. Erasmus, *Handbook of the Christian Soldier* (CWE 66:69).
31. Erasmus, *Handbook of the Christian Soldier* (CWE 66:34–35).
32. Erasmus, *Handbook of the Christian Soldier* (CWE 66:69).

throughout the history of the church. This concern of his was prominent, for instance, in his debate with Martin Luther over free choice. Erasmus observed that the authority of Scripture is not the issue. "I confess that it is right that the sole authority of Holy Scripture should outweigh all the votes of all mortal men. But the authority of the Scripture is not here in dispute. The same Scriptures are acknowledged and venerated by either side. Our battle is about the meaning of Scripture."[33] In this particular debate, Erasmus argued that Scripture upholds free choice, whereas Luther appealed to Scripture to limit, or bind, choice. The question about the authority to interpret, lurking in the background, is a key point of debate that, in many ways, leads to the Protestant Reformations and would shape the future course of biblical interpretation.[34]

Martin Luther

As the most prominent figure of the early Protestant Reformations, the assumptions of Martin Luther (1483–1546) about Scripture and its interpretation have wielded a lasting influence on subsequent Protestant exegesis. Like Erasmus and other Renaissance humanists, Luther was interested in returning to the written sources in their original languages, Hebrew and Greek. Beginning in 1521, while in protective custody in Wartburg Castle, he began his translation of the New Testament from Erasmus's Greek edition into his own native German, followed later by his translation of the Old Testament from Hebrew into German. Luther's Bible became the Scriptures of German Lutheranism.

With regard to the senses of Scripture, recall that in the late medieval period—following in the steps of Hugh and Andrew of Saint-Victor, Thomas Aquinas, and Nicholas of Lyra—there was renewed interest in the literal sense, which the humanists tended to stress. In this context, how did Luther view the use of allegory as a tool in biblical interpretation? Usually the most direct way to find a commentator's opinion on this question is to check for comments on Galatians 4, where the apostle Paul offered his own allegorical interpretation of Sarah and Hagar. In his lectures on Galatians from 1535, Luther does not disappoint. First of all, unlike Erasmus, we see that Luther immediately places a wedge between Paul and Origen and distances himself from Origen. Because one cannot deny that Paul uses and affirms "allegory," Luther revives the ancient Antiochene strategy of claiming that Paul's allegorizing should not be confused with Origen's use of the same term. At any

---

33. Erasmus, *De libero arbitrio*, 43.

34. In addition to the primary sources, see a summary of Erasmus and Luther's debate on free choice in Ozment, *Age of Reform*, 290–317.

rate, Luther is not complimentary of standard medieval exegesis. He thinks, first, that the association of "Jerusalem above" (Gal. 4:26) with the heavenly Jerusalem, as John Cassian and others had understood it, is incorrect. The Jerusalem above, according to Luther, is simply the church. He goes on to deride the application of the "four senses of Scripture," by which "unlettered monks and scholastic doctors . . . misinterpreted almost every word of Scripture." They "tore Scripture apart into many meanings and robbed themselves of the ability to give sure instruction to human consciences."[35] "Many meanings" result in the uncertainty of any meaning.

At the same time that he rejects a certain type of allegory and the quadriga in general, Luther proceeds to interpret Galatians 4 beyond the letter. Commenting on the same verse (4:26), he says: "This allegory teaches in a beautiful way that the church should not do anything but preach the Gospel correctly and purely and thus give birth to children. In this way we are all fathers and children to one another, for we are born of one another. I was born of others through the Gospel, and now I am a father to still others, who will be fathers to still others."[36] Luther claims that this extension of Paul's allegory, which is not overt in the biblical verse itself, is taught in the text. Whatever Luther means by his comments against allegorizing, he apparently does not mean to exclude all spiritual interpretation beyond the letter.

Rather than a blanket prohibition against allegory, Luther puts some limits to it. At Galatians 4:24, where Paul introduces the word "allegory," Luther points out that allegories alone cannot prove doctrine, but that they illustrate matters taught elsewhere in the literal sense. This limit holds true even for Paul, who used "more substantial arguments" in other places to prove the same point. "For it is very fine, once the foundation has been properly laid and the case has been firmly established, to add some kind of allegory."[37] This is essentially the same point that Thomas Aquinas made when he said that any spiritual interpretation must be taught somewhere in the literal sense.

Luther further curtails allegorical interpretation by limiting its practice to knowledgeable exegetes. "Unless someone has a perfect knowledge of Christian doctrine, he will not be successful at presenting allegories."[38] Luther posits that he would not have handled the allegory in the way Paul did. "Not everyone has the skill to play around with allegories."[39] The sentiment that only experienced interpreters should try their hand at allegory echoes Gregory

35. Luther, *Galatians* (LW 26:440).
36. Luther, *Galatians* (LW 26:441).
37. Luther, *Galatians* (LW 26:435–36).
38. Luther, *Galatians* (LW 26:433).
39. Luther, *Galatians* (LW 26:438).

of Nyssa and others who assumed that it is not for everyone. Many Protestant Reformers felt the same about biblical interpretation in general.

Luther was simply a participant in an ongoing conversation that began long before him about the senses of Scripture. Medieval exegesis evidenced a shift toward the letter that continued into the early modern period.[40] As Nicholas of Lyra spoke of a double literal sense, the humanist Jacques Lefèvre d'Étaples (Jacobus Faber Stapulensis, ca. 1455–1536), whose exegesis influenced Luther's, folded the spiritual sense within the one literal sense, a literal sense that "coincides with the Spirit."[41] Although Lefèvre's strategy is different from Nicholas's, they both retain spiritual senses in the literal. Luther is close to this strategy, one that will become explicit among later Protestants.[42] Luther passed on to Protestants a legacy of rejecting the quadriga and deriding allegory, but at the same retaining the use of spiritual senses that go beyond the mere letter. As such, early Protestants developed various strategies for pulling off this new, sometimes precarious balance between the rejection and the retention of spiritual interpretations.

Luther's interpretation of Galatians is also a fine place to see his well-known distinction between law and gospel at work. In Paul's allegory, he "shows the distinction between the Law and the Gospel very clearly."[43] The promises of the law are conditional, leaving people in doubt of their salvation, for no one keeps the law perfectly. The promises of the new covenant, by contrast, are unconditional: "they do not demand anything of us."[44] The gospel sets free from the law.[45] For those who believe in Christ, Luther claims, the entire law has been abrogated. This abrogation includes not only the civil and ceremonial law but also and especially the moral law, which contributes nothing to salvation. The gospel teaches that grace alone and faith justify apart from the law and its works.[46]

Luther did not simply equate law with the Old Testament and gospel with the New. Grace and gospel are present in the Old Testament. But gospel— God's gift of righteousness and the doctrine of justification by grace through faith, especially as articulated by Paul in Romans and Galatians—became central. As a hermeneutical key, this doctrine would be decisive in many ways for later German Lutheran biblical scholarship, particularly scholarship on

40. See Muller, "Biblical Interpretation in the Era of the Reformation."

41. Lefèvre d'Étaples, "Introduction to Commentary on the Psalms," 297–301. See Oberman's discussion in *Forerunners of the Reformation*, 286–91.

42. On Luther's exegesis, see further Pelikan, *Luther the Expositor*; Kolb, *Martin Luther and the Enduring Word of God*.

43. Luther, *Galatians* (LW 26:444).

44. Luther, *Galatians* (LW 26:437).

45. Luther, *Galatians* (LW 26:441).

46. Luther, *Galatians* (LW 26:446–49).

the New Testament and Paul, which viewed these teachings as Paul's central dogma. For Luther, it meant that the Epistle of James, which apparently contradicts Romans 4 by teaching justification by works, should not be counted "among the chief books."[47] For nineteenth-century Lutherans, the underlying law-gospel distinction would lead to questioning the authenticity of Pauline letters that did not center on this definition of gospel.

As for the question of authority, Luther's view of Scripture's primary authority emerged clearly in the course of his debate with Johann Eck at the Leipzig Disputation of 1519. Eck got Luther to admit that the decrees of popes and councils have erred and that they should be subordinate to Scripture. The following year, Luther expressed his perspective more sharply in his address *To the Christian Nobility of the German Nation*. One of the "walls" that the Roman Church has used to protect itself from criticism and reform is the idea that "only the pope may interpret Scripture."[48] Luther set about to demolish this wall of a papal monopoly on the interpretation of Scripture. Again, both sides prioritized Scripture. The question was, Who has the exclusive authority to interpret Scripture? Luther's answer is clear: it is not the pope or even councils. Rather, baptized Christians, all of whom are priests, have a right to interpret Scripture.[49]

As it turns out, despite their different perspectives on free choice, both Erasmus and Luther express a similar view of the relationship between Scripture and tradition. They both recognize Scripture as the primary authority and source for Christian doctrine. Luther's insistence that popes and councils can err does not mean that no councils were correct or that councils should not be heard. It is consistent, moreover, with Erasmus's admission that Scripture "should outweigh all the votes of all mortal men." With these two figures, it is a question of which church fathers are to be heard and how much of that subordinate weight should be given to their collective voices.[50] Already by Luther's day, however, more extreme views were developing that either gave no weight to church tradition or, alternatively, gave equal weight to tradition and Scripture.

Perspicuity and the Authority to Interpret

In a dispute such as that between Erasmus and Luther on free choice, who has the authority to interpret Scripture and to settle the debate? This contested

47. Luther, *Preface to the Epistles of St. James and St. Jude* (LW 35:395–98).
48. Luther, *To the Christian Nobility* (LW 44:133–34).
49. Luther, *To the Christian Nobility* (LW 44:135–36).
50. On Luther's use of the tradition in exegesis, see Pelikan, *Luther the Expositor*, 71–88.

question, exemplified in the exchange between Erasmus and Luther, had been brewing since the late medieval period and would haunt the sixteenth century, whose controversies brought to light "the problem of the criterion of truth."[51] The schisms that resulted from the sixteenth-century Reformations are, in large part, the working out of different answers to this question regarding authority. The authority of Scripture per se, affirmed by all sides, was not the question: what was at stake was the authority to interpret it. "All sides of the many debates that persisted throughout the Middle Ages were in search of an authoritative determination of the biblical text."[52] Who gets to interpret Scripture? Is church tradition authoritative? Which traditions? The late medieval church, which tended to add to the confusion, simply did not have—or at least did not effectively employ—the resources to deal with the kinds of fundamental questions raised by Protestant Reformers. But answers were certainly given, and it is important to notice the range of opinions when it comes to the role of church tradition in the interpretation of Scripture.

In order to understand this debate regarding authoritative interpretation, we must back up a bit. The relationship between Scripture and church tradition was raised earlier, in the discussion about Irenaeus and the gnostics (chapter 2). The oral tradition, passed down from the apostles, functioned as an authoritative key for biblical interpretation. Indeed, the oral tradition and the written tradition coincided in the church as two sides of the same coin: they informed one another and were not to be separated, and each was legitimized by its claim to apostolicity. After the time of Irenaeus, however, the oral tradition, no longer linked to anyone's living memory of the apostles, continued to expand. As the centuries advanced, the oral tradition was no longer equated with the apostolic rule of faith and liturgy known to Irenaeus and his contemporaries in the Great Church. Eventually the tradition of the church came to include whatever the teaching magisterium of the church decided, whether or not a basis could be found in Scripture. As a result, there came to be a sharper separation between the ever-developing tradition of the church and its stable biblical text. In light of this separation, sides were chosen: some subordinated the church's teaching to Scripture and criticized that teaching in light of Scripture, whereas others came to emphasize the supreme authority of the church's teaching office, and of the pope as its representative, to interpret Scripture.[53]

51. Popkin, *History of Scepticism*, 1–17.
52. Levy, *Holy Scripture and the Quest*, xi.
53. E.g., see the options discussed ca. 1375 in John Brevicoxa, *De fide et ecclesia*, trans. in Oberman, *Forerunners of the Reformation*, 67–92.

Accordingly, the question of the role of unwritten tradition in authoritative interpretation (already addressed by Irenaeus) became more pressing in the Western church, with its developed hierarchy and with the increasing power of the pope to interpret and legislate (never envisioned by Irenaeus), a papal power that was contested by various theologians and especially by the Council of Constance (1414–18).[54] With regard to this relationship between Scripture and church tradition, a debate that preceded the Reformation, Heiko Oberman distinguished between what he called Tradition I and Tradition II.[55]

With Tradition I, Scripture and church teaching are both normative—that is, they still coinhere—but Scripture maintains priority above extrabiblical church tradition. Oberman associates Tradition I with the early church, and it remained a genuine catholic and medieval option, as exemplified by Thomas Aquinas: "Nevertheless, sacred doctrine makes use of these [philosophical] authorities as extrinsic and probable arguments; but properly uses the authority of the canonical Scriptures as an incontrovertible proof, and the authority of the doctors of the Church as one that may properly be used, yet merely as probable. For our faith rests upon the revelation made to the apostles and prophets who wrote the canonical books, and not on the revelations (if any such there are) made to other doctors."[56] Thomas then proceeds to quote Augustine to the same effect. Thomas's opinion that Scripture is primary was echoed in the late medieval period by Thomas Bradwardine, John Wyclif, Jan Hus, and later Reformers, as well as by Thomas Aquinas's most able sixteenth-century interpreter, Cardinal Cajetan (Thomas de Vio).

In contrast, Tradition II sees Scripture and extrabiblical church teaching as coequal norms in Christian doctrine. Among those who held this opinion are the late medieval theologians William of Ockham, Pierre d'Ailly, Jean Gerson, and Gabriel Biel, as well as the Ingolstadt theologian and opponent of Luther, Johann Eck. This two-source view was codified at the Council of Trent (1545–63) and therefore became *the* Roman Catholic view: "The council clearly perceives that this truth [of salvation] and rule [of conduct] are contained in written books and in unwritten traditions which were received by the apostles from the mouth of Christ himself, or else have come down to us, handed on as it were from the apostles themselves at the inspiration

---

54. For helpful background to the council and the late medieval problem of Scripture's authority and its interpretation, see Levy, *Holy Scripture and the Quest*.

55. Oberman, *Harvest of Medieval Theology*, 365–412; Oberman, *Forerunners of the Reformation*, 53–120; Oberman, *Dawn of the Reformation*, 280–89.

56. *ST* Ia.i.8 ad 2.

of the holy Spirit."[57] This statement implies that not all doctrinal truth may be found or anticipated in Scripture.[58] Such influence of the church, past and present, is what is meant by unwritten traditions.

As this passage from Trent also implies, the question of where authority for interpretation resides relates to whether Scripture is sufficient in itself and whether it is perspicuous. The doctrine of sufficiency asserts that Scripture reveals what is necessary for salvation without need of any supplement. Scripture's sufficiency, however, is contingent upon its perspicuity or clarity. The doctrine of perspicuity states that Scripture is clear about all that one must believe and do for salvation. Most advocates of perspicuity immediately grant that many passages of Scripture are obscure. The occasional obscurity, though, indicates that those same passages do not concern matters of first importance, or, if they do, then they are handled more clearly elsewhere. That which is necessary is clear somewhere in Scripture. The Westminster Confession of Faith (1647) well summarizes over a century of Protestant argumentation: "All things in Scripture are not alike plain (*perspicua*) in themselves, nor alike clear unto all; yet those things which are necessary to be known, believed, and observed for salvation are so clearly (*perspicue*) propounded and opened in some place of Scripture or other, that not only the learned, but [also] the unlearned, in a due use of ordinary means, may attain unto a sufficient understanding of them."[59]

The questions of sufficiency and perspicuity are eminently relevant to the matter of authority and the use of church tradition in biblical interpretation. On the one hand, if Scripture is sufficient and perspicuous on its own, then there is little or no need for an accompanying oral tradition maintained by the church's teaching magisterium. If, on the other hand, Scripture is insufficient and obscure, then the oral tradition and teaching magisterium are essential for supplementing and clarifying Scripture. Gerald Bray has summarized the hermeneutical debate in the early modern period: "The key issue which distinguished Protestants from Catholics was whether Scripture was

57. Council of Trent, Session 4, Decree 1 (April 8, 1546), in Tanner, *Decrees of the Ecumenical Councils*, 2:663.

58. Before it was changed, the original wording of this decree stated that the truth is contained "*partly* in written books, *partly* in unwritten traditions" (emphasis added), thus underscoring the insufficiency of Scripture. It is not clear why the Tridentine theologians modified the statement from its original wording, but it is enough to notice that the final wording does not exclude the meaning of the original wording—namely, that Scripture is insufficient without unwritten tradition. See Pelikan, *Reformation of Church and Dogma*, 277.

59. The Westminster Confession of Faith 1.7, in Schaff, *Creeds of Christendom*, 3:604. For more on perspicuity in Reformed theology, see Muller, *Post-Reformation Reformed Dogmatics*, 2:322–40.

self-interpreting, or whether it required the teaching authority of the church to make it plain."[60] The reformer Philip Melanchthon seems to agree. Addressing the Paris theologians who condemned Luther in 1521, he writes, "This is, as I see it, the sum of the controversy. And here I ask you, my masters, has Scripture come forth in such a manner that its certain meaning can be established without the interpretation of the councils, the fathers, and of the schools, or not?"[61]

Those who emphasized biblical obscurity the most also tended to stress the role of external biblical interpretation and the need to supplement Scripture with church tradition. Specifically, the Roman Church's insistence on the need for the teaching magisterium (ultimately vested in the papacy) to step in and interpret Scripture was a corollary to its claim of biblical obscurity. Thus again the Council of Trent declared: "No one . . . shall dare to interpret the sacred scriptures either by twisting its text to his individual meaning in opposition to that which has been and is held by holy mother church, whose function is to pass judgment on the true meaning and interpretation of the sacred scriptures."[62] According to the most formidable defender of Tridentine Catholicism against the Protestants, the Jesuit Robert Cardinal Bellarmine (1542–1621), the Protestant opinion that the sense of Scripture is clear (*clarissimus*) is "manifestly false, for Scripture itself presents testimony concerning its own difficulty and obscurity." Rather, the church, represented by the Spirit-filled council of bishops and the pope, must interpret Scripture and make its meaning plain. Without the accompanying oral traditions, Bellarmine contends, Scripture is not a sufficient rule.[63]

By contrast, those who emphasized biblical perspicuity the most also tended to insist that Scripture is sufficient and that there is no need for the church's tradition or teaching magisterium to come alongside and clarify Scripture or supplement its content. The Bible is already clear because it is self-interpreting. In its extreme formulation, perspicuity implies that no church tradition should have a voice in biblical interpretation. In practice, this meant that individual readers now had the authority to interpret.

If Erasmus was concerned about Reformers coming along and reading Scripture without any regard for the preceding tradition, then his concern applies less to Luther than it does to the so-called Radical Reformers. The

60. Bray, *Biblical Interpretation*, 192.

61. Melanchthon, *Luther and the Paris Theologians*, 73.

62. Council of Trent, Session 4, Decree 2 (April 8, 1546), in Tanner, *Decrees of the Ecumenical Councils*, 2:664.

63. Bellarmine, *Disputationes de controversiis Christianae fidei* 3.1, 3; 4.4, in *Opera omnia*, 1:96, 102, 119.

Radicals saw postapostolic ecclesiastical tradition as bankrupt, since they traced the institutional church's apostasy back to its early days, when it was "destroyed and ruined . . . by Antichrist."[64] Practices that have no explicit sanction in the New Testament, such as infant baptism, were prohibited. For many Anabaptists, anything that was not expressly commanded or exemplified in the New Testament was proscribed, without any conscious consideration of church tradition.[65]

With regard to the authoritative interpretation of Scripture, all Protestants were united in their rejection of the pope's supreme exegetical authority and in their affirmation that Scripture is the primary rule of faith and practice. Since the early twentieth century, this view has been summed up with the motto "Scripture alone" (*sola scriptura*). This slogan, however, is simplistic and can be misleading.[66] *Sola scriptura* was not cited as a slogan by the Reformers, and it leaves the impression that there is no room for church tradition, as Jean Gerson used the phrase when he opposed it.[67] Few Reformers, however, felt that there was no voice whatsoever for the historic church. For this reason, Luther rarely used the phrase *sola scriptura*, and he opposed the idea that no commentary on Scripture is needed.[68] In general, the Reformers were especially keen to listen to the church fathers, assuming the general principle that the earlier the testimony, the more reliable, for the stream is purest at its source (*ad fontes*). For these figures, *sola scriptura* would have meant that "Scripture alone" is the primary, not necessarily the sole, authority. In light of the phrase's ambiguity, rather than *sola scriptura*, a slightly more accurate term might be *prima scriptura* (Scripture first), inasmuch as Scripture was regarded as the primary, but not the only, voice in theology. Within these bounds lay a broad range of opinion on how much sway church tradition should hold, but there was general agreement that it was an important lens for reading Scripture. Thomas fits here, as does Luther, who held a "critical reverence" for the early Christian writings.[69]

Then there were the Radical Reformers, who eschewed church tradition, typically regarded it as a source of error in theology, and cited it almost always

64. Philips, *Confession*, 207.

65. For example, congregational singing. See Grebel, *Letters to Thomas Müntzer*, 75, 79. This is an early articulation of what would later be known as the Reformed Regulative Principle.

66. Van den Belt, "*Sola Scriptura*: An Inadequate Slogan," traces the origin of the slogan and offers several arguments against its continued use.

67. See the discussion in Oberman, *Forerunners of the Reformation*, 289.

68. See the discussion of Luther's opposition to *sola scriptura* in Wengert, *Reading the Bible with Martin Luther*, 16–21.

69. This is how Jaroslav Pelikan describes the attitude of Luther and his colleagues toward the patristic tradition. See Pelikan, *Development of Christian Doctrine*, 55.

as an example of how not to interpret Scripture. For those who grant no say at all to the historic Christian tradition, a more fitting characterization of their position might be *nuda scriptura* (bare Scripture), signifying that the Bible is the only relevant voice.[70] This "Bible only" position is itself a radicalization of Tradition I—that is, a radical rejection of tradition—and a reaction to medieval theologians who filled the biblical silence with their own teachings under the category of tradition.[71]

Between the two extremes of Tridentine Catholicism and Radical Reform fell most of mainstream Protestantism, which, against the former, stressed perspicuity as a way to counter the Roman Catholic attempt to regulate biblical interpretation but, against the latter, also saw the benefit of church tradition as a lens for biblical interpretation. At any rate, as it related to religious authority, the issue of biblical perspicuity was central, with Protestants advocating perspicuity of the text to the individual reader and Roman Catholics upholding the necessary role of the ecclesiastical magisterium in interpreting a more or less obscure text.[72]

Figure 5.1

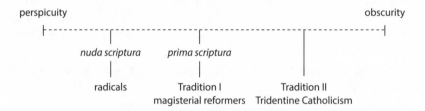

As noted above, we can observe that Erasmus upheld the voice of the church fathers in the interpretation of difficult matters. If there is a controversy about the interpretation of Scripture, and the authority of the early church fathers is invoked, some Reformers would reject those ancient writers on the ground that they are only humans. Yet, as Erasmus points out, these same Reformers, humans as well, then proceed to offer their own interpretations. What's

70. B. Gregory, *Unintended Reformation*, 95, collapses all Protestants into this view of *nuda scriptura*, denying any difference between, say, Luther and the Radicals on their use of tradition. But despite what Luther and other magisterial Reformers at times said, and despite the fact that they did subordinate tradition to Scripture (as did Thomas Aquinas, Erasmus, and others), their use of tradition is clearly more positive than that of the Radicals.

71. As Oberman speculates in *Forerunners of the Reformation*, 60.

72. For more detailed treatment of these and related issues, see S. Schreiner, *Are You Alone Wise?*, 79–207.

more, some of them claim the Holy Spirit as the source of their interpretations. Erasmus admits that this description may not apply to Luther or to all Reformers.[73] In fact, the difference between Erasmus and Luther seems to be a disagreement that falls within the scope of *prima scriptura*, or Tradition I, within which there could be a spectrum of positions. The "Bible only" view that he describes is more typical of the Radical Reformers, specifically the "spiritualists." His concern, however, is legitimate. "What am I to do," asks Erasmus, "when many bring diverse interpretations?"[74] It is necessary that some human interpret. It might as well be church fathers as anyone else. He seems afraid that Protestants have opened Pandora's box and that, in rejecting the interpretation of one pope, they have simply introduced the interpretations of many "popes," with no criteria for discrimination. His fear would eventually prove legitimate.

John Calvin

Of all the Protestant Reformers, John Calvin (1509–64) is the one most often cited as the forerunner of modern exegesis. For this reason, Calvin, who wrote commentaries on nearly every book of the Bible, is the one sixteenth-century figure who is most likely to be consulted and quoted in a modern historical-critical commentary. There is some good reason for this reputation, yet it does not tell the whole story.

Calvin was a trained lawyer as well as an accomplished writer and commentator. His first book, published in 1532, was a commentary on the Stoic philosopher Seneca's treatise *On Clemency* (*De clementia*), and it established his credentials as a humanist scholar. The same philological skills that he used to exegete the classics would serve him well in his biblical interpretation. In the preface to his first biblical commentary in 1540, on the Letter to the Romans, Calvin discusses the method that he would pursue in this commentary and all others to follow. Some of these principles are worth examining.[75]

First, Calvin tells readers that he intends to write with "clear brevity." He contrasts his method with those of the Lutheran reformer Philip Melanchthon and of his own Strasbourg colleague Martin Bucer. On the one hand,

73. Erasmus, *De libero arbitrio*, 45.
74. Erasmus, *De libero arbitrio*, 46.
75. In fact, as with most of the sketches in this book, there is too much to examine in this survey, and the literature on Calvin's exegetical method is extensive. For a fine study of Calvin's exegetical principles, see Holder, *John Calvin and the Grounding of Interpretation*. For other surveys, see Steinmetz, "John Calvin as an Interpreter of the Bible," and Muller, "Hermeneutic of Promise and Fulfillment."

Melanchthon's commentaries treated the main points but frequently omitted discussion of important difficulties in the biblical text. On the other hand, Bucer's commentaries were exhaustive and thus exhausting, too large and wordy for a common person to use. Calvin was aiming for the right balance between these two styles.[76] Included in "brevity" is Calvin's decision to leave out many doctrinal topics that might arise as one engages with the biblical text. At the time, many commentators still mixed theological and dogmatic issues with the exegetical. Recall how, especially in the scholastic environment of study in the late medieval universities, a harder distinction began to form between biblical and doctrinal studies. For Calvin, although there is no separation between the two, there is nevertheless a distinction that enables him to focus on the concerns most proximate to the text. Therefore, alongside his commentaries, Calvin did provide a theological handbook, the *Institutes of the Christian Religion*, which went through several editions between 1536 and 1559. In the *Institutes*, he generally avoids prolonged exegesis. Instead, amid the doctrinal discussion Calvin provides biblical citations to point readers both to Scripture and to the extended interpretation in his commentaries. Calvin's ideal reader, not to mention the ideal scholar of Calvin today, should read the *Institutes* with constant reference to the commentaries.

Second, Calvin states that it is almost the sole task of the interpreter to "lay open the mind of the writer" (*mens scriptoris*), which is to say, to discover authorial intent.[77] Elsewhere he states, "It is not the business of a good and judicious commentator to seize eagerly on syllables, but to attend to the design (*consilium*) of the speaker."[78] By attending to the *mens scriptoris*, Calvin is not making an earth-shattering suggestion. The mind, or meaning, of the original author had always been a concern of the responsible exegete. For Calvin, though, especially on this side of the Renaissance, with its emphasis on returning *ad fontes*, discerning the "mind of the writer" required a respect for that writer's situation that had not always been valued. The prominence he gives to explaining the mind of the writer—that it is "almost his only [*unicum*] task"—demanded philological examination and investigation of historical contexts.

Calvin's respect for historical contexts can be illustrated from his commentaries. In the first place, many passages that had been traditionally taken as straight-line prophecies of Christ were interpreted by Calvin without a direct christological fulfillment. Take, for instance, Genesis 3:15, a passage

76. Calvin, "Epistle Dedicatory to Simon Grynaeus," xxiii–xxvi; *Calvini opera*, 10/2:402–6.
77. Calvin, "Epistle Dedicatory to Simon Grynaeus," xxiii; *Calvini opera*, 10/2:403.
78. Calvin, *Harmony of the Evangelists*, 1:299, on Matt. 5:39; *Calvini opera*, 45:184.

referred to as the protoevangelium because it is commonly interpreted as the first announcement of the gospel: "I will put enmity between you [the serpent] and the woman, and between your seed and hers; he will crush your head, and you will strike his heel" (NIV). About this verse, Calvin writes, "I interpret this simply to mean that there should always be the hostile strife between the human race and serpents, which is now apparent; for, by a secret feeling of nature, man abhors them. . . . For he declares that there shall be such hatred that, on both sides, they shall be troublesome to each other; the serpent shall be vexatious towards men, and men shall be intent on the destruction of serpents."[79]

It is only several paragraphs later that Calvin mentions Christ, and when he does, it is to say that Christ is not in view here:

> There is, indeed, no ambiguity in the *words* here used by Moses; but I do not agree with others respecting their *meaning*; for other interpreters take the seed for *Christ*, without controversy; as if it were said, that some one would arise from the seed of the woman who should wound the serpent's head. Gladly would I give my suffrage in support of their opinion, but that I regard the word *seed* as too violently distorted by them; for who will concede that a *collective* noun is to be understood of one man *only*?[80]

Calvin goes on to say that it is indeed collective humanity, presumably the church, who will conquer the serpent, which he does associate more directly with Satan, and that it is certainly by Christ that humanity conquers Satan. But Calvin explicitly denies the association between the woman's seed and Christ; the reference is to humanity in general.[81]

Note that Calvin, like a good humanist, appeals to grammar, a philological reason, for dismissing Christ as the referent of seed.[82] It is not that he thinks predictive prophecy is impossible, as later modern commentators will come to assume. He does not even rule out actual, direct prophecies of Christ in the Old Testament. He is willing, however, to go where the grammar and history lead. Like some of his Antiochene predecessors, he thus exhibits a certain reluctance to find as many types and prophecies of Christ as some

79. Calvin, *Genesis*, 167–68, on Gen. 3:15.

80. Calvin, *Genesis*, 170, on Gen. 3:15.

81. Calvin was not unique among early Reformers in his interpretation of Gen. 3:15. Before Calvin, Johannes Oecolampadius denied that "seed" here is primarily a reference to Christ, though he seems more willing than Calvin to grant the christological application. Oecolampadius, *Exposition of Genesis*, 184–85.

82. This reason seems to undermine Paul's discussion of "seed" and "seeds" in Gal. 3:16. Cf. Calvin's discussion in *Galatians and Ephesians*, 94–96, on Gal. 3:16.

of his contemporaries found. Rather, he attempts to make sense of the Old Testament first in its historical context, a context that, of course, does not refer explicitly to Jesus. For this reason, some of Calvin's opponents accused him of a "Judaizing" interpretation.[83]

Another example of Calvin's attention to the *mens scriptoris* (meaning of the writer) comes in his commentary on the book of Psalms. There was a general recognition in the commentary tradition, going back at least to the fourth century, that several psalms refer neither to David's time nor to the time of the Babylonian exile, but instead to the struggles and persecution of the Jewish people leading up to and following the Maccabean revolt in the second century BC. The fact that this was standard fare in the patristic, medieval, and Reformed tradition confirms that such questions about the context and occasion of biblical documents were not invented by Calvin or the Reformation. Calvin assigned seven psalms to the Maccabean situation (44, 74, 79, 85, 106, 123, and 129), half as many as the Antiochene Theodore of Mopsuestia applied to that occasion. Thus Calvin, like his predecessors, agreed that certain psalms were written about the Maccabean period.

Interestingly, where Calvin differs from the exegetical tradition is on the question of who actually authored these Maccabean psalms. Previously there had been a consensus that these same psalms were penned by either David or some contemporary of his, a writer, at any rate, who spoke in the person of someone who is absent, a common and ancient rhetorical technique known as prosopopoeia. That is, these particular psalms speak, from centuries earlier, with the perspective of a second-century BC Jew. In contrast to this consensus of commentators, however, Calvin believed that these psalms were actually composed during the Maccabean period. Again, it is not that Calvin thought it was impossible for an inspired writer to speak prophetically in the person of someone else. But he repeatedly claimed that these psalms speak straightforwardly and "historically" (*historice*). It is a testimony to Calvin's historical sensitivity in interpretation that, absent any textual or theological reason for seeing it otherwise, he viewed these psalms as coming from the very people who lived through the hardships that they describe.[84]

Furthermore, Calvin's emphasis on the *mens scriptoris* (intention of the writer) leads him to stress the literal sense of the text and to denigrate "allegory." He rejects Origen's interpretation of 2 Corinthians 3:6—namely, that the letter that kills is the literal sense and the Spirit that gives life is the spiritual,

---

83. See Pak, *Judaizing Calvin*.
84. On Calvin's interpretation of the Maccabean psalms, including the history of exegesis on this topic, see Stanglin, "Adopted in Christ."

allegorical sense. To Calvin's mind, this influential interpretation by Origen led to the unhealthy domination of allegorization in biblical interpretation.[85]

As with Luther and others, Calvin's thoughts on allegory are revealed also in his commentary on Galatians 4. Consistent with Thomas Aquinas and Luther, Calvin observes that Paul's argument would not be convincing on its own, but it functions well as a confirmation of other sound arguments.[86] Where Paul mentions allegory in Galatians 4, Calvin takes the opportunity to blame Origen for "torturing Scripture, in every possible manner, away from the true sense" and for inspiring generations of interpreters to bury the "pure meaning of Scripture" under false interpretations. The "true meaning of Scripture," Calvin asserts, "is the natural and obvious meaning." Paul's allegorical interpretation was justified, according to Calvin, because it was consistent with the literal sense, which he accuses Origen of despising.[87] Again like Luther, Calvin takes the "Jerusalem above" to be a reference to the earthly church, not to heaven.[88]

Calvin's stress on the *mens scriptoris* is further reflected in his comments on the parable of the good Samaritan, especially when they are contrasted with the interpretations of Origen, Augustine, and other predecessors. As he concludes his comments on the parable, Calvin writes, "The allegory which is here contrived by the advocates of free will is too absurd to deserve refutation. According to them, under the figure of a wounded man is described the condition of Adam after the fall, from which they infer that the power of acting well was not wholly extinguished in him, because he is said to be only *half-dead*."[89] Thus Calvin rejects the popular allegory claiming that, since Jesus describes the beaten and robbed man as "half-dead," he must also have been half-alive. And this half-alive man, who signifies fallen humanity in need of rescue, must then be capable of some action or at least of the willingness to be rescued. Such a reading, popular among some interpreters, was rejected by Calvin and other Augustinians on the doctrinal grounds that it is Pelagianizing.[90] This medieval interpretation, along with its application, was possible only because of the patristic reading that interprets the Samaritan as Christ. But Calvin would have none of it, as he continues:

85. Calvin, *Corinthians*, 174–75, on 2 Cor. 3:6. Calvin's view is predominant among modern commentators.
86. Calvin, *Galatians and Ephesians*, 134, on Gal. 4:21.
87. Calvin, *Galatians and Ephesians*, 135–36, on Gal. 4:22.
88. Calvin, *Galatians and Ephesians*, 140–41, on Gal. 4:26.
89. Calvin, *Harmony of the Evangelists*, 3:62, on Luke 10:30.
90. See Calvin, *Inst.* 2.5.19.

As little plausibility belongs to another allegory, which, however, has been so highly satisfactory, that it has been admitted by almost universal consent, as if it had been a revelation from heaven. This *Samaritan* they imagine to be Christ, because he is our guardian; and they tell us that *wine was poured*, along with *oil*, into the wound, because Christ cures us by repentance and by a promise of grace. They have contrived a third subtlety, that Christ does not immediately restore health, but sends us to the Church, as *an innkeeper*, to be gradually cured. I acknowledge that I have no liking for any of these interpretations; but we ought to have a deeper reverence for Scripture than to reckon ourselves at liberty to disguise its natural meaning [*germanum eius sensum*]. And, indeed, any one may see that the curiosity of certain men has led them to contrive these speculations, contrary to the intention of Christ [*Christi mentem*].[91]

As he has focused on the mind of the writer, so in this case Calvin appeals to the "mind of Christ"—that is, the intention of the original speaker—to rule out an allegory that he sees as inconsistent with the "genuine sense" of Scripture. The focus on authorial intention is a reaction to what are viewed as allegorical interpretations that are not based on the literal sense. At least in this case, if the allegory is not intended by the author, then it is illegitimate. For this reason, Calvin was hesitant to interpret any biblical story allegorically that was not already interpreted as such in Scripture. Speaking of this parable, he said, "Allegories ought to be carried no farther than Scripture expressly regulates, so far are they from forming a sufficient basis on which to found dogmas."[92]

Based again on Calvin's preface to his Romans commentary, a third point is clear: biblical exegesis should be undertaken for the "good of the church."[93] This stated goal places Calvin squarely in the long tradition of biblical interpretation that precedes him. As David Steinmetz put it, "Calvin's interests extended to questions of authorship, historical background, philology, and rhetoric. Yet he never allowed such questions to dominate his exegesis, which had as its constant goal the edification of the church."[94] As much as Calvin is an heir of Renaissance humanism, and as much as his historical sensibility impels him to stress authorial intention, it does not cause him to view Scripture as simply a historical artifact written to ancient people. Indeed, Scripture is written to the ancient church, but it is also intended for the church in sixteenth-century Geneva, intended for God's people of all time, intended

91. Calvin, *Harmony of the Evangelists*, 3:62–63, on Luke 10:30; *Calvini opera*, 45:614.
92. Calvin, *Inst.* 2.5.19.
93. Calvin, "Epistle Dedicatory to Simon Grynaeus," xxiv–xxvi; *Calvini opera*, 10/2:403–4.
94. Steinmetz, "John Calvin as an Interpreter of the Bible," 288.

for us and for our benefit. In this sense, God intends Scripture to be employed for a purpose beyond the purposes envisioned by its human authors.

The implications of reading Scripture in this way are evident throughout Calvin's commentaries. They can be illustrated in any of his commentaries, but perhaps there is no better place to see his principles at work than in the commentary on Psalms. Psalm 2, a traditionally messianic psalm, provides a good test case. He assumes David to be the author: given this assumption, he is careful to give proper attention to the psalm's original context. Although the psalm is quoted multiple times in the New Testament, Calvin does not immediately jump to an exposition of its first-century application. The nations that rage against the "anointed one" (Messiah/Christ) are the many enemies who opposed David, God's anointed.[95] When the text declares, "You are my son; this day I have begotten you" (2:7), most commentators traditionally took the "son" to be Jesus Christ, following Hebrews 1:5, and "this day" to be the eternal day in which God the Son was eternally begotten. In contrast, Calvin attends first to the historical context. The son is a reference to David, who, because he is the anointed king, may be called the son of God. Calvin then specifically rejects the reference to the eternal day. Instead, the day of begetting is a figure of speech indicating when God made David's kingship manifest.[96] Once again, one can see why some of Calvin's critics accused him of a "Judaizing" interpretation.

While Calvin always has before him the historical context of Psalm 2, he also looks to the christological meaning. In general, he regards David as a type of Christ par excellence. Thus these and other elements in Psalm 2 apply to David and his kingdom, but they also apply to Christ and his kingdom prophetically, not, Calvin insists, allegorically.[97] For Calvin, Christ is the scope of Scripture. Commenting on Romans 10:4, Calvin writes: "The law had been given for this end, to lead us as by the hand to another righteousness: nay, whatever the law teaches, whatever it commands, whatever it promises, has always a reference to Christ as its main object; and hence all its parts ought to be applied to him. . . . We have then here a remarkable passage, which proves that the law in all its parts had a reference to Christ; and hence no one can rightly understand it, who does not continually level at this mark."[98] In this way, even if Calvin stressed the original historical context of the Old Testament, he also was open to seeing Christ in the Old Testament either directly or indirectly.

95. Calvin, *Psalms*, 9–13, on Ps. 2:1–3.
96. Calvin, *Psalms*, 17–18, on Ps. 2:7.
97. Calvin, *Psalms*, 11–12, on Ps. 2:1–2.
98. Calvin, *Romans*, 384–85, on Rom. 10:4.

Exegesis for "the good of the church" also looks to the present. Throughout his interpretation of Psalm 2, immediate application is a recurring theme as Calvin exhorts readers to think and act in light of the psalm's message. The psalm is nothing if it is not a word for the church. As Calvin makes clear in his preface to the Psalms commentary, the Psalter is "an anatomy of all the parts of the soul," for the whole range of human emotions is represented in it, "as in a mirror."[99] The reader is invited, as it were, to share in the range of emotions with the psalmist. So David, the chief psalmist, becomes an example of imitation and a point of comparison for Calvin, similar to the way Gregory I identified with Job because of his illness.[100] In this way, the reading of the Psalter and of Scripture in general can be a deeply personal experience. Similarly, the faithful community of Israel is a model for the Christian church. Calvin's desire to identify with the circumstances of the psalmists may be why he gives such attention to the original authors and their historical context, as he does when identifying some authors as second-century BC figures.

Because of Calvin's attention to human authorial intent and historical context, it may be tempting to view Calvin as an early proponent of historical-critical exegesis. Calvin's exegetical practice may reflect the long transition between medieval and modern critical exegesis, but in nearly every respect, he is closer to medieval than to modern critical exegesis, and he should be interpreted in the former context. All of Calvin's guiding hermeneutical principles, including the stress on authorial intent, are, as we have seen, typical of patristic and medieval biblical interpretation.[101] If there is anything new or any significant difference in Calvin, it is one of degree, to be found in his generally increased emphasis, as a good humanist, on philological and historical concerns within the biblical text. Overall, his aims in biblical interpretation are consistent with the aims of most of his premodern predecessors.

Post-Reformation Orthodoxies

Throughout the course of the sixteenth and seventeenth centuries, a wide range of exegetical works continued to appear, from popular-level sermons to the most technical, philological commentaries. Doctrinal and moral instruction

---

99. Calvin, "Piis et ingenuis lectoribus salutem," *Calvini opera*, 31:15; Calvin, *Psalms*, xxxvii, "To the Godly and Ingenious Readers."

100. Gregory I, "Letter to Leander" 5, trans. Kerns, 54.

101. After citing H.-J. Kraus's elaboration of eight exegetical principles of Calvin, Richard Muller observes that "not a single principle noted here separates Calvin definitively from the medieval exegete"; cf. Kraus, "Calvin's Exegetical Principles," with Muller, "Hermeneutic of Promise and Fulfillment," 69.

continued to be linked closely with exegesis of Scripture, which still appealed to traditional lines of interpretation. But in the wake of new and hardening denominational lines, exegesis was put in service of a rising number of competing confessions of faith. By the end of the sixteenth century, the Western Latin church was divided along the clear confessional lines of Roman Catholic, Lutheran, Reformed, and Anglican, alongside a variety of Radicals. As examples, we may look briefly at select Roman Catholic, Lutheran, and Reformed figures.

After the Council of Trent, as may be expected, Roman Catholic interpreters continued to uphold both the equal authority of received church tradition with that of Scripture as well as the full legitimacy of the spiritual sense. At the same time, like nearly everyone in the wake of the Renaissance, their best exegetes were fully engaged in the careful examination of the literal sense. The Jesuit Cornelius à Lapide (1567–1637), professor of exegesis at Leuven, is the most popular and enduring Roman Catholic commentator from the early modern period and a good example of an exegete who pursued the literal and spiritual senses rigorously. Throughout his vast commentaries on Scripture, he cites classical sources, Arabic and Syriac translations of Scripture, and church fathers. On the parable of the good Samaritan in particular, not only does he give attention to philological matters and the literal sense, but he also suggests that the parable is "founded on incidents of at that time frequent occurrence, and is therefore a true history," citing Jerome for support. Yet, throughout the discussion of the parable, Lapide also provides allegorical interpretations from John Chrysostom, Ambrose, Augustine, Gregory the Great, and others. The Samaritan is Christ, as Augustine said, but we must also "imitate the Samaritan."[102] Lapide's work is a prime example of technical commentary that attends to literal and spiritual senses, is intended for the scholar as well as for the church, and is in line with Tridentine Catholicism.

Among the Lutherans, the controversialist Matthias Flacius Illyricus (1520–75) composed a well-known manual of biblical interpretation titled *Key to Sacred Scripture* (*Clavis scripturae sacrae*, 1567). As one would expect from an admirer of Luther, Flacius emphasizes the importance of the literal sense and many basic principles for examining it, including the law-gospel distinction.[103] His work is also characterized by a number of points that show just how traditional his approach was. First of all, Flacius stresses the importance of the interpreter's own skill and experience, especially with regard to difficult Scriptures. "I confess that the Scriptures present several difficulties, and that,

102. Lapide, *Great Commentary*, 257–62.
103. Flacius Illyricus, *Sacred Scriptures*, 74–75, on the law-gospel distinction.

no matter how many remedies I prescribe, they will still in no way be well-suited for the unschooled. For this reason, the inexperienced reader deserves to keep a distance from the reading of Sacred Scripture."[104] The hearer of any teaching—or, in this case, of Scripture—must be "in the proper condition."[105] The student of theology and of Scripture must be spiritually well rounded, having a sense of contrition for sin and of justification, the testimony of the Spirit, a knowledge of temptations, wrestling with Satan, frequent prayer, and obedience to God. The corruption of morals impedes understanding.[106]

Flacius employs the *analogia scripturae*, the comparison of similar portions of Scripture to shed light on obscure passages.[107] He also recommends the use of the *analogia fidei*, a brief catechetical instruction that comes from Scripture. Every interpretation of Scripture should be in harmony with this basic summary of doctrine.[108] Against the Roman Catholic view of tradition, Flacius denies that church fathers and predecessors have authority, and he warns against paying excessive attention to what they say.[109] He does emphasize that Scripture should be interpreted like any other book; that is, the interpreter should understand the author's argument and the book's scope.[110] At the same time, however, Scripture is not like any other book, for the scope and argument of all Scripture is Christ.[111] These and similar principles—including Christ as the scope of all Scripture, the priority of the Holy Spirit in guiding interpretation, and viewing New Testament allegories and typologies as application but not interpretation of Old Testament Scripture—continued to be features of Lutheran orthodoxy after the Formula of Concord (1580).[112]

Two Reformed theologians may be taken as examples that reflect the ongoing application of the exegetical principles inherited from their medieval and Reformation predecessors. Neither of these figures is unique, but they were both important in their time, and they typify the mainstream post-Reformation thought that would influence later generations of orthodox and evangelical Protestantism.

William Perkins (1558–1602), the most popular English Reformed theologian and preacher at the turn of the seventeenth century, well represents

104. Flacius Illyricus, *Sacred Scriptures*, 65–66.
105. Flacius Illyricus, *Sacred Scriptures*, 89.
106. Flacius Illyricus, *Sacred Scriptures*, 91–92.
107. Flacius Illyricus, *Sacred Scriptures*, 64–65, 87, 102–3.
108. Flacius Illyricus, *Sacred Scriptures*, 77, 79.
109. Flacius Illyricus, *Sacred Scriptures*, 84–85.
110. Flacius Illyricus, *Sacred Scriptures*, 73.
111. Flacius Illyricus, *Sacred Scriptures*, 69.
112. For an overview of Lutheran orthodox interpretation of Scripture, see R. Preus, *Theology of Post-Reformation Lutheranism*, 315–39.

the general interpretive presuppositions of "Reformed orthodoxy" into the eighteenth century. Among the Reformed who were later called Puritans, he was a major biblical interpreter whose influence was substantial as well as international.[113] Throughout his commentaries and treatises, the methods of scholasticism, common in the post-Reformation period, are evident in Perkins's use of syllogisms and distinctions.[114] Particularly with the Protestant focus on Scripture as the primary rule of faith and practice, such logic was indispensable for determining the legitimacy of certain practices in worship.[115] According to Perkins, necessary deductions from Scripture are just as binding as Scripture's explicit commands and approved examples.[116] Although commentaries from this era were frequently technical and focused on issues of textual criticism and original languages, Perkins's commentaries were not primarily philological, so he did not appeal to the languages as closely as Calvin or some of his nearer contemporaries did. Instead, Perkins's concerns were overtly homiletical and theological.

Perkins also epitomizes the standard Protestant handling of the spiritual senses. In his discussion of "allegory" from Galatians 4, he attributes to the "Papists" the ancient acknowledgment of the "double sense of Scripture, one *literal*, the other *spiritual*." He then describes the threefold distinction within the spiritual sense, offering the word "Jerusalem" as an example of the quadriga, as had been done for over a millennium before him.[117] After explaining the fourfold sense, Perkins adds, "But I say to the contrary, that there is but one full and entire sense of every place of Scripture, and that is also the literal sense, sometimes expressed in proper, and sometimes in borrowed or figurative speeches. To make many senses of scripture, is to overturn all sense, and to make nothing certain. As for the three spiritual senses (so called) they are not senses, but applications or uses of scripture."[118] Properly speaking, according to Perkins, there is only one sense of Scripture—the literal, which may also

113. See McKim, "Perkins, William"; also Patterson, *Perkins and the Making of a Protestant England.*

114. As were many of his contemporaries, Perkins was also influenced by the logical and rhetorical methods made famous by Pierre de la Ramée (1515–72), who in turn was a product of scholasticism and humanism. See McKim, *Ramism in William Perkins' Theology*, 60, 69–70, 129; and Ong, *Ramus, Method, and the Decay of Dialogue*, 199.

115. See, e.g., the distinction between general and specific commands in Perkins, *Warning against the Idolatrie*, 685, col. 1.c.

116. Cf. Westminster Confession of Faith 1.6, in Schaff, *Creeds of Christendom*, 3:603: "The whole counsel of God, concerning all things necessary for his own glory, man's salvation, faith, and life, is either expressly set down in Scripture, or by good and necessary consequence may be deduced from Scripture."

117. Perkins, *Galatians*, 304. I have modernized the spelling in quotations from Perkins.

118. Perkins, *Galatians*, 304–5; cf. Perkins, *Arte of Prophecying*, 737, col. 2.b.

include figurative language. Perkins's concern is clear: multiple senses lead to uncertainty of meaning. The assertion of only one sense is the common Protestant reaction to the perceived chaos of spiritual senses not properly linked to the literal sense.

Because of his strong support of the literal sense and grammatical exegesis, it is understandable why some interpreters might see here a clear line of demarcation between Perkins and the premodern exegetes who precede him. As we have seen, however, Perkins is simply following a long line of catholic interpreters since the medieval period who emphasize the one, literal sense. In addition, it is an error to equate Perkins's literal sense with more limited, modern notions of human authorial intent or "original sense."[119] Like Luther, who decried allegorical interpretation yet simultaneously practiced it, Perkins also acknowledged a fuller meaning of Scripture in ways consistent with patristic and medieval exegesis.

First of all, as did Calvin and other Reformers before him, Perkins singles out particular biblical books as aids to the interpretation of the whole canon. He recommends that Bible students first read Romans and the Gospel according to John, which serve as interpretive keys to the New Testament, after which the student should move on to the Old Testament books.[120] This order enables a typological and christological reading.

Furthermore, as Perkins claims that there is only one literal sense, he goes on to say that the literal and spiritual senses "are not two senses, but two parts of one full and entire sense."[121] That is, spiritual meaning is included within the literal sense as a "part" of it. Because God's Word is still for today's church, spiritual applications are necessary and flow from the intended meaning of Scripture.

In acknowledging that the one literal sense can be either properly or figuratively interpreted, he ponders how one should determine the difference. If a "proper" (in other words, literalistic) interpretation is "against common reason, or against the analogy of faith, or against good manners [morals], they are not then to be taken properly, but by figure."[122] If these guidelines sound familiar, it is because they are basically the same rules that Origen used to determine whether and how quickly one should move on to the spiritual sense. From this statement, it is also clear that Perkins admits the same traditional boundaries to biblical interpretation. Later he observes that "the principal means of the interpretation of Scripture, is Scripture itself. And it

119. Sheppard, "Interpretation of the Old Testament," 48–52.
120. Perkins, *Arte of Prophecying*, 736, col. 2.
121. Perkins, *Galatians*, 305.
122. Perkins, *Galatians*, 305.

is a means, when places of Scripture are expounded by the analogy of faith, by the words, scope, and circumstances of the place."[123] In other words, the historical context of the literal sense, the analogy of Scripture providing its own interpretation, and the analogy of faith all control biblical exegesis.

Thus the one literal sense still allowed for christological interpretation of the Old Testament as well as a chastened amount of allegorizing. Perkins leaves room for allegorizing in the sermon as long as the allegories are used sparingly and soberly, they are fitting to the matter at hand, and they are not used alone to prove any point of faith.[124] An example of allegorization is his interpretation of Leviticus 11, a description of clean animals that chew the cud, which he says signify those who engage in holy meditations.[125] This allegory, reminiscent of the *Epistle of Barnabas* and the standard patristic interpretation of the dietary laws of Moses, reflects a practice that is not frequent in Perkins, but is also not out of character. In their allegories, as in their theology and exegesis as a whole, Perkins and other Protestants were not trying to be original or novel.

Finally, the importance of tradition is not lost on Perkins. The historic Christian tradition functions as a kind of confirmation of exegetical conclusions. "We are able to justify our interpretation of Scripture for the main points of religion, by the consent of Fathers, and Councils, as well as they of the Church of Rome."[126] The Roman Church does not have a monopoly on the appeal to the church fathers, who also support Protestant interpretations. Perkins's contemporary and fellow Englishman Richard Hooker (1554–1600) spoke similarly of the use of tradition in theology: "Neither may we in this case lightly esteem what hath been allowed as fit in the judgment of antiquity, and by the long continued practice of the whole Church; from which unnecessarily to swerve, experience hath never as yet found it safe."[127]

Francis Turretin (1623–87), not known as a commentator as much as the paragon of seventeenth-century Reformed orthodoxy in Geneva, also reflects interpretive presuppositions and approaches that are in continuity with the biblical exegesis of his Protestant predecessors. He helps set the tone and becomes a touchstone for subsequent generations of conservative Protestant theologians and exegetes. In light of the Protestant treatment of the quadriga described thus far, it is instructive to see how Turretin handles the senses of Scripture. Like the other writers discussed in this chapter, Turretin was

---

123. Perkins, *Galatians*, 311.
124. Perkins, *Arte of Prophecying*, 751, col. 2.a.
125. See Perkins, *Cases of Conscience*, 82–83.
126. Perkins, *Galatians*, 311.
127. Hooker, *Laws of Ecclesiastical Polity* 5.7.1 (2:27).

concerned that multiple senses of Scripture lead to doubt and ambiguity in interpretation. He thus rejects the fourfold sense in favor of "only one true and genuine sense," the literal sense, which may be either simple and historical or composite and typological.[128] Thus literal does not mean literalistic. The truth conveyed in a passage of Scripture is "only one and simple," not multiple and therefore uncertain. The importance of the perspicuity of Scripture is evident in Turretin's claim that the sense is single and straightforward.[129]

Although he seems to marginalize the spiritual sense of Scripture, Turretin also makes room for an interpretive approach that is largely in step with medieval exegesis. For instance, echoing Perkins's similar distinction, to the one sense of Scripture Turretin adds the diverse applications of Scripture—that is, its "theoretical and practical uses," the former of which corresponds to allegory and anagogy, the latter to tropology.[130] He, moreover, approvingly quotes Thomas Aquinas's claim that the literal sense is the meaning intended by the Holy Spirit, even allowing that many things, including typological and christological interpretations, may be connoted by a single set of words.[131]

The mystical sense, embraced in the literal sense, is proper when it is grounded in the Scriptures themselves—namely, when an inspired New Testament writer provides the allegory. These unique, divinely inspired cases may be used to prove and support doctrine. Unsurprisingly, Turretin is less enthusiastic about allegorical interpretations offered by later, uninspired human interpreters. If an allegory is given for the purpose of illustration, then it is suitable, as long as the interpreter does not intend it as proof of a doctrine. But if the extrabiblical allegory is intended to prove a doctrine or for mere pleasure, then it is improper. Origen once again is singled out as the first Christian culprit who employed this approach and "often ran into extravagance."[132]

Even as he denigrates Origen for his extravagant allegories, Turretin, like Origen, ponders when a passage should be taken figuratively. When a passage makes no sense in its most literal meaning, or when a passage is contrary to the "analogy of faith" and "any received doctrine," then it must be interpreted figuratively.[133] Turretin would not open the door to the same sort of spiritual interpretations common to Origen, but it is worth recalling that, for the same reasons, Origen was motivated to dig deeper than the literal sense.

128. Turretin, *Institutes* 2.19.1–4 (1:149–50).
129. On Turretin's doctrine of perspicuity, see his *Institutes* 2.17 (1:143–47).
130. Turretin, *Institutes* 2.19.6 (1:150–51).
131. Turretin, *Institutes* 2.19.3, 5, 13 (1:150–52).
132. Turretin, *Institutes* 2.19.15 (1:152).
133. Turretin, *Institutes* 2.19.18–19 (1:153).

Allowing for the diversity of seventeenth-century Reformed exegesis and doctrine of Scripture, there is still a fundamental unity of concerns and expressions, illustrated here by Perkins and Turretin. Scholastic methodology, typical of the academic context of post-Reformation Protestant theology, is evident in doctrinal and exegetical treatises. Perkins and Turretin both eschew the quadriga in general and allegory in particular, and they advocate only one sense of Scripture—the literal. Nevertheless, the literal sense embraces a fuller sense that allows for typological and christological readings of the Old Testament, and they think of the three spiritual senses as legitimate in terms of uses or applications. For Perkins, there is a place for allegorical interpretation, but Turretin is less willing to allegorize beyond the specific instances in the New Testament. And both writers acknowledge that Scripture must be taken figuratively when its literal sense contradicts the rule of faith and other Scriptures.

Principles of Early Modern Exegesis

Like all periods in history, the early modern period must be viewed in terms of both continuity and discontinuity with the period that preceded it. With regard to continuity, the similarities between Protestant Reformers and their medieval forebears should be emphasized, if only to counter the popular but erroneous belief that the Reformers were the first practitioners of modern exegesis. Rather, all the figures under consideration in this chapter presuppose most of the important features of premodern exegesis.

1. *Continuity of premodern approaches*. Early modern exegetes maintain a robust doctrine of biblical inspiration. They take for granted the unity of Scripture and the analogy of Scripture, as well as all the principles that flow from this conviction. Clear passages help explain the obscure ones, and the relationship between the Old and New Testaments is characterized by true types and antitypes, promises and fulfillments. All of Scripture in its diverse unity points to Christ, who remains "the scope and argument of all of Scripture."[134] These beliefs about Scripture enable spiritual interpretations or applications that go beyond the literal sense and human authorial intent. Scripture is written for all God's people, revealing a word of doctrine and ethics for the church today. The reader or hearer must be virtuous, illuminated by the Holy Spirit, in order to understand and apply the true message of Scripture. Such features, common to virtually all premodern exegesis, figure prominently in most sixteenth-century approaches to Scripture. These

---

134. Flacius Illyricus, *Sacred Scriptures*, 69.

assumptions of both Roman Catholic and Protestant orthodoxies continued well into the modern period and were never entirely lost to a broad range of ecclesiastical interpreters.

Because of the continued and assumed importance of these features to the exegetical task, it is proper to regard early Protestant exegesis as closer in spirit to the medieval period than to the later, modern period. The continuities notwithstanding, certain discontinuities are also evident in this early modern period that would influence exegesis in subsequent centuries. These features were not full-blown at the beginning of the early modern period. Indeed, most of them can be traced to the high or late medieval period. It is a time of slow (by today's standards) transition to modern exegesis, the seeds of which can be seen in the figures examined above, but only in hindsight. Drawn from the evidence considered in this chapter, here is a summary of the most important developments, whose evolution was often simultaneous and mutually reinforcing.

2. *Diminishing authority of tradition.* The doubt regarding the reliability of tradition that was typical of the Renaissance extended to questions about the church's teaching. As Luther confessed, and much to the chagrin of Johann Eck, popes and councils can err. For Protestants, therefore, tradition became a questionable criterion of truth. To be sure, in the late medieval church, before the Reformation, the belief that tradition is subordinate to Scripture and the belief that it is equal and supplementary—that is, Oberman's Tradition I and Tradition II, respectively—coexisted. The two coexisted in tension, yes, but in the same fellowship of believers. On the other side of the Reformation, both theories continued to persist in the West, but now confessionally at odds, no longer in fellowship with or even within shouting distance of one another. Post-Tridentine Catholics held fast to an elevated view of tradition independent of Scripture, whereas Protestants subordinated tradition without quite specifying its role.

Among the Protestants who subordinated tradition to Scripture, many continued to value the role of tradition. Early in the Reformation (1521), Melanchthon defended Luther against the Roman Catholic claim that he was opposed to all fathers and councils.[135] Calvin affirmed that the analogy of faith remains a true test for every interpretation of Scripture.[136] Hooker's appreciation for historic tradition, expressed above, reflected the sentiment of many. But alongside such appreciation stood Reformers such as the Radicals who excluded church tradition altogether, resulting in *nuda scriptura* as the only

---

135. Melanchthon, *Luther and the Paris Theologians*, 74.
136. Calvin, *Inst.* 4.17.32.

source of religious authority or voice apparently worth hearing. The late medieval tension that had been building between church tradition and Scripture forced a choice regarding the authority of the historic tradition. The Protestant marginalizing of that tradition, exhibited in part in this chapter, is one of the primary indicators of the transition from premodern to modern exegesis, laying the groundwork for the later expulsion of church tradition from consideration in exegesis. It is not yet discernible in the *comma Johanneum* episode with Erasmus, but when it comes to textual criticism and controversial commentary, the church and its dogma would come to have decreasing authority and influence. Later biblical scholars would be less likely to care what the church thought, and interpretation depended increasingly on the individual exegete.

The beginning of this period is marked by traditional dogmatic interpretations in conjunction with increasingly historical and sometimes skeptical methods. The emerging tendency to read Scripture apart from the lens of church tradition would result in the gradual rending of the church's doctrine from biblical foundations. The distinction between theology and exegesis that arose during the high medieval period became sharper during the Reformation. With the aid of Erasmus's Greek text and Latin translation, Luther could pose a biblical argument against five of the seven sacraments. Later in the same century, Socinians would reject the doctrine of the Trinity also on biblical grounds. All this was possible because tradition came to be seen not as an aid to exegesis, but as a hindrance.

3. *One literal sense, with the spiritual sense in flux.* Emphasis on the single literal sense goes hand in hand with a neglect of the manifold spiritual sense. And the fortunes of the literal sense had been on the rise for a long time. The marginalizing of the spiritual senses—allegorical, tropological, and anagogical—began well before the Reformations when scholars reacted against what they saw as the loss or at least obfuscation of the literal sense. Andrew of Saint-Victor and Nicholas of Lyra downplayed the spiritual senses. Since the prevailing exegesis seemed to ignore the text itself, reforming exegetes viewed the spiritual senses as the vehicles for absurd interpretations with no basis in the literal sense. Because the proper controls on the spiritual sense had not been consistently applied and allegorizers had often lost their way, allegory came to be regarded as a feeble prop for novel and controversial doctrines.

Protestant Reformers, already at odds doctrinally and ecclesiastically with Rome, blamed the obfuscation of the literal sense ultimately on the pope. As William Tyndale wrote, "The literal sense is become nothing at all. For the pope hath taken it clean away, and hath made it his possession."[137] In line with

---

137. Tyndale, *Obedience of a Christian Man*, 339.

the late medieval perception that the spiritual senses were getting out of hand, the standard Protestant approach was to claim that Scripture had only one legitimate sense, the literal, and that any spiritual senses or applications were subsumed under the literal. In commentaries and sermons alike, the emphasis on the literal was joined with polemic against the quadriga. "Allegory," which tended to stand for the abuse of the entire spiritual sense, was well on its way to ghettoization. As with the Antiochenes, so also for Protestants: Origen, who stood in a long line of allegorical interpreters, was somehow pegged as the father of allegory and thereby became the bogeyman of exegesis. For Calvin and Turretin, allegorization is discouraged to the point that only the allegories in the New Testament are legitimate. Not only is Origen not a proper model for allegorical interpretation, but the implication is that the apostles themselves are not always proper models for exegesis. This conclusion is a departure from the premodern view. In the early church there may have been some debate between Alexandrians and Antiochenes regarding exactly what Paul was doing in his use of "allegory," but that Paul's exegetical method was something to be imitated was unquestioned.

It is important to reiterate that Protestant exegetes of the early modern period did not reject the spiritual sense wholesale, as would later exegetes, but maintained the legitimacy of spiritual applications arising from the biblical text. Luther led the way in his eagerness both to lampoon the abuse of allegory and to advocate its proper use.[138] From one perspective, this approach does not differ substantively from the historic claim that the doctrine and morals communicated in the spiritual senses must be built on the foundation of the literal sense. It was inevitable, however, that the significance and role of the spiritual senses were now in question and left to individual interpreters to articulate. Simply to admit that there is only one sense led to increasing focus on that literal sense, which in turn included a de-emphasis on the spiritual sense.

4. *Human authorial intent.* Discerning the intent of the human author has always been basic to understanding any text. No interpreter discussed in this book would disagree. But Protestants often regarded the spiritual sense, as outlined in the quadriga, as something foreign to the text, something that introduced ambiguity because it allowed for multiple levels of interpretation and thus multiple truths. The common concern was that multiple meanings rendered any meaning uncertain. In response, the literal, or grammatical, sense came to be associated more closely with the human author's intended meaning. In order to limit the ambiguity, interpreters began to focus on the

---

138. For another early Protestant example of doing both, see the discussion of the four senses in Tyndale, *Obedience of a Christian Man*, 339–65.

one truth intended by the author. This does not mean that every early modern exegete emphasized the human author's situation to the same degree. Most exegetes, however, became increasingly satisfied with pursuing a single truth in each text. Thus Erasmus, who advocated the spiritual sense, looked for the one key or point to the parables, and Calvin spoke of a "genuine sense" of the text, claiming more pointedly that to discover authorial intent is almost the only task of interpretation. Again, beginning with authorial intent, as most interpreters of this period do, is not what distinguishes early modern from premodern exegetes. But when traditional interpretations and the spiritual sense began to decline, then authorial intent—communicated in the "natural" or "grammatical" sense—was bound to become more prominent, a process that takes further shape in this period.

5. *Renaissance methods*. Focus on the grammatical sense and human authorial intent went hand in hand with increasing scrutiny of the Bible as a historical document. With regard to all received ancient texts, Renaissance humanists sought truth and applied their skepticism by means of their philological tools. Eventually these means would be applied most vigorously to Scripture. Attention to its historical context was paramount. For true understanding of the biblical text, the interpreter was required to go back to the sources—that is, to the Hebrew, Aramaic, and Greek languages. This requirement applied to ministers as well, for the magisterial reform movements encouraged an educated, well-trained preaching ministry in reaction to what they perceived as poorly trained parish priests. In addition to linguistic analysis, the Renaissance rediscovery of and renewed appreciation for classical rhetoric led to greater interest in rhetorical analysis. Going back to the sources also meant a new focus on textual criticism, for the received text itself was also a tradition that was not indubitable.

All of these philological emphases sat well with reform-minded individuals, whose doubts about the late medieval church's teachings and practices were finding expression in the Protestant world. The Reformations are, at least in their handling of texts, the religious effect of the Renaissance and the new medium of typography. The Reformers simply intensified the existing shift toward the letter by emphasizing the text and philology in biblical interpretation. Thus it was Protestants more than Roman Catholics who embraced the humanist methods of interpretation, though no Western exegetes were immune to the humanist influence. The Roman Catholic Council of Trent officially recognized the use of the Latin Vulgate as Scripture, and the Vulgate went through later revisions. At the same time, Roman Catholics were free to engage in original-language biblical study and, based on their use of the same humanist tools, generally produced as fine and technical commentaries as did any Protestants. The gravitation toward the literal sense and away from allegorical interpretation, however, did not happen as quickly or as drastically for Roman Catholics as it did for most Protestants.

The impulse of the Renaissance to return to the original sources and to question venerable tradition expressed itself theologically in Reformation and post-Reformation exegesis. In this specific period of transition, the differences are quantitative, not qualitative. It is difficult to point to substantive changes between premodern and early modern exegesis. They are often matters of degree. Earlier, premodern exegetes acknowledged the foundational importance of the literal sense and, in order to do it justice, gave attention to human authorial intent, historical background, the literal sense, and philological tools. Early modern exegetes now intensified their pursuit of the literal sense and the means for arriving there, increasingly at the expense of the spiritual sense and what had been regarded as divine authorial intent. To the Reformers, rejecting the autonomy of the pope's biblical interpretation meant that unbridled allegory was to be reined in by the literal sense of the Scripture and the sole intention of its human authors, which could allegedly be understood apart from the Roman Church's interpretations. The results of the Renaissance handling of texts, now in the context of new ecclesiastical and political institutions, would come to fruition in the modern period. Although the Reformers did not practice what would come to be modern historical-critical exegesis, they are progenitors in a line that, along with many factors, would lead to it. To the degree that the transition to historical-critical exegesis involved the loss of the spiritual sense and the exclusion of dogma, the narrative of this transition is necessarily focused on Protestant rather than Roman Catholic trajectories.

––––––

The figures presented in this chapter, each in their own way, reflect the budding of the seeds that were planted in the premodern era. Whereas certain characteristic approaches to the text in the sixteenth and seventeenth centuries appear to be in continuity with patristic and medieval approaches, in retrospect from the modern point of view, some of these features could look more like tendencies that would blossom during the so-called Enlightenment.

6

The Rise of Historical-Critical Exegesis

The interpretation of Scripture is of two kinds. For the one interpretation merely and simply describes its true sense; but the other interpretation, in addition, elicits some doctrines from this sense, which doctrines it applies to the use of the hearers and readers. For the most part, professors in the schools are occupied with the former interpretation, but preachers employ the latter in the church and for the people.

—Étienne de Courcelles[1]

The office of the interpreter is not to add another [interpretation], but to recover the original one; the meaning, that is, of the words as they struck on the ears or flashed before the eyes of those who first heard and read them. . . . The intelligent mind will ask its own questions, and find for the most part its own answers. The true use of interpretation is to get rid of interpretation, and leave us alone in company with the author.

—Benjamin Jowett[2]

We modern theologians are too proud of our historical method, too proud of our historical Jesus, too confident in our belief in the spiritual gains which our historical theology can bring to the world.

1. Courcelles, *Institutio* 1.14.9, in *Opera*, 31.
2. Jowett, "Interpretation of Scripture," 338, 384.

> The thought that we could build up by the increase of historical
> knowledge a new and vigorous Christianity and set free new spiri-
> tual forces, rules us like a fixed idea, and prevents us from seeing
> that the task which we have grappled with and in some measure
> discharged is only one of the intellectual preliminaries of the great
> religious task.
>
> —Albert Schweitzer[3]

Admittedly, John Josias Conybeare (1779–1824) is not an outstanding figure in the history of biblical interpretation. He was professor of Anglo-Saxon and later of poetry at Oxford. In the field of humanities, he is celebrated as the "first English popularizer of *Beowulf*,"[4] or at least a popularizer for scholars. His groundbreaking work on the epic poem, post-humously published in *Illustrations of Anglo-Saxon Poetry* (1826), produced large selections of the Old English text with modern English paraphrase and commentary, along with literal Latin translations.[5] My interest in Conybeare concerns the final work of his life, the Bampton Lectures at Oxford in 1824. After delivering the lectures, he sent the final manuscript for their publication on June 7, 1824, four days before his untimely death.[6]

Conybeare's chosen topic was the history and development of the spiritual sense of Scripture in exegesis. Yet it is not primarily for his historical narra-tive and assessments, which are often judicious, that I mention Conybeare's work. In the midst of his examination, he also provides occasional indications of his own thoughts on the emerging, modern approach to biblical interpre-tation. Like nearly everyone else in the early nineteenth century, he stands somewhere in the prolonged, indefinite borderland between premodern and modern exegesis. He is interesting, though, because he recognizes his position and defines the boundary.

In his opening lecture, Conybeare observes that there has been a reaction to the abuse of the spiritual sense of Scripture. In recent years, he says, a school of thought has arisen that has not yet come to England, though it is perhaps already influencing its divinity students. It is especially prominent in the "protestant churches of continental Europe." It discards all spiritual and allegorical interpretations, "including in one sweeping and indiscriminate

---

3. Schweitzer, *Quest of the Historical Jesus*, 399.
4. Magennis, *Translating "Beowulf,"* 50.
5. Conybeare, *Illustrations of Anglo-Saxon Poetry*, 30–167.
6. Conybeare, *Bampton Lectures*.

censure the human expositions of Origen and Augustin [*sic*], of [Johannes] Cocceius and [Campegius] Vitringa, and the inspired parallelisms of the Epistle to the Hebrews." Conybeare goes on to say that this movement is led by men of great erudition in small matters of literary detail, "but little distinguished by any of the higher powers of intellect, and yet less by the reasonable and pious submission of that intellect to the revealed word and will of its great author."[7]

Conybeare is clearly troubled by what he considers to be an overreaction against the spiritual sense of Scripture. In contrasting the two excesses, he does not mince words about which is the greater threat. On the one hand is "the fanciful and enthusiastic misapplication of scriptural language and imagery," and on the other hand "the yet more dangerous and culpable mis-application of learning and of talent which would deprive the word of light and life of its spiritual, nay, of its very prophetic and authoritative character."[8] To Conybeare's mind, the abuse of spiritual interpretation is better than its total neglect.

In his closing lecture, Conybeare seeks a more balanced approach. He is definitely no enthusiastic allegorist, but he does see a place for a secondary, spiritual sense, as long as it is tied to and flows from the literal.[9] Even so, his fear about the imbalance remains. After speaking about the messianic scope of the entire Old Testament, in its parts and whole, he warns that if this "master-key" is taken away, then the door will be closed to divine truth. The contents behind that door, "under this self-called rational view, may be thought to open a wider field for the exertions of human ingenuity, for the free and luxuriant speculations of conjectural criticism; but, on the score of intelligibility, as well as upon that of Christian faith and Christian edification, the loss is incalculable."[10] In other words, the so-called rational approach to Scripture may seem to limit human speculation, but in reality it opens the door to another kind of speculation, one that is ultimately devastating to the church's faith.

Conybeare was prescient. Not only did he testify to the shift that was happening still in his day, but he also accurately predicted the influence it would have on those who practice biblical interpretation and the effect on the church for whom it is supposedly practiced. This chapter will sketch some of the influential factors and figures leading to the situation that Conybeare decries and the repercussions that followed from it. The aim is to describe the underlying assumptions of modern exegesis, to explain how they came

7. Conybeare, *Bampton Lectures*, 6–8.
8. Conybeare, *Bampton Lectures*, 10.
9. Conybeare, *Bampton Lectures*, 320–29.
10. Conybeare, *Bampton Lectures*, 330.

to be, and ultimately to contrast these assumptions with premodern exegesis. The concern is summed up well by Carl Braaten and Robert Jenson: "The historical-critical method was originally devised and welcomed as the great emancipator of the Bible from ecclesiastical dogma and blind faith. Some practitioners of the method now sense that the Bible may have meanwhile become its victim."[11]

Remonstrants

If John Calvin and other Reformers were not quite the harbingers of modern historical-critical method that some theologians have assumed and not the ones directly responsible for the shift to modern exegesis, then we must continue the story to see clearer evidence of the transition. Although many writers from the late sixteenth to the mid-seventeenth centuries reflect the assumptions of the emerging modern exegesis, two in particular represent early and explicit examples of the next phase in this gradual development: the Remonstrant theologians Simon Episcopius (1583–1643) and Étienne de Courcelles (1586–1659). Remonstrants were the Dutch Arminians who, like Jacob Arminius (1559–1609) before them, resisted the Reformed doctrines of absolute predestination and irresistible grace. After Arminius's death, this group was expelled from the Dutch Reformed Church and, after a few years of exile, occupied a marginal place in Dutch religious life. Despite their small numbers then and their comparative obscurity now, Remonstrant theologians and biblical scholars were highly respected and influential throughout European academia. Episcopius, a former student of Arminius, was the first professor of theology at the Remonstrant Seminary in Amsterdam, and Courcelles was his successor.

Episcopius and Courcelles stand out for the prominence they gave to two ideas that were important to all Protestant doctrines of Scripture: biblical perspicuity and the priority of the literal sense. First, as we have seen, perspicuity means that, although there may be some obscure passages, Scripture is crystal clear about everything that is necessary to believe and to do. Perhaps no one in the seventeenth century emphasized this doctrine of perspicuity more than did the Remonstrants.

This new emphasis on perspicuity is seen first in their optimistic view of reason's ability to interpret Scripture. The perspicuous text is comprehensible when the reader approaches it with, as Episcopius puts it, "natural reason."

11. Braaten and Jenson, introduction to Braaten and Jenson, *Reclaiming the Bible for the Church*, ix.

Scripture is clear to all readers who are "gifted with common reason."[12] Cour-celles, who was a friend of René Descartes and translator of the *Discourse on Method*, also stresses the role of reason and that anyone, regenerate or unregenerate, can grasp the doctrines necessary for salvation.[13]

That Episcopius's view of perspicuity was controversial even among Prot-estants is evident in the opposition he encountered against it. His Reformed opponents accused him of holding an optimistic anthropology that dismissed the inner illumination of the Holy Spirit. In response, Episcopius insisted that "common sense" or "right reason [*ratio recta*]" is sufficient for under-standing the Bible's literal sense.[14] Yes, the Holy Spirit's illumination is needed for the supernatural work of faith and obedience, but nothing more than natural reason is necessary merely to comprehend the words of Scripture. To understand the words of Scripture, he claimed, is distinct from believing and obeying unto salvation.

To be sure, Episcopius's innovation is not in his insistence on the use of "right reason," an ancient virtue that all Christian interpreters have acknowl-edged. Right reason is simply the faculty on the human side ensuring that perspicuous Scripture will be perspicuously understood. After all, reasoning is inevitable. In this light, his opponents' alarm at the use of reason was over-stated. But what his opponents seem to have detected correctly is the more optimistic view of reason, which is apparently not as bad off as the will and affections. This view became typical of the Remonstrants and of the com-ing age of Enlightenment. For Episcopius, the reading and understanding of Scripture was not necessarily a spiritual exercise, but a rational one. The new implication, contrary to premodern interpretation up to this point, is that one can fully grasp the meaning of Scripture without being a believer. Courcelles, in emphasizing the role of reason throughout the tradition, sidesteps the issue of just how important reason has now become. Typical of the zeitgeist, Courcelles does not seem to appreciate the degree to which human reason, supposedly void of passions, can yet deceive and be deceived.

The Remonstrant emphasis on perspicuity is seen also in the suggestion that, for reason to function properly, it must remain unaffected by any other influ-ence. In the task of interpretation, then, Scripture must be engaged without the interference of the affections or any presuppositions. Episcopius emphasized the need to cast off all hindrances when interpreting Scripture. Courcelles

12. See Episcopius, *Disputationes theologicae tripartitae*, part 1, 3.1–3 and part 3, 3.1; in *Operum theologicorum*, part 2:391, 445.

13. Courcelles, *Institutio* 1.13.1, in *Opera*, 26–27; cf. 1.14.7, in *Opera*, 30.

14. See Episcopius, *Confessio* 1.14, 16 ([1622], 6–7); ET, *Arminian Confession of 1621*, trans. Ellis, 41–43.

warned against ignorance, prejudice, and affections clouding one's interpretation, urging readers to "free ourselves from these impediments."[15] This
attitude is consistent with what Descartes wrote in his first epistemological
rule in the *Method*: "Avoid precipitous judgment and prejudice."[16]

Second, along with the emphasis on reason's ability to clarify Scripture, the
Remonstrant theologians took the late medieval and Reformation prioritizing
of the literal sense to the next level. Though Episcopius does not explicitly
reject the spiritual sense, he appears to collapse the spiritual sense into the
grammatical, or literal, sense. For Episcopius, certainly the only legitimate
typologies and allegories are those already expressed in Scripture, as Calvin
also seemed to indicate.[17] Discovering "the intention of the one who uttered
the words," revealed in the literal sense, is the task of interpretation.[18]

With both of these Remonstrant theologians, we see a focus on the literal-
historical sense to the near exclusion of any spiritual-allegorical sense. Human
authorial intent took center stage and became the primary touchstone of meaning. For Courcelles, this meant that the biblical text should be interpreted like
any other text.[19] As for other historical texts, so also for the Bible, no spiritual
or divine meaning is to be legitimately discovered beyond the literal sense.
This focus on the literal sense and human authorial intent led to increased
attention to the original languages and textual criticism.

The Remonstrant approach to Scripture is a very early example of what
became commonplace in later Remonstrants such as Jean LeClerc (1657–
1736), who taught in the Remonstrant Seminary for most of his career,
and in modern exegesis generally. Some observations about its implications
are in order. The ecclesiastical context of the Remonstrants was a factor
in their view of biblical interpretation. Like other minority groups in the
post-Reformation period, the Remonstrants felt the sting of religious intoler-
ance. Their marginal status led them to interact with other marginal groups
and opinions that they probably would not have otherwise encountered
or so quickly entertained. It is fairly clear, for instance, that the Remonstrants' historical approach to Scripture based on right reason was partly
influenced by the writings of the anti-trinitarian Fausto Sozzini (Faustus
Socinus, 1539–1604).[20] In addition, given the reality of post-Reformation
ecclesial division and unprecedented war, religio-political unity, or at least

15. Courcelles, *Institutio* 1.14.7, in *Opera*, 30.
16. Descartes, *Discourse on Method*, 10.
17. Calvin, *Inst.* 2.5.19.
18. [Episcopius,] *Apologia pro confessione*, fol. 36r.
19. Courcelles, *Institutio* 1.24.7, in *Opera*, 30.
20. Daugirdas, "Biblical Hermeneutics of Socinians and Remonstrants."

toleration, was the goal. This goal of toleration was explicit in the work of the Remonstrant scholar Hugo Grotius, who was also a celebrated commentator on Scripture and whose approach was consistent with that of the Remonstrant theologians.[21] Remonstrants emphasized the simplicity of the perspicuity of the one literal sense in order to promote unity on the basis of Scripture, a unity that apparently could not be achieved on the basis of confessions or overwrought interpretations. The method was the way to peace. What the Leiden humanist Joseph Scaliger said ultimately applies to Scripture: "Theological disputes all stem from ignorance of grammar."[22] As Descartes wanted to apply his rationalist method to every academic discipline and philosophical question, in hopes of defeating skepticism and discord and finding certainty and unity, so a rational method of interpreting the Bible was intended to lead to unity and concord.

The Remonstrant stress on perspicuity, following in the footsteps of their Protestant forebears, did not lead to greater interpretive unity (much less religio-political unity). Instead, ironically, the exegetical methods of Renaissance philology, combined with Protestant doctrine, led to greater obscurity—an obscurity that could be adequately addressed only by scholars. As Erasmus and others had advocated, everyone should have access to Scripture, and Protestants usually stressed the obligation of all Christians to read their Bibles. But how were the people, who were obliged to read the Bible regularly, supposed to cope with the demands of correct interpretation? The same philologists who told the people to read the Bible could not produce a firmly established text. Nevertheless, they cheerfully published texts with a dizzying array of variant readings, as did Courcelles, whose Greek New Testament of 1658 boasted a "gathering of variant readings fuller than any other."[23] The same biblical scholars who told the common people to read this uncertain text said it must be done properly in the ancient languages, which they could not read. The Bible should be read by all, but it is inaccessible to nearly all. Fortunately, as Courcelles mentioned, the "experts" have produced translations.[24] But whose translation, with which expert's annotations, was correct? Moreover, how was the Protestant church to apply and gather relevant doctrines from Scripture if it was not written

21. The definitive study of Grotius is by Nellen, *Hugo Grotius*. For a summary of Grotius's contributions to biblical interpretation, see Reventlow, *History of Biblical Interpretation*, 3:209–23.

22. Attributed in Turner, *Philology*, 59.

23. Courcelles, "Praefatio ad lectorem," in *Novum testamentum*, fols. 002r–002v. Courcelles optimistically claimed that one "can easily discern the true reading from the false." Courcelles, *Institutio* 1.3.6, in *Opera*, 7.

24. Courcelles, *Institutio* 1.14.2, in *Opera*, 29.

for them, but only to the ancients? The literal-historical sense alone, apart from the spiritual senses, would appear to be burdened with the impossible task of serving as a foundation for doctrinal meaning and a defense for traditional dogma.[25]

That biblical studies was becoming primarily an academic enterprise, without reference to its continued churchly use, is implied when Courcelles wrote: "The interpretation of Scripture is of two kinds. For the one interpretation merely and simply describes its true sense; but the other interpretation, in addition, elicits some doctrines from this sense, which doctrines it applies to the use of the hearers and readers. For the most part, professors in the schools are occupied with the former interpretation, but preachers employ the latter in the church and for the people."[26] He distinguishes and advocates two kinds of biblical interpretation. Exegesis as pure description yields the "true sense," and it is reserved for the experts and scholars. Doctrine and morals and other applications, however, are in the purview of the preachers. Courcelles promotes as clearly as possible the distinction that will later be known as that between biblical and dogmatic theology.

In sum, like the Radicals of the sixteenth century, the Remonstrants of the seventeenth century promoted the perspicuity of Scripture with no "prejudices." Since doctrinal presuppositions are hindrances to the objective interpretation of authorial intent, they should be abandoned in exegesis. The new, cutting-edge exegesis would be one that expels tradition from any influence. What began as a "radical" position in the early seventeenth century would, by the end of the same century, begin to emerge as the mainstream Protestant position. The increasing focus on human reason's ability to interpret a clear Scripture by seeking the original human author's intent, without reference to the spiritual senses or traditional Christian doctrine, presages the full-orbed historical-critical method of the modern period.

Benedict de Spinoza

The approach to Scripture reflected by the Remonstrants would soon become part of the air breathed in Enlightenment-era Europe. Those principles were taken to the next level by the philosopher Benedict (Baruch) de Spinoza (1632–77), who lived at least outwardly as a faithful Jew until his excommunication from the synagogue in 1656. To put it mildly, Spinoza was controversial; as

25. For more on Episcopius and Courcelles's biblical exegesis and its consequences, see Stanglin, "Rise and Fall of Biblical Perspicuity."
26. Courcelles, *Institutio* 1.14.9, in *Opera*, 31.

Jonathan Israel puts it, he "emerged as the supreme philosophical bogeyman of Early Enlightenment Europe."[27]

Spinoza is mentioned in most introductory Old Testament courses as one of the first scholars to deny that Moses had anything to do with the authorship of the Pentateuch: "It is plainer than the noonday sun," Spinoza announces, "that the Pentateuch was not written by Moses but by someone else who lived many generations after Moses."[28] More broadly, his *Theological-Political Treatise* (1670) has been called "the most important seventeenth-century work to advance the study of the Bible and religion generally."[29] His immediate aim was to make more room for individual freedom in the Dutch Republic by weakening the authority of the church and the legitimacy of its theology, though he would also claim that such freedom should not undermine true piety.[30] Everyone in society should be free both to think and to say anything,[31] and he intended to exercise his freedom.

The search for the right "method," always necessary to any discipline, became a watchword in the Enlightenment. Proper methodology leads to true knowledge. In its more optimistic iterations, it is possible to tell whether something is true simply by examining the idea with the correct method. If the right method in any field could be discovered and followed, certainty would result. Again, in an age of doubt, certainty was at a premium. Descartes wanted mathematical certainty in philosophy. So, like Descartes and other Enlightenment thinkers, Spinoza exalted method. Throughout the *Treatise*, he pursued his "method for interpreting the sacred volumes."[32] Interpreting Scripture, he wrote, is analogous to interpreting nature—that is, analogous to employing the scientific method.[33]

The success of the method depends on the capability of human reason to implement it. Typical of the Enlightenment, Spinoza exalts uncorrupted human reason and its ability to discover truth. He states that nothing expressly taught in Scripture conflicts with the natural understanding.[34] The "natural light of reason" is the rule of interpretation that is common to all people; thus the "highest authority to interpret Scripture rests with each

27. Israel, *Radical Enlightenment*, 159; see 159–74 on Spinoza.

28. Spinoza, *Treatise*, 122; see 118–29 for his own arguments and his appeal to the much earlier arguments of Ibn-Ezra (1089–1164); cf. Turner, *Philology*, 60.

29. J. Preus, *Spinoza and the Irrelevance of Biblical Authority*, x. On Spinoza's *Treatise*, see Israel, *Radical Enlightenment*, 275–85; Israel, in his introduction to Spinoza, *Treatise*, viii–xxxiv.

30. Cf. Spinoza, *Treatise*, 6; Israel, in his introduction to Spinoza, *Treatise*, viii.

31. Spinoza, *Treatise*, 11.

32. Spinoza, *Treatise*, 9.

33. Spinoza, *Treatise*, 98–99, 102.

34. Spinoza, *Treatise*, 9.

individual."[35] Scripture is perspicuous enough for salvation. There is no need for supernatural illumination.[36]

Furthermore, correct execution of the method requires objectivity in the process. It is necessary to "free our minds from theological prejudices."[37] Having noted the apostasy of the early church and the impurity of the established church's theology, Spinoza presumed to go back to the Bible, "to make a fresh examination of Scripture with a free and unprejudiced mind, and to assert nothing about it, and to accept nothing as its teaching, which I did not quite clearly derive from it."[38] Only the opinions expressed in Scripture should be allowed in its interpretation.[39]

Without attempting an exhaustive account of Spinoza's method, a few salient features must be noted. Spinoza drew an important distinction between the "true sense of Scripture" and the "truth of things." On the one hand, the true or "genuine sense of a passage" is what the human author believed and intended to convey. On the other hand, the "truth of things" is what we know to be actually true according to the natural light of reason.[40] Though these two categories may overlap, they are distinct. Spinoza offers an illustration. If the Bible says, "God is fire," then we cannot immediately deny its literal intention on the basis of our philosophical reason that testifies otherwise. The meaning depends on what the human author believed. If we are to decide whether the human author "Moses" believed God is fire or he intended it only metaphorically, then it must be on the basis of other statements within Moses's writings.[41] So it is not that Scripture should be accommodated to reason; that would be to impose modern thought and categories on the ancients. Neither should our reason be accommodated to Scripture, which would impose ancient thought and categories on us.[42] Scripture and our theology are distinct domains, but they have been confused and thought of as one. This confusion is why Spinoza insists that, in order to understand the Bible, it must be read without any theological prejudice or presupposition. Once the distinction is secure, then there will be many things in the biblical writings that "we are now able to dispense with."[43]

35. Spinoza, *Treatise*, 116–17.
36. Spinoza, *Treatise*, 111.
37. Spinoza, *Treatise*, 98, 112.
38. Spinoza, *Treatise*, 7–9.
39. Spinoza, *Treatise*, 100.
40. Spinoza, *Treatise*, 100, 109–15. Israel discusses this distinction in his introduction, xi–xiii.
41. Spinoza, *Treatise*, 100–101. As it happens, Spinoza does find other passages in "Moses" that indicate the immaterial view of God.
42. Spinoza, *Treatise*, 186.
43. Spinoza, *Treatise*, 169.

According to Louis Dupré, it was Spinoza who "proposed a new, subjective principle of exegesis, namely, the intention of the author. This, of course, had been virtually absent from the ancient belief that the author served as a mere mouthpiece of divine communications."[44] It is an exaggeration to suggest that premodern interpreters were not concerned with authorial intent. But the point is well taken that authorial intent now had nothing to do with divine intent or inspiration, rendering the belief in inspiration superfluous and perhaps even inimical to biblical interpretation thus understood.

In order to comprehend the true sense of Scripture, which is the author's meaning, Spinoza asserted that a history of the Bible must be reconstructed that explains the circumstances of each book: "the life, character and particular interests of the author of each individual book, who exactly he was, on what occasion he wrote, for whom and in what language," and so on. The better we know the author's mind and personality, the more able we are to explain his meaning.[45] Spinoza emphasizes the diversity of views among the authors, observing that the apostles disagreed widely about the foundations of religion.[46] This primary attention to the historical circumstances behind each individual document would become a hallmark of historical-critical exegesis. Doing justice to the historical setting means also attending to the original languages, an essential principle that has dominated exegesis since the Renaissance. For Spinoza, who wrote a Hebrew grammar, Hebrew is of utmost importance, for even the New Testament writers used Hebrew idioms translated into Greek.[47]

Even as he exalts the method, Spinoza is not sanguine about the available evidence. Most aspects of the historical background of the biblical books, he admitted, are lost to us.[48] This lack of evidence applies also to the ancient Hebrew language itself, perfect knowledge of which is impossible. Spinoza points to the many ambiguities of the language, including the lack of vowels and punctuation in the original texts.[49] The method is therefore limited by limited data. It appears that confidence in the method and its results should increase proportionate with the increase of research and information. Thus later generations are not discouraged by the limits that Spinoza points out, but rather they are inspired to reconstruct the history on the basis of ever-changing research.

44. Dupré, *Enlightenment*, 252.
45. Spinoza, *Treatise*, 101.
46. Spinoza, *Treatise*, 161.
47. Spinoza, *Treatise*, 100.
48. Spinoza, *Treatise*, 109–11.
49. Spinoza, *Treatise*, 106–9.

Spinoza insists that he is not intending to undermine all of Scripture by casting doubt on certain parts, but that instead he is attempting to uphold Scripture. In fact, he claims, a thing is sacred only insofar as it is treated as such. As long as people make sacred use of Scripture, it is sacred. But when it is neglected or abused, a once-sacred thing can cease to be sacred. Scripture will remain sacred as long as it is used properly and moves people to devotion to God and to the universal divine law, which, according to Spinoza, can be naturally known.[50] The true religion, the true word of God, is summed up in the love commands and the simple truths that Jesus taught.

G. E. Lessing

Like Spinoza, the deist Gotthold Ephraim Lessing (1729–81) was neither a theologian nor a biblical commentator, though he had a deep interest and influence in both fields. Now a century after Spinoza, Lessing was a leading figure of the German Enlightenment who reflected a new, more rigorous, and skeptical approach to history that characterizes modern exegesis. In his famous essay "On the Proof of the Spirit and of Power" (1777), Lessing comments on a passage in Origen's *Contra Celsum* (*Against Celsus*) in which Origen also quotes the apostle Paul. In the opening book of Origen's response to Celsus, Origen claims that Christians have proofs superior to those of pagan Greek philosophy. Citing 1 Corinthians 2:4, where Paul mentions the "proof of the Spirit and of power," Origen interprets the proof of the Spirit as fulfilled prophecies and the proof of power as miracles.[51]

Lessing was not convinced. He posits that, if he had lived at the time of Christ and seen for himself the fulfillment of the prophecies and the powerful wonders, then he would be able to submit his intellect to these demonstrations and believe in Christ. As it is, though, the proof of spirit and of power, the fulfilled prophecies and miracles, are not still in the eighteenth century fulfilled prophecies and miracles. They are human reports of fulfillment and human reports of miracles, not the same as seeing it for oneself. Such reports "have to work through a medium which takes away all their force."[52]

For Lessing, historical truths of any kind, in the Bible or not, cannot enjoy the same kind of certainty as something immediately available to one's senses. For Lessing, according to Dupré, "no knowledge is less certain than

---

50. Spinoza, *Treatise*, 153, 164–66, 169.
51. See Origen, *Contra Celsum* 1.2.
52. Lessing, "Proof of the Spirit," 51–52.

the historical one."[53] Lessing wonders why the historical events recorded in the Bible are treated as if they are infinitely more reliable than they in fact are. Furthermore, even if they are taken as valid, Lessing doubts that a particular historical truth should be able to prove a theological proposition. "But to jump with that historical truth to a quite different class of truths, and to demand of me that I should form all my metaphysical and moral ideas accordingly; to expect me to alter all my fundamental ideas of the nature of the Godhead because I cannot set any credible testimony against the resurrection of Christ: if that is not a μετάβασις εἰς ἄλλο γένος [*metabasis eis allo genos*, shifting to another genus], then I do not know what Aristotle meant by this phrase."[54] Anything that could be used to bolster a theological proposition about Christ would be merely another historical claim. Lessing would like to believe with certainty, but he cannot, because there is "the ugly, broad ditch" that he cannot walk or even leap across.[55]

The ugly, broad ditch would become a metaphor for the chasm between an alleged historical event and a normative theological proposition. For Lessing, the historical event (even assumed as a certain fact) and present theological understanding are two mutually exclusive categories, with no clear link. More devastatingly, though, the history is not certain for Lessing and his contemporaries. The ditch seems to reflect also the wide chronological gap and the resulting uncertainty about what the Bible records. The upshot is that, when mathematical certainty became the standard, skepticism was the outcome for anything falling short of such certainty. Since the biblical witness is not as reliable as one's own senses, it is therefore not reliable at all. Combined with a growing philosophical naturalism that saw the cosmos as a closed system and ruled out the possibility of miracles—David Hume's assault on miracles comes to mind[56]—biblical narratives were soon subjected to historical skepticism. Efforts were made to cut through the religious bias of the biblical writers, to get behind the text to find out what really happened.

The Science of Biblical Studies

As we have seen, in the medieval period the university became a rival setting to the monastery and church liturgy for the reading and study of Scripture. It was primarily in that setting that *sacra pagina* (sacred page, biblical studies) came

53. Dupré, *Enlightenment*, 191.
54. Lessing, "Proof of the Spirit," 54.
55. Lessing, "Proof of the Spirit," 55.
56. Hume, "Miracles."

to be clearly distinguished from *sacra doctrina* (sacred doctrine, theological studies). But it was in the early modern and Enlightenment-era universities of Protestant Europe that these concepts finally came to be separated. What emerged was the scholarly, scientific discipline of biblical studies.

Michael Legaspi refers to this process as the transition from a "scriptural Bible" to an "academic Bible."[57] The development was aided by several factors already discussed. As a scientific pursuit, biblical studies required objectivity in scientific investigation. Just as a scientist should not conduct an experiment with his mind already made up, there was an emphasis on reading the Bible without theological prejudice—that is, apart from later doctrinal categories—in order to discover the intended meaning of the human author, by which is meant anyone responsible for what became the finished text, including earlier, oral tradents. Objectivity is thought to be the means to correct understanding, and this goal of understanding could be, and really should be, accomplished apart from ecclesiastical contexts. Scientific examination encouraged questioning and scrutinizing, dissecting the text of the Bible into its individual parts, which meant not only the individual books but also the diverse layers that lay behind those books. In order to fully understand the text, scholars had to pursue the history behind the materials that came to constitute the Bible. The execution of these and related assumptions in biblical interpretation is what I mean by historical-critical, or modern, exegesis. Human authorial intent is the goal, and it can be discovered through the means of philological analysis and research into historical backgrounds and context. The purpose here is not to collapse all modern exegesis into historical-critical or to imply that all modern exegetes were alike; strictly speaking, the historical-critical approach, itself capable of many nuances, was but one exegetical model during the modern period. Our interchangeable use of the designations, however, reflects the fact that historical-critical assumptions were becoming commonplace toward the close of the Enlightenment period. The emergence of the historical-critical method is not the whole story of exegesis in the modern period, but it is its genius.[58]

As implied in these assumptions, the object of study is the biblical text apart from any theological construct placed on it from the outside. Spinoza had already distinguished the meaning intended by the ancient human author from the truth of fact, observing that they do not always overlap. This distinction between, on the one hand, the theology believed and presented by the biblical

57. Legaspi, *Death of Scripture*, viii.
58. John Barton fervently resists designating modern exegesis as the "historical-critical method," for he denies that it is either strictly historical or a method. See Barton, *Nature of Biblical Criticism*, 31–68.

author(s) and, on the other hand, our own understanding of truth (theological and otherwise) is perhaps the first step of historical-critical exegesis, and it was articulated most famously by Johann Philipp Gabler (1753–1826).

In 1787, as professor in the University of Altdorf, J. P. Gabler delivered his inaugural lecture on the topic of the "distinction between biblical and dogmatic theology." He begins his discourse by lamenting the contention of religious opinions and the discord among Christian denominations. Such divisions are due, he says, not only to the occasional obscurity of Scripture, but also to the custom of reading one's own opinions into Scripture—that is, the failure to distinguish between biblical and dogmatic theology.[59] Biblical theology is what the biblical authors believed and intended to communicate; it is static on the pages of Scripture. Dogmatic theology represents later attempts to systematize and apply those biblical thoughts; it changes with each age and individual theologian. The two have been confused and combined into one thing. By disentangling the two, Gabler means to exclude all allegorical and spiritual senses, indeed all theological formulations, that go beyond human authorial intent.[60]

Part of the confusion, Gabler implies, is in the traditional use of classic sayings (*dicta classica*),[61] meaning places in Scripture frequently called on to prove a doctrinal point. These passages are also called prooftexts (*dicta probantia*). The assumption is that biblical texts, in the subsequent history of interpretation, have been lifted from their context and placed together with other unrelated passages, giving them a new, dogmatic context in an attempt to prove doctrines unknown to the original authors. The solution is to put these passages back into their respective contexts, and if the interpreter seeks to glean any doctrinal ideas from them, the ideas must be consistent with the text's own era and place of origin.[62]

For Gabler, the pursuit of biblical studies is not merely for the sake of historical curiosity. The research should go on to inform the church's doctrine. Once biblical theology has been isolated and then accurately described, the interpreter can, as Gabler puts it, discern the "undoubted universal ideas . . . which alone are useful in dogmatic theology." Upon those foundations, then, one can build "a dogmatic theology adapted to our own times." This dogmatic theology, of course, should be in harmony with "the principles of human reason."[63]

---

59. Gabler, "Oration."
60. Gabler, "Oration," 498.
61. See the passing reference in Gabler, "Oration," 501.
62. Gabler, "Oration," 499.
63. Gabler, "Oration," 501.

The seeds of later developments are evident in Gabler's speech. But it should be remembered that, although some philosophers and scholars had little stake in defending traditional Christian faith, most of the early practitioners of historical-critical exegesis were pious believers who were trying to restore unity to the fragmented churches and to society by objective, scholarly engagement with the Bible.[64] As it turns out, though, the focus on the Bible as a merely human book effectively excluded consideration of it as a divinely inspired book. As biblical studies became separated from the question of inspiration, it also ceased to be normative for the modern church and its doctrinal formulations.

Bible Only

In general, American Christianity amplified the European Protestant tendency to return to simple Christianity and to cast off traditions that they dismissed as recent innovations in church history. This deep desire to tread their own path without the baggage of previous generations, combined with the optimism, populism, and occasional anti-intellectualism so characteristic of the new American republic, influenced biblical interpretation. Whether the results were historically orthodox, wildly unorthodox, or somewhere in between, the common factor in much of American Protestantism was the vocal rejection of traditional, ecclesiastical modes of biblical interpretation.

The severing of biblical interpretation from traditional dogma, pioneered in sixteenth-century Protestantism especially among the Anabaptists and represented so vividly in the eighteenth century by Gabler, came to full expression in the Unitarianism of William Ellery Channing (1780–1842). Channing was an early leader in the American Unitarian movement that began to flourish around the turn of the nineteenth century. The Unitarian impulse was rational and antitraditional but, at the same time, intensely biblical in the sense of what we called *nuda scriptura*, the approach of reading the Bible without any influence from previous interpretations. In a speech that Channing delivered for an ordination ceremony in Baltimore in 1819, he laid out the chief principles of Unitarian Christianity, the first of which related to biblical interpretation.

Channing acknowledged that Unitarians are accused of an excessive reliance on reason in their interpretation of Scripture. He countered that Scripture's meaning should be sought in the same manner as the meaning of any other book, and reason is therefore necessary.[65] Despite the limits of reason, all

64. See Legaspi, *Death of Scripture*, 9, et passim.
65. Channing, "Unitarian Christianity," 367–68.

interpreters, including the avowed opponents of his rationalism, appeal to reason in defense of their own opinions. The potential for reason to err does not imply that it cannot be used for anything or that it errs more egregiously in religion than in other fields,[66] a point that Étienne de Courcelles had made a century and a half earlier. Channing put his reasonable hermeneutic in the service of a Unitarian—which is to say, classically heretical—view of God, regarding trinitarianism as "irrational and unscriptural."[67]

Alongside Spinozan pantheists, Enlightenment deists, and freethinking Unitarians such as Channing, a large percentage—surely the majority—of Christian theologians during the nineteenth century sought to employ the presuppositions and methods of modern exegesis in the context of a traditional orthodoxy that affirmed biblical inspiration. On the North American scene, Alexander Campbell (1788–1866), the leading figure in the American Restoration (Stone-Campbell) Movement, is a case in point.

Campbell, born and raised in Ireland, immigrated to the new American republic and soon severed ties with the Presbyterianism of his youth. He was the founding president of Bethany College in (West) Virginia and a champion of reform and simple, biblical Christianity. With the help of others, he led a movement that sought Christian unity by returning to the Bible alone for the rule of faith and practice, eventually spawning Churches of Christ, Christian Churches, and the Disciples of Christ.[68] *Nuda scriptura* was Campbell's approach. After all, it was the bias of traditional interpretations that led to and continues to foster denominational divisions. "They all take from the Bible such parts as suit their respective theories. They also select from the fathers and from tradition certain other parts of their systems. We profess to take the whole Bible and nothing from the sects, nor the Fathers."[69] To drive home his point that postbiblical influence is unnecessary for the proper interpretation of Scripture, Campbell wrote, "Nothing discovered by any man, that has lived since John wrote the Apocalypse, is of any virtue in religion; nay, indeed, is no part or parcel of Christianity."[70] As his father, Thomas Campbell, put it, we should accept in our faith and practice nothing that is "not as old as the New Testament."[71] The Campbells' skepticism of the positive use of Christian tradition in biblical interpretation was common among Protestants, and

66. Channing, "Unitarian Christianity," 369.
67. Channing, "Unitarian Christianity," 371.
68. For an accessible historical survey of biblical interpretation among these groups, see Boring, *Disciples and the Bible*.
69. A. Campbell, "Calvinism and Arminianism," 326.
70. A. Campbell, "Anecdotes, Incidents and Facts," 280.
71. T. Campbell, *Declaration and Address*, 19. On the implications of this phrase, see Stanglin, "Restorationism and Church History."

especially among American Protestants.[72] The European impulse to throw off the old traditions became impulsive in the New World. American Christianity tended to be ahistorical in every aspect, not least in biblical exegesis.

In light of the emphasis on the Bible only, the interpretation of Scripture was of utmost importance to Alexander Campbell and his reformation movement. He was influenced by a Baconian inductive approach (that is, the scientific method), and like most Enlightenment thinkers he assumed that this was the most reliable way to truth and knowledge in human endeavor. It was a method that all could affirm and that would yield agreeable, if not entirely uniform, conclusions. In an essay on biblical interpretation, he writes:

> Great unanimity has obtained in most of the sciences in consequence of the adoption of certain rules of analysis and synthesis: for all who work by the same rules, come to the same conclusions. And may it not be possible, that in this divine science of religion, there may yet be a very great degree of unanimity of sentiment and uniformity of practice amongst all who acknowledge its divine authority? Is the school of Christ the only school in which there can be no unanimity—no proficiency in knowledge? Is the Book of God the only volume which can never be understood alike by those who read and study it?[73]

Since the diversity of biblical interpretation contributes to denominational divisions, Campbell wanted to bring more unity to the enterprise. Such guileless optimism is characteristic of the Enlightenment and especially of nineteenth-century America. From a post-Enlightenment perspective that acknowledges the limits of and confusion within the hard sciences themselves, one must acknowledge also the impossibility of everyone coming to the same understanding, even if everyone could agree on a method. At the same time, there is something to be said for coming to some agreement of method. At least there would be some boundaries around the results, some conclusions that would be excluded, some semblance of commonality. The benefit is similar to agreeing on the definition of terminology before a conversation, in order to ensure that people are not talking past one another.

Campbell distinguishes three levels or degrees of inspiration in the texts of Scripture; that is, not all passages are equally inspired. Inspiration proper, as he defines it, concerns knowledge of supernatural things "beyond the reach of human intellect." A secondary degree of inspiration comes in the form of divine aid in recalling facts already known (either directly or indirectly)

---

72. E.g., see the discussion in Hatch, *Democratization of American Christianity*, especially 179–83.
73. A. Campbell, "Bible—Principles," 13.

by the human writer. The Holy Spirit thus keeps the writers from error. The third kind of text requires no divine aid at all and is thus not inspired. These passages declare matters that are "quite natural and common, for which inspiration is neither claimed nor pretended." In all of these instances, even in the "apparently uninteresting" matters, there is great value and importance in the words, reflecting the life and faith of the apostolic church. Moreover, even with the highest degree of inspiration, the human writers had complete freedom to choose their own style and words and means of communicating the truth.[74]

Even in its inspiration, then, the Bible comes in simple human language. As such, it is to be interpreted by the same rules as "any other book." The meaning of the text is to be "philologically ascertained"; there is no need for special rules or a divine dictionary or grammar.[75] As with any other book, Campbell does admit that there can be more than the literal or grammatical sense in Scripture. But, like Protestants before him, he is worried about, and reacting against, excessive allegorizations that are not tied to the literal sense.[76] Campbell thus takes the classic Protestant angle of folding the spiritual sense into the literal. Years earlier, he had dismissed the double, triple, and quadruple sense of Scripture as a relic of the past, soon to be confined only to the enthusiastic and weak minds among the denominations.[77]

Campbell goes on to enumerate seven "cardinal rules of interpretation."[78] Most of his principles have to do with interpreting the Bible as one would any other book from the ancient world. In fact, his first six rules would apply equally to the interpretation of any ancient document. For instance, the first rule states, "Consider first the historical circumstances of the book." As we have already seen, the identification of the historical background is the point of departure for modern exegesis. The third rule states, "To understand the meaning of what is commanded, promised, taught, . . . the same philological principles, deduced from the nature of language, or the same laws of interpretation which are applied to the language of other books, are to be applied to the language of the Bible." Notice the limitation of any allegorical readings in the sixth rule: "In the interpretation of symbols, types, allegories, and parables, this rule is supreme. Ascertain the point to be illustrated; for comparison is never to be extended beyond that point—to all the attributes, qualities, or circumstances of the symbol, type, allegory, or parable." In other

74. A. Campbell, "Bible—Principles," 15–17.
75. A. Campbell, "Bible—Principles," 17.
76. A. Campbell, "Bible—Principles," 21–22.
77. A. Campbell, "Double Sense of Scripture," 38.
78. A. Campbell, "Bible—Principles," 15, 23.

words, find the one point taught in the type or parable, and limit the interpretation to that main point.

These six rules are common to modern grammatical-historical interpretation. Campbell's seventh rule, however, is aimed at the heart of the interpreter and may be the one factor for him that distinguishes biblical interpretation from every other interpretive exercise. That rule is the cultivation of "humility," which brings the interpreter into the "understanding distance," a place where God's word can truly be heard and understood.[79] Humility is necessary to open our ears to hear God's voice. By giving attention to the character of the interpreter, Campbell is in line with the premodern tradition and not typical historical-critical exegesis. Without the proper disposition, the reader will miss the point. "Now, while the philological principles and rules of interpretation enable many men to be skillful in biblical criticism, and in the interpretation of words and sentences, who neither perceive nor admire the *things* represented by those words, the sound eye contemplates the things themselves, and is ravished with the spiritual and divine scenes which the Bible unfolds."[80] Channeling Augustine's semiotics (intentionally or not), Campbell recognizes that an interpreter may grasp the words but miss the realities to which these signs point. He assumes an ultimate end to which these words are the means. The reader should have "one aim" and "one ardent desire": to know the will of God. The humble, teachable reader will be given the grace of true understanding (God "giveth grace to the humble, " James 4:6), a certainty of knowledge "to which the man of letters alone never attained, and which the mere critic never felt."[81]

Nothing observed here about Campbell's approach to Scripture is unique. His case is worth noting because of the larger phenomenon that he exemplifies: an American frontier Protestant orthodoxy that was optimistic about the gains of modern exegetical methods and dismissive of spiritual or allegorical interpretations that promote uncertainty and division, but at the same time one that maintained the spiritual nature of Scripture and its sole, direct authority for current faith and practice.

A third and final example of the Anglo-American historical-critical method come of age, with its emphasis on the Bible only, takes us back to England. Benjamin Jowett (1817–93) was professor of Greek at Oxford and well known for his translations, especially of Plato. He was part of the Broad Church Movement, a liberal Protestant reaction to the Anglo-Catholic Oxford Movement

79. A. Campbell, "Bible—Principles," 23.
80. A. Campbell, "Bible—Principles," 24, with spelling modernized.
81. A. Campbell, "Bible—Principles," 24.

within the Church of England. Whereas the Oxford Movement valued, among other things, a return to the patristic tradition, the Broad Church Movement generally did not, a fact that is evident in writers like Farrar and Jowett. Jowett wrote a lengthy essay on biblical interpretation that appeared in 1860, in which he provides a clear statement of the principles and aims of the kind of modern, historical-critical exegesis that he advocated.[82]

Like so many before him, Jowett is motivated by his concern about the diversity of interpretation, a problem exacerbated in the wake of the Reformation. It is the same Scripture read by all, but there is little agreement about its meaning.[83] The task of the interpreter, Jowett claims, is not to add another meaning to the words, but to recover the original meaning that the original readers and hearers would have understood. The interpreter must imagine himself as a disciple of Christ or Paul and disregard everything that followed after that period. "The history of Christendom is nothing to him. . . . All the after-thoughts of theology are nothing to him." Whatever we do not understand about Scripture cannot be resolved by the conjectures of the church fathers. The interpreter should approach the text with no grand theory of interpretation.[84] The point is to "get rid of interpretation,"[85] by which he means any system of thought external to the Bible that would influence or predetermine its interpretation. The aim is simply this: "*Interpret the Scripture like any other book.*"[86]

Many of the figures discussed in this book might agree, in a qualified sense, that Scripture should be read like other books—not any book, perhaps, but other great works of literature. It is also true that previous thinkers found meanings in those other books that go beyond the letter. Not so for Jowett. For him, Scripture has only one meaning, the meaning intended by the human author and received by the original readers, thus ruling out fourfold interpretation.[87] It is the interpreter's job "to place himself as nearly as possible in the position of the sacred writer. That is no easy task."[88] It requires knowing the "inner and outer life" of the writers and their contemporaries. It often means choosing an interpretation that goes against received tradition but is more consistent with the historical setting.[89]

82. Jowett, "Interpretation," 330–433. This is the same essay chosen by David Steinmetz to represent the aims and presuppositions of modern exegesis. Steinmetz, "Superiority of Pre-critical Exegesis."

83. Jowett, "Interpretation," 330.

84. Jowett, "Interpretation," 338.

85. Jowett, "Interpretation," 384.

86. Jowett, "Interpretation," 377, emphasis original.

87. Jowett, "Interpretation," 338, 419.

88. Jowett, "Interpretation," 378.

89. Jowett, "Interpretation," 378–79.

In his own day, Jowett was a controversial figure and considered by some to be "unsound" in his theology.[90] Nevertheless, like Alexander Campbell on the American scene, Jowett strove to be a faithful Christian. Although the Bible was to be read like any other book, he still felt that Scripture, because of its content, shines above other books.[91] He also believed in the superintendence of the Spirit in its production.[92] His aim was to bring clarity to Scripture and thereby to promote unity in the church. Back on the Continent, however, not all interpreters seemed to prioritize these spiritual and ecclesiastical goals.

Getting "Behind the Text"

On the European continent, the assumptions behind the historical-critical method in its Enlightenment setting were being driven to their logical conclusions in the nineteenth century. Certain philosophical assumptions about the closed nature of the universe deeply influenced biblical interpretation. It became increasingly common among the intelligentsia to conceive of God, if he exists at all, in a deistic or pantheistic way. As such, miracles, defined as violations of the uniformity of the laws of nature, by definition do not happen.[93] This presupposition a priori rules out divine inspiration of Scripture and any miracles that it reports, including predictive prophecy, the parting of the waters, and the raising of the dead, to name a few.

Along with the new philosophical assumptions, there were new doubts about the identities and aims of the biblical authors. Once the anachronisms in the Pentateuch proved that a hand later than Moses composed the books, it would eventually be open season on the other books of the Bible. If predictive prophecy is ruled out, again a priori, then any apparent prediction that was fulfilled must have been written after the fulfillment. For instance, the Synoptic Gospels, which predict the fall of Jerusalem, must have been written after its destruction in AD 70.[94]

Pseudonymity also was suspected regarding books whose authorship had never before been questioned. The skepticism that had been reserved for

90. L. Campbell, "Introduction," ix. Jowett was admired by others. In 1885, Frederic W. Farrar, who had little patience for those who affirmed the spiritual sense of Scripture, dedicated his history of biblical interpretation to Jowett.

91. Jowett, "Interpretation," 375.

92. Jowett, "Interpretation," 382.

93. Hume, "Miracles," 111: "A miracle is a violation of the laws of nature; and as a firm and unalterable experience has established these laws, the proof against a miracle, from the very nature of the fact, is as entire as any argument from experience can possibly be imagined."

94. This assumption was popularized in the eighteenth century by, among others, Voltaire. See Dupré, *Enlightenment*, 252.

indisputable anachronism would evolve into skepticism about any aspect of a document that might strike an individual reader as anachronistic. For instance, if the Pastoral Epistles reflect an institutional church and attention to creedal formulas, then they could not have been written by Paul or anyone else before AD 70. New Testament books that exhibit such characteristics came to be called "early catholic," a handy Protestant phrase that had the practical effect of subordinating these documents within the canon. The Johannine Epistles were written by a school of John's followers; the Deutero-Paulines were forged by a later admirer of Paul.

Whether pseudonymous or simply anonymous, historical narratives in both Testaments were judged to be composed long after the events that they describe. The longer the gap between the narrated time and the time of narration, the less historically reliable the books were thought to be. Whether it was memory lapse, the accretion of later details and stories, or theological interpretation and symbolism, the stories were hopelessly tainted with the ideas and biases of later writers who redacted the received material to suit their own agendas. Such is the context of the famous Documentary Hypothesis of Julius Wellhausen (1844–1918), who carved up the Pentateuch into four distinct main sources (the Yahwist, Elohist, Deuteronomic, and Priestly sources), inspiring later exegetes to follow the trails of new, hypothetical authorial occasions. These and other developments encouraged scholars to look behind the finished textual composition to discover—that is, speculate about—the circumstances in which the texts were originally composed and used, especially in an oral setting. The term "setting in life" (*Sitz im Leben*) indicates the prehistory and use behind the written text, but it came to refer more generally to the author's original occasion and circumstances in life.

On the one hand, the Bible, as it stands, became a historical artifact, a record of what ancient Jews believed about God and Jesus of Nazareth. The text was a witness to the history of religions. But on the other hand, given the impossibility of the miracles it reports, the predictions it seems to make, the later words it puts into the mouths of Moses and Jesus, the Bible is, to the modern critic, an accumulation of layers that must be peeled away. Its accounts cannot be taken as they stand, at face value. Hence historical-critical exegesis, in addition to the other principles named thus far, became preoccupied with what really happened "behind the text." It was now the exegete's job, qua historian, to peel away not only the interpretive traditions of later Christian theology but also the layers resident in the Bible itself, to jettison anything that seems historically unlikely. If we may call this whole set of concerns historical-critical exegesis, then no school of thought reflects it better than the Tübingen school, and no project epitomizes it more than the various quests for the "historical Jesus."

The Tübingen school refers to the historical and exegetical approaches associated with professors at the University of Tübingen from about 1835 to 1860. Its most famous representative was the revisionist church historian Ferdinand Christian Baur (1792–1860). Baur and his followers attributed most of the New Testament writings, including most of the Pauline Epistles, to the so-called early catholic period of the second century. Influenced by a long history of Lutheran interpretation that took justification by grace through faith as Paul's central dogma, any document in which that doctrine was not central was suspect. According to Baur, these later writings reflect the synthesis between Jewish, Petrine Christianity and Gentile, Pauline Christianity, conspicuous especially in the Acts of Apostles. But it was another Tübingen professor, David Friedrich Strauss (1808–74), who contributed more specifically to a new reading of the Gospels.[95]

In 1835 D. F. Strauss published his massive work *Life of Jesus* (*Leben Jesu*). Strauss asserts that the early church took the Gospels to be supernatural history; since rationalism has dispensed with the supernatural aspect, it now is time to question the historicity of the Gospels. Strauss prefers the category of myth, by which he means theological ideas couched in story form.[96] With this language, he seeks to preserve the essence of the Christian faith, upholding the "eternal truths" behind Christ's miracles and resurrection, even while casting doubt on these events as "historical facts."[97] He is partly motivated by comparing the Bible with the stories told in other ancient religions; if the others are dismissed as false, then there is no good ground for accepting the biblical stories of divine agency and miracles as historically factual.[98]

The goal, then, is to go behind the text to separate what is historical or factual from what is not. To this end, Strauss describes various types of myths that may be found in the Gospels.[99] He also delineates the negative and positive "criteria by which to distinguish the unhistorical in the Gospel narrative."[100] The picture of Jesus that could stand up to historical scrutiny would eventually be called the "Jesus of history," to be contrasted with the "Christ of faith" that is presented, with all its accompanying myth and legend, in the New Testament.

95. On the Tübingen school, see Harris, *Tübingen School*. On Strauss, see Baird, *History of New Testament Research*, 1:246–58; and Frei, *Eclipse of Biblical Narrative*, 233–44.

96. Strauss, *Life of Jesus*, xxix.

97. Strauss, *Life of Jesus*, xxx.

98. Strauss, *Life of Jesus*, 69.

99. Strauss, *Life of Jesus*, 86–87.

100. Strauss, *Life of Jesus*, 87–92.

Two trajectories emerged from Strauss's influential work. Most scholars were captivated by the quest for the historical Jesus, with its seemingly endless scrutiny of biblical and historical records, speculation about what really happened, and inconclusive debates over the meaning of the evidence. Strauss's list of criteria would be taken up in subsequent studies, and similar form-critical criteria of authenticity would continue to guide the quests for the historical Jesus up to the present day.[101]

Others, however, recognized the difficulty of historical certainty and the impossibility of a bias-free search. They reacted against historicism, finding the quests to be dubious. Albert Schweitzer famously concluded that the Jesus of historical speculation ended up looking too much like a self-portrait of the researchers themselves. Schweitzer called the result a "half-historical, half-modern, Jesus."[102] Nineteenth-century theologians offered people a Jesus who was "too small" because he was made to conform to their own standards. According to Schweitzer, they weakened his commands, turning his denial of the world into our acceptance of it.[103] For all of Schweitzer's historical contextualization of Jesus as an eschatological prophet, he concludes that "it is not Jesus as historically known, but Jesus as spiritually arisen within men, who is significant for our time and can help it."[104]

Many, like Schweitzer, focused their attention instead on the Christ of faith. Contemporary with Strauss, Søren Kierkegaard anticipated the downplaying of the significance of historical evidence. Kierkegaard's Danish writings became influential in German translations around the turn of the twentieth century, and they were especially persuasive among the so-called neo-orthodox theologians. Reacting against liberal Protestant theology, Karl Barth distinguished between *Geschichte* and *Historie*, asserting that the latter is of little importance theologically. Rudolf Bultmann took up the category of myth, discussed in Strauss, and engaged in a project of demythologizing the Bible. A more recent example is Luke Timothy Johnson, who takes the Jesus Seminar's positivistic, historical-critical methods to task, replacing it with his own historical minimalism.[105]

101. Cf., e.g., Meier, *Roots of the Problem and the Person*, 168–84; Keener, *Historical Jesus*, 155–59; Stein, *Jesus the Messiah*, 46–49; Blomberg, *Historical Reliability of the Gospels*, 246–54; Blomberg, *Jesus and the Gospels*, 186–87. For an overview of historiographical issues related to Jesus, see McKnight, *Jesus and His Death*, 3–46.
102. Schweitzer, *Quest of the Historical Jesus*, 396.
103. Schweitzer, *Quest of the Historical Jesus*, 398.
104. Schweitzer, *Quest of the Historical Jesus*, 399.
105. See Barth, *Church Dogmatics*, IV/1:335–36. On Bultmann, see Baird, *History of New Testament Research*, 2:280-86; Livingston et al., *Modern Christian Thought*, 2:157–61; and Keener, *Historical Jesus*, 7–10. See also Johnson, *Real Jesus*, 81–166.

Principles of Historical-Critical Exegesis

The principles and approaches discernible in the late medieval and early modern periods came of age in the eighteenth and nineteenth centuries. The modern approach to the Bible reflected in this chapter continued to dominate the academic study of the Bible throughout the twentieth century and up to the present day. As with premodern exegetes, no two modern exegetes are exactly alike. There may not be one actual instance of the Platonic form of a modern exegete. Although no one exegete may conform to all the features we have identified as modern exegesis, there are basic, interconnected assumptions that together are identifiable as modern historical-critical exegesis and, in nearly every respect, contrast with premodern exegesis.

1. *Doubt.* There can be no doubt that one of the most influential features of intellectual life in the early modern West was doubt. New knowledge and discoveries were casting new doubt on old traditions, whether geographical, scientific, philosophical, or theological. An epistemological crisis was at hand that injected doubt into nearly everything. What used to be certain was not anymore. In such a climate, venerable and sacrosanct ecclesiastical traditions, both dogmatic and biblical, could no longer go unquestioned. Skepticism was applied to received doctrines, to the allegorical interpretations used in their support, and even to the very text of Scripture. The systematic doubt that found famous expression in Descartes's writings had been brewing for centuries before him, but it came to fruition in the modern period and continues up to today, especially when it comes to the Bible and its content.

2. *Perspicuity and right reason.* In contrast to the Roman Catholic emphasis on Scripture's obscurity, a position that had justified the institutional church's authority in interpretation, Protestants had from the beginning of the Reformations insisted on the perspicuity or clarity of Scripture, especially with regard to doctrines necessary for salvation. The early Reformers generally coupled the doctrine of perspicuity with a reliance on the Holy Spirit's aid in interpretation. By the early seventeenth century, however, some Protestant groups such as the Remonstrants stressed the preeminence of right reason for correct interpretation, apart from any direct help of the Spirit.

Again, it is not that right reason was not important before the modern period. Humans, and particularly Christians, had always valued reason. But they realized that it is severely limited and could easily falter, and it is therefore not a sound first principle or foundation for theology. For Calvin, "The testimony of the Spirit is superior to all reason."[106] The new factor in the modern period was just how important reason had become in epistemology. In the "Age of

---

106. Calvin, *Inst.* 1.7.4.

Reason," reason became the final arbiter of truth. As John Locke said, "*Reason must be our last Judge and Guide in every Thing.*"[107] Reason was now a "vital, progressive force."[108] Because the Bible was seen as perspicuous, and because human reason was capable of solving problems, there was an optimism that the one true meaning can be uncovered. There was generally less appreciation for the limits of reason, but rather an assumption that reason could penetrate through any obscurity and that readers would know when they are misusing or neglecting reason. This exaltation of reason touched nearly everyone during and after the Enlightenment. In contrast to the Augustinian and Anselmian view of "faith seeking understanding," an otherwise orthodox thinker such as Alexander Campbell could write, "With me, consistency must precede faith."[109]

Concern for the correct, scientific method rose to prominence, along with the hope that unity could be achieved in interpretation and among interpreters. The prospect for unity was music to the ears of those who lived through the cacophony of political and religious strife that characterized early modern Europe. If the interpreter would simply approach the Bible in the same objective, reasonable way that the scientist approached nature, then, as long as enough information is available, the single message of any passage could be discerned. (Of course, the scientific method is not as objective as it was once believed to be.) If enough relevant data are not available, then historical investigation is necessary to complete the exegetical method and arrive at an agreeable conclusion. In any case, all prejudices, biases, and hindrances to objective, reasonable interpretation should be set aside, including all theological convictions that are not spelled out in the text under consideration.

3. *Single, literal meaning of human author.* Modern exegetes, in reaction to the multivalence of premodern interpretation and in a noble attempt to rein in uncertain interpretations, restricted the meaning of Scripture to one sense, the literal sense. This process began in earnest in the medieval period and was carried further by Protestants, who quickly came to assert that Scripture has only one sense. That one sense, though, still allowed for christological and spiritual applications that had always been connected to it. In the modern period, the literal sense came to be narrowly identified with the single meaning intended by the human author. As Brevard Childs summarizes this shift: "The historical sense of the text was construed as being the *original* meaning of the text as it emerged in its pristine situation. Therefore, the aim of the

---

107. Locke, *Essay concerning Humane Understanding* 4.19.14, 4th ed., 427, emphasis original; see 4.17 on reason, 4th ed., 404–17. See also Descartes, *Discourse on Method*, part 2, trans. Cress, 7.
108. Livingston et al., *Modern Christian Thought*, 1:7.
109. A. Campbell, "Trinitarianism, Arianism, and Socinianism," 158. Campbell writes these words while defending his basically orthodox views on the Trinity.

interpreter was to reconstruct the original occasion of the historical reference on the basis of which the truth of the biblical text could be determined. In sum, the *sensus literalis* [literal sense] had become *sensus originalis* [original sense]."[110] Meaning was to be located somewhere in the space occupied by what the human author intended and the original recipients understood. Outside of the undisputed Letters of Paul, the human author rarely meant an identifiable individual; it included the back-history of oral traditions, literary antecedents, and final redactors.[111] But if historical critics could seek truth in a possible history behind the final form, they would. This literal sense gradually was seen to exclude predictive—and therefore christological—utterances that did not relate to the author's situation. What does the text mean? It means the one thing that the human author, at whatever stage, intended. Biblical exegesis, therefore, was reduced to the search for the sole intent of the human author.

Figure 6.1

Paul:	Letter		Spirit	
			/ \	
Origen:	Body	Soul		Spirit
			/ \	
Quadriga:	Literal	Tropological	Allegorical	Anagogical
Alternative Order:	Literal	Allegorical	Tropological	Anagogical
	(history)	(faith)	(love)	(hope)
Early Modern Protestant:	Literal (with typological and christo-logical meaning and spiritual application)			
Modern Historical-Critical:	Literal (authorial intent)			

Early modern Protestant exegesis folded the spiritual sense into the literal. Gradual marginalization of the spiritual sense became its total loss in modern historical-critical exegesis.

4. *Loss of spiritual senses.* In the late medieval and early modern periods, the fortunes of the spiritual sense can be traced from Nicholas of Lyra through

110. Childs, "Sensus Literalis," 89.

111. John Barton denies that modern exegesis, which he calls "biblical criticism," is concerned primarily with authorial intent, countering that it is concerned also with the many layers "between the earliest strata and the finished product." See Barton, *Nature of Biblical Criticism*, 69–116, here 70. In fact, however, this is precisely what is meant by author(s) in "authorial intent."

Luther to the Remonstrants. And it is a long, gradual story that moves from merely favoring the literal sense, to subsuming the spiritual sense under the literal sense, to marginalizing the spiritual sense, to, in subsequent generations, eliminating the spiritual sense altogether. For the Protestant Reformers, the one literal sense embraced spiritual interpretations. Yet the transition from considering the spiritual sense as a distinct category—the second category in the twofold sense—to folding it into the literal sense already implied a demotion of the spiritual sense. What began with the marginalization of spiritual meanings, as well as any other applications beyond what the human author intended, moved to the wholesale rejection of any fuller sense. That is, the marginalization finally became an utter loss. It was only natural that focus on the one literal sense would gradually result in the loss of the spiritual senses and any concept of fuller meaning.

If Scripture was sufficient and clear in necessary matters, and tradition was unnecessary, then the study of Scripture should focus on the literal sense, which came to be equated with and referred to also as the grammatical sense. The literal sense was narrowed to authorial intent and a literalistic account of what actually happened. If doctrinal, moral, or eschatological concepts— that is, the stuff of the threefold spiritual sense—were not explicit in the text, then those interpretations were eventually abandoned. Without any spiritual meaning, the Bible could be viewed merely as a historical document. It is true that churchmen might continue to apply biblical texts however they liked, but such applications were not to be confused with the real meaning of the passage.

For an increasing number of biblical interpreters during the Reformation, the only acceptable allegorical interpretations were those that the inspired New Testament writers provided. Thus began the notion, contrary to early and medieval thought, that the apostles, with their spiritual exegesis, are not models of exegesis for later generations.

5. *Uninspired and diverse.* Focus on the human author was accompanied by the eventual rejection of traditional notions of inspiration. Once inspiration was questioned, it was not a divine word for the church anymore. For modern exegesis, the Bible came to be treated increasingly as a gathering of merely human documents, the writing and collecting of which had nothing to do with special divine inspiration. For deists, pantheists, and skeptics, their philosophical point of view ruled out inspiration from the start. For others who personally held to a doctrine of inspiration, the modern exegetical method could be implemented usually without reference to inspiration. That is, since interpretation is a merely historical pursuit, then neutrality is demanded when it comes to inspiration and authority.

Since there was no acknowledgment of a single divine author of the various biblical books, unity of theological purpose and scope could no longer be taken for granted. Fixation on each author and his unique situation led interpreters to emphasize diversity, theological and otherwise, among the human authors. The assumption became one of disunity and contradiction, which renders exegetically unsound the age-old practice of using one Scripture to explain another. Neither could one appeal to prooftexts throughout the canon of Scripture in order to support doctrinal propositions, for the exegete now cannot presume that one biblical author agrees theologically with another on any matter. The burden of proof is on the interpreter to find any unity at all, say, between the Letters of Paul and those of Peter or John.

6. *Free from dogma*. The distinction between *sacra pagina* and *sacra doctrina* that became explicit in the high medieval period developed into an outright disjunction in the modern period, resulting in a tenuous relationship between biblical text and church doctrine. The dissolution of the bond between biblical theology and systematic theology, articulated so clearly by Gabler, affected influence in both directions. First and more obviously, the received tradition of the church was to have no influence on exegesis. Biblical interpretation, reduced to discernment of the human author's intent, should not be shaped by any doctrinal presuppositions external to the specific human author under consideration. Sound exegesis requires the exclusion of all theological prejudices. The interpreter is liberated from the constraints of dogma, free to interpret for oneself. The explicit hermeneutical use of the rule of faith, the *analogia fidei*, was no more. One is to read and see the Bible anew.

Second, from the other direction, this separation severely limited the sort of impact that Scripture could have on the church's current theology. With the removal of the spiritual senses, doctrinal formulation had to be done, if at all, exclusively at the level of the literal sense, which is to say, human authorial intent. For instance, if it is agreed that the author of Genesis 1:26 did not know about and therefore did not intend to teach anything about the Trinity, then this and any other Old Testament passage cannot be used to support trinitarianism. Or, to expand on Spinoza's example, if the exegete determines that the authors of Deuteronomy (4:24) and Hebrews (12:29) thought that God is to be identified as literal fire, but for reasons external to those books we know better, then our theology really should not be bound by Scripture. If present belief in God's incorporeality should not affect our reading of the Bible, then the Bible's various statements about God can be more easily dismissed as nothing more than ancient mythology and therefore irrelevant to our thinking about God.

Thus, if the written word is merely a human word by and about and for the ancients, then there is naturally less interest in it as an infallible guide for our own theology or philosophy. As such, the Bible is an ancient, fallible book to be examined, not a divine revelation to be revered, and certainly not a guide to doctrine. As Henri de Lubac said, to moderns the Bible is "a book that interests them, but which does not concern them."[112]

7. *Historical criticism and academic precision.* If a biblical text is to be properly understood, then the author's singular intent must be discerned and explained in one single interpretation. The discovery of this one sense, then, requires philological and historical labor. If authorial intent is the end goal of modern exegesis, then a number of tools are employed as the means to that end. Scholarly research, aided especially by archaeology, has been indispensable for contextualizing the biblical documents.[113]

Premodern exegetes assumed that the literal-historical sense is what the text says and that, in a straightforward narrative, history is related in the text. Moderns, however, lost the priority of the narrative and became preoccupied with the question of historicity, eventually separating history from text.[114] They increasingly claimed that the historical, what really happened, is seldom narrated in the text, but is more often to be found before and behind the text. Recognition that the biblical documents were not simply dropped from heaven, but that they have a past, led to intense historical investigation and reconstruction of the past. Historicity was equated with truth, and the index of meaning became located behind the text. This interminable investigation into the history behind the biblical text led both to speculation and to skepticism, which did not take the text at face value, but instead located the truth in form-critical theories about the transmission of oral traditions. Skepticism became the default attitude toward the biblical text.

The premium placed on a scholarly method that could be implemented by the use of objective reason, which enjoyed its heyday during the Enlightenment, called for precision of interpretation. At least since the time of Origen, interpretive method had been important. But the Enlightenment brought a new optimism for the method's ability to resolve uncertainty. The method required a range of philological and historical skills that belonged only to

---

112. Lubac, *Medieval Exegesis*, 2:81.

113. Again, contra John Barton, who denies that modern exegesis is preoccupied with questions of history. See Barton, *Nature of Biblical Criticism*, 187: "Biblical criticism is first and foremost a literary procedure, which tries to construe and understand the biblical texts in their context." In fact, this goal entails the means and therefore the importance of historical research.

114. See Frei, *Eclipse of Biblical Narrative*, 51–65; Legaspi, *Death of Scripture*, 6; Green, "Which Conversation Shall We Have?," 141.

scholars. Close reading and interpretation of Scripture became equated with scholarly historical and philological engagement. Ministers in training were taught the method, a method that was in many ways inimical to Christian faith. And the heirs of the same Protestant movement that once endorsed perspicuity now relegated the careful study of Scripture to the halls of academia. What Jonathan Sheehan said about Luther became the modern Protestant legacy: "The prophet Luther was a figure overshadowed by that of the scholar Luther."[115] In contrast to the premodern era, the reading of Scripture was no longer considered worship. Whereas the primary context for interpretation had been the church and its liturgy, it was now the university with its scholarly methods. Scholarly societies with no connection to the church could now gather their members to scrutinize the Bible.

Either way, whether one was Roman Catholic or Protestant, still the laity depended on an expert, professional class to help make Scripture perspicuous. But among Protestants, that professional class was more often situated in the university, not in the church. In the context of the rise of the modern, secular nation-state, there was an antagonistic relationship of university (once handmaid of the church, now of the state) versus the church. This kind of academic biblical study did not foster unity; rather, it created more fragmentation, or at least sustained the existing fragmentation, among Christians.

8. *Irrelevance of virtue.* When the light of common reason, apart from the light of the Holy Spirit, is made the primary and ultimately sole qualification for the exegetical task, then the virtue of the interpreter is not considered essential for interpretation. This implication is in stark contrast to all premodern exegesis, which assumed that only a virtuous person, illuminated by the Spirit, can truly grasp the significance of Scripture. For modern exegesis, comprehension of the Bible has nothing to do with the presence or absence of faith, hope, and love. To be sure, certain other virtues are required: neutrality, philological acumen, historical knowledge, and the like. A very popular handbook of exegesis by the German scholar Johann A. Ernesti, in its English translation, speaks at length about the "requisites of a good interpreter" and includes an appendix by Karl A. G. Keil on the "qualifications of an interpreter"; the requisites and qualifications are all intellectual and could just as easily describe an atheist or a scoundrel.[116] Once the act of interpreting the Bible is secularized—that is, seen no longer as a sacred act—then an unbeliever can be just as skilled in the task as a believer. Indeed, since the believer brings to exegesis a host of doctrinal presuppositions or baggage, then the

115. Sheehan, *Enlightenment Bible*, 8.
116. See Ernesti, *Elements of Interpretation*, 2–5, 119–24.

unbeliever may actually have the advantage in unbiased interpretation. What was once the church's book, read and expounded in the context of its life and liturgy, was now studied in the halls of the academy. The inhabitants of these halls, even if they were supported by churches, usually conducted their research apart from the church's life and liturgy and eventually apart from any reference to faith.

As we have seen, most modern exegetes did not deny faith, and many maintained a robust doctrine of inspiration. Those who maintained the faith, though, had their work cut out for them as they accepted other presuppositions that were more amenable to skeptics than to believers. Theologically conservative scholars, including fundamentalists and most evangelicals, found themselves in a precarious position, seeking to defend Christian orthodoxy after conceding most of the assumptions of modern exegesis. For, like their liberal Protestant counterparts, conservative Protestants also dismissed spiritual senses and allegorical interpretation, focused on human authorial intent, and treated the Bible merely as a repository of literalistic claims of fact. Conservatives and liberals only differed on whether those claims were literally true or literally false. Whether modern interpreters believed in divine inspiration or not, such a belief was not necessary for their brand of exegesis. The philological, historical enterprise, freed from confessional frameworks, became the genius of modern exegesis, and it could be practiced by anyone with the scientific know-how.

Reactions to the Historical-Critical Method

Modern historical criticism is the exegetical model that has dominated academic biblical studies for a couple of centuries. During the last third of the twentieth century, however, an increasing number of interpreters began to voice discontent with the historical-critical approach to Scripture. It is not simply that they called into question the conclusions of so-called higher criticism. In fact, throughout the modern period, contrary to the critical consensus, conservative commentators had strenuously defended such notions as traditional authorship and historical reliability. But they had typically done so on the basis of modern assumptions. Neither was the new discontent motivated merely by an indifferent or skeptical attitude toward historical knowledge, as was prominent among the neo-orthodox. Rather, the new criticisms, which did not come from fundamentalists, conservatives, or neo-orthodox, cut to the heart of modern exegesis. They denied that the text has any stable meaning, its author any discernible intention, and its interpreter any objective, unbiased perspective.

The approaches that deny these and other assumptions of modern hermeneutics were labeled deconstructionist and poststructuralist. They go hand in hand with postmodern thought, which, as Jean-François Lyotard famously defined it, is "incredulity toward metanarratives."[117] For the devout postmodern, all textual meaning depends on and is subject to the reader, who creates whatever meaning the reader wishes. The reader, not the text or its original author, becomes the chief factor in interpretation.

This is not the place to rehearse the postmodern critique of modern hermeneutics or to offer a full-blown critique of the critique.[118] In short, much of the postmodern impulse is consistent with the principles of premodern exegesis. There is more to interpretation than recovering the intent of the human author, if that recovery is even possible. There may not be only one, single truth to discover in a single passage. The community that receives the text is not unbiased in its reception, but plays a role in shaping the interpretation. In these and other areas, postmodern interpretation has been instrumental in chastening the hubris of the historical-critical method and thus has opened the door to the reconsideration of premodern exegesis.

At the same time, postmodernism went too far in its critique. In reaction to the modern emphasis on discovering the single, true meaning of the text, postmodernism claims that there is no objective truth. Postmodern exegesis, therefore, tends to deny that authorial intent is discernible at all or that the text has any meaning apart from an interpreter. The reader alone is decisive. Claims such as these, all related to the suspicion of metanarratives, are themselves part of a metanarrative of which we may justly be suspicious.

This shift in biblical hermeneutics may be seen, for instance, in the proliferation of postmodern readings. Postmodern interpreters rightly criticized the modern assumption that an exegete could and should approach the biblical text with complete objectivity and neutrality. The observation that bias is impossible to avoid led to the prescriptive advice that objectivity should not even be attempted. Once a vice for the modern literary scholar to avoid, "eisegesis," reading one's own interpretation into the text, was turned into

117. Lyotard, *Postmodern Condition*, xxiv. For a useful introduction to postmodernism, see Grenz, *Primer on Postmodernism*. Note also the various styles of Christian engagement with postmodernism found in writers such as Wells, *Above All Earthly Pow'rs*; and J. Smith, *Who's Afraid of Postmodernism?* And for a powerful critique of postmodernism and pluralism as a philosophy, see Alvin Plantinga, *Warranted Christian Belief*, 422–57.

118. For both, see Vanhoozer, *Is There a Meaning in This Text?* See also the brief assessment of postmodern exegesis in Bockmuehl, *Seeing the Word*, 50–55.

a postmodern virtue. Postmodern interpreters are encouraged to approach the text with a critical literary theory of some sort or another that governs how the text is interpreted. In many cases, this move means that readers are overt about their biases, and interpretation is self-consciously perspectival.

Not only are different exegetical perspectives encouraged, but since there is no objective meaning in the text itself and no interpretive control on the meaning that can be imposed on a text, there is also no way to assess the value of one interpretation over another. As in other areas of culture influenced by postmodernism, evaluation is unnecessary and incongruent with the presupposition that meaning is provided by the individual interpreter. Thus postmodern biblical readings are as varied as the disciplines and interests of the interpreters. The resulting fragmentation is bewildering. A sense of the diversity is evident in the program units associated with the Society of Biblical Literature and its annual meeting, the premier conference for biblical scholars. Here are some of the ways that interpreters in this society describe their different hermeneutical lenses (simply insert "hermeneutics," "theory," or "criticism" after the following entries): African, African American, animal, Asian and Asian American, Eastern Orthodox, ecological, ethnic Chinese, feminist, gender, ideological, Islanders, Jewish, Korean, Latino/a and Latin American, Latter-Day Saints, LGBTI/Queer, metaphor, minoritized, performance, postcolonial, psychological, social-scientific, and trauma. Identity hermeneutics, not unlike identity politics, results in endless division.

Some of the practitioners of these approaches would no doubt defend the thoroughgoing postmodern line that there is no meaning in the text itself that is not provided by the interpreter. Others, however, would still fall back on the historical-critical method as the default instrument for investigating issues such as historical background and authorial intent, to the extent that those questions matter. In either case, functionally, it is more in the realm of current application where the postmodern reading fits. In this way, postmodern hermeneutics can coexist more or less comfortably in the same society as historical criticism. Even as postmodern and perspectival readings proliferate, the underlying assumptions of the modern historical-critical model still dominate the academy when it comes to purely historical, descriptive questions about the background and origin of the biblical text.

Part 2

Letter and Spirit

7

(Ir)Reconcilable Differences?

"The king led me into the wine cellar" [Song 1:4]. . . . In this cellar there are four large jars full of honeyed sweetness, whose names are simple history, allegory, morality, anagogy. . . . The doorway to this storeroom—that is, to holy Scripture—is the correct faith; but the key, humility. He who wants to enter into the storeroom of the Lord—that is, into holy Scripture—must enter through doorway and key, namely, through faith and humility.

—Eadmer of Canterbury[1]

"Why do you spend money for that which is not bread?" [Isa. 55:2]. You, that is, who follow the letter that kills, not caring about spiritual understanding nor beauty and morality, but about a superfluity of gloss.

—Peter Cantor[2]

By identifying the literal sense with the original sense the task of biblical interpretation has become a highly speculative enterprise. The literal sense of the text no longer functions to preserve fixed literary parameters; rather, because of the preoccupation of exegesis with origins, the literal sense dissolves before the hypothetical

1. Eadmer of Canterbury, *Liber de Sancti Anselmi similitudinibus* 194 (PL 159:707D, 708C).
2. Peter Cantor, *On Isaiah*, quoted in Smalley, *Bible in the Middle Ages*, 243n1.

191

reconstructions of the original situations on whose recovery correct
interpretation allegedly depends.

—Brevard Childs[3]

The previous chapters, though not entirely free of assessment, attempted
to offer a reliable analysis of the dominant interpretive approaches in
the history of exegesis and to understand the principles and presuppositions
behind those approaches. It remains now to inquire into the prescriptive task.
That is, in light of the preceding account of the history of biblical interpretation, it is time to take stock of the differences between premodern and modern
principles of exegesis and, with this knowledge in mind, to ask what Christian
biblical interpretation should look like today.

My contention is that each approach, if pursued without restraint, differs
from the other so much as to be nearly incompatible. And alas, the distinct
approaches are frequently separated from one another and portrayed and
practiced without restraint. But if they are reunited and accompanied by
the proper controls, then the approaches need not be antagonistic but rather
complementary. In order to develop this thesis, we need to explore the weaknesses of each approach on its own, what each looks like unchecked, and
then consider the proper controls and strengths that can bring them into
harmony. First, though, where do the main differences lie between premodern
and modern exegesis?

Differences between Approaches

There may be other ways to discuss exegetical tendencies throughout two
millennia of biblical interpretation than by dividing them into premodern and
modern. Certainly there are more complex modes. These categories, though,
reflect the most significant watershed in this history and therefore can justifi-
ably serve as points of departure. As should be clear throughout the previous
chapters, premodern exegesis is not a monolithic entity whose practitioners
rigidly followed a uniform method. Instead, it is a category that circumscribes
a vast array of figures, including Alexandrians and Antiochenes, Gregory of
Nyssa and Nicholas of Lyra, and even Luther and Calvin. The same is true
of modern exegesis, which includes all manner of orthodox believers and
heterodox skeptics, trinitarians, Unitarians, and pantheists alike.

3. Childs, "Sensus Literalis," 90.

The question at hand regards what is peculiar to each sweeping category. To paint with a broad but accurate stroke, we have seen that premodern interpretation focuses more on the "spirit" of the text and all that the spiritual sense entails, whereas the modern approach focuses on the "letter" of the text and all that the literal sense came to mean. In other words, if biblical interpretation is meant to be twofold, of the letter and of the spirit, then premodern exegesis affirms both but emphasizes the spiritual, while modern exegesis dispenses with the spiritual and emphasizes the literal, understood narrowly as human authorial intent. For the sake of this discussion, premodern exegesis may be identified more with the spiritual sense and its most celebrated interpretive technique, allegory; modern exegesis may be identified more with the literal sense, which, in historical-critical interpretation, is reduced to human authorial intent.

These different emphases had all kinds of implications that can be regarded variously as either repercussions or causes. With ancient exegesis, which stressed the spiritual sense, the reading and interpretation of Scripture were carried out primarily, if not exclusively, in a spiritual—that is to say, liturgical—context. Scripture was the church's book, read through the lens of the church's dogma, and handled (literally and figuratively) by believers in a reverent and religious way. After a very long moment of transition that led to modern exegesis, the Bible was read, by believers and unbelievers alike, apart from confessional frameworks and dogmatic biases, and just as often outside of any specifically spiritual or liturgical setting.

A précis such as this is not intended to obscure certain complexities. There is a real sense in which depicting the two options as "allegory" and (or, versus) "the literal sense" is not an adequate account of premodern and modern interpretation. On the one hand, premodern interpreters were, or at least were supposed to be, interested in the literal sense. On the other hand, some modern interpreters, lay and professional alike, are apt to see in biblical narratives all kinds of allegorical meanings. It is also not the case that modern exegetes are careful with details and that premoderns were haphazard. Premodern interpreters could spend a copious amount of ink on the details of meanings, distinctions, etymologies, and intertextual connections of individual words. They were not uncritical readers.

As Frances Young points out, there is actually a great deal of overlap in the exegetical methods of different eras. She claims that the chief difference between ancient and modern exegesis has to do not so much with methods as with presuppositions and worldviews, with assumptions and big-picture questions. As such, there is more going on in the exegetical process than a strict choice between literal and allegorical. To the degree that they are useful descriptions, it is better to think of them on a spectrum, with something like woodenly literalistic on one end and entirely metaphorical or allegorical on the other.[4] Where particular exegetes lie on the spectrum depends in part on their individual and cultural assumptions about the biblical text and God's relation to it.

And, with regard to exegetical results, these cultural assumptions can be more meaningful than methods. From this perspective, from one era to another (or, as in this book, from one chapter to the next) the differences appear to be fairly minor, of degree but not of kind. But, skipping over a few centuries, the transition from premodern to modern may appear to be qualitative. That is, the differences of degree seem to amount to a difference of kind. The culture of interpretation shifts so much between ancient and modern that, if ancient and modern Christians were to sit down together to study the same text of Scripture, it might seem as if they were looking at completely different texts. Too many degrees of separation on the spectrum make the continuity difficult to see.

Using the image of a spectrum as a point of departure, I add that much of the difference in approach to the biblical text is evident in the sorts of questions interpreters lead with or find to be of utmost importance to the exegetical task. In other words, which questions point to the text's true meaning and are the sine qua non of exegesis? On one end of the spectrum, one might ask, What does this text tell us about God and his relationship with his people? What are the questions that the biblical text itself raises? What should we believe, do, and hope for? What is the message for the church? Such questions are, generally speaking, the primary concern of premodern exegesis. On the other end, one might ask, What did the ancient author(s) intend to convey? What did the original audience understand? What really happened? These questions are, generally speaking, the primary concern of modern exegesis. These two sets of questions both aim to uncover truth, yet they represent very different approaches to the biblical text. What if an interpreter had to choose only one or the other set of questions as the true index of meaning? Happily, we are not forced to choose one apart from the other. Both types of questions are important; they need not be mutually exclusive or irreconcilable. But some interpreters have indeed chosen to claim one set of questions to the near exclusion of the other.

Such questions probe to the heart of one of the primary concerns of this book: In light of the various historical trajectories, how should Christians proceed with responsible and faithful biblical interpretation? What can be

4. See the discussion in F. Young, *Biblical Exegesis*, 119–39.

done to ease the tension often felt between theological and historical approaches to Scripture? What are the advantages and disadvantages of each method? Are the approaches irreconcilable? If they are irreconcilable, then it will be difficult or impossible to retrieve anything of value from both. In this case, an interpreter must choose one or the other or neither approach. But if the approaches are not mutually exclusive, then an interpreter might find something worth retrieving and putting into practice from both approaches.

The historical survey has also shown that these two approaches have often been portrayed as contraries. Indeed, the modern historical-critical method of exegesis was based on the rejection of a fuller, spiritual sense. With good reason, then, some scholars have suspected that these approaches are irreconcilable. At the end of his account of the rise of modern academic study of the Bible, Michael Legaspi stresses the incompatibility of the two ways of reading the Bible: "I believe that the scriptural Bible and the academic Bible are fundamentally different creations oriented toward rival interpretive communities. Though in some ways homologous, they can and should function independently if each is to retain its integrity."[5]

In order to judge whether the approaches are indeed irreconcilable or two mutually exclusive pursuits, we must see what each could look like on extreme ends of the spectrum.

The Real Problem

Exegesis can go wrong in all sorts of ways. For our present purposes, however, we want to see how landing on one side of the spectrum between literal and spiritual can lead to imbalance. In other words, very few interpreters are all letter or all spirit, but the closer they come to either extreme, the more liable they are to err.

Allegory Unbridled

The primary complaint lodged against the distinct spiritual sense, often condensed into "allegory" by its opponents, is that it is not tied sufficiently to the literal sense. Allegory runs amok when it is severed from the literal sense and the interpreter effectively ignores the literal sense in its literary and historical contexts. It encourages spiritual speculation that is removed from the literal sense. One worry is that the search for multiple meanings

5. Legaspi, *Death of Scripture*, 169. Levering, *Participatory Biblical Exegesis*, 141, also notes the challenge of harmonizing premodern with historical-critical exegesis.

undermines the stability of any meaning whatsoever and—here is the rub—
that interpreters will find in Scripture only what they already believe or want
to prove. Frederic Farrar states the concern clearly: "When once the principle
of allegory is admitted, when once we start with the rule that whole passages
and books of Scripture say one thing when they mean another, the reader
is delivered, bound hand and foot, to the caprice of the interpreter. He can
be sure of absolutely nothing except what is dictated to him by the Church,
and in all ages the authority of 'the Church' has been falsely claimed for the
presumptuous tyranny of false prevalent opinions."[6] Farrar went on to reject
the quadriga in particular as a tool of the Roman Church. It encouraged the
doctrine of Scripture's obscurity, ensuring that only the magisterium could
interpret it.[7] In short, the admission of allegorical interpretation means admit-
ting the worst kind of eisegesis: reading into the text whatever one wills—in
this case, whatever the teaching magisterium wills. Interpretation is limited
only by the interpreter's imagination. In a sense, the meaning is too wide
open and needs to be narrowed.

To be fair, the history of theology has time and again proved this concern
to be valid. From the Protestant perspective, medieval allegorical exegesis was
often used to bolster a controversial Roman doctrine. One example is the
famous bull issued by Pope Innocent III in 1198, *Sicut universitatis conditor*.
In this bull, Innocent offered an allegorical interpretation of the fourth day of
creation (Gen. 1:14–19). The "greater light," the sun, was the pope, and the
"lesser light," the moon, was the king. Based on this questionable interpretive
move, the pope explained that the dignity of the civil, temporal ruler is inferior
to that of the spiritual ruler, and the king derives his inferior authority from
the pope, just as the moon derives its light from the sun.[8]

Another problem with neglecting the literal sense in favor of the spiritual
sense is the tendency to dismiss a text too quickly as absurd, ahistorical, or
impossible. The difficulty may come in the form of a detail in a command or
in a narrative that is at first puzzling and therefore is set aside. Contributing
to this problem is the very rule articulated by Origen: any text that is impossible to reconcile on the literal level should be understood only in a spiritual
way. But this rule is valid only if the literal sense is actual nonsense. As we
have seen, Origen made this move with some of the food laws in the Old
Testament. He could not allow any literal sense to the prohibitions against
eating what were translated as goatstags and griffins.[9] Origen, as well as

6. Farrar, *History of Interpretation*, 239.
7. Farrar, *History of Interpretation*, 296–300.
8. Innocent III, *Sicut universitatis conditor*, 117–18 (PL 214:377).
9. Origen, *Princ.* 4.3.2.

others, misunderstood the animals mentioned in Deuteronomy 14:5, 12, and Leviticus 11:3.[10] Rather than digging deeper or entertaining the possibility of mistranslation or misunderstanding of the Hebrew terms for fauna, he interpreted the laws only spiritually. Similarly, Augustine tended to dismiss the literal restriction against boiling a goat in its mother's milk, a command that later commentators struggled with on the literal level.[11] These cases show why one should never say that an event certainly never happened as narrated in Scripture or that a law given in Scripture was impossible to carry out.

The difficulty on the literal level may also come in the form of a doctrinal or moral challenge. For example, another common interpretive rule was that nothing should be interpreted literally about God that is not proper or fitting of God. This rule is certainly useful when it comes to some of the anthropomorphic and anthropopathic depictions of God in Scripture. But this same rule could also be used to dismiss any hard saying about who God is or about his moral expectations for his people or, for that matter, any difficult teaching that needs to be heard. For instance, most Christians are well aware that some of Jesus's hard sayings should be viewed as hyperbolic. When Jesus says that the one who looks at a woman lustfully ought to gouge out his right eye (Matt. 5:28–29), readers understand that this should not be taken literally, for the fault lies not with the right eye, and that action alone will not remedy a sinful heart.[12] In fact, Christians are so skilled at this kind of spiritual interpretation that they can easily miss the force of the statement and the gravity of the sin. The point of these sorts of passages is to get readers to pay more rather than less attention to Scripture and its teaching. One of the main tasks of Scripture is to confront, challenge, and overturn our thinking. Unless the interpreter's thought is already sufficiently formed by Scripture, reliance on the spiritual sense could be a cover for ignoring the hard texts and avoiding the necessary struggle.

In a certain sense, then, hasty reliance on the spiritual sense unnecessarily restricts and discounts valid meanings that could be conveyed by the literal sense. John Goldingay expresses a similar concern that Christocentric, trinitarian, and creedal readings will narrow and determine the message of Scripture to us. "The aim of interpretation is to enable the Scriptures to confront us, widen our thinking, reframe our thinking, rescue us from our narrowness and deliver us from the way our thinking and lives are decisively shaped by our being modern or postmodern, Western or non-Western people.

10. Origen, *Princ.* 4.3.2, ed. Butterworth, 464nn5–6.
11. For this example, see Smalley, *Bible in the Middle Ages*, 303–6.
12. Origen makes this point in *Princ.* 4.3.3.

The vocation of theological interpretation is to encourage that process and not let it be constrained by christocentrism, trinitarianism or an unqualified submission to the Christian tradition."[13] For Goldingay, because the Bible is about God, "historical exegesis" on its own is sufficiently theological.[14] It is a legitimate concern that the lens or window through which the text is viewed becomes the very object of viewing, thus obscuring what was the ostensible object. In a similar vein, Alexander Campbell argues against reading Scripture through the lens of any creed, for interpreters will only find in the Bible the content of what they already believe. "If I must examine the Bible through the creed, then the creed is my eyes—my artificial eyes, (for it cannot be my natural eyes)—my spectacles. If my spectacles are green glass, the Bible is also green; if blue, the Bible is blue; and as is the creed, so is the Bible to me. I am a Calvinist, or an Arminian, or a Fullerite, according to my spectacles or my creed, my 'established opinions, customs, and regulations.'"[15] According to Campbell, presuppositions impede the objectivity necessary for discerning the truth. When a reader approaches the Bible through the lens of any philosophy or system of thought other than the Bible itself, it obscures the message of the Bible.

Perhaps only a few interpreters have taken the spiritual sense to the extremes against which Campbell and Goldingay warn. Without proper checks, however, it does not take much imagination to see how interpreters could exploit the spiritual sense to prove what they already believe or want to believe.

Historical Criticism Unbridled

If the problems associated with allegorical interpretation relate to the neglect of the literal sense, then it should come as no surprise that, with regard to Christian interpretation, the most significant problems associated with historical criticism relate to the neglect of the spiritual sense. The historical-critical method may be described as focusing on the literal sense alone, understood narrowly as the one meaning intended by the human author. This narrowing to a single historical event—with a single human author in a particular place with one message to be received by one audience at one point in time—certainly expresses an important truth about the provenance of every text in the Bible. But when this point is emphasized and taken to its logical conclusion, when historicity becomes the sole focus, then two problems arise for biblical interpretation.

13. Goldingay, *Do We Need the New Testament?*, 176; see 157–76 for his fuller critique.
14. Goldingay, *Do We Need the New Testament?*, 157–60.
15. A. Campbell, "Reply," 209.

The first problem has to do with the inscrutability of that single historical event of composition. Take the central pursuit of modern exegesis: authorial intent (whoever the author or authors of the text or behind the text may be). Although the intent behind some and perhaps most texts is clear (as in Luke 1:1–4 and John 20:30–31), statements of intent are not exhaustive explanations, and the intent behind entire documents and individual passages alike can be notoriously elusive. The further removed the author is from the context of today's reader and the less that is known about the author's original context, the more difficult it is to discern that author's intent. If there is any uncertainty in interpreting a particular text, then skepticism is the result, for the mind of the author is ultimately impenetrable.

Even if one knows the biblical author's precise intent, recall that modern critics for various reasons came to see biblical narratives as historically unreliable. The text itself, even the author's intent, is viewed with skepticism. John Dominic Crossan, famous for his search for the real Jesus behind the biblical text, admits this approach: "There is an ancient and venerable principle of biblical exegesis that states that, if it looks like a duck, walks like a duck, and quacks like a duck, it must be a camel in disguise."[16] This sort of skepticism, of course, is not "ancient and venerable," but thoroughly modern. The truth, what really happened and what was really said, lies behind the text.

There is a difference between, on the one hand, affirming that a narrative account rarely depicts an event as a camera would have recorded it and, on the other hand, judging the text as guilty until proved innocent. It is one thing to think critically and carefully about the text; it is quite another thing to begin with the assumption that the text is covering up (intentionally or not) the real truth. Historical criticism has tended to the latter, with the presumption of unreliable history, seeking to shift the burden of proof to anyone who takes any story or testimony in Scripture at face value. Related to skepticism about historicity is the presumption of diversity and difference among the biblical authors, to the degree that the onus for finding any overarching unity is on the interpreter.

Take, for example, the well-known problem of the authorship of the Pastoral Epistles, which most scholars consider pseudonymous. Arguments for pseudonymity that appeal to a different style and theology in comparison to Paul's "authentic" letters are ultimately circular, begging the question about the control group and ignoring the multiple explanations for the different style and theology belonging to Paul and/or his amanuenses. Evidence that allegedly points to a second-century date—concern for church polity,

16. Crossan, "Why Jesus Didn't Marry," 5.

creedal formulas, delay of the parousia, and so on—could also reasonably reflect the concerns of Paul's later years. In addition to plausible defenses of Pauline authorship based on the Pastorals themselves, patristic testimony to their authenticity is unanimous (which is not the case for some other New Testament books). Although the case for the pseudonymity of the Pastorals is, at best, indecisive, based as it is on speculations that are often uncritical and unquestioned, it has nevertheless somehow become a dogma in New Testament scholarship.[17]

Ignorance about an author's identity and intent, the lack of evidence about the oral and written sources that precede the finished products, skepticism about what is narrated in those finished products, and other obstacles have not stopped scholars from reconstructing the historical scenarios that allegedly lie behind the texts. Otherwise sound and measured reconstructions can, in the hands of historical critics, become excessively speculative. For instance, the rather obvious truth that there is some relationship of dependence among the Synoptic Gospels has led some scholars not merely to posit the existence of the hypothetical written document Q but also to speak of its multiple layers of redaction and to provide a critical edition of Q, complete with its own concordance.[18]

What lies behind the text, whether we mean the layers of sources behind the text itself or the events as they really happened, becomes the object of interminable speculation. And the speculation is not limited only to plausible scenarios; scholars appear eager to defend any reconstruction that is merely possible. After all, almost any scenario, even if implausible, can be imagined as possible.[19]

Ironically, one of the common criticisms leveled by moderns against allegorical interpretation is that it leads to speculation far removed from the text at hand and that it serves as a means to show off the creativity of the interpreter. Yet the historical-critical method, as generally practiced, includes no less speculation, albeit of a different flavor. Unrestrained, premodern spiritual speculation has been traded in for unrestrained, modern historical speculation. J. J. Conybeare was correct two centuries ago in observing that modern critical exegesis, in comparison with premodern exegesis, "may be thought to open a wider field for the exertions of human ingenuity, for the free and

17. For an accessible overview of this issue, see Johnson, *Writings of the New Testament*, 375–82.

18. Robinson, Hoffmann, and Kloppenborg, *Critical Edition of Q*. See also Mack, *Lost Gospel*; Kloppenborg, *Q, the Earliest Gospel*; Borg, *Lost Gospel Q*.

19. For a memorable critique of such speculative reconstructions, see Lewis, "Modern Theology and Biblical Criticism," 152–66.

luxuriant speculations of conjectural criticism."[20] The speculations of the historical-critical method on any given text equal or exceed the speculations involved in many allegorical interpretations. "Instead of achieving a new level of objectivity by restricting the primary sense of the text to its literal meaning, the plain sense has become the captive of countless speculative theories of historical and literary reconstruction."[21]

Another irony related to the issue of speculation is the modern exegete's more fundamental criticism that the spiritual sense, by allowing multiple meanings, put the notion of any single meaning in doubt. The presence of multiple senses, Farrar claimed, "is subversive of all exactitude."[22] In order to curtail the ambiguity that accompanies multiple senses, historical-critical exegesis attempts to provide objectivity and exactitude by pursuing the one single meaning. But because authorial intent is ultimately inconclusive and its pursuit entails speculation, modern exegetes rarely achieve consensus or any "exactitude" on the one true meaning of the text. From macro-questions about an author's overall theology to micro-questions about the exact meaning of a single word or phrase, there is little agreement among commentators. As turning the pages of any exhaustive modern commentary will reveal, nearly every verse of the Bible is contested or contestable, having at least two or three possible interpretations. Interpretive certainty is no easier for modern exegesis to achieve than it was for premodern exegesis. Some solutions are more certain, perhaps, but other matters once held as certain are now doubted.

Besides, "exactitude," defined as the absence of any and all ambiguity in the affirmation of the one true meaning of the text, may not be the point of reading Scripture. Multiplicity of interpretations is not necessarily a problem for a premodern reader, who, like Augustine, could find great benefit in multiple interpretations.[23] But the proliferation of commentaries with competing interpretations and solutions undermines an allegedly objective scientific method aimed at finding the one true meaning. To say, as the historical critic seems obliged to admit, that there is one true authorial intent on which interpretation of a particular biblical document must be based, but we cannot be sure which possible interpretation is certainly correct—that is not obviously better than simply allowing multiple meanings from the start. Because of the problem of historical inscrutability, the modern exegete, bound to the original

20. Conybeare, *Bampton Lectures*, 330.
21. Childs, "Sensus Literalis," 90–91.
22. Farrar, *History of Interpretation*, 296.
23. Augustine, *De doctrina Christiana* 2.6.7–8, trans. Green, 32–33; *Civ.* 11.19, trans. Dyson, 472–73.

historical event behind the text, must defer the question of truth in hope that more historical work will be done.

From a Christian perspective, a second main problem arises for modern exegesis when exclusive focus is turned to the literal sense, understood as historicity and authorial intent, apart from the spiritual sense: the exclusion of faith from biblical interpretation. It is not that a Christian cannot practice historical-critical exegesis. It is, rather, that faith commitments (Christian or otherwise) are expected to play no role whatsoever in interpretation. Objectivity, which is to say, no disposition, is really the only disposition required. As a purely descriptive endeavor, historical-critical exegesis practices something like methodological atheism. To be fair, this aim for neutral objectivity originated in the context of unbridled allegory, and it seemed like the best answer to interpreters who would read their own preconceptions into any text and call it exegesis. As a solution to this problem, however, not only are personal beliefs and feelings set aside (as if doing so were truly possible), but also the faith of the historic church.

The method of interpretation has to be scholarly and scientific, which means that the object of investigation must be handled accordingly. Apart from all personal commitments, the Bible becomes little more than an ancient artifact to be scrutinized by scientific, scholarly processes. As the orthodox Presbyterian Charles Hodge claimed, "The Bible is to the theologian what nature is to the man of science."[24] Hodge went on to explain at great length the similarities between the scientific and theological methods.[25] The problem with Hodge's exposition is not that there are no similarities. Rather, it is that everything he describes about correct interpretation is on the level of intellectual exercise, and the task that he describes, theological as well as scientific, may just as well be carried out by the disinterested scholar. In modern exegetical theory, little room is given for appreciation, love, and wonder of the object of study—qualities that Hodge no doubt possessed—particularly as they might aid interpretation. Interest is seen not as a help but a hindrance, a skewing factor; disinterest is the interpretive virtue.

An admittedly extreme illustration might show how the historical-critical method, absent any and all spiritual import, tends to treat the Bible. Contrast two ways to study a human being: on the one hand, the careful investigation conducted by lovers on their honeymoon with, on the other hand, the careful investigation conducted by a scientist on a cadaver or by a medical examiner at an autopsy. Utilizing all the right methods and tools, the scientist examines

24. Hodge, *Systematic Theology*, 1:10.
25. Hodge, *Systematic Theology*, 1:10–15.

the body with precision and comes to discover many things about the deceased person. Now a lover comes to know his spouse no less and no less precisely than the scientist would know a cadaver. But the knowledge gained by each is far different, and the methods for gaining the knowledge are equally different. The lover and the scientist could even be the same person. If so, the scientific examination, to be objective and thorough, should remain unaffected by any feelings of the lover acting later as scientist. There are two totally different sets of facts, ends, and motivations—two completely different relationships toward the known object. And, we must admit, what is known by the lover about his spouse is, except perhaps in a medical emergency, much more important than what a scientist can know about a cadaver subjected only to academic study.

Lest this illustration seem dubious, consider how a biblical text is treated in a technical commentary in the classic, historical-critical genre. It is typically carved up like a cadaver. A conventional example is found in what is perhaps the most comprehensive modern commentary on Song of Songs. The commentator treats the poem's first instance of "kiss" (Song 1:2) thus: "Kiss," in most places in the Old Testament, "is a matter of at least one mouth applied to a variety of objects—mouth, lips, hands, feet, an idol, a calf."[26] In its exhaustive discussion of the word "kiss," the commentary proceeds to leave no philological stone unturned. The reader of the commentary, arguably given too much information about a kiss, is not left with the feeling of love that is "more delightful than wine" (Song 1:2 NIV). Gone is the genuinely human passion that the word "kiss" would normally evoke—memories of a first kiss, the anticipation of a kiss, the unexpected kiss, the quotidian kiss, the short and affectionate kiss, the long and sensuous kiss. Anyone who has spent much time kissing will sense that the critical commentary leaves something to be desired. And anyone who has spent much time with historical-critical exegesis will recognize that this is not an isolated example.

Rather than providing a definition of "kiss" or a discourse on its linguistic cognates, when Bernard of Clairvaux comes to the word "kiss" in Song of Songs, he speaks immediately of "the grace released by the touch of those lips" and of how "I ask to be kissed by the kiss of his mouth." Here the joy of the kiss is not quenched. "O happy kiss, and wonder of amazing self-humbling which is not a mere meeting of lips, but the union of God with man. The touch of lips signifies the bringing together of souls."[27] By invoking the themes of grace, longing, and union, the allegorizer Bernard actually comes closer than

26. Pope, *Song of Songs*, 297; Bray, *Biblical Interpretation*, 164, cites this example to make a similar point.
27. Bernard of Clairvaux, *Sermons on the Song of Songs*, Sermon 2, trans. Evans, 215–17.

the modern exegete to conveying the significance of a kiss. His description is not of a cadaver, but of a living, vibrant reality.[28]

The scholarly style of investigation typical of a historical-critical commentary is reminiscent of an old scene from *The Simpsons* in which the brilliant scientist Professor Frink is a substitute teacher for a kindergarten class. He is trying to explain to the five-year-old children how a corn-popper push toy works. As he moves the toy on its wheels back and forth in front of him and the balls dance with the movement, he describes how "the compression and expansion of the longitudinal waves cause the erratic oscillation—you can see it there—of the neighboring particles." One of the children interrupts to ask, "Can I play with it?" The professor barks, "No, you can't play with it! You won't enjoy it on as many levels as I do."[29] It is not that there should be no enjoyment on the scientific level. The problem is that he thinks no one can or should enjoy it except on that level. In his obsession with the scientific explanation, along with his resolve to inflict it on an unwilling audience, he has obscured the true end of the toy.

What if Scripture was not intended to be dissected and picked apart in the way that historical criticism often advocates? David Steinmetz described the tension that many scholars came to recognize in the latter half of the twentieth century: "No one wanted to abandon historical-critical exegesis as an approach to Scripture, but it was increasingly clear to many historians that the historical-critical method was a marvelous instrument for answering some questions posed by the text but clumsily inarticulate in dealing with others."[30]

Not everyone who practices the historical-critical method treats the biblical text merely as the object of scientific study and bars all spiritual significance from consideration. Indeed, there are very few who would devote themselves to deep study of Scripture who do not have, or did not at one time have, some spiritual interest in the book. It is beyond dispute, however, that the method's purpose is to provide a merely historical account of the text and to exclude the biases of the church's faith and its spiritual purposes from exegesis. It encourages dispassionate, value-neutral investigation of an object that is otherwise meant to evoke the affections as well as doctrinal and moral judgments. More to the point, on the assumption that meaning is limited to human authorial intent, Christ would be excluded from the Old Testament, and anyone who

28. In the history of interpretation, from Origen onward, it is the modern commentator who is the anomaly here, not Bernard.

29. *The Simpsons*, season 6, episode 21, "The PTA Disbands," directed by Swinton O. Scott III, written by Jennifer Crittenden, aired April 16, 1995, on Fox.

30. Steinmetz, "Doing History as Theologians," 179.

thinks otherwise, including the New Testament writers, is doing violence to the text. Christian ends simply are not in view.

Perhaps the starkest differences between extreme allegory and extreme historical criticism are due to genre and purpose, or telos. As different as an autopsy is from a honeymoon or the scientific explanation of the push toy from a child playing with it, so is the difference between a historical-critical commentary and a sermon. They address different audiences for different purposes. They ask and answer a different set of questions.

This recognition of two extremes, though, leads back to the question of whether these two different approaches can ever work in harmony. How can the spiritual sense avoid entirely subjective interpretations that make the Bible into a prooftext for prior opinions? How can historical criticism be employed in a way that does not constantly undermine Christian faith? Can we live in both worlds, and can they be the same world? The approaches can be compatible, but only with the proper controls in place, the most important of which is that each approach is allowed to contribute to the discussion.

Proper Controls

The past abuse of these two broad approaches to Scripture does not nullify any and all proper use. If certain limits or controls are observed, the two approaches need not be directly opposed to one another.

Allegory within Limits

The primary concern of those who oppose the spiritual sense, as we have seen, is that there are no limits or controls to what one can find in Scripture. That is, once one admits meaning beyond the literal sense, there is nothing to stop interpreters from imposing their own meanings on the text and calling it spiritual exegesis. Although instances of unbridled allegory are all too easy to find throughout the history of interpretation, this is not how the spiritual sense was intended to be used. It is clear that early Christian interpreters, especially since the time of Irenaeus, have advocated the use of proper limits on the spiritual sense. In fact, all of the following controls were acknowledged by premodern interpreters, as demonstrated in earlier chapters.

1. *Sensus literalis*. If biblical interpretation should be twofold and spiritual interpretation errs most egregiously by passing over the literal sense, then the first solution is to tie the spiritual sense to the literal, as traditional premodern interpreters have always maintained. The literal sense is the first

step. All interpretation must first take seriously the actual words of the text. One must read the lines before one reads between the lines. With regard to the spiritual sense, interpretation should be connected to and based on the literal sense of the passage in question.

Tools of the historical-critical method are often helpful here. Begin with questions of historical contextualization and human authorial intent. When the literal sense does not make immediate sense to us, we cannot thereby assume that it did not make sense to the original author or audience. Spiritual interpretation should not bypass the hard work of historical, grammatical, and contextual understanding.

2. *Analogia scripturae*. The wider principle of using clear Scriptures to help explain obscure ones can be applied to spiritual interpretation. A proposed spiritual interpretation should not contradict other plain passages of Scripture. As Thomas Aquinas put it, do not extract from a text a spiritual interpretation that is not taught elsewhere in the literal sense. Thomas's rule shows both the importance of other Scriptures and the priority of the literal sense.

These first two points can be applied in evaluating an allegorical interpretation mentioned above. The sun and moon allegory of Innocent III fails the test of the plain sense of other passages, for the jurisdictional superiority of the ecclesiastical over the civil authority is not plainly taught elsewhere in the literal sense of Scripture. The topic of church and state is broached in Mark 12:17 and Romans 13:1–7, but not in a way that supports Innocent's claim. Such passages give no more ground for believing that the pope is the sun than for anyone to claim, "I am the sun; you are the moon. Therefore, do as I say." Early Protestants can perhaps be pardoned for their aversion to allegory. But one did not have to be a Protestant to recognize the problem. Dante Alighieri (1265–1321) and Stephen Langton (ca. 1150–1228) before him were among the medieval figures who objected to Innocent's allegory for its undermining of the literal sense.[31]

3. *Analogia fidei*. Any Christian interpretation must agree with the fundamental points of the faith handed down by the apostles and reflected in the whole of Scripture. Interpretation must arise from and be confirmed by the church. For premodern interpreters who emphasized spiritual interpretation, the content of Christian faith was always understood as being a necessary boundary. Exegesis was understood as allegory within confession. What Beryl Smalley said of Langton is true in general: "He has a test for the content of allegory. It must conform to the Christian faith."[32] Again, in the case of In-

31. See Smalley, *Bible in the Middle Ages*, 261–62, 306–7.
32. Smalley, *Bible in the Middle Ages*, 261.

nocent's allegory, the doctrinal point that he sought to teach was not part of the faith of the ancient fathers but was a more recent and always controversial teaching that really gained ground in the eleventh century.

Overarching unity is the key assumption underlying the *analogia scripturae* and the *analogia fidei*. The unity of the faith of the prophets and the apostles is reflected in the basic theological unity of the Scriptures that they composed, all inspired by the one Spirit of God. The point is that any interpretation of a part must fit the whole—the whole canon of Scripture and the whole rule of faith.

If these boundaries are respected and observed, then the spiritual sense will not be a pious front for "anything goes." If the literal sense means anything and if other Scriptures and the rule of faith bracket out certain interpretations, then it will at least make it more difficult to read whatever one wills into Scripture.

Historical Criticism within Limits

The chief concern with the historical-critical method is the reduction of meaning to a compositional moment or historical event—that is, a single truth—that sometimes is impenetrable and always excludes any significance that might transcend the human author's intent. Even if all modern exegetes are not so reductionistic in practice, there is nothing inherent in the method that is particularly Christian. If it is to be practiced by Christians, therefore, something else must come alongside it. Within proper limits, the tools of the historical-critical method can be put into the service of a Christian reading of Scripture.

Many of the shortcomings of the historical-critical method, from a Christian point of view, can be alleviated by attending to some of the same controls that ought to accompany spiritual interpretation, but applied from a different direction. Unlike premodern interpretation, which assumed the use of the *analogia fidei* and *analogia scripturae* even if it occasionally forgot them, these same controls are not native to modern exegesis, but are positively excluded by it. But a historical approach to Scripture that is consciously Christian cannot do without them.

1. *Spiritual sense*. If biblical exegesis should be twofold, then the literal and the spiritual approaches must balance one another. If historical-critical exegesis errs by ignoring any spiritual sense, then the solution begins with recognizing the legitimacy of both aspects of Christian biblical interpretation. Although the literal sense is the first step, the modern exegete must realize that it is only the *first* step. That is, finding what the original human author

intended and what the original audience understood may be a great place to start, but it is not necessarily the place to finish.

It is the historical-critical method of literal exegesis that positively excludes presuppositions, particularly theological assumptions. But if Christ is the scope of all Scripture, if all Scripture points to God, if all Scripture is useful for doctrinal and moral instruction, then the spiritual sense is inherent in Scripture. The *analogia fidei* is a factor here. The rule of faith, along with the literal sense of Scripture, supplies the content for spiritual interpretation. Without a Christian theological lens, there is nothing really Christian about biblical interpretation, especially when it comes to the Old Testament. Take, for example, the Song of Songs. From a modern exegetical perspective, there is really no internal evidence for thinking that this song is about anything more than the love between a man and a woman. If this were the only proper interpretation, however, then it would not be in the Jewish or Christian canon.

Most Christian exegetes, even those otherwise committed to the historical-critical method, recognize that biblical interpretation should draw out the text's significance for today's church and application in new situations. The point advocated here, though, is that doctrinal or moral application is not simply an afterthought but may be a legitimate, fuller "sense" of Scripture, even if not obviously intended by the human author.

2. *Analogia scripturae.* One might say that modern historical-critical ex-egetes discovered radical theological diversity—diversity in the Old and New Testaments, not to mention in the early church. The incontestable fact of diversity, though, has managed to obscure an overarching unity that is also clearly present in Scripture, a unity that flows from the one God and the story of redemption in Christ. As such, whereas premodern exegetes needed simply to be reminded that interpretations should fit with the whole of Scripture and the rule of faith, which they saw as fundamentally in harmony, modern exegetes tend to deny the harmony. The fixation on theological diversity among the biblical authors, with their individual concerns, undermines any real sense of a common thread, leading most modern scholars to dismiss any legitimate role for *analogia scripturae*.

The diversity notwithstanding, there is yet a unity to Scripture that no historian should ignore. Biblical authors of both Old and New Testaments consciously employed stories and words from earlier biblical documents. New Testament writers used similar concepts and words to describe their common beliefs. Intertextuality and a shared faith reflect an underlying unity that legitimates the use of Scripture to explain Scripture. Pointing to other biblical passages for commentary can be illuminating without undermining the integrity and distinctive voice of a particular book under investigation.

3. *Interpretive humility*. Another limit to extreme interpretations concerns the disposition of the interpreter. Specifically, humility must be at the top of the list of exegetical virtues. To be sure, humility is not reserved for modern critics only. Since pride is a sin that can attach itself to any fallen human who pursues any interpretive approach, humility is indispensable for anyone who would seek truth through either the literal or the spiritual sense. It is not that a prideful person cannot possibly understand and teach a true interpretation, but that such a person is less likely to listen to the wisdom of others, less likely to admit ever being wrong, and thus more likely to obfuscate the biblical message, perhaps even without knowing it.

Again, such obfuscation can result from spiritual interpretations and speculative allegories, which can suffer from lack of humility. The doctrine taught in Innocent III's sun and moon allegory, besides being unfounded in the literal sense, also served to bolster his own position. The allegory might have been more believable had its proponent not been the prime beneficiary. Humility helps one listen; it puts a person within range of hearing and understanding Scripture.

If humility can help rein in spiritual interpretations, it should be even more effective for those who focus on the literal sense. The scientific approach to the Bible, though no less speculative than spiritual exegesis, tends to be no less confident in its conclusions. As Luke Timothy Johnson has said, the historical-critical method "has tended to be overly critical of the tradition and insufficiently critical of itself."[33] Premodern and postmodern approaches have chastened the hubris involved in limiting textual meaning to a single, discoverable authorial intent. Publication and advancement in historical-critical exegesis, moreover, are contingent on uncovering something novel in Scripture, which often entails finding someone else with whom to differ. Of course, some interpretations surely come closer to the mark than others. But since academia advances by negative criticism, the scholarly system tends to promote pride in oneself and in one's own interpretation.

Along with interpretive humility goes the call to limit historical speculation and skepticism and to stop prejudging the text as unreliable. Critical editions of Q, second-century dates for the Pastorals, and the like should each be seen for what it in fact is: one of many possible reconstructions to explain a historical question that is tangential to the spiritual point of the canonical text. Theories about a document's author or occasion are only as strong as, and thus should receive only as much credence as, the internal and external evidence warrants. For instance, mirror reading should not assume that every

33. Johnson, *Real Jesus*, 171.

instruction or exhortation is meant to address a specific problem in the church. We can know that the Philippian church was plagued with pride, division, and strife not simply because Paul urges the church to humility, unity, and joy, but because he calls out Euodia and Syntyche by name for their inability to get along (Phil. 4:2). With matters that cannot be confirmed internally or externally, speculation should be limited. Humility of interpretation is an effective antidote to overweening speculation, regardless of one's exegetical approach. Let the text stand innocent until proved guilty. When modern speculation runs far afield from the text, a simple and careful reading of the biblical text is sometimes all it takes to gain a clear understanding. Theories that eschew wild speculation in favor of a careful and humble reading of the text often, for this reason, turn out to be the truly radical theories in modern scholarship. A saying attributed to longtime Yale New Testament professor Nils Dahl is apt: "An exegete should have the courage to state the obvious."

We have seen some of the extreme voices and the proper limits that should be applied to them. With these checks and balances in mind, what does it look like to balance letter and spirit? What can the church today learn from giving attention to literal and especially neglected spiritual interpretations?

8

A Way Forward

And when you devote yourself to the divine reading, uprightly and with a faith fixed firmly on God seek the meaning of the divine words which is hidden from most people. Do not stop at knocking and seeking, for the most necessary element is praying to understand the divine words.

—Origen[1]

Truth, not eloquence, is to be sought for in Holy Scripture. Each part of the Scripture is to be read with the same Spirit wherewith it was written.

—Thomas à Kempis[2]

Retrieval Exegesis

In this survey of the history of biblical interpretation, an important aim is to be instructed by the past for the sake of the present and future. What should be recovered from this history? This question about exegesis is related to the larger task of so-called retrieval theology. To ask what should be retrieved from the history of doctrine is not a recommendation for the slavish replication of

1. Origen, "Letter of Origen to Gregory Thaumaturgus," 4, trans. Slusser, 192.
2. Thomas à Kempis, *Of the Imitation of Christ*, 1.5 (p. 17).

211

the past, whether of the first, fourth, sixteenth, or any other century. It is rather to learn from history. It is to take the best of the past and allow it to inform Christian faith and practice today. It means to value historical perspective. Of course, the voices of the historical church are not judge and jury. Like us, they all stand under Scripture. But those voices from the past are witnesses, voices that today's church should not fail to hear.

What is true for the history of theology in general is also true for the history of biblical interpretation in particular. Thus we ask: What should be retrieved from the history of exegesis? Which principles and approaches to Scripture would be beneficial for the present task of biblical interpretation? Which of these approaches from the past have been muffled or silenced but need to be heard again? What can be learned from our ancestors in the faith, devout Christians who approached these narratives from a perspective different from that of most modern Westerners?

As an exercise in retrieval exegesis, I make a number of suggestions that arise from this historical survey of biblical interpretation and the limits to be placed on extreme methods mentioned in the previous chapter. Most of the suggestions are drawn from the premodern period. These suggestions do not constitute an exhaustive list of principles or techniques for biblical interpretation, much less a step-by-step guide to exegesis. The suggestions that come across as very basic may best be taken as good reminders. Other suggestions, perhaps, are less common in contemporary discussions of exegesis and thus deserve more careful consideration. Some suggestions may raise more questions than can be answered in this short space. Indeed, a chapter or book could be written on each of them. All their implications cannot be drawn out here; yet if these suggestions provoke further thought and more responsible, holistic biblical interpretation, then their purpose will be served.[3]

Literal-Spiritual Exegesis

As Augustine wrote at the beginning of one of his commentaries on Genesis, "All divine scripture is twofold."[4] To use the apostle Paul's language, biblical interpretation is of the letter and of the spirit. Although there is a distinction between the two approaches, there should be no separation. Premodern interpreters of Scripture were one in their belief that the sacred text has both

3. It should be pointed out that there are many commentaries, series of commentaries, and even journals that practice theological interpretation of Scripture, often seeking to put into practice the best principles of premodern exegesis. See, e.g., the Brazos Theological Commentary on the Bible and *Journal of Theological Interpretation*.

4. Augustine, *Literal Meaning of Genesis* 1.1.1 (WSA I/13:168).

a literal and a spiritual sense or meaning. The literal sense is the basis for and points to the spiritual sense; the spiritual sense arises from and is linked to the literal. One approach without the other results in a partial, incomplete reading and likely a distorted reading. To invoke Origen's analogy, just as human nature is composed of body, soul, and spirit and would be lacking without any one of them, so also biblical interpretation must have in view the body, soul, and spirit of the text in order to be whole. They should not be torn apart. If we pay attention to the literal sense alone apart from the spiritual senses, the Bible is a mere historical curiosity and a dead letter. If we seek only the spiritual senses without basis in the literal sense, then our faith and practice will more likely be based on our preferences than on divine revelation in the text.

Letter

Acknowledgment of twofold exegesis means, first of all, that sufficient attention should be paid to the literal sense. However much we may want to say in favor of spiritual interpretation as it was practiced in centuries past—indeed much will be said below—it must not imply that one should bypass the literal-grammatical sense. By "literal" sense, premodern Christians meant the actual words of the text in their context, not necessarily a "literalistic" account. The literal sense, what the words say and plainly mean on the most basic level, if it is possible to discern that, is the foundation and control of all subsequent interpretation and application.

Modern exegesis has taught readers of the Bible to seek the original intention of the authors and how their writings would have been received by the original recipients. It is a good and necessary endeavor to begin with the question of what the text meant in its original context. We should not make the text say just anything we want it to say. Depending on their genre, most texts have a more or less narrow range of possibilities of meaning.

To the degree that attention to the literal sense and the author's meaning entails historical examination, the gains of modern historical research and the best tools of historical criticism should be employed. The progress made in the modern era to understand Scripture in its ancient context is essential for responsible exegesis. The tools of historical, philological, and archaeological research are means to the end of discerning authorial intent. Historical research, especially by means of archaeology, has opened up the cultural and linguistic world of the ancient Near East in ways hardly imagined before the modern era. Knowledge of Koine Greek and advances in textual criticism have increased understanding of the New Testament. As a result, the contextual world of the Bible has been illumined, and this knowledge must not be ignored. We should not pretend that modern exegesis never happened or that the knowledge acquired through the historical-critical method is irrelevant to Christian biblical interpretation.

The modern exegete's impulse to discover authorial intent comes with a legitimate call to look behind the text for clues to its meaning. After all, the lack of historical contextualization can lead to gross misunderstanding of a text. Even the recognition that we do not possess the exact words (ipsissima verba) of a narrated speech means that we are a degree removed from the facts of the history. Such searches can be carried out, however, without undue speculation or venturing too far behind. For instance, if in a letter Paul describes himself as a prisoner (Eph. 3:1; 4:1) and he writes about the spiritual "armor of God" in terms of physical armor (Eph. 6:10–18), it does not take much imagination to picture Paul writing or dictating in proximity to a Roman soldier, drawing a contrast between earthly war and the battle that is "not against flesh and blood." An interpretive move like this one is fairly intuitive. In the case of the Letter to the Romans, any careful reader can see that Paul is addressing a Jew-Gentile conflict. But the epistle is neither merely a general exhortation to unity that all first-century churches needed nor, much less, Paul's systematic theology. Rather, Paul is tackling a problem specific to a church that has been deprived of its Jewish members for about six years, a scenario corroborated externally by Acts 18:1–2 and Suetonius's *Life of Claudius*.[5] Although Paul's epistle can be largely understood without reference to the Claudian edict, this very likely background circumstance sheds light on the text of Romans.[6]

Spirit

In addition to the literal sense, twofold exegesis also calls the believer to attend to the spiritual sense. For premodern Christians it is the spiritual meaning of Scripture, not its literal meaning, that is of ultimate importance, because it is a spiritual end to which Scripture points. The spirit, though logically subsequent to the letter, is what brings life (2 Cor. 3:6), and it is the spiritual sense that yields knowledge of doctrine and morals. At this point, a Christian exegete trained in the historical-critical method, and one who is already devoted to making spiritual applications, may be questioning the legitimacy of the spiritual sense. Why is spiritual interpretation, particularly as a distinct category, needed?

The clearest answer to this question surfaces when one considers the purpose, or telos, of Scripture. Scripture is not an end in itself, but a means to other

5. See Suetonius, *Vita Claudii* 25.4. See also Donfried, *Romans Debate*.
6. For further reflections on authorial intent, see Fowl, "The Role of Authorial Intention."

ends. What are these goals of Scripture? According to 2 Timothy 3:16–17, all inspired Scripture is "profitable for doctrine, for reproof, for correction, for instruction that is in righteousness." In other words, the goal of Scripture is to train its readers in doctrine and morals. This sort of training then equips the believer "for every good work." These sacred letters "grant wisdom for salvation" (2 Tim. 3:15). The "goal [τέλος, telos] of the instruction is love" (1 Tim. 1:5). All these are spiritual ends. But not "every inspired Scripture" is clearly instructive or spiritually edifying on the literal level. It is therefore the spiritual sense, guidance by the Holy Spirit, that allows readers to elicit from such texts what is instructive for Christian faith and practice—that is, what is in fact the intended spiritual function of Scripture.

Elsewhere, Paul calls Christ the "telos of the law for everyone who believes" (Rom. 10:4). Paul makes a similar point when he writes, "The law has become our tutor, leading to Christ" (Gal. 3:24). In other words, the law—or more broadly, the revelation of God to his people—is meant to point his people to Christ. But not every law or special revelation from God clearly points to Christ. It is the spiritual sense, therefore, that enables one to read the Old Testament text christologically and, ultimately, to be accepted as Christian canon. If Scripture is to be read in a Christian way, then it must be interpreted spiritually; it must have meaning that goes beyond the original authorial intent. Scripture is, in a word, multivalent. Limiting Scripture to one meaning and marginalizing further spiritual meanings and applications would be an impoverished way to read the Old Testament, making it irrelevant to Christians (and to Jews as well). The text need not mean merely one thing.

And this kind of spiritual interpretation of Scripture—christological, doctrinal, moral—is precisely what we see happening in the New Testament. Paul claims that the exodus story, which nowhere mentions Christ and is not literally or historically a message that was directed to first-century Christians, "happened typologically" and "was written for our instruction" (1 Cor. 10:11). As such, he interprets the story christologically and applies its doctrine and morals to the Corinthian church (1 Cor. 10:1–13). Throughout his writings, whether the ancient command regards circumcision, sacrifice, diet, or treatment of animals, Paul is eager to emphasize a spiritual interpretation and application. His recurring contrast between letter and spirit (Rom. 2:29; 7:6; 2 Cor. 3:6–8), always in the context of the interpretation and application of the law, makes sense as a hermeneutical key for the reading and application of Scripture.[7]

---

7. This traditional reading is admittedly and not unexpectedly contrary to the conclusions of many modern exegetes. See, e.g., Furnish, *II Corinthians*, 199–200; T. Schreiner, *Paul, Apostle of*

As noted earlier, this method was, from the beginning of Christian exegesis, understood as having been taught by Jesus himself to his first disciples (Luke 24:45). The things written in the Law, the Prophets, and the Psalms (Writings)—that is to say, in the whole Old Testament—were written about Christ (Luke 24:44). Even Jesus's own sayings and actions were often best interpreted allegorically, and he chastised his disciples for not knowing better (Mark 4:10–20; 8:14–21). The apostles followed this method of interpretation, notably in the New Testament, which then became the model for Christian exegesis and, I would add, models for us.[8] Many more examples could be given to show that the spiritual sense is assumed by the New Testament authors. The distinct spiritual sense, therefore, is not the invention of the pope, as many Protestants have alleged.

A survey of these biblical passages also makes clear what the earliest readers and writers of Scripture regarded as the goals of Scripture. Scripture was not written in order to be scientifically examined or understood on one level alone. Without doubt, historical knowledge and scientific examination have their proper roles as tools for understanding Scripture. But whatever the authors' intentions were, at the human or divine level, they were not hoping to provide fodder for academic dissertations and monographs. The earliest recipients, at least, did not treat Scripture thus. They did not read for historical curiosity or intellectual stimulation alone. If it was written and compiled for the goals of spiritual instruction and moral formation, to draw people nearer to Christ and to God, then a reader is not only justified in interpreting with such ends in mind but is also obliged to do so. That some modern exegetes for a couple of centuries have had different goals—different from those of the original biblical authors and their audiences and of roughly seventeen centuries of Christian interpreters—is of little consequence to this point.

As all premodern interpreters recognized, not every biblical text demands a spiritual interpretation that is distinct from the literal sense, because many texts contain the spiritual point directly in the literal sense. When Scripture says that God is love, there is certainly much to explore, but the spiritual point is clear enough on the literal level. The moral point of "Love your neighbor," whose application is endless, is embedded in the literal sense. The same is true when the text is already explicitly christological. For this reason,

---

God's Glory, 134–35; Witherington, *Paul's Letter to the Romans*, 177. For a summary of the issues and history of the letter-spirit theme in 2 Cor. 3:6, see Hafemann, *Paul, Moses, and the History of Israel*, 1–35; Hafemann declares that seeing the letter-spirit contrast as primarily an apologetic strategy for Paul's apostolic ministry does not negate its hermeneutical significance (33).

8. This point has been emphasized throughout this study. It is also prominent in Leithart, *Deep Exegesis*, vii–viii, 34, 37.

christological interpretation of an otherwise nonchristological text is mostly reserved for the Old Testament. Typically, the New Testament is, on the literal level, already about Christ.

It could be that Christian historical-critical exegetes who initially question the need for spiritual interpretation will see this description and say that they are already doing this, inasmuch as they find in the text spiritual applications for the church today. Such application is commendable, and it is worth recognizing that these exegetes are, in practice, transcending the historical-critical method. They are not far from the approach of literal-spiritual interpretation. Spiritual interpretation is something more, though, than application of an ancient text. It is the willingness to say that, while this Old Testament text is about David, it is also about Christ. The spiritual interpretation is not merely an added application: if it is true, it is in some sense meant to be found in the text. The spiritual aspect is not something separate from exegesis, confined only to a sermon. Since the Bible is intended to be a means to spiritual formation and union with God, then it is the sermon, the homily with literal and spiritual insight into the text, rather than the technical commentary that should be regarded as the definitive genre of exegesis.

Spiritual interpretation is not simply about finding the one correct doctrine or ethical conclusion or christological reference. It is more inclusive, all-embracing in its scope. It is the exuberance, reminiscent of Origen's exegesis, of a living church engaging a living text. Spiritual interpretation not only enables readers to enter the world of Scripture but also frees readers to see their own world through Scripture. In this way, spiritual interpretation authorizes and makes sense of the "This is that" sort of interpretation that is often seen in the New Testament and patristic interpretation of the Old Testament, when "that" is something new and apparently far removed from the original "this."

It is a mode of interpretation—or better, of appropriation—that invites us to think biblically. Scripture becomes part of our grammar, and its stories and sayings shape our own lives, becoming the idiom or inside language through which we experience the world. It is as much the Bible interpreting us as it is we who are interpreting the Bible. Its stories become our stories, the lens through which we interpret our reality. Such a disposition toward the text, common among ancient interpreters, allowed them to employ the biblical idiom in unique contexts, primarily liturgical, but also ordinary and mundane. Using Scripture thus does not disregard or efface its original context but gives it a new context. Something like this is going on in much of premodern interpretation, including the New Testament's interpretation of the Old.

Let me illustrate this point with a canon other than Scripture. In my immediate family, we have a shared canon of oral material from which we freely quote. We are eminently familiar with it in its context, not because we have ever read it on a page (we have not), but because we have heard it many times. The corpus that I have in mind is mostly comedy, including film (from *Mad World* to *The Princess Bride*), television (from *Looney Tunes* to *The Simpsons*), and stand-up comedy (especially Jim Gaffigan). When we begin quoting, sometimes we have the words verbatim; if we get a few words wrong, then we may help each other get them right or just move on.[9] Why do we quote? This body of material provides words and attitudes that help us engage and make sense of our experiences, or they simply help us share a cheap laugh amid the experience, or they do both. For instance, if my son says, "Good idea," and I snap in reply, "Of course it's a good idea!" we laugh because we know the context of the line in a famous movie. Although the phrase has been removed from its original context and has been placed in a new context, it is an analogous context. More important, without forgetting the original context of the lines, we also tacitly know which parts of that context apply in the present situation and which do not. No, I am not really angry or condescending, as is the case in the movie. But, yes, at the same time, it (whatever "it" may be) really is a good idea, perhaps obviously good. "This is that." It is intertextuality at work, though no "text" is actually involved, and the "work" of interpreting and appropriating comes intuitively for the insiders who are familiar with the canon.

The shared biblical idiom, the insider language and literature of Scripture, functions for the church in a similar way. Premodern exegetes had a distinct advantage in this regard: they were familiar with the contents of Scripture, and some of them were walking concordances. Everyone heard Scripture at length in the liturgy. Clergy and monks, the primary interpreters of Scripture before the printing press, read Scripture on their own and, especially in the monastery, recited the Psalms on a regular basis. Their memory was trained for retaining what was heard. Scripture was on their heart, so intertextual connections between Old and New Testament or between the Bible and their lives of work and worship were second nature.

If we are to understand Scripture and learn from the apostolic and patristic examples of exegesis, then it is important to understand how the ancients themselves used it. The problem is that late modern people are not so familiar with this biblical idiom. As a culture, we have other, more familiar canons.

9. F. Young, *Biblical Exegesis*, 133, speaking about early patristic cross-referencing in a looser oral context: "To reproduce exactly was not felt to be incumbent upon one who quoted a document."

The secular educated class does not recognize the origin or context of some of the most memorable stories and celebrated sayings from Scripture.[10] Sadly, the same goes for Christians, clergy and laity alike, who seem less biblically literate than ever before. Since we rely not on our memory but on pages, concordances, and screens, we do not allow the words into our hearts. The biblical stories will never become our stories if we do not know them. Our memories are not trained like those of our ancestors, though they seem effective enough in areas of less importance. I have heard of a church leader who, when a fellow Christian in conversation quotes from a well-known television show or movie, asks the person also to quote something from Scripture. What if this leader were really ambitious and asked people to quote something from Scripture not randomly but regarding the topic at hand? Spiritual exegesis, of course, requires more than biblical literacy, but not less. Full-orbed spiritual interpretation perishes for lack of knowledge.

Spiritual exegesis is much more than can be summed up in this section or fully exemplified by the figures in previous chapters. It is much more about the attitudes, dispositions, and goals than about any particular methods. Opening the door to spiritual interpretation is simply allowing the text to speak to the hearts and minds of believers who seek God's face. It is to regard the reading of Scripture as a liturgical act, a discipline of prayer. Because it is already sacramental, the literal is at the same time spiritual.[11] By engaging in spiritual reading, believers let timeless words fill their being and, from there, address ever new times and places. Through these words believers hear God speaking a message of faith, love, and hope. The spiritual sense is simply spiritual understanding, spiritual truth, unfolding from the plain words in their literal understanding. Above all, perhaps, to read spiritually is to approach inspired Scripture expecting to be transformed and renewed by God's Spirit, seeking to hear and find God and to become like God, realizing that the spiritual goal of Scripture will probably elude those who do not pursue it. The search helps make the discovery possible.

Quadrigal Questions

Perhaps what needs to be retrieved, as an effective way to strike the exegetical balance of twofold interpretation, is the so-called quadriga of the Middle

10. For instance, a book review editor of the *New York Times* was apparently puzzled by a poem that referred to "plucking out your eye and cutting off your hand or foot if it offends you," dismissing the concept as "strange." As reported by Reno, "While We're at It," 66.

11. Boersma, *Scripture as Real Presence*, 53–55.

Ages. This blossoming of the spiritual sense led to a fourfold interpretation: the literal (what the text says), allegorical (what is to be believed), tropological (what is to be done), and anagogical (what is to be hoped)—the last three corresponding to the theological virtues of faith, love, and hope. It could go without saying that the quadriga is foreign to the way most ministers and professional exegetes approach Scripture and to the way most seminaries teach the discipline of biblical interpretation. I submit, however, that the quadriga provides a good model for how the church ought to read Scripture today, and it reflects the four types of questions that readers ought to be asking.[12]

First, although the literal or historical sense of the quadriga was not the same as what came to be the more narrow literalism reflected by many readers, in several ways it does correspond to the kind of description and investigation familiar to the historical-critical method. What did the text mean in its original setting? What does the text actually say on its surface? What does it mean on the historical and grammatical level? What is the argument or scope of the text? Second, on the basis of this text, what should we believe? What does it teach, allegorically or otherwise, about the faith? Third, what should we do? How should we behave? What does it teach, tropologically or otherwise, about the moral life of love to which we are called? Fourth, what should we hope for? What does the text teach, anagogically or otherwise, about God's eternal intentions for his people? These questions are connected, as Peter Leithart points out: "The literal sense of the text opened out into a christological allegory, which, because Christ is the head of his body, opened out into tropological instruction and, because Christ is the King of a kingdom here yet also coming, into anagogical hope."[13] Not all three levels of the spiritual sense will be obvious in each and every text. But the questions should be asked. Perhaps other questions should be asked that do not easily fit into any of these four categories. But these are conversation starters.

There are many practical consequences of this approach. The quadriga encourages holistic exegesis that will ask many of the questions necessary for understanding and attend to the different goals of Bible reading. If there is any question about historical background or authorial intent that would help illuminate the text, then there are tools for this purpose. If there is any question about the message for the church today, and there always is, then there are tools for this purpose as well. A reader or setting that inclines

12. The Roman Catholic Church still cites Augustine of Dacia's couplet, along with a discussion of the quadriga, in the *Catechism of the Catholic Church* 115–19, Doubleday ed., 38–39.

13. Leithart, *Deep Exegesis*, 207.

unilaterally to the historical questions should be challenged to inquire into the three spiritual senses. Conversely, a reader or setting that inclines to spiritual interpretation should be shown how attention to the literal sense can enhance spiritual understanding and sound application. Exegesis that is unapologetically literal and spiritual refuses to leave the task of interpretation to only one set of questions.

I have often heard, and probably at one time given, advice to ministers that their time spent in critical exegesis must be supplemented at other times with devotional reading. Specifically, the idea is that careful study in preparation for a sermon or Sunday school class is separate from and does not "count" for personal Bible study. This is a false dichotomy, and there's no reason why the one shouldn't promote the other and why Bible reading cannot be both intellectually and spiritually stimulating. The distinction need not be blurred, but neither should the activities be conceived as two entirely different tasks. Whatever historical and grammatical investigation goes into study, it is in vain, given the stated purposes of Scripture, if it does not end in spiritual insight for oneself and one's congregation. Whatever spiritual edification or feeling is gained from personal meditative reading, *lectio divina*, or the like, it is less helpful if it is not accompanied by contemplation on the meaning of the words and basic understanding of their context. Devotional reading and scholarly reading need not be at odds.

Holistic exegesis that follows the quadriga is also less likely to encounter throwaway passages—that is, verses or sections of the Bible that seem to promote, at best, only historical curiosity. Just as Origen would not pass over the details of the Israelite travel narrative out of Egypt, there are passages whose spiritual message is waiting to be uncovered. Each and every passage of Scripture is profitable. Basil spoke for all ancient exegetes when he said that "in the inspired words, there is not one idle syllable."[14]

As with all steps of exegesis, there is no one right chronological order and no indisputable logical order to the process. In that sense, exegesis in general and the fourfold approach in particular are not an exact science or recipe to follow. What one learns to do at first in a rudimentary way will become natural with practice. The quadrigal questions, perhaps intuitive to some laypersons, are reminders to all readers of what to look for in Scripture in light of the spiritual end for which it is given.

If literal-spiritual exegesis, as it was ideally conceived in the premodern church, is taken seriously, other important practical implications flow from the attention given to the spiritual sense.

14. Basil of Caesarea, *Hexaemeron* 7.11 (*NPNF²* 8:89).

Regulated Reading

Before modern exegetes excluded all theological presuppositions from bibli-cal interpretation, an essential feature of premodern biblical exegesis was the insistence on interpreting Scripture within the boundaries set by the rule of faith (*regula fidei*) and the whole of Scripture. In other words, premodern ex-egetes read Scripture overtly through a theological lens. The reason is simple, and it is as true now as it was then: *nuda scriptura*, or "Bible only-ism," does not guard against false teaching. From one side, the rule of faith can function as a limit to the spiritual sense: allegorical interpretations must not go beyond the bounds of the ancient, catholic faith. From another side, the rule of faith also excludes certain interpretations that appear to be based on a literalistic reading—interpretations that are, after all, thoroughly biblical and literal as well as thoroughly heretical. As Spinoza admitted, "Every heretic has his text."[15] The early church knew it and warned against "the unlearned and unstable" who distort Paul's Letters and the rest of the Scriptures (2 Pet. 3:15–16). Peter Lom-bard claimed that even heretics adhere "stubbornly to the words of Scripture."[16]

The exegete must, as Irenaeus insisted, have the correct hypothesis (ὑπόθεσις, *hypothesis*) or principle, the right lens, which for him was the *regula fidei* (rule of faith), the oral proclamation of the faith passed down from the apostles. Although its function is different from later creeds, its content is summed up well in the ancient creeds of the church, especially the Apostles' and the Niceno-Constantinopolitan Creeds. As we have seen, this rule of faith comes alongside Scripture and is itself informed by the whole of Scripture. As re-gards exegesis, the faith expressed in the rule—belief in Father, Son, and Holy Spirit—serves as a lens for reading Scripture and regulates the range of possible interpretations of Scripture.

What about objectivity? What about letting Scripture speak for itself? Is it possible to be objective and still be guided by the rule of faith? As Jaroslav Pelikan once asked, "Is it possible for exegesis today to assert the sovereignty of Scripture over tradition . . . and simultaneously to affirm a continuity and affinity with the tradition and dogma of the Christian centuries?"[17] The two can coexist. Christians can conduct an objective search for truth that allows Scripture to speak to and challenge them on its own terms. But complete neutrality or detachment is neither possible nor desirable.

The myth of the pure neutrality of reason has been effectively debunked in philosophy now for centuries, and the similar myth of hermeneutical

---

15. Spinoza, *Treatise*, 178.
16. Peter Lombard, *Sentences* 2.96.4, trans. Silano, 72.
17. Pelikan, *Luther the Expositor*, 258.

neutrality has been similarly debunked in biblical studies now for decades. When we apply a lens through which Scripture is read, we accept the postmodern insight that no reader is entirely unbiased and that everyone reads through a lens. One's reading will be "ruled" or regulated by something. Which grid or lens should we bring to our reading of Scripture? No shortage of options has been provided. Just like identity politics, we have identity hermeneutics. Modern academia has made a cottage industry of reading and applying the text through this, that, or the other lens, usually based on race, gender, and sexual preferences, analogous in some ways to a spiritual sense. As important and inescapable as some of these perspectives may be, they should be subordinate to the first principle of Christian exegesis: the rule of faith.

As we employ the rule of faith as the primary lens that supersedes all others, we engage in unapologetically Christian reading. Robert Jenson speaks about the creed, which is roughly equivalent to the content of the rule of faith, as a "critical theory" for reading Scripture. "The church cannot simply opt out of modernity's critical pathos; we may not be of the world, but we are in it, and all in it now are critics. The question has to be 'Following *what* critical theory, and penetrating to *whose* agenda, should the church read its Scripture?' . . . The community positioned to perceive what a scriptural text is truly up to is the church, and the creed is the set of instructions for discerning this agenda."[18] Yes, Christians have an agenda for reading and interpreting their Scripture, and that agenda is the rule of faith—the combined practices, beliefs, and worldview of the community that wrote, received, and submitted to Scripture. The Bible is the church's book, and its correct interpretation can only happen in conversation with the church and its doctrine. It is not a postmodern rejection of truth and meaning in the text, but the affirmation of a true lens that helps readers see the truths in the text.[19]

The rule of faith does not include everything that any or every church has ever asserted. As the tradition developed beyond the ancient rule, it is subordinate to Scripture. As an aspect of this Christian lens, though, biblical interpretation is also informed by the broad, historic Christian tradition. The tradition influences our biblical interpretation, whether or not we acknowledge it. Even the most anticreedal, traditionless Christians, on occasion, unwittingly read Scripture

18. Jenson, *Canon and Creed*, 81.
19. O'Keefe and Reno note that bringing a lens to a discipline is not unique to biblical exegesis. For instance, one learns how to be a scientist in community, learns how certain rules apply to examination and observation, learns the virtues and skills needed for the discipline, and so on. O'Keefe and Reno, *Sanctified Vision*, 114–28.

through the lens of received tradition.[20] To acknowledge the tradition of biblical interpretation and application, we invite the voices of the past to have a seat at the table. It does not mean that every individual interpretation throughout history is valid or worth following. From one perspective, the tradition is a multiform cacophony of voices. But from another perspective, as Vincent of Lérins said, we are interested in what is believed "by all."[21] What we need to hear are not the individual voices alone, but the chorus.[22] As in jurisprudence, some legal cases are more important than others, and over time it becomes clear which cases and decisions set major precedents.[23] Scripture belongs to the church and is meant to be interpreted within the church and in light of its past. Any approach that pretends not to be influenced by the past, that intentionally ignores the history of doctrine, and that excludes a large part of the communion of saints is needlessly robbing itself of centuries of wisdom.

When it came to the role of tradition in biblical interpretation, Protestants, like many medieval theologians, were one in their rejection of the pope's monopoly on biblical interpretation. It was not exactly clear, however, which interpretive authority to put in place of the papacy. The eventual rejection, in some circles, of any ecclesiastical authority to interpret would lead to an authority crisis: Who ought to interpret? Is it the individual reader? What should be done in the face of competing interpretations? *Sola scriptura*, if it is *nuda scriptura*, excludes one pope by inviting infinite popes and their interpretations, with the predictable consequence of endless divisions over interpretation.[24] One of the Roman Church's earliest and most persistent criticisms of Protestantism to this day is the lack of unity that resulted from rejecting the magisterium's right to interpretation. By rejecting all tradition and the rule of faith that united the earliest Christians, many Protestants threw out the proverbial baby with the bathwater.[25]

20. For a discussion, along with concrete examples, see Stanglin, "Restorationism and Church History."

21. Vincent of Lérins, *Commonitory* 2.6 (*NPNF*[2] 11:132).

22. Pelikan, *Emergence of the Catholic Tradition*, 122: "Listen to the chorus more than to the soloists."

23. Giulio Silano provides an extended analogy between a casebook and Peter Lombard's *Sentences*. See Silano's introduction to Peter Lombard, *Sentences*, 1:xix–xxvi. This seems to be a helpful way to think about the whole Christian tradition.

24. Although Brad Gregory's discussion of *sola scriptura* lacks much needed nuance, this much seems true, especially of what we have called *nuda scriptura*: "From the outset of the Reformation to the present day, the insistence on *sola scriptura* and its adjuncts has produced and continues to yield an open-ended range of incompatible interpretations of the Bible, with centrifugal social and wide-ranging substantive implications for morality" (B. Gregory, *Unintended Reformation*, 205).

25. For more on the rule of faith as a hermeneutical lens and means to greater unity, see Stanglin, "Restoration Movement."

It is not that the tradition is infallible, especially with regard to doctrinal matters that are not specified in the rule of faith. A novel interpretation of the literal sense of Scripture, one that has never been conceived in two millennia, could be the correct one. As reported earlier, some advances in our knowledge of ancient history, particularly that of the ancient Near East, enhance this possibility. The point, though, is that a biblical interpreter should have a very good reason for differing from the chorus of voices.

This lens that regulates Christian biblical interpretation—the rule of faith, other Scriptures, the great tradition—provides a wide boundary within which exegesis can operate. At the edges of that boundary, the rule of faith may challenge or exclude a rogue interpretation. Timothy George compares it to a guardrail that helps keep travelers on the right path when they find themselves on a dangerous highway.[26] But within that boundary, space is carved out for many true interpretations that are in keeping with the literal sense and with the rule of faith and that do justice to the multivalence of Scripture. Regulation of interpretation by the rule of faith should not limit Scripture's ability to challenge the reader, and it should not stifle imaginative interpretation and application. Good speculation, within the proper bounds, need not be stifled.

Virtue of the Interpreter

A recurring theme throughout the history of interpretation is the need for virtuous interpreters. From the New Testament's warning that "not many should become teachers" (James 3:1) and its concern about the "unlearned and unstable" who distort Scripture (2 Pet. 3:16), to Origen and Gregory of Nyssa's advice that interpreters should possess insight from the Holy Spirit, to Luther's caution that not everyone has the skill to allegorize, the church has always recognized that biblical interpretation can be a challenge. In light of the history, what sort of skills and virtues should an interpreter of Scripture possess? What kind of people should the church form for the practice of sound exegesis?

If balanced interpretation embraces both the literal and spiritual dimensions, then the ideal reader can skillfully attend to both aspects of exegesis. First of all, adequate care for the literal sense requires someone who is adept in literature, the biblical languages, and grammar and has relevant knowledge of ancient history and the cultural world in which the biblical documents were forged. In short, it is someone who can read and seek to

26. George, *Reading Scripture with the Reformers*, 123.

understand a text from a vastly different time and place. Modern exegetical handbooks, universities, and seminaries have historically emphasized this group of skills, although the rigor of training in these areas has declined in recent years.

What has often been neglected in formal educational institutions and in churches alike is not so much a skill set as a virtue set that was more commonly promoted and present in the premodern church. The ideal interpreter is not just someone who can diagram a sentence in Greek, though that certainly helps. In addition to such skill, it is someone who also is indwelt by the Spirit, infused with virtues that fit the task. Again, the question comes back to the nature of the task at hand. Recall that Episcopius (1583–1643) and other modern theologians claimed that human reason without the Holy Spirit is sufficient for understanding Scripture, though the Spirit would be necessary to lead one to believe and to obey. But according to Scripture itself and virtually all premodern interpreters, one has not grasped Scripture properly if one is not led to faith and obedience. If the ultimate goal of Scripture is to instruct readers in Christian faith and morals and lead them to union with God, then the reader should be someone who desires such formation and ends, someone who is looking for instruction and edification in faith and morals, someone who bears the fruit of the Spirit. The hearer should be in "the proper condition."[27] This is someone who has the humility to listen before speaking. One who loves the text and its subject matter for the very reasons that they ought to be loved is the one best equipped to seek and find the telos of the text. Holiness is a key to understanding where Scripture would lead us, for only the pure in heart will see God.[28] The point is not to form a panel of judges to assess an exegete's virtue, but to draw attention to an important qualification that is nearly universally ignored. If Scripture's purpose is to point to God, then its ideal interpreters should be those who desire that end.

In addition to skills and virtues, the ideal interpreter of Scripture should be saturated by Scripture and immersed in its idiom, as well as informed about the faith summed up in the rule of faith or creed. Only when readers have been permeated with biblical literature will they be able to see the intertextual connections in Scripture and then be able to make the connections to the faith and life of the church. Only then will Bible readers be equipped to see their world through the eyes of Scripture. If the church wants to cultivate good

27. Flacius Illyricus, *Sacred Scriptures*, 89.

28. The role of sanctity in spiritual interpretation is examined in O'Keefe and Reno, *Sanctified Vision*, 128–39.

interpreters, then it should prioritize once again the goal of basic biblical and theological literacy, a process that begins in homes and churches.

As the study of church history in general opens up a world of wisdom and broad perspective, so the study of the history of interpretation provides exegetical insight and perspective that we miss when we consult only the most recent commentators. Whether or not we agree with their exegetical conclusions, more often than not our older brothers and sisters will help us see the beauty and glory of the God revealed in Scripture, the telos of which is Christ.

Exegetical Cases

The retrieval of the best of ancient exegesis does not assume that every attempt at allegorical interpretation will be correct and arrive at true meaning, any more than every historical-critical exegesis hits the mark. Some interpreters on both sides have overstepped their appropriate bounds. But, as we have noticed, such instances of abuse do not imply that the whole enterprise of either literal or spiritual interpretation is therefore invalid and has no proper use. What, though, is the proper use?

First of all, by promoting the spiritual sense alongside the literal sense, I am not advocating all-out allegorizing. For eager allegorizers and their audiences who regularly pay no attention to the literary and historical contexts, they need a good dose of the literal sense. For eager literalists, they could be encouraged to go beyond the letter. That is, the balance should be sought and the twofold sense united.

For those who do move on to spiritual interpretation, I agree with many premodern figures who insist that only the skilled, only the spiritually mature, only those who know what they are doing should attempt allegorical interpretations. Just as only the skilled should practice allegory, only someone who effectively handles the literal sense should try to move on to the spiritual senses. An essential part of "knowing what they're doing" is the ability first to place the biblical text in its original context and understand it on the literal, historical level. Indeed, the goal of Bible reading is to ascend ever higher into a spiritual union with God, but the ascent does not begin at the top. The literal sense may not be the end goal, but it is foundational as the first step. We must learn to walk before we can run, to flap our wings before ascending in flight.

For example, in the midst of an allegorical interpretation, if one wants to say that the two coins that the good Samaritan handed to the innkeeper are the two sacraments that Christ gave the church, then such an interpretation is on firm ground since the two sacraments are commanded elsewhere in the literal sense of Scripture and are part of the earliest church's doctrine and practice. But an elaborate allegory of the good Samaritan parable, expected by most premodern congregations, would probably be a distraction in a sermon today. At any rate, first the congregation should hear the main point of the parable: love for one another. Any further, spiritual interpretation or allegorical elaboration should be tied to the main point of the literal sense. The connection between love and the sacraments is not far-fetched at all: Christ's gift of the sacraments is an expression of his love for his rescued people.

After all is said, then, what does it look like to put these principles into practice? What does it mean to be mindful of both letter and spirit? In an effort to lend more shape to the principles recommended for retrieval, I offer here brief discussions of several biblical texts, most of which have been broached in previous chapters. The discussions that follow are not detailed interpretations or comprehensive exegeses, either on the literal or the spiritual side. As with the observation about the good Samaritan above, they are more like notes intended to illustrate how letter and spirit can work in harmony within their proper limits—almost like notes in preparation for an exegesis done in preparation for a sermon. Some of these discussions interact with premodern exegetes, at times agreeing and at other times disagreeing with them. They assume some familiarity with each text and the potential problems of interpretation. They are, especially when it comes to spiritual interpretation, not the only interpretive possibilities. They are simply attempts to show the principles being put into practice. These texts are treated in canonical order, and in each case a reason for their selection is given. The final example is a homily, given in the midst of a baptismal liturgy, that seeks to demonstrate how premodern exegetical methods—in this case, typology—may be used in the service of the church.

Genesis 1:16: The Greater and Lesser Lights

The reason for addressing Genesis 1:16 is to revisit the allegory posited by Pope Innocent III and to show how an allegorical interpretation can remain within the proper limits. As we observed earlier, Innocent III's allegorical interpretation of the sun and moon, the greater and lesser lights, as the superiority of the ecclesiastical over the civil authority fails to convince because it is not taught anywhere in the literal sense of Scripture and, in fact, seems to miss the point of the New Testament's message about the church's relation to the state.

If one is inclined to an allegorical interpretation of the fourth day of creation, a better way would be to suggest that Christ is the sun and that we, his people, are the moon. This association certainly passes the test of agreement with other Scriptures and the rule of faith. It is taught elsewhere in the literal sense that Christ is the head of his body, the church (Eph. 5:23; Col. 1:18); there is no controversy about Christ's preeminence. Scripture also declares that Christ is "the light of the world" (John 8:12) and that his people, too, are "the light of the world" (Matt. 5:14). How can both Christ and his people be the light? The light does not come from us; as all good things come from the Father of lights (James 1:17), we merely reflect the greater light. As the moon reflects the sun's light, we are mirrors that look to Christ and reflect his glory (2 Cor. 3:18). The multiple scriptural connections and the prevalence of the theme of light throughout Scripture suggest this allegorical interpretation and the link to Genesis 1. Augustine does something similar when, in his meditation on the fourth day of creation, he refers to God's people as lights of the world that should not be hidden under a bowl.[29]

Genesis 1–11: Problems with Literalism

For well over a century now, I believe it is safe to say, the primeval history of Genesis 1–11 has been the most hotly debated portion of Scripture, and so it is with some reluctance and much trepidation that I broach the topic. The point in raising it here is not to resolve all the problems but to point to some of the ways that principles of a premodern approach could help readers today avoid some of the more dangerous pitfalls associated with a literalistic interpretation.

As we have seen, the early church fathers as a whole tended to read allegorically what they regarded as difficult or nonsensical texts from the Old Testament. As such, early Christians generally did not take the creation accounts in Genesis as literal in every detail, or at least not merely literal. Although they usually considered the earth to be only a few thousand years old, they based this belief on a figurative interpretation of the six days of creation, along with the absence of any widespread scientific evidence to prove an "old" earth.[30] If Genesis 1 refers to literal, twenty-four-hour days, how could there be days

29. Augustine, *Confessions* 13.19.25. Much more could be said by way of spiritual interpretation of the fourth day of creation. See, e.g., Basil of Caesarea, *Hexaemeron*; Ambrose of Milan, *Hexameron*; Augustine, *Literal Meaning of Genesis*.

30. For a brief summary of the interpretation of Gen. 1 and the age of the earth from the patristic to the post-Reformation period, see D. Young and Stearley, *Bible, Rocks, and Time*, 33–46.

without the movement of the sun, moon, and stars, which were not created until the fourth day? Early Christians recognized that, in this case, bogging down in a merely literal reading raises more problems than it solves.

Indeed, the church fathers assumed that if a biblical text is nonsensical on its surface, then this very difficulty is a literary clue to the parabolic nature of the text, under which one should seek the deeper, spiritual meaning. Recall, for instance, how Origen dismissed the literal sense of aspects of the narratives in Genesis 1–3. The numerous, insurmountable difficulties with the literalistic interpretation of the text are clues that the spiritual meaning should be sought. In other words, the very fact that one is asking about the location of Eden in relation to the four rivers, about Cain's wife and the other people whom he feared, about the longevity of the characters, or about the "sons of God" and their mating with the daughters of men—that very fact indicates that one is asking the wrong questions. The presence of so many fabulous elements in these texts presents a challenge to any simplistic, literal-historical interpretation. This is not to suggest that God could not have actualized a paradisiacal garden or a walking, talking snake. It is simply to acknowledge the numerous historical, scientific, geographical, and literary problems that arise when this account is taken literally. All those irreconcilable questions that people bring are indications that it is being read incorrectly.

At the same time, there is a difference between saying that it could not have happened that way and that it probably did not happen that way. If I am reading the genre of Genesis 1–11 correctly—as something akin to parable or, in Origen's terms, allegory—then to ask about its historicity is about as appropriate as asking about the historicity of the good Samaritan or prodigal son. Could there have been a merciful Samaritan and a lost son, and could all the things have actually happened as told? Of course! Could God accomplish creation in 144 hours, become incarnate to walk in a garden, and the like? Without a doubt. But in both cases, fixation on the historical question often leads one to miss the point of the narratives. It is not a question of divine omnipotence or even the reliability of Scripture. It is rather a question of genre, and the clue in the case of Genesis 1–11 is its mythological language and contradictions.[31] This is Origen's point, one well worth considering.

A literalistic reading, moreover, does not solve all interpretive problems but is subject to multiple interpretations of its own. In fact, a literalistic reading

31. These characteristics are to be contrasted with later narratives in the Old Testament and especially the New Testament, which, as they proceed, are narrated chronologically closer to the events, tend to reflect more historical sobriety over mythological language, exhibit contradictions in smaller or minor details, and clearly make historical claims with appeals to supporting proof, as, for example, in the case of Jesus's resurrection.

of Genesis 1 could be used in various ways to support ideas and worldviews that we would presume to be not necessarily biblical and to be definitely out of step with what we now know about the cosmos. How, for instance, might a traditional Neoplatonist of late antiquity read Genesis 1 in a literalistic fashion? In *Timaeus*, where Plato records his story about God and creation, he mentions the four basic elements: earth, air, fire, and water.[32] A Neoplatonist could, without great difficulty, see Genesis 1 as consistent with the Platonic view of physical reality and read the four elements into the Genesis account. The first verse of Genesis mentions the creation of heaven and earth, and the second verse speaks of spirit and water. For Plato, fire is the highest element that represents heaven. *Ruach* (Hebrew) or *pneuma* (Greek) can be translated variously as spirit, wind, or air. Thus, in the beginning, God created fire (heaven), earth, air (spirit), and water.[33] In this way, a certain literal interpretation of the biblical text could turn it into a sort of ancient science textbook pronouncing on physics that, we now know, is greatly mistaken. In addition to this ancient possibility, it is well known how an early modern, literalistic reading of Scripture was used to support the scientific theory of geocentrism, or how a modern, literalistic rendering of Genesis 1 has creation actually being completed, from beginning to end, in six days, or 144 hours. Such interpretations turn the biblical text into another kind of science textbook that pronounces on astronomy and provides a timetable of geological history.

Biblical scholars now recognize that, regardless of what the biblical authors may have personally believed about physics and astronomy, Genesis 1 was not primarily intended as what we might call a science textbook. The theological message—that God is transcendent and powerful, the source of all being; that he created freely; that he loves and cares for his entire creation; that he intends to communicate his goodness and grace to creation, so that humanity might reflect his glory and image in holy worship—is the primary purpose of the creation account in Genesis 1.[34] Such readings are not to be confused with the spiritual interpretations of early Christians; there are many differences, but the motivations are similar. The Genesis text is not a treatise on physical science; instead, it is a theological cosmogony, in the style of epic poetry, that makes claims about the nature and character of the God who created.

Once again, the difference between premodern interpretations and modern, literalistic interpretations stems in part from the kinds of questions asked of

32. Plato, *Timaeus* 31B–32C, et passim.
33. Augustine, *Civ.* 8.11, reports this interpretation and says that some Christians use these similarities as proof that Plato was directly or indirectly influenced by the Old Testament.
34. For recent treatments of Gen. 1, see W. Brown, *Seven Pillars of Creation*, 33–77; Walton, *Lost World of Genesis One*; Walton, *Genesis 1 as Ancient Cosmology*.

Genesis 1–11 and of Scripture in general. Modern readers tend to focus more on questions of historicity, science, textual background, date, provenance, authorship, and human authorial intent. All these are important questions for guiding one's interpretation. Premodern interpreters, however, tended to be more interested in what the biblical text teaches about God, Christ, his people, his intentions for his people—in short, doctrine and morality. The questions one asks of the text will influence what one finds in the text and which answers one deems most important. Premodern interpreters often did not address questions of historicity when it came to passages in Genesis 1–11; when they did, there seems to have been a wide degree of latitude. But they rarely got lost in the literal sense without addressing doctrine and ethics.[35] The concerns of premodern interpreters, vis-à-vis those of modern interpreters, seem to be more in line with the theological concerns of the biblical writers themselves.

Another example of the dangerous possibilities of literalistic interpretation focuses on the aftermath of the second creation account, told by the so-called Yahwist source in Genesis 3, in which a certain literal reading could easily raise intractable theological problems. In fact, the gnostic sect known as the Ophites (*ophis*, "serpent") took these texts literally and, accordingly, glorified the serpent of Genesis 3, honoring it as God.[36] In a sense, the serpent appears to be the only good character in the story. He alone tells the truth and appears to want to help Eve acquire valuable knowledge. On this reading, what could the true literalist infer about God? God is the one lying about the penalty for eating the forbidden fruit, he is vindictive, and he jealously guards his position by banishing the cursed couple who are on their way to becoming his equal. Make no mistake—this rendering is one logically coherent way of reading the text literally. If it sounds far-fetched, it is only because orthodox Christians have a traditional interpretation of the text that, bounded by the rule of faith, smooths over some of these difficulties. Thus the rule of faith excludes incorrect, literalistic interpretations.

Inquiring into human authorial intent, the foremost question for historical-critical understanding, is also of little help in understanding Genesis 3. What was the original intent for this text? An etiology of some sort, but what? It could be about the discovery of sex, the origin of clothing, how the snake lost

---

35. For instance, the Antiochene exegete Theodoret of Cyrus inquired into the narrated oddities and details of Gen. 1–11, but those questions were balanced by more profound and more strictly theological questions. See Theodoret of Cyrus, *Questions on the Octateuch*, vol. 1.

36. On the Ophites and the veneration of the serpent, see Origen, *Contra Celsum* 6.24, 28, 30; Epiphanius of Salamis, *Panarion* 37, in *Panarion: Book I*, 241–48; *Secret Book of John* 11, in *Nag Hammadi Scriptures*, 116.

its legs, why people hate snakes, why childbirth is painful, why work is painful, where natural evil comes from, or how sin and death came to be. Given its composition during the exile, it could be an allegory for the Babylonian exile from the promised land. Were all these points equally important to the human author, whoever and whenever he was? Were any of these points intended? Who could really know? What about the protoevangelium, the promise of victory for the woman's seed over the serpent, which was probably not in the human author's mind? If interpretation is restricted to or always based on authorial intent, then passages such as this one will remain a puzzle for any interpretation, especially for Christian interpretation.

Regardless of whether the original Yahwist author personally thought that the married Adam lacked a rib or that death and pain began with a historical fall, the main point of the text is the revelation of theological truth and archetypes that are consistent with the rule of faith and the whole of Scripture. Indeed, the writers of the New Testament indicate that this passage is full of meaning beyond the surface-level account. For example, the earliest church identified the serpent as a type of Satan (John 8:44; Rev. 12:9), saw Adam's loss of innocence as the story of all people (Rom. 5:12–21), and came to view the curse on the snake as the protoevangelium. To be sure, even modern Christians who insist on merely literal interpretations acknowledge these recurring typologies that are not explicitly present in the Genesis text itself.

Anyone who feels strongly about their literalist reading of Genesis 1–11 ought to gain some humility when they realize that most premodern Christians, who were just as devoted to God and the inspiration of his Word as they are, did not share their concerns or perhaps their same beliefs about the text. We are encouraged to read Genesis as, above all, a Christian book, and to avoid getting mired in a literalistic reading that causes us to be antagonistic to science or to miss the spiritual point of the text.

Psalm 137: Imprecation

As did David Steinmetz in his classic manifesto on premodern exegesis, in the introductory chapter I also raised the issue of Psalm 137. Because of its apparent endorsement of slaughtering the enemy's babies, this is one of the most notoriously difficult psalms to read individually, much less to sing in a liturgical setting. How can it possibly be put to Christian use? In short, if read merely on the literal level, it cannot.

But if Psalm 137 is read spiritually, then the Jerusalem for which one longs is the church, the faithful soul, and the heavenly kingdom desired by those in exile. As Steinmetz said, the psalm could become "a lament of those who long for the establishment of God's future kingdom and who are trapped in this disordered and troubled world, which with all its delights is still not their home."[37] In this sense, God's exiled people still long for Jerusalem. The ultimate enemies of the faithful are not physical Edomites or Babylonians, but spiritual enemies, the flesh that must be put to death. The imprecations against them are condemnations of the world, the flesh, the devil. As Steinmetz says, "If you grant the fourfold sense of Scripture, David sings like a Christian."[38] And if there is any type of literature meant to be taken symbolically and figuratively, surely poetry and song qualify.

This kind of allegorical interpretation goes back at least to Origen, who does this very thing with Psalm 137. The righteous destroy every instance of evil, down to the infant sin that has just been implanted. The infants of Babylon—a word that, Origen says, means confusion—are the confused thoughts of evil implanted in the soul. Thus God's command to destroy evil and its children is not at all contrary to Jesus's command to love enemies.[39] Any imprecatory psalms that speak about enemies and their defeat are, spiritually, about the powerful danger of sin and the war to be waged against evil, against the principalities and powers of this dark age.

As explained earlier in the historical survey, one feature of premodern exegesis was the ability to smooth over difficulties by appealing to a fuller spiritual sense, as Origen famously does. This approach was no longer possible once the spiritual sense had been eliminated. But, contrary to some criticisms, spiritualizing a biblical text is not always the easy way out; it is not always a way to ignore difficult teaching. In this case, that criticism is turned on its head. Literal interpretation alone, which tends to see Psalm 137 as nothing more than a curiosity (and an embarrassing one at that), allows the reader to dismiss the Christian meaning and thus the moral challenge. And it has become common among Christians to read the psalm precisely in this way, merely as a historical testimony that finds little or no positive spiritual value or application in it. But taking words seriously does not always mean taking them literally, as the apostles discovered on more than one occasion (for instance, Mark 8:14–21). The real challenge comes not from the literal but from the spiritual interpretation: Do we take evil as seriously as the psalmist takes the "Babylonians"? Is sin our hated enemy? Do we long to conquer it and its offspring? Do we really consider ourselves to be engaged in a spiritual

37. Steinmetz, "Superiority of Pre-critical Exegesis," 31.
38. Steinmetz, "Superiority of Pre-critical Exegesis," 31.
39. Origen, *Contra Celsum* 7.22.

battle? Do we desire the coming of God's kingdom as intensely as the psalmist did? Without this or a similar interpretation, Psalm 137 would have little
justification for its place in the Christian canon or worship.

Isaiah 7 and Matthew 1: Immanuel

In a well-known promise and fulfillment, Matthew quotes from Isaiah 7:14
(LXX) that a virgin would conceive and give birth to a son and name him Immanuel, or God with us. When Origen deals with this text, he insists that Immanuel is a straight-line prophecy of Jesus. The Hebrew word עַלְמָה (*almah*),
he argues, can mean virgin, and so the LXX is correct to translate it as virgin
(παρθένος, *parthenos*). In addition to the legitimacy of the translation, Origen
observes that it would not be much of a sign to King Ahaz "if a young woman
not a virgin bore a son."[40] But one could also ask whether a child who would
not appear for seven more centuries is much of a sign for Ahaz. By contend-
ing that the sign was not given in Ahaz's time, in the eighth century BC, but
was fulfilled only in Jesus, Origen and many Christian interpreters after him
have missed out on an important dimension of the text. In this case, greater
attention to the historical and literary contexts, inspired by the historical-
critical method, actually aids the christological and spiritual interpretations.

First of all, beginning with the Gospel text, the wider context of Matthew displays a marked interest in the Old Testament from the beginning
of chapter 1 and throughout the book. He was writing to show that Jesus
was the fulfillment of God's promises to Israel, including twelve instances
of the introductory formula "this fulfills the word spoken through . . ."
Jesus fulfills, fills up, brings to completion, and perfects the Old Testament
types. The fact of Matthew's general interest in the Old Testament, the
specific reference to fulfillment, and the fact that Jesus is never actually
called Immanuel—all invite readers to consider the Old Testament context
in which this name appears, a context that Matthew and his audience of
Jewish Christians knew well.

Isaiah's call (Isa. 6:1–7) stands at the beginning of the section having to
do with the Syro-Ephraimite war. It is a trying time, and the long reign of
Uzziah has just ended. The vision of Isaiah seems to begin with the picture of
the earthly temple (6:1, 3), but it also seems to be absorbed by the heavenly
temple, in which he sees the Lord. Isaiah's guilt is taken away. God's presence
is a prominent theme here. Isaiah says he will go and preach for God. The
people will be so hardened that they are unable to repent. It is a prophecy of

40. Origen, *Contra Celsum* 1.34–35.

destruction, but with the destruction is the prophecy of the remnant (6:13). God is present for punishment and for grace.

It is 734 BC, and King Ahaz of Judah is worried that the kings of Aram and of Ephraim will attack Jerusalem. He is outside Jerusalem, personally making sure that the city is secure and prepared for a siege. Isaiah meets the king out there and says, "Their plans against Jerusalem will not last" (7:7). Through Isaiah the Lord tells Ahaz to ask for a sign, to which he replies, "I don't need a sign." The Lord will give him a sign anyway: a maiden will give birth to a son and name him Immanuel (God with us). A brief time limit is set before which the plans of those two kings will be thwarted and their own lands devastated.

Based on the historical sense, Immanuel is a boy who was born in the 730s BC, a specific sign for King Ahaz. As Immanuel (God with us), this boy is a sign of God's presence with his people, a theme carried forward from the previous chapter. God's presence means two things: salvation for those who trust (7:16) and judgment for those who don't (7:17). Immanuel is the sign of both salvation and judgment: God is present to save his people from enemy attack, and he is present to bring punishment on Ahaz's family, eventually removing them from the throne during the Babylonian exile.

In Isaiah 7–9, there are other names and descriptions of Isaiah's sons (8:1). Then comes the figure in 9:6–7 and his description. The sons that are born of woman are taking on more divine characteristics. All the symbolic names used throughout Isaiah are intended to show that God is with his people.

Why does Matthew take up this sign and apply it to Jesus? Matthew knew Jesus as the ultimate fulfillment of God's presence with us. God himself is personally present in the form of a man, dwelling with us. Like that pillar of cloud and fire, like the rock in the desert, like the tabernacle and the temple, like Immanuel, Christ is God's glory in the flesh.

When we see an Old Testament text mentioned as fulfilled in the New Testament, the temptation is simply to ignore the Old Testament context and skip directly to the christological interpretation. But there is no need to suggest that for Ahaz there was no contemporary sign, an eighth-century BC Immanuel. When we see what Immanuel meant in the original context, it helps us to understand why Matthew appealed to this verse and how it truly applies to Jesus.

Like the Isaianic Immanuel, God's presence in Jesus signifies salvation for his people and judgment for unbelievers. God's presence confronts us in Christ, and two responses are possible. This response of either faith or offense is clear in the Gospel of Matthew and can be traced and seen throughout the document. We know Jesus Christ as the sign of salvation (1:21), but we often fail to see that he is also the sign of judgment (11:6; 23:34–38). These points in Matthew become clearer when one gives full attention to the context in Isaiah and sees the sign for what it was in its original time and place. As with other so-called messianic prophecies, there is an original fulfillment that the earlier writer had in mind, one that applied to the immediate Old Testament community. There is also a sense in which Jesus the Messiah more perfectly fulfills the meaning behind the original prophecy. What does it mean that Jesus is our Immanuel? It means that, in Jesus and in the Spirit whom he sent, God is still with us to the end of the age (Matt. 28:20).

Matthew 6:11 / Luke 11:3: Daily Bread

The importance of inquiring into historical context and the help that it can provide for understanding the literal and spiritual senses can be amply illustrated, as in Isaiah 7. At the same time, the inadequacy of restricting meaning to authorial intent or historical context, along with the impulse to pit literal versus spiritual, can hinder exegesis. Sometimes the willingness to relinquish the pursuit of authorial intent when it is ambiguous, along with an openness to the compatibility of literal and spiritual interpretations and aid from other Scriptures, can facilitate theologically responsible exegesis. A case in point is the phrase in the middle of the Lord's Prayer, translated woodenly, "Our bread that is daily give us today" (Matt. 6:11).

Two words complicate this otherwise straightforward petition: daily bread. First, the meaning of ἐπιούσιος (*epiousios*), traditionally translated as "daily," is unclear. As Origen correctly noticed, it is apparently a neologism.[41] It was presumably made up to represent whatever Jesus said in Aramaic. A made-up word is not always a problem. If there are examples of its use in other contexts, if we know the building blocks or etymology of the new construction, if early translations are in agreement, then we have clues. Sadly, none of this is the case with ἐπιούσιος. It is used nowhere in Greek literature except in Christian references to the Lord's Prayer.[42] Its etymology is debatable, and the early translations into Syriac and Latin are not uniform. Based on differing etymologies and early translations, ἐπιούσιος could mean either daily, necessary and essential, supersubstantial (that is, supernatural), or for tomorrow.[43]

41. Origen, *De oratione* 27.7 (PG 11:509C; ACW 19:96–97).
42. In the first century, Matt. 6:11; Luke 11:3; *Didache* 8:2.
43. For the range of translation possibilities, see Betz, *Sermon on the Mount*, 396–400; BDAG 376–77.

What is the significance of the different possibilities? Consider first the connotations of "daily" bread. A reader who has a basic knowledge of Scripture
will be reminded of the manna provided in the desert to sustain the traveling
Israelites, "bread from heaven" for "each day" (Exod. 16:4). One will also
recall the regulations for collecting the manna (Exod. 16:4–5, 16–26). What
were the principles behind those rules? Ultimately, the manna reflected Israel's
dependence on God for survival, who gave them enough for each day, and
enough on the sixth day for two days, but not enough to hoard.

In the exodus story, is the bread daily or necessary? Yes, it is both. Although
the two words, "daily" and "necessary," have different etymologies and very different meanings in Greek, in the specific context of food, their semantic range
overlaps enough to be almost synonymous. Bread that is essential for survival
is going to come regularly or daily. This same combination of ideas is taken up
a few paragraphs later in the Sermon on the Mount, when Jesus encourages
his disciples not to worry about what they will eat tomorrow, for their Father
knows what they need (Matt. 6:25–34). So which is the proper translation for
ἐπιούσιος, daily or necessary? In this context, each seems to imply the other.
The ambiguity of the word is a rare case, to be sure, but it calls into question
any exegesis that seeks certainty in authorial intent and in the exact etymology.

The second main question, distinct but also related to the first, is the
meaning of "bread." This time, of course, it is not about translation, but
bread could nevertheless be open to interpretation. On the one hand, most
modern readers would interpret the bread here as physical food, and if asked
to stretch the meaning a bit, might realize that it includes all things necessary
for physical life. Such is Calvin's interpretation, that "Christ speaks here of
bodily food." More broadly, it is a prayer "that we may receive all that is
necessary for the present life." Even here, though, Calvin restricts the meaning to "temporal blessings."[44] On the other hand, there is a long tradition
of seeing this bread as something other than physical, indicated in Jerome's
and Erasmus's translation of ἐπιούσιος as "supersubstantial," against which
Calvin was reacting. Origen dismisses those who think that Jesus was telling
us to pray for "material bread" and writes to "refute their error." As support, Origen cites many instances in the Gospels where bread clearly means
spiritual food.[45] What should we make of the two alternatives? And can other
Scriptures or authorial intent help?

First of all, there is no reason to go as far as Origen and insist that the
petition has nothing to do with physical bread. Scripture in general and Jesus

44. Calvin, *Harmony of the Evangelists*, 1:323, on Matt. 6:11.
45. Origen, *De oratione* 27.1–6 (ACW 19:92–96).

in particular show concern for human physical needs, yet with neither too much nor too little wealth. Proverbs 30:8 says, "Give me neither poverty nor riches" (NIV). Why? As the following verse says, both extremes would lead to temptation (30:9). Instead, the prayer is that God would give me "my daily bread," as the NIV translates it. A more accurate translation would render the Hebrew as the bread "necessary" or sufficient for me (Prov. 30:8). But again, as in the Lord's Prayer, what is essential, when it comes to food, turns out to be daily. The LXX here dispenses with the word "bread": "order what is necessary and sufficient for me" (Prov. 30:8 NETS). What is necessary includes food, but bread or food has become a cipher for all sustenance. Give what is necessary to sustain me.

As we have seen, Calvin came this far in relating the bread to physical blessing.[46] But it does not require a hermeneutical leap to include under the category of essentials not only physical sustenance but also spiritual sustenance. In fact, a good case can be made that, if "essential" or "necessary" is the idea in the Lord's Prayer, as it is in Proverbs 30, then what is truly essential is the spiritual sustenance.

And this is where Origen's point is relevant and Calvin did not go far enough. An imagination already shaped by Scripture will easily recognize the rich symbolism of bread. Without naming all instances, the most obvious spiritual interpretation of bread is perhaps in John 6:32, where, on the heels of physically feeding the five thousand, Jesus contrasts the bread of Moses with the "true bread" given by the heavenly Father. The language of John 6:32 actually echoes the language of the Lord's Prayer: the "Father . . . gives . . . bread." But what is the "true bread" given by the Father? It is spiritual nourishment and strength, God's commands, and the Word of God himself, the bread of life (John 6:35). It is supersubstantial bread, bread that sustains "for tomorrow," through eternity. Seeking this bread calls for shunning spiritual junk food, the false nourishment that fills up but makes the consumer unhealthy. Solid, healthy, chewable food is for the spiritually mature.

In the case of this petition in the Lord's Prayer, Origen rejected the physical or literal interpretation, and Calvin bypassed the figurative or spiritual. It should be clear, however, that both the literal and the spiritual interpretations can coincide without doing violence to one another. In fact, the concepts of physical and spiritual come together in the eucharistic bread. In Holy

---

46. It is possible that Calvin's rejection of the spiritual sense was intensified by the tendency of some interpreters to regard supersubstantial bread as the bread that transubstantiates in the Mass, a doctrine that he, of course, rejected.

Communion, the physical bread that strengthens our physical lives is the body of Christ that also nourishes our spiritual lives.

We can return to the question of authorial intent. Which meaning did Jesus intend? Which meaning did Matthew intend? Attention to authorial intent and historical background may exclude some interpretations. But it is just as clear that an appeal to authorial intent, especially as an attempt to determine the one true meaning or translation and to decide for either literal or spiritual interpretation against the other, would be a dead end. Did either Jesus or Matthew mean only physical bread or only spiritual bread? In Matthew's church, as the Gospel was heard and the Lord's Prayer was recited around the Lord's Table, can a eucharistic connotation be excluded? Did Jesus or Matthew intend that? Does it matter? The fact that there are no definitive answers to the authorial intent of this small but rich phrase points to the inherent weakness of limiting meaning to this criterion.

1 Peter 3:18–22: Baptism Now Saves You[47]

We all like to hear rescue stories. We hate the bad news when tragedy strikes, but we like to hear about deliverance. How many rescue stories do you remember hearing in the context of the recent earthquake and tsunami in Japan? Did you hear about the four-month-old girl who was swept from her parents' arms when the tsunami wave crashed into their home, and was found three days later in the rubble, wood, and mud, crying but otherwise unharmed? Or the sixty-year-old man who, after the earthquake, went back to his house, and then the wave came and swept his roof away, with him on top of it? He was found two days later about ten miles out to sea, sitting on top of his floating roof! Or the seventy-year-old woman whom rescuers pulled out of her toppled home four days after the quake? I know some were rescued nine days after the disaster started. Yes, we love to hear rescue stories. We hate the bad news of disaster that sets it up, but we love hearing about someone being saved.

The story told in Scripture doesn't have to go very far before we run into the bad news. The creatures who were made for eternal fellowship with God chose instead to be their own gods. Through selfishness and rebellion, we humans have thrust ourselves into the disastrous situation from which we need rescue. And from Genesis 3 onward, the whole story of the Bible is one long rescue story—the greatest rescue story ever told. Think about this

47. I preached this sermon on the occasion of my eldest child's baptism, in the context of a baptismal liturgy, on Easter morning, April 24, 2011, in Searcy, Arkansas. I have resisted the temptation to update the opening illustration.

rescue story and what it tells us about the rescuer. It tells of a God who did not scrap the project, but decided to redeem the fallen creation. We hear of a God who revealed himself to his people, who rescued them time and time again, who gave them laws for their own good, who was present among them for their salvation, who became Son of Man so they might become sons and daughters of God.

When we think about the process of salvation, we also cannot help but think about God's amazing grace, the undeserved gift, that he died for us while we were still enemies and sinners, that he loved us when we were unlovable. We think about the faith that he has granted to us, that he enables us to cooperate in this salvation by accepting his gift. So we know we must believe and trust God, whom we know to be trustworthy. Part of that saving faith involves, by the help of his Spirit, turning to God in repentance, a change of heart and mind that involves sorrow for the sin and brokenness we have participated in, and new resolve to leave behind that old way of life, which really is a way of death.

And, in addition to all these things, we rightly associate salvation with baptism, and baptism with salvation. No Christian creed or document speaks more highly of baptism than does the New Testament. In baptism, the New Testament tells us, we are clothed with Christ, sins are washed away and forgiven, the gift of the Holy Spirit is poured out, and we are saved. It is the working of God, the objective moment at which God has chosen to seal his promise of adoption in us. Of course, baptism would mean nothing without everything I've already said about the story of redemption, God's grace, and the gift of faith. Yet baptism is the visible moment of rescue.

Let us think about salvation in terms of one of the first rescue stories in the Bible. The disaster? The largest tsunami ever. The deluge. The flood. Actually, the disaster that brought it on started long before—violence!—when, in Genesis 4, Cain killed his brother Abel out of jealousy; when, later in that chapter, Lamech promised, not sevenfold, but seventy-sevenfold revenge on his enemies. And then, Genesis 6:5 tells us, every inclination of the human heart was nothing but evil. Verse 11 says that the earth was corrupt and full of violence. Humanity had corrupted themselves *and* the good land on which God had placed them. In response to human violence, God inflicted a punishment that fit their depraved crimes, but also set the stage for one of the most famous rescue stories in all recorded history. This is a familiar story, but let us pause to highlight three features of this rescue story.

First, it is a story of judgment on sin. Think of how the earth looked at the beginning of creation. Before the gradual process of creation was complete in Genesis, the earth was covered in water (Gen. 1:2). The second and third days of creation involved God bringing order out of the chaos, erecting boundaries not to be crossed by the water, separating water from water, and then the land from the water—all this to make something that, at the end, was pronounced "very good."

But sin proliferated exponentially, faster than compound interest, and an unpaid debt accumulated; the people and land that were created very good became evil, beyond recognition. When the standard for goodness, God, is abandoned, chaos and disorder reign. The chaos that existed before God separated the waters returned. So, to keep pace with humanity's choice, God reversed the process of creation and let it go its way, and the waters reverted to their original, chaotic mess. Like our boys' bringing order to their room by cleaning it, and somehow the process is quickly reversed. Legos seem to come from above and below to cover the room again. Likewise, from above and below, the floodgates were opened and the waters came to cover the earth again. This is not just a mere little children's story for Sunday school about the first zoo. This is the undoing, the reversal, of creation itself. Sin, in all its chaos and disorder, had full rein and was brought to its destructive completion. The water is about judgment.

Second, right in the midst of the judgment on sin, in the very bosom of this return to chaos and destruction of creation, is situated the story of salvation. Think of a large Google Map view, and then zoom in on it. In a vast and endless sea of death and destruction sits a little boat of hope for the future, saved through the water. The very means of destruction was also the means of rescue. I think we often miss the saving role of water in the flood story: for those in the ark, the *water* made the salvation possible.

Salvation from what? Saved from the evil world of corruption and violence of which Noah and his family wanted no part. Saved from the punishment coming to that disordered creation that wanted no part of God. Saved from it all, the ark was the one sacred space left in all creation. The one place where God was feared and his word heeded. It was a place where all were welcome, but only a few, eight in all, chose that space. The ark was the one place left where creation still had some semblance of order, and for that reason, it was the means of rescue, lifted by the water above the death and destruction. The water is about salvation.

Third, at the end of the story, there was new life. In the wake of the flood and the safe landing of the life raft, there was a new start for those who disembarked. The water over the earth, which destroyed every living thing, also cleansed the earth and renewed it. The water that brought death also made new life possible. Like washing a dirty car, yes, the water destroys: it wipes out all the things that need wiping out. The defilement of human sin and violence had been washed away, and the earth made a clean start. Imagine walking back out on the pristine planet, after the water has receded, as its soil sees sunlight again for the first time. It was a new creation, a re-creation, as if a dying and a coming back to life.

And after taking all this in, what could Noah say, what could he do? There was only one fitting response: he built an altar and worshiped God, thanking him for this incredible deliverance. Humanity got a second chance. Would Noah and his offspring live perfectly from here on out? No. According to the text of Genesis 9, Noah and his sons held out, at the most, as long as it takes for vines to grow and wine to ferment—so a year or two. Even with the new beginning, Noah was still a son of Adam, prone to sin. Though rescued and given a second chance, Noah and his offspring still had to wait for an even greater deliverance.

This is such an exciting rescue story that it is picked up at least four times in the New Testament. Let us give attention to one of those, 1 Peter 3:18–22:

> For Christ also suffered once for sins, the righteous one for the unrighteous ones, so that he might bring you to God, on the one hand, having been killed in the flesh, but, on the other hand, having been made alive in the spirit, in which having gone he proclaimed also to the spirits in prison, to those who at one time disobeyed when the patience of God waited in the days when Noah constructed an ark in which a few, that is, eight souls, were saved through water. This antitype, baptism, also now saves you, not the putting away of the filth of flesh but the appeal of a good conscience to God, through the resurrection of Jesus Christ, who is at the right hand of God, having gone into heaven as angels and authorities and powers submit to him.

Note a few things in this text. First of all, Jesus's death, resurrection, and ascension are central events, a point to which we will return in a moment. Next, the story of Noah is introduced, and a kind of comparison is given. Jesus, so to speak, went to proclaim victory over those who were disobedient in Noah's day. Then he says that the water symbolizes baptism. The idea expressed is that of type and antitype, technical terms for foreshadowing and reality. The Old Testament type foreshadows the antitype, which is the reality. The floodwaters foreshadow and point to baptism.

All this raises an important question. How is baptism like the flood? Why does 1 Peter make this comparison? We can give exactly the same answers that we gave when we spoke of three features of the flood story.

First, baptism represents judgment against sin. In baptism, as in the flood, something is being destroyed. What is it? Sin. Immediately after his discussion of baptism as dying with Christ in Romans 6, Paul says in verse 6, "For we know that our old self was crucified with him so that the body ruled by sin might be done away with" (NIV). Baptism means judgment against the old self and thus the death of the old self. Just as we often miss the saving aspect of the floodwaters, conversely we often miss the judgment aspect in the waters of baptism.

Baptism symbolizes what Christ has already accomplished: the destruction of every power, ruler, and authority, and the destruction of every fiber of our own being that is opposed to God. To be baptized involves the willful rejection of a way of life—really, a way of death—that the world approves, the utter renunciation of Satan and the ways of this world, the stubborn refusal to be corrupted by the sin and violence of the earthly city. Those baptized in the early church symbolized this renunciation—this rebellion—by turning west, facing the direction of everything that opposes God, and spitting. And so, to the degree that the old self has followed those ways, this renunciation is personal. The self, too, the flesh, is to be renounced, judged, and put to death.

This death is exhibited in baptism by being covered, or buried, in water. Immersion underwater, by someone else, is about the most vulnerable thing a person can do. In the pool, kids will go underwater just fine on their own, but most kids will do everything they can to avoid being dunked by someone else. There is a moment of breathlessness, no wind, no spirit. A few seconds of this, and a person could get very uncomfortable. This is, after all, a way to kill someone. Immersion underwater bears the semblance of death. It is judgment against sin.

Second, baptism is the moment of salvation. Salvation from what? Rescued from the evils of the world that stand against God, delivered from the punishment that awaits everything and everyone outside the sacred space. First Peter 3:21 says that baptism now saves you. First Peter and I are not saying that there is something magic in the water. What we are saying is that God chooses to use visible and tangible signs in creation to make his promises manifest. He ties a rainbow, as it were, around his finger and shows it to us to remind himself and us of his covenant of mercy. He uses ordinary bread and a cup to reseal our union with him and provide sanctifying grace. He also uses ordinary Red Sea water and Jordan River water and Arkansas water to work wonders. By God's grace, baptism, the very means and moment of destruction, is also the means and moment of salvation.

Third, baptism is the inauguration of a new creation. The death of the old self enables the resurrection of the new self. The putting away—not of literal dirt, but the washing away of sin—brings a spiritual cleansing. The death of the old self means life for the new. Whoever is in Christ is a new creation; the old has passed away, the new has come (2 Cor. 5:17). As Noah and his family walked onto a renewed creation with a second chance, and as Jesus walked out of the tomb on that first Easter Day, baptism is a fresh start of new life. In Romans 6, Paul says that in baptism we are raised to walk in newness of life.

Will this new life be one of perfection? Probably not. We still live in this in-between time, when we are still children of Adam even as we are children of God. But has something changed? Absolutely. We have died to sin. How can we live in it any longer? We cannot be enslaved to sin and overpowered by it. Baptism is our pledge and appeal of a good conscience before God. It is Pentecost extended, the pouring out of God's Holy Spirit to lead us through temptation, and even leading us beyond sin to repentance when necessary. This new life is not perfect, but with resurrection power and the help of the Holy Spirit, it is a striving toward perfection.

Finally, according to Romans 6, baptism is a re-presentation of the death, burial, and resurrection of Christ, and as such, baptism unites us with Christ's death, burial, and resurrection. And in Colossians 3, notice how Paul mentions the death, resurrection, and ascension of Christ to the right hand of the Father. "Therefore, if you have been raised together with Christ, seek the things above, where Christ is seated at the right of God. Set your minds on the things above, not on the things on the earth. For you died, and your life has been hidden with Christ in God. When Christ is made manifest, your life, then also you will be made manifest with him in glory" (3:1–4). In baptism, not only do we follow in Christ's footsteps, but we are also united with his dying and rising and exaltation. It is the sealing of God's promise in us of the death of our self that will no longer condemn us or rule in us; it is the promise of our own future bodily resurrection and our subsequent exaltation to the presence of God.

What can we say, what can we do, in light of the deliverance God has accomplished? Like Noah, we worship the God who has saved us from certain death. Thanks be to God for his salvation, for our deliverance, and for every rescue story we have the privilege to hear about and witness. Let us stand in awe of God's love and of the mighty deeds that he has wrought.

Bibliography

The following entries include the works cited and used in the book, as well as some additional resources for further reading and research.

Ambrose of Milan. *Hexameron, Paradise, and Cain and Abel*. FC 42. New York: Fathers of the Church, 1961.

The Apostolic Fathers: Greek Texts and English Translations. 3rd ed. Edited and translated by Michael W. Holmes. Grand Rapids: Baker Academic, 2007.

Athanasius. *Epistola ad Afros* 2. In *NPNF²*, vol. 4.

———. *Festal Letter* 39. In *NPNF²*, vol. 4.

Augustine. *De civitate Dei contra paganos*. ET, *The City of God against the Pagans*. Translated by R. W. Dyson. Cambridge Texts in the History of Political Thought. Cambridge: Cambridge University Press, 1998.

———. *The Confessions*. Translated by Maria Boulding. *WSA* I/1.

———. *De doctrina Christiana*. ET, *On Christian Teaching*. Translated by R. P. H. Green. Oxford World's Classics. New York: Oxford University Press, 1997.

———. *Enchiridion*. In *WSA* I/8.

———. *The Literal Meaning of Genesis*. In *WSA* I/13.

———. *Questions on the Gospels*. Translated by Roland Teske. In *WSA* I/15 and I/16.

———. *Works of Saint Augustine*. 2nd ed. Hyde Park, NY: New City Press, 2012–.

Aune, David E. *Revelation 6–16*. Word Biblical Commentary 52B. Nashville: Nelson, 1998.

Ayres, Lewis. "'There's Fire in That Rain': On Reading the Letter and Reading Allegorically." *Modern Theology* 28, no. 4 (2012): 616–34.

Baird, William. *History of New Testament Research*. 3 vols. Minneapolis: Fortress, 1992–2013.

Barth, Karl. *Church Dogmatics*. Vol. IV/1, *The Doctrine of Reconciliation*, Part 1. Translated by Geoffrey W. Bromiley. Edinburgh: T&T Clark, 1956.

Barton, John. *Holy Writings, Sacred Text: The Canon in Early Christianity*. Louisville: Westminster John Knox, 1998.

———. *The Nature of Biblical Criticism*. Louisville: Westminster John Knox, 2007.

Basil of Caesarea. *The Hexaemeron*. In *NPNF²*, vol. 8.

Bede. *The Ecclesiastical History of the English People*. Oxford World's Classics. New York: Oxford University Press, 1994.

Behr, John. *Asceticism and Anthropology in Irenaeus and Clement*. Oxford Early Christian Studies. Oxford: Oxford University Press, 2000.

Bellarmine, Robert. *Disputationes de controversiis Christianae fidei adversus huius temporis haereticos, De verbo Dei*. In *Opera omnia*, vol. 1. Naples: Joseph Giuliano, 1856.

Bernard of Clairvaux. *Sermons on the Song of Songs*. In *Selected Works*. Translated by G. R. Evans. CWS. Mahwah, NJ: Paulist Press, 1987.

Betz, Hans Dieter. *The Sermon on the Mount: A Commentary on the Sermon on the Mount, Including the Sermon on the Plain*. Hermeneia. Minneapolis: Fortress, 1995.

Biblia patristica: Index des citations et allusions bibliques dans la littérature patristique. 7 vols. Paris: Éditions du Centre national de la recherche scientifique, 1975–2000.

Blomberg, Craig L. *The Historical Reliability of the Gospels*. Nashville: B&H Academic, 2016.

———. *Interpreting the Parables*. Downers Grove, IL: InterVarsity, 1990.

———. *Jesus and the Gospels*. Nashville: Broadman & Holman, 1997.

Blowers, Paul M., ed. *The Bible in Greek Christian Antiquity*. Notre Dame, IN: University of Notre Dame Press, 1997.

———, ed. *In Dominico Eloquio/In Lordly Eloquence: Essays on Patristic Exegesis in Honor of Robert Louis Wilken*. Grand Rapids: Eerdmans, 2002.

———. "The *Regula Fidei* and the Narrative Character of Early Christian Faith." *Pro Ecclesia* 6, no. 2 (1997): 199–228.

Bockmuehl, Markus. *Seeing the Word: Refocusing New Testament Study*. Studies in Theological Interpretation. Grand Rapids: Baker Academic, 2006.

Boersma, Hans. *Scripture as Real Presence: Sacramental Exegesis in the Early Church*. Grand Rapids: Baker Academic, 2017.

Boles, Paul C. "Allegory as Embodiment: The Function of History in Origen's *Genesis Homily*." *Journal of Theological Interpretation* 10, no. 1 (2016): 87–101.

Bonner, Gerald. "Augustine as Biblical Scholar." In *Cambridge History of the Bible*, 1:541–63.

Borg, Marcus J., ed. *The Lost Gospel Q: The Original Sayings of Jesus*. Berkeley: Ulysses, 1996.

Boring, M. Eugene. *Disciples and the Bible: A History of Disciples Biblical Interpretation in North America*. St. Louis: Chalice Press, 1997.

Boxhorn, Marcus Zueris van. *Nederlandsche historie, behelsende de staat van de Nederlandsche kerk voor der hervorming*. Utrecht: Hermannus Ribbius, 1700.

Braaten, Carl E., and Robert W. Jenson, eds. *Reclaiming the Bible for the Church*. Grand Rapids: Eerdmans, 1995.

Bradley, James E., and Richard A. Muller. *Church History: An Introduction to Research, Reference Works, and Methods.* Grand Rapids: Eerdmans, 1995.

Bray, Gerald L. *Biblical Interpretation: Past and Present.* Downers Grove, IL: InterVarsity, 2000.

Brazos Theological Commentary on the Bible. Grand Rapids: Brazos Press, 2005–.

Brevicoxa, John. *De fide et ecclesia.* Translated in Oberman, *Forerunners of the Reformation,* 67–92.

Brown, Dennis. "Jerome and the Vulgate." In Hauser and Watson, *A History of Biblical Interpretation,* 1:355–79.

Brown, William P. *The Seven Pillars of Creation: The Bible, Science, and the Ecology of Wonder.* New York: Oxford University Press, 2010.

Butterfield, Herbert. *The Whig Interpretation of History.* 1931. Reprint, New York: Norton, 1965.

Caird, G. B. *The Language and Imagery of the Bible.* Philadelphia: Westminster, 1980.

Cairns, Earle E. *Christianity through the Centuries: A History of the Christian Church.* 3rd ed. Grand Rapids: Zondervan, 1996.

Calvin, John. Calvin's Commentaries. In 22 vols. Calvin Translation Society. Reprint, Grand Rapids: Baker, 1996.

———. *Commentary on a Harmony of the Evangelists, Matthew, Mark, and Luke.* Vols. 1–2 in CC 16. Vol. 3 in CC 17.

———. *Commentary on the Book of Psalms.* CC 5–6.

———. *Commentary on the Epistle of Paul the Apostle to the Romans.* CC 19.

———. *Commentaries on the Epistles of Paul to the Corinthians.* CC 20.

———. *Commentaries on the Epistles of Paul to the Galatians and Ephesians.* CC 21.

———. *Commentaries on the First Book of Moses Called Genesis.* CC 1.

———. "The Epistle Dedicatory to Simon Grynaeus." In *Commentary on the Epistle of Paul the Apostle to the Romans.* CC 19.

———. *Institutes of the Christian Religion.* Edited by John T. McNeill. Translated by Ford Lewis Battles. Library of Christian Classics 21–22. Philadelphia: Westminster, 1960.

———. *Ioannis Calvini opera quae supersunt omnia.* Edited by G. Baum, E. Cunitz, and E. Reuss. Brunswick: Schwetschke, 1863–1900.

The Cambridge History of the Bible. Edited by P. R. Ackroyd, C. F. Evans, G. W. H. Lampe, and S. L. Greenslade. 3 vols. Cambridge: Cambridge University Press, 1963–70.

Cameron, Michael. *Christ Meets Me Everywhere: Augustine's Early Figurative Exegesis.* Oxford Studies in Historical Theology. New York: Oxford University Press, 2012.

Campbell, Alexander. "Anecdotes, Incidents and Facts," *Millennial Harbinger,* 3rd series, 5 (1848): 280–83.

———. "The Bible—Principles of Interpretation." *Millennial Harbinger,* 3rd series, 3 (1846): 13–24.

———. "Calvinism and Arminianism." *Millennial Harbinger,* 3rd series, 3 (1846): 322–29.

————. "The Double Sense of Scripture." *Millennial Harbinger*, 1st series, 1 (1830): 38–40.

————. "Reply." *Christian Baptist* 5 (1827): 208–11.

————. "Trinitarianism, Arianism, and Socinianism." *Millennial Harbinger*, 1st series, 4 (1833): 153–60.

Campbell, Lewis. Introduction to *Theological Essays of the Late Benjamin Jowett*, edited by Lewis Campbell, ix–xx. London: Henry Frowde, 1906.

Campbell, Thomas. *Declaration and Address of the Christian Association of Washington*. In *The Quest for Christian Unity, Peace, and Purity in Thomas Campbell's "Declaration and Address": Text and Studies*, edited by Thomas H. Olbricht and Hans Rollmann. Lanham: Scarecrow Press, 2000.

Cassian, John. *The Conferences*. Translated by Boniface Ramsey. ACW 57. New York: Newman Press, 1997.

Catholic Church. *Catechism of the Catholic Church*. New York: Doubleday, 1995.

Channing, William Ellery. "Unitarian Christianity." Delivered at the Ordination of Rev. Jared Sparks in The First Independent Church of Baltimore on May 5, 1819. http://www.transcendentalists.com/unitarian_christianity.htm. In *The Works of William E. Channing*, 367–83. Boston: American Unitarian Association, 1890.

Chesterton, G. K. *Orthodoxy*. Nashville: Thomas Nelson, 2000.

Childs, Brevard. "The Sensus Literalis of Scripture: An Ancient and Modern Problem." In *Beiträge zur alttestamentlichen Theologie: Festschrift für Walther Zimmerli zum 70. Geburtstag*, edited by Herbert Donner, Robert Hanhart, and Rudolf Smend, 80–93. Göttingen: Vandenhoeck & Ruprecht, 1977.

Clement of Alexandria. *Paedagogus*. In *ANF*, vol. 2.

————. *Stromata*. In *ANF*, vol. 2.

Conybeare, John Josias. *The Bampton Lectures for the Year MDCCCXXIV: Being an Attempt to Trace the History and to Ascertain the Limits of the Secondary and Spiritual Interpretation of Scripture*. Oxford: Oxford University Press, 1824.

————. *Illustrations of Anglo-Saxon Poetry*. London: Harding & Lepard, Pall Mall, East, 1826.

Cook, John Granger. *The Interpretation of the New Testament in Greco-Roman Paganism*. 2000. Reprint, Peabody, MA: Hendrickson, 2002.

Courcelles, Étienne de. *Institutio religionis Christianae*. In *Opera theologica*. Amsterdam: Daniel Elzevier, 1675.

————. "Praefatio ad lectorem." In *Novum testamentum*. Amsterdam: Elzevier, 1658.

Courtenay, William J. "The Bible in the Fourteenth Century: Some Observations." *Church History* 54, no. 2 (1985): 176–87.

Crossan, John Dominic. "Why Jesus Didn't Marry." *CSER* [*Committee for the Scientific Examination of Religion*] *Review* [Amherst, NY] 1, no. 1 (2006): 5–10. Cf. http://www.beliefnet.com/entertainment/movies/the-da-vinci-code/why-jesus -didnt-marry.aspx.

Crouzel, Henri. *Origen: The Life and Thought of the First Great Theologian*. Translated by A. S. Worrall. San Francisco: Harper & Row, 1989.

Daugirdas, Kestutis. "The Biblical Hermeneutics of Socinians and Remonstrants in the Seventeenth Century." In *Arminius, Arminianism, and Europe*, edited by Th. M. van Leeuwen, Keith D. Stanglin, and Marijke Tolsma, 89–113. Brill's Series in Church History 39. Boston: Brill, 2009.

Davis, Ellen F., and Richard B. Hays. "Nine Theses on the Interpretation of Scripture." In *The Art of Reading Scripture*, edited by Ellen F. Davis and Richard B. Hays, 1–5. Grand Rapids: Eerdmans, 2003.

de Jonge, H. J. "Erasmus and the Comma Johanneum." *Ephemerides theologicae Lovanienses* 56, no. 4 (1980): 381–89.

DelCogliano, Mark. Introduction to Gregory I, the Great, *Moral Reflections on the Book of Job*, 1:1–45.

de Lubac. *See* Lubac, Henri de.

Descartes, René. *Discourse on Method*. Translated by Donald A. Cress. Indianapolis: Hackett, 1980.

Diodore of Tarsus. *Commentary on Psalms 1–51*. Translated by Robert C. Hill. Atlanta: Society of Biblical Literature, 2005.

———. "Preface to the *Commentary on Psalm 118*." In Froehlich, *Biblical Interpretation in the Early Church*, 87–94.

Dionysius the Areopagite. *Pseudo-Dionysius: The Complete Works*. Translated by Colm Luibheid. CWS. Mahwah, NJ: Paulist Press, 1987.

Dodd, C. H. *The Parables of the Kingdom*. London: Nisbet, 1935.

Donfried, Karl P., ed. *The Romans Debate*. Rev. ed. Peabody, MA: Hendrickson, 1991.

Dove, Mary. "Literal Senses in the Song of Songs." In Krey and L. Smith, *Nicholas of Lyra*, 129–46.

Dupré, Louis. *The Enlightenment and the Intellectual Foundations of Modern Culture*. New Haven: Yale University Press, 2004.

Eadmer of Canterbury. *Liber de Sancti Anselmi similitudinibus*. In PL 159.

Ebeling, Gerhard. *The Word of God and Tradition: Historical Studies Interpreting the Divisions of Christianity*. Translated by S. H. Hooke. Philadelphia: Fortress Press, 1968.

Egeria: Diary of a Pilgrimage. Translated by George E. Gingras. ACW 38. New York: Newman, 1970.

Epiphanius of Salamis. *Panarion: Book I (Sects 1–46)*. Translated by Frank Williams. Leiden: Brill, 1997.

Episcopius, Simon. *Apologia pro confessione sive declaratione sententiae eorum, qui in foederato Belgio vocantur Remonstrantes*. N.p., 1630.

———. *Confessio, sive declaratio, sententiae pastorum, qui in foederato Belgio Remonstrantes vocantur*. Harderwijk: Theodore Daniel, 1622. ET, *The Arminian Confession of 1621*. Translated by Mark A. Ellis. Eugene, OR: Pickwick, 2005.

———. *Disputationes theologicae tripartitae, olim in Academia Leydensi, tum publice, tum privatim duobus Collegiis, habitae*. In *Operum theologicorum: Pars altera*, part 2. Rotterdam: Arnold Leers, 1665.

Epistle of Barnabas. In *Apostolic Fathers*.

Erasmus, Desiderius. *The Handbook of the Christian Soldier*, in *CWE* 66.

———. "Letter 182, to Christopher Fisher (1505)." In *CWE* 2.

———. *De libero arbitrio*. ET, *Luther and Erasmus: Free Will and Salvation*. Library of Christian Classics. Philadelphia: Westminster, 1969.

———. *Novum instrumentum omne, diligenter ab Erasmo Roterodamo recognitum et emendatum*. Basel: Johannes Froben, 1516.

———. "To the Reader (1515)." In *CWE* 3.

Ernesti, Johann A. *Elements of Interpretation*. Translated by Moses Stuart. Andover: Flagg & Gould, 1822.

Eusebius. *Ecclesiastical History*. Translated by Kirsopp Lake and J. E. L. Oulton. 2 vols. LCL 153 and 265. Cambridge, MA: Harvard University Press, 1926–32.

Farkasfalvy, Denis M. "Theology of Scripture in St. Irenaeus." *Revue Benedictine* 78, nos. 3–4 (1968): 319–33.

Farmer, William R., and Denis M. Farkasfalvy. *The Formation of the New Testament Canon: An Ecumenical Approach*. New York: Paulist Press, 1983.

Farrar, Frederic W. *History of Interpretation*. Bampton Lectures. New York: Dutton, 1886.

Fee, Gordon, and Douglas Stuart. *How to Read the Bible for All Its Worth*. 3rd ed. Grand Rapids: Zondervan, 2003.

Ferguson, Everett. *Backgrounds of Early Christianity*. 2nd ed. Grand Rapids: Eerdmans, 1993.

———, ed. *The Bible in the Early Church*. Studies in Early Christianity 3. New York: Garland, 1993.

———. "Irenaeus' *Proof of the Apostolic Preaching* and Early Catechetical Instruction." In Studia Patristica 18, no. 3:119–40. Kalamazoo, MI: Cistercian Publications, 1989.

———. "The Muratorian Fragment and the Development of the Canon." *Journal of Theological Studies* 44, no. 2 (1993): 691–97.

———. *The Rule of Faith: A Guide*. Eugene, OR: Cascade, 2015.

———. "Using Historical Foreground in New Testament Interpretation." In *Biblical Interpretation: Principles and Practice*, edited by F. Furman Kearley, Edward P. Myers, and Timothy D. Hadley, 254–63. Grand Rapids: Baker, 1986.

Ferguson, Everett, and Abraham J. Malherbe. Introduction to Gregory of Nyssa, *The Life of Moses*.

Flacius Illyricus, Matthias. *How to Understand the Sacred Scriptures*. From *Clavis Scripturae sacrae*. Translated by Wade R. Johnston, tractatus I. Saginaw, MI: Magdeburg, 2011.

Fowl, Stephen E. "The Role of Authorial Intention in the Theological Interpretation of Scripture." In *Between Two Horizons: Spanning New Testament Studies and Systematic Theology*. Edited by Joel B. Green and Max Turner, 71–87. Grand Rapids: Eerdmans, 2000.

———, ed. *The Theological Interpretation of Scripture: Classic and Contemporary Readings*. Oxford: Blackwell, 1997.

Frei, Hans W. *The Eclipse of Biblical Narrative: A Study in Eighteenth and Nineteenth Century Hermeneutics*. New Haven: Yale University Press, 1974.

Fried, Johannes. *The Middle Ages*. Translated by Peter Lewis. Cambridge, MA: Belknap Press of Harvard University Press, 2015.

Froehlich, Karlfried. *Biblical Interpretation from the Church Fathers to the Reformation*. Variorum Collected Studies Series. Burlington, VT: Ashgate, 2010.

———, ed. *Biblical Interpretation in the Early Church*. Sources of Early Christian Thought. Philadelphia: Fortress, 1984.

———. *Sensing the Scriptures: Aminadab's Chariot and the Predicament of Biblical Interpretation*. Grand Rapids: Eerdmans, 2014.

Furnish, Victor P. *II Corinthians*. Anchor Bible. New York: Doubleday, 1984.

Gabler, Johann P. "An Oration on the Proper Distinction between Biblical and Dogmatic Theology and the Specific Objectives of Each." In *The Flowering of Old Testament Theology: A Reader in Twentieth-Century Old Testament Theology, 1930–1990*, edited by Ben C. Ollenburger et al., 492–502. Winona Lake, IN: Eisenbrauns, 1992.

Gavrilyuk, Paul L. "Scripture and the *Regula Fidei*: Two Interlocking Components of the Canonical Heritage." In *Canonical Theism: A Proposal for Theology and the Church*, edited by William J. Abraham, Jason E. Vickers, and Natalie B. Van Kirk, 27–42. Grand Rapids: Eerdmans, 2008.

George, Timothy. *Reading Scripture with the Reformers*. Downers Grove, IL: IVP Academic, 2011.

———, ed. *Reformation Commentary on Scripture*. Downers Grove, IL: IVP Academic, 2011–.

Goldingay, John. *Do We Need the New Testament? Letting the Old Testament Speak for Itself*. Downers Grove, IL: InterVarsity, 2015.

Gordon, Bruce, and Matthew McLean, eds. *Shaping the Bible in the Reformation: Books, Scholars, and Their Readers in the Sixteenth Century*. Leiden: Brill, 2012.

Grafton, Anthony. *Forgers and Critics: Creativity and Duplicity in Western Scholarship*. Princeton: Princeton University Press, 1990.

Grant, Robert M., and David Tracy. *A Short History of the Interpretation of the Bible*. 2nd ed. 1984. Reprint, Minneapolis: Fortress, 2005.

Grebel, Conrad. *Letters to Thomas Müntzer, September 5, 1524*. In Williams and Mergal, *Spiritual and Anabaptist Writers*, 71–85.

Green, Joel B. "Which Conversation Shall We Have? History, Historicism and Historical Narrative in Theological Interpretation: A Response to Peter van Inwagen." In *"Behind" the Text: History and Biblical Interpretation*, edited by Craig Bartholomew, C. Stephen Evans, Mary Healy, and Murray Rae, 141–50. Grand Rapids: Zondervan, 2003.

Greer, Rowan A. Introduction to Theodore of Mopsuestia, *The Commentaries on the Minor Epistles of Paul*, translated by Rowan A. Greer, ix–xliv. Atlanta: Society of Biblical Literature, 2010.

Gregory, Brad S. *The Unintended Reformation: How a Religious Revolution Secularized Society*. Cambridge, MA: Belknap Press of Harvard University Press, 2012.

Gregory of Nyssa. *The Life of Moses*. Translated by Everett Ferguson and Abraham J. Malherbe. CWS. New York: Paulist Press, 1978.

Gregory I, the Great. "Letter to Leander." In *Moral Reflections on the Book of Job*, vol. 1.

———. *Moral Reflections on the Book of Job* [= *Moralia*]. Translated by Brian Kerns. Vol. 1. Collegeville, MN: Liturgical Press, 2014.

Grenz, Stanley J. *A Primer on Postmodernism*. Grand Rapids: Eerdmans, 1996.

Hafemann, Scott J. *Paul, Moses, and the History of Israel: The Letter/Spirit Contrast and the Argument from Scripture in 2 Corinthians 3*. Paternoster Biblical Monographs. Eugene, OR: Wipf & Stock, 2005.

Hall, Christopher A. *Reading Scripture with the Church Fathers*. Downers Grove, IL: InterVarsity, 1998.

Hamilton, Victor P. *The Book of Genesis: Chapters 1–17*. New International Commentary on the Old Testament. Grand Rapids: Eerdmans, 1990.

Hanson, R. P. C. *Allegory and Event: A Study of the Sources and Significance of Origen's Interpretation of Scripture*. 1959. Reprint, with introduction by Joseph W. Trigg. Louisville: Westminster John Knox, 2002.

Harris, Horton. *The Tübingen School: A Historical and Theological Investigation of the School of F. C. Baur*. New ed. Grand Rapids: Baker, 1990.

Harrisville, Roy A., and Walter Sundberg. *The Bible in Modern Culture: Baruch Spinoza to Brevard Childs*. 2nd ed. Grand Rapids: Eerdmans, 2002.

Hatch, Nathan. *The Democratization of American Christianity*. New Haven: Yale University Press, 1989.

Hauser, Alan J., and Duane F. Watson, eds. *A History of Biblical Interpretation*. 3 vols. Grand Rapids: Eerdmans, 2008–17.

Hayes, John H. *Hebrew Bible: History of Interpretation*. Nashville: Abingdon, 2004.

Heine, Ronald E. *Origen: Scholarship in the Service of the Church*. Christian Theology in Context. Oxford: Oxford University Press, 2010.

———. "Reading the Bible with Origen." In Blowers, *The Bible in Greek Christian Antiquity*, 131–48.

———. *Reading the Old Testament with the Ancient Church: Exploring the Formation of Early Christian Thought*. Grand Rapids: Baker Academic, 2007.

Hengel, Martin, and Roland Deines. *The Septuagint as Christian Scripture: Its Prehistory and the Problem of Its Canon*. Translated by Mark E. Biddle. New York: T&T Clark, 2002.

Hill, Robert C. Introduction to Theodore of Mopsuestia, *Commentary on the Twelve Prophets*, translated by Robert C. Hill, 1–34. Washington, DC: Catholic University of America Press, 2004.

———. *Reading the Old Testament in Antioch*. Leiden: Brill, 2005.

Hodge, Charles. *Systematic Theology*. Vol. 1. New York: Charles Scribner's Sons, 1871.

Holder, R. Ward. *John Calvin and the Grounding of Interpretation: Calvin's First Commentaries*. Studies in the History of Christian Traditions 127. Leiden: Brill, 2005.

————, ed. *A Companion to Paul in the Reformation*. Brill's Companions to the Christian Tradition 15. Leiden: Brill, 2009.

Holder, R. Ward, and Kathy Ehrensperger, eds. *Reformation Readings of Romans*. New York: T&T Clark, 2008.

Hooker, Richard. *Of the Laws of Ecclesiastical Polity*. 2 vols. London: J. M. Dent, 1907.

Houghton, H. A. G. *The Latin New Testament: A Guide to Its Early History, Texts, and Manuscripts*. Oxford: Oxford University Press, 2016.

Huizinga, Johan. *The Autumn of the Middle Ages*. Translated by Rodney J. Payton and Ulrich Mammitzsch. Chicago: University of Chicago Press, 1996.

Hume, David. "Of Miracles." Excerpted from his *An Enquiry concerning Human Understanding*. In *Dialogues concerning Natural Religion*, edited by Richard H. Popkin, 107–25. 2nd ed. Indianapolis: Hackett, 1998.

Hurtado, Larry W. *The Earliest Christian Artifacts: Manuscripts and Christian Origins*. Grand Rapids: Eerdmans, 2006.

Ignatius of Antioch. *To the Philadelphians. To the Trallians. To the Smyrnaeans*. In *Apostolic Fathers*.

Innocent III. *Sicut universitatis conditor*. In *Documents of the Christian Church*, edited by Henry Bettenson and Chris Maunders, 117–18. 4th ed. New York: Oxford University Press, 2011.

Irenaeus of Lyons. *Adversus haereses*. In *ANF* 1.

————. *Proof of the Apostolic Preaching*. Translated by Joseph P. Smith. ACW 16. Westminster, MD: Newman, 1952.

Israel, Jonathan I. Introduction to Spinoza, *Theological-Political Treatise*, viii–xxxiv.

————. *Radical Enlightenment: Philosophy and the Making of Modernity, 1650–1750*. Oxford: Oxford University Press, 2001.

Jenson, Robert W. *Canon and Creed*. Interpretation. Louisville: Westminster John Knox, 2010.

John Chrysostom. *The Gospel of St. Matthew*. In NPNF[1], vol. 10.

Johnson, Luke Timothy. *The Real Jesus: The Misguided Quest for the Historical Jesus and the Truth of the Traditional Gospels*. San Francisco: HarperSanFrancisco, 1996.

————. *The Writings of the New Testament: An Interpretation*. 3rd ed. Minneapolis: Fortress, 2010.

Josephus, Flavius. *Antiquities of the Jews*. In *The Complete Works of Flavius Josephus*. Translated by William Whiston. Chicago: Thompson & Thomas, n.d.

Journal of Theological Interpretation. Winona Lake, IN: Eisenbrauns, 2007–.

Jowett, Benjamin. "On the Interpretation of Scripture." In *Essays and Reviews*, 330–433. London: John W. Parker & Son, 1860.

Justin Martyr. *Dialogue with Trypho*. In *Writings of Saint Justin Martyr*.

————. *First Apology*. In *Writings of Saint Justin Martyr*.

————. *Writings of Saint Justin Martyr*. Translated by Thomas B. Falls. FC 6. New York: Christian Heritage, 1948.

Kannengiesser, Charles. *Handbook of Patristic Exegesis*. 2 vols. Leiden: Brill, 2004.

Keener, Craig S. *The Historical Jesus of the Gospels*. Grand Rapids: Eerdmans, 2009.

Kelly, J. N. D. *Early Christian Doctrines*. Rev. ed. New York: Harper Collins, 1978.

Kloppenborg, John S. *Q, the Earliest Gospel: An Introduction to the Original Stories and Sayings of Jesus*. Louisville: Westminster John Knox, 2008.

Kolb, Robert. *Martin Luther and the Enduring Word of God: The Wittenberg School and Its Scripture-Centered Proclamation*. Grand Rapids: Baker Academic, 2016.

Kraus, Hans-Joachim. "Calvin's Exegetical Principles." Translated by Keith Crim. *Interpretation* 31, no. 1 (1977): 12–18.

Krey, Philip D. W. "The Apocalypse Commentary of 1329: Problems in Church History." In Krey and L. Smith, *Nicholas of Lyra*, 267–88.

Krey, Philip D. W., and Lesley Smith, eds. *Nicholas of Lyra: The Senses of Scripture*. Leiden: Brill, 2000.

Kristeller, Paul Oskar. *Renaissance Thought: The Classic, Scholastic, and Humanist Strains*. New York: Harper & Row, 1961.

Kugel, James A., and Rowan A. Greer. *Early Biblical Interpretation*. Library of Early Christianity. Philadelphia: Westminster, 1986.

Lamarche, Paul. "The Septuagint: Bible of the Earliest Christians." In Blowers, *The Bible in Greek Christian Antiquity*, 15–33.

Lapide, Cornelius à. *The Great Commentary of Cornelius à Lapide: S. Luke's Gospel*. Translated by Thomas W. Mossman. 3rd ed. London: John Hodges, 1892.

Lauro, Elizabeth Ann Dively. *The Soul and Spirit of Scripture within Origen's Exegesis*. Leiden: Brill, 2005.

Leclercq, Jean. *The Love of Learning and the Desire for God: A Study of Monastic Culture*. Translated by Catharine Misrahi. New York: Fordham University Press, 1961.

Lefèvre d'Étaples, Jacques. "Introduction to Commentary on the Psalms." In Oberman, *Forerunners of the Reformation*, 297–301.

Legaspi, Michael C. *The Death of Scripture and the Rise of Biblical Studies*. Oxford Studies in Historical Theology. New York: Oxford University Press, 2010.

Leinsle, Ulrich G. *Introduction to Scholastic Theology*. Translated by Michael J. Miller. Washington, DC: Catholic University of America Press, 2010.

Leithart, Peter J. *Deep Exegesis: The Mystery of Reading Scripture*. Waco: Baylor University Press, 2009.

Lessing, G. E. "On the Proof of the Spirit and of Power." In *Lessing's Theological Writings*, selected and translated by Henry Chadwick, 51–56. Stanford: Stanford University Press, 1957.

The Letter of Aristeas. In *Old Testament Pseudepigrapha*, vol. 2. Edited by J. H. Charlesworth. Garden City, NY: Doubleday, 1985.

Levering, Matthew. *Participatory Biblical Exegesis: A Theology of Biblical Interpretation*. Notre Dame, IN: University of Notre Dame Press, 2008.

Levy, Ian Christopher. *Holy Scripture and the Quest for Authority at the End of the Middle Ages*. Notre Dame, IN: University of Notre Dame Press, 2012.

Lewis, C. S. "Modern Theology and Biblical Criticism." In *Christian Reflections*, edited by Walter Hooper, 152–66. Grand Rapids: Eerdmans, 1995.

Lischer, Richard. *Reading the Parables*. Interpretation. Louisville: Westminster John Knox, 2014.

Livingston, James C., and Francis S. Fiorenza, with Sarah Coakley and James H. Evans. *Modern Christian Thought*. 2nd ed. 2 vols. Minneapolis: Fortress, 2006.

Locke, John. *An Essay concerning Humane Understanding: In Four Books*. 4th ed. London: Awnsham & John Churchill & Samuel Manship, 1700.

Lombard, Peter. *See* Peter Lombard

Longenecker, Richard N. *Biblical Exegesis in the Apostolic Period*. 2nd ed. Grand Rapids: Eerdmans, 1999.

Louth, Andrew. *The Origins of the Christian Mystical Tradition: From Plato to Denys*. New ed. Oxford: Oxford University Press, 2007.

Lubac, Henri de. *History and Spirit: The Understanding of Scripture according to Origen*. Translated by Anne Englund Nash. San Francisco: Ignatius Press, 2007.

———. *Medieval Exegesis: The Four Senses of Scripture*. 3 vols. Ressourcement. Grand Rapids: Eerdmans, 1998–2009.

Luibheid. *See* Dionysius the Areopagite

Luther, Martin. *Galatians*. In *LW* 26.

———. *Preface to the Epistles of St. James and St. Jude*. In *LW* 35.

———. *To the Christian Nobility of the German Nation*. In *LW* 44.

Lyotard, Jean-François. *The Postmodern Condition: A Report on Knowledge*. Translated by Geoff Bennington and Brian Massumi. Theory and History of Literature. Minneapolis: University of Minnesota Press, 1984.

Mack, Burton L. *The Lost Gospel: The Book of Q and Christian Origins*. San Francisco: HarperSanFrancisco, 1993.

Madigan, Kevin. *Medieval Christianity: A New History*. New Haven: Yale University Press, 2015.

Magennis, Hugh. *Translating "Beowulf": Modern Versions in English Verse*. Cambridge: Brewer, 2011.

Martens, Peter W. *Origen and Scripture: The Contours of the Exegetical Life*. Oxford: Oxford University Press, 2012.

Matter, E. Ann. "The Church Fathers and the *Glossa Ordinaria*." In *The Reception of the Church Fathers in the West: From the Carolingians to the Maurists*, edited by Irena Backus, 1:83–111. Leiden: Brill, 1997.

McDonald, Grantley. *Biblical Criticism in Early Modern Europe: Erasmus, the Johannine Comma and Trinitarian Debate*. Cambridge: Cambridge University Press, 2016.

McDonald, Lee Martin. "Lists and Catalogs of New Testament Collections." In McDonald and Sanders, *The Canon Debate*, 591–97.

McDonald, Lee Martin, and James A. Sanders, eds. *The Canon Debate*. Peabody, MA: Hendrickson, 2002.

McGinn, Bernard. *The Presence of God: A History of Western Christian Mysticism*. 6 vols. in 7. New York: Crossroad, 1991–2017.

McKim, Donald K., ed. *Historical Handbook of Major Biblical Interpreters*. Downers Grove, IL: InterVarsity, 1998.

———. "Perkins, William." In *Historical Handbook of Major Biblical Interpreters*, edited by Donald K. McKim, 231–35. Downers Grove, IL: InterVarsity, 1998.

———. *Ramism in William Perkins' Theology*. American University Studies: Series 7, Theology and Religion. New York: Peter Lang, 1987.

McKnight, Scot. *Jesus and His Death: Historiography, the Historical Jesus, and Atonement Theory*. Waco: Baylor University Press, 2005.

Meier, John P. *A Marginal Jew: Rethinking the Historical Jesus*. Vol. 1, *The Roots of the Problem and the Person*. Anchor Bible Reference Library. New York: Doubleday, 1991.

Meister Eckhart. *Meister Eckhart: The Essential Sermons, Commentaries, Treatises, and Defense*. Translated by Edmund Colledge and Bernard McGinn. CWS. New York: Paulist Press, 1981.

Melanchthon, Philip. *Luther and the Paris Theologians*. In *Melanchthon: Selected Writings*. Translated by Charles Leander Hill. Minneapolis: Augsburg, 1962.

Methodius of Olympus. *On the Resurrection*. In PG 18.

Muller, Richard A. "Biblical Interpretation in the Era of the Reformation: The View from the Middle Ages." In Muller and Thompson, *Biblical Interpretation*, 8–13.

———. "The Hermeneutic of Promise and Fulfillment in Calvin's Exegesis of the Old Testament Prophecies of the Kingdom." In Steinmetz, *The Bible in the Sixteenth Century*, 68–82.

———. *Post-Reformation Reformed Dogmatics*. Vol. 2, *Holy Scripture*. 2nd ed. Grand Rapids: Baker Academic, 2003.

Muller, Richard A., and John L. Thompson, eds. *Biblical Interpretation in the Era of the Reformation*. Grand Rapids: Eerdmans, 1996.

The Nag Hammadi Scriptures. Edited by Marvin Meyer, with Wolf-Peter Funk et al. San Francisco: HarperOne, 2007.

Nellen, Henk J. M. *Hugo Grotius: A Lifelong Struggle for Peace in Church and State, 1583–1645*. Translated by J. C. Grayson. Boston: Brill, 2014.

Nellen, Henk J. M., and Jan Bloemendal. "Erasmus's Biblical Project: Some Thoughts and Observations on Its Scope, Its Impact in the Sixteenth Century and Reception in the Seventeenth and Eighteenth Centuries." *Church History and Religious Culture* 96, no. 4 (2016): 595–635.

Nicholas of Lyra. "Commentary on Exodus 3." In *The Theological Interpretation of Scripture: Classic and Contemporary Readings*, edited by Stephen E. Fowl, 114–28. Oxford: Blackwell, 1997.

———. "Incipit prologus." In PL 113.

———. "Prologus in moralitates." In PL 113.

———. "Prologus secundus." In PL 113.

Nicholas of Lyra et al. *Biblia sacra cum glossa ordinaria primum quidem a Strabo Fuldensi monacho . . . et postilla Nicolai Lyrani Franciscani*. Vol. 1. Douai: Baltazar Bellerus, 1617.

Oberman, Heiko A. *The Dawn of the Reformation: Essays in Late Medieval and Early Reformation Thought*. 1986. Reprint, Grand Rapids: Eerdmans, 1992.

————. *Forerunners of the Reformation: The Shape of Late Medieval Thought Illustrated by Key Documents*. Translations by Paul L. Nyhus. New York: Holt, Rinehart & Winston, 1966.

————. *The Harvest of Medieval Theology: Gabriel Biel and Late Medieval Nominalism*. 3rd ed. 1983. Reprint, Grand Rapids: Baker Academic, 2000.

Oden, Thomas C., and Christopher H. Hall, eds. ACCS. Downers Grove, IL: InterVarsity, 1998–2010.

Oecolampadius, Johannes. *An Exposition of Genesis*. Translated by Mickey L. Mattox. Milwaukee: Marquette University Press, 2013.

O'Keefe, John J., and R. R. Reno. *Sanctified Vision: An Introduction to Early Christian Interpretation of the Bible*. Baltimore: Johns Hopkins University Press, 2005.

Ong, Walter J. *Ramus, Method, and the Decay of Dialogue: From the Art of Discourse to the Art of Reason*. Cambridge, MA: Harvard University Press, 1958.

Origen. *Commentary on the Gospel according to John, Books 13–32*. Translated by Ronald E. Heine. FC 89. Washington, DC: Catholic University of America Press, 1993.

————. *Contra Celsum*. Translated by Henry Chadwick. Cambridge: Cambridge University Press, 1965.

————. *De oratione*. In PG 11. ET in *Prayer; Exhortation to Martyrdom*. Translated by John J. O'Meara. ACW 19. Westminster, MD: Newman, 1954.

————. *De principiis*. ET, *On First Principles*. Translated by G. W. Butterworth. Foreword by John C. Cavadini. Notre Dame, IN: Ave Maria Press, 2013.

————. *Homilies on Genesis and Exodus*. Translated by Ronald E. Heine. FC 71. Washington, DC: Catholic University of America Press, 1982.

————. *Homilies on Jeremiah; Homily on 1 Kings 28*. Translated by John Clark Smith. FC 97. Washington, DC: Catholic University of America Press, 1998.

————. *Homilies on Luke*. Translated by Joseph T. Lienhard. FC 94. Washington, DC: Catholic University of America Press, 1996.

————. "Letter of Origen to Gregory Thaumaturgus." In *St. Gregory Thaumaturgus: Life and Works*. Translated by Michael Slusser. FC 98. Washington, DC: Catholic University of America Press, 1998.

Ozment, Steven. *The Age of Reform, 1250–1550: An Intellectual and Religious History of Late Medieval and Reformation Europe*. New Haven: Yale University Press, 1980.

Pagels, Elaine. *The Gnostic Paul: Gnostic Exegesis of the Pauline Letters*. 1975. Reprint, New York: Continuum, 1992.

Pak, G. Sujin. *The Judaizing Calvin: Sixteenth-Century Debates over the Messianic Psalms*. Oxford Studies in Historical Theology. New York: Oxford University Press, 2009.

Patte, Daniel, and Vasile Mihoc, eds. *Greek Patristic and Eastern Orthodox Interpretations of Romans*. Romans through History and Culture 9. New York: Bloomsbury T&T Clark, 2013.

Patterson, W. B. *William Perkins and the Making of a Protestant England*. Oxford: Oxford University Press, 2014.

Peckham, John C. "Epistemological Authority in the Polemic of Irenaeus." *Didaskalia* 19, no. 1 (2008): 51–70.

Pelikan, Jaroslav. *The Christian Tradition: A History of the Development of Doctrine.* 5 vols. Chicago: University of Chicago Press, 1971–89.

———. *Development of Christian Doctrine: Some Historical Prolegomena.* New Haven: Yale University Press, 1969.

———. *The Emergence of the Catholic Tradition (100–600).* Vol. 1 (1971) of *The Christian Tradition.*

———. *Luther the Expositor: Introduction to the Reformer's Exegetical Writings.* In *LW,* Companion Volume. St. Louis: Concordia, 1959.

———. *Reformation of Church and Dogma (1300–1700).* Vol. 4 (1984) of *The Christian Tradition.*

———. *The Reformation of the Bible/The Bible of the Reformation.* New Haven: Yale University Press, 1996.

———. *Whose Bible Is It? A Short History of the Scriptures.* New York: Penguin, 2005.

Perkins, William. *The Arte of Prophecying, or, a Treatise concerning the Sacred and Onely True Manner and Methode of Preaching.* In *Workes,* vol. 2.

———. *A Commentarie, or, Exposition upon the five first Chapters of the Epistle to the Galatians.* London: John Legatt, 1617.

———. *A Warning against the Idolatrie of the Last Times, and an Instruction Touching Religious or Divine Worship.* In *Workes,* vol. 1.

———. *The Whole Treatise of the Cases of Conscience, Distinguished into Three Bookes.* In *Workes,* vol. 2.

———. *The Workes of the Famous and Worthie Minister of Christ, in the Universitie of Cambridge, M. W. Perkins.* 3 vols. Cambridge: John Legate et al., Printer to the University of Cambridge, 1608–13.

Peter Lombard. *The Sentences.* 4 vols. Translated by Giulio Silano. Toronto: Pontifical Institute of Mediaeval Studies, 2007–10.

Philips, Obbe. *A Confession.* In *Spiritual and Anabaptist Writers: Documents Illustrative of the Radical Reformation,* edited by George Huntston Williams and Angel Mergal. Library of Christian Classics. Philadelphia: Westminster, 1957.

Philo. *On Abraham. On Joseph. On Moses.* Translated by F. H. Colson. LCL 289. Cambridge, MA: Harvard University Press, 1935.

Pietersma, Albert, and Benjamin G. Wright, eds. *A New English Translation of the Septuagint.* New York: Oxford University Press, 2007. Corrected and emended, 2014, http://ccat.sas.upenn.edu/nets/edition/.

Plantinga, Alvin. *Warranted Christian Belief.* New York/Oxford: Oxford University Press, 2000.

Pope, Marvin H. *Song of Songs.* Anchor Bible. Garden City, NY: Doubleday, 1977.

Popkin, Richard H. *The History of Scepticism from Erasmus to Spinoza.* Berkeley: University of California Press, 1979.

Preus, J. Samuel. *Spinoza and the Irrelevance of Biblical Authority.* Cambridge: Cambridge University Press, 2001.

Preus, Robert D. *The Theology of Post-Reformation Lutheranism: A Study of Theological Prolegomena*. St. Louis: Concordia Publishing House, 1970.

Radner, Ephraim. *Time and the Word: Figural Reading of the Christian Scriptures*. Grand Rapids: Eerdmans, 2016.

Ramsey, Boniface. Introduction to John Cassian, *The Conferences*, 5–24.

Rashdall, Hastings. *The Universities of Europe in the Middle Ages*. 2 vols. in 3. Oxford: Clarendon, 1895.

Reno, R. R. "While We're at It." *First Things*. August/September 2017, 66–69.

Reventlow, Henning Graf. *History of Biblical Interpretation*. 4 vols. Atlanta: Society of Biblical Literature, 2009–10.

Robinson, James M., Paul Hoffmann, and John S. Kloppenborg, eds. *The Critical Edition of Q: A Synopsis Including the Gospels of Matthew and Luke and Thomas with English, German, and French Translations of Q and Thomas*. Hermeneia. Minneapolis: Fortress, 2000.

Rocca, Gregory P. *Speaking the Incomprehensible God: Thomas Aquinas on the Interplay of Positive and Negative Theology*. Washington, DC: Catholic University of America Press, 2004.

Rorem, Paul. *Pseudo-Dionysius: A Commentary on the Texts and an Introduction to Their Influence*. New York: Oxford University Press, 1993.

Roukema, Riemer. "The Good Samaritan in Ancient Christianity." *Vigiliae Christianae* 58, no. 1 (2004): 56–74.

Rylaarsdam, David. *John Chrysostom on Divine Pedagogy: The Coherence of His Theology and Preaching*. Oxford Early Christian Studies. Oxford: Oxford University Press, 2014.

Saebø, Magne, ed. *Hebrew Bible/Old Testament: The History of Its Interpretation*. 3 vols. in 5. Göttingen: Vandenhoeck & Ruprecht, 1996–2015.

Salomon, David A. *An Introduction to the "Glossa Ordinaria" as Medieval Hypertext*. Cardiff: University of Wales Press, 2012.

Sandys-Wunsch, John. *What Have They Done to the Bible? A History of Modern Biblical Interpretation*. Collegeville, MN: Liturgical Press, 2005.

Schaff, Philip, ed. *The Creeds of Christendom, with a History and Critical Notes*. 6th ed. 3 vols. 1931. Reprint, Grand Rapids: Baker, 1998.

Schreiner, Susan E. *Are You Alone Wise? The Search for Certainty in the Early Modern Era*. Oxford Studies in Historical Theology. New York: Oxford University Press, 2010.

Schreiner, Thomas R. *Paul, Apostle of God's Glory in Christ: A Pauline Theology*. Downers Grove, IL: InterVarsity, 2001.

Schweitzer, Albert. *The Quest of the Historical Jesus: A Critical Study of Its Progress from Reimarus to Wrede*. Translated by W. Montgomery. London: Adam & Charles Black, 1910.

The Secret Book of John. In *The Nag Hammadi Scriptures*. New York: HarperOne, 2007.

Sheehan, Jonathan. *The Enlightenment Bible: Translation, Scholarship, Culture*. Princeton: Princeton University Press, 2005.

Sheppard, Gerald T. "Interpretation of the Old Testament between Reformation and Modernity." In William Perkins, *A Commentary on Hebrews 11*, edited by John H. Augustine, 46–70. Pilgrim Classic Commentaries. New York: Pilgrim Press, 1991.

Sheridan, Mark, ed. *Genesis 12–50*. ACCS. Downers Grove, IL: InterVarsity, 2002.

———. *Language for God in Patristic Tradition: Wrestling with Biblical Anthropomorphism*. Downers Grove, IL: IVP Academic, 2015.

Silano, Giulio. Introduction to Peter Lombard, *The Sentences*, 1:xix–xxvi.

Silva, Moisés. *Has the Church Misread the Bible? The History of Interpretation in the Light of Current Issues*. Foundations of Contemporary Interpretation 1. Grand Rapids: Academie, 1987.

Simonetti, Manlio. *Biblical Interpretation in the Early Church: An Historical Introduction to Patristic Exegesis*. New York: T&T Clark, 2002.

Smalley, Beryl. *The Study of the Bible in the Middle Ages*. New York: Philosophical Library, 1952.

Smith, James K. A. *Who's Afraid of Postmodernism? Taking Derrida, Lyotard, and Foucault to Church*. Grand Rapids: Baker Academic, 2006.

Smith, Lesley. *The Glossa Ordinaria: The Making of a Medieval Bible Commentary*. Leiden: Brill, 2009.

Spinoza, Benedict de. *Theological-Political Treatise*. Edited by Jonathan Israel. Cambridge Texts in the History of Philosophy. Cambridge: Cambridge University Press, 2007.

Stanglin, Keith D. "Adopted in Christ, Appointed to the Slaughter: Calvin's Interpretation of the Maccabean Psalms." In *Biblical Interpretation and Doctrinal Formulation in the Reformed Tradition: Essays in Honor of James De Jong*, edited by Arie C. Leder and Richard A. Muller, 69–93. Grand Rapids: Reformation Heritage Books, 2014.

———. "'Baptized in the Sea': An Invitation to Typological Interpretation." *Leaven: A Journal of Christian Ministry* 21, no. 2 (2013): 70–74.

———. "*Bona Conscientia Paradisus*: An Augustinian-Arminian Trope." In *Church and School in Early Modern Protestantism: Studies in Honor of Richard A. Muller on the Maturation of a Theological Tradition*, edited by Jordan J. Ballor, David S. Sytsma, and Jason Zuidema, 361–72. Studies in the History of Christian Traditions 170. Boston: Brill, 2013.

———. *The Missing Public Disputations of Jacobus Arminius: Introduction, Text, and Notes*. Boston: Brill, 2010.

———. "Restorationism and Church History: Strange Bedfellows?" *Christian Studies* 26 (2013–14): 21–32.

———. "The Restoration Movement, the Habit of Schism, and a Proposal for Unity." *Christian Studies* 28 (2016): 7–20.

———. "The Rise and Fall of Biblical Perspicuity: Remonstrants and the Transition toward Modern Exegesis." *Church History* 83, no. 1 (2014): 38–59.

———. "*Spiritus Propheticus*: Spirit and Prophecy in Calvin's Old Testament Exegesis." *Calvin Theological Journal* 50, no. 1 (2015): 23–42.

Stein, Robert H. *Jesus the Messiah: A Survey of the Life of Christ*. Downers Grove, IL: InterVarsity, 1996.

————. *The Method and Message of Jesus' Teachings*. Philadelphia: Westminster, 1978.

Steinmetz, David C., ed. *The Bible in the Sixteenth Century*. Durham, NC: Duke University Press, 1990.

————. "Doing History as Theologians." *Calvin Theological Journal* 50, no. 2 (2015): 174–80.

————. "John Calvin as an Interpreter of the Bible." In *Calvin and the Bible*, edited by Donald K. McKim, 282–91. New York: Cambridge University Press, 2006.

————. "The Superiority of Pre-critical Exegesis." *Theology Today* 37 (1980): 27–38.

————. *Taking the Long View: Christian Theology in Historical Perspective*. Oxford: Oxford University Press, 2011.

Stevenson, James, ed. *Creeds, Councils, and Controversies: Documents Illustrating the History of the Church, AD 337–461*. Revised by W. H. C. Frend. 3rd ed. Grand Rapids: Baker Academic, 2012.

Stewart, Columba. *Cassian the Monk*. Oxford Studies in Historical Theology. New York: Oxford University Press, 1998.

Strauss, David Friedrich. *The Life of Jesus Critically Examined*. 2nd ed. Translated by George Eliot. New York: Macmillan, 1892.

Stuhlmacher, Peter. *Historical Criticism and Theological Interpretation of Scripture: Toward a Hermeneutics of Consent*. Translated by Roy A. Harrisville. Minneapolis: Fortress, 1977.

Suetonius. *Lives of the Caesars*. Translated by J. C. Rolfe. 2 vols. LCL 31 and 38. Cambridge, MA: Harvard University Press, 1914.

Tanner, Norman P., ed. *Decrees of the Ecumenical Councils*. Vol. 2, *Trent to Vatican II*. Washington, DC: Georgetown University Press, 1990.

Taylor, Marion Ann, ed. *Handbook of Women Biblical Interpreters: A Historical and Biographical Guide*. Grand Rapids: Baker Academic, 2012.

Tertullian. *Against Marcion*. In *ANF* 3.

————. *On Prescription against Heretics*. In *ANF* 3.

Teske, Roland. "The Good Samaritan (Lk 10:29–37) in Augustine's Exegesis." In Van Fleteren and Schnaubelt, *Augustine: Biblical Exegete*, 347–67.

Theodore of Mopsuestia. *Letter to the Galatians*. In *The Commentaries on the Minor Epistles of Paul*, translated by Rowan A. Greer, 2–169. Atlanta: Society of Biblical Literature, 2010.

Theodoret of Cyrus. *The Questions on the Octateuch*. Vol. 1, *On Genesis and Exodus*. Translated by Robert C. Hill. Library of Early Christianity 1. Washington, DC: Catholic University of America Press, 2007.

Thomas à Kempis. *Of the Imitation of Christ*. Philadelphia: Henry Altemus Co., n.d.

Thomas Aquinas. *Summa theologiae*. Latin/English edition. Translated by Laurence Shapcote, OP. Edited by the Aquinas Institute. 8 vols. Lander, WY: Aquinas Institute, 2012.

Thompson, John L. *Reading the Bible with the Dead: What You Can Learn from the History of Exegesis That You Can't Learn from Exegesis Alone*. Grand Rapids: Eerdmans, 2007.

Torjesen, Karen Jo. *Hermeneutical Procedure and Theological Method in Origen's Exegesis*. Patristische Texte und Studien 28. Berlin: de Gruyter, 1985.

Turner, James. *Philology: The Forgotten Origins of the Modern Humanities*. Princeton: Princeton University Press, 2014.

Turretin, Francis. *Institutes of Elenctic Theology*. 3 vols. Translated by George Musgrave Giger. Edited by James T. Dennison Jr. Phillipsburg, NJ: P&R, 1992.

Tyconius. *The Book of Rules*. Translated by William S. Babcock. Texts and Translations 31. Atlanta: Scholars Press, 1989.

Tyndale, William. *The Obedience of a Christian Man*. In *The Works of the English Reformers: William Tyndale and John Frith*, edited by Thomas Russell, 1:163–379. London: Ebenezer Palmer, 1831.

Valla, Lorenzo. *On the Donation of Constantine*. Translated by G. W. Bowersock. Cambridge, MA: Harvard University Press, 2008.

van den Belt, Henk. "*Sola Scriptura*: An Inadequate Slogan for the Authority of Scripture." *Calvin Theological Journal* 51, no. 2 (2016): 204–26.

van Fleteren, Frederick. "Principles of Augustine's Hermeneutic: An Overview." In Fleteren and Schnaubelt, *Augustine: Biblical Exegete*, 1–32.

van Fleteren, Frederick, and Joseph C. Schnaubelt, eds. *Augustine: Biblical Exegete*. New York: Peter Lang, 2001.

Vanhoozer, Kevin J. *Is There a Meaning in This Text? The Bible, the Reader, and the Morality of Literary Knowledge*. Grand Rapids: Zondervan, 1998.

van Liere, Frans. *An Introduction to the Medieval Bible*. New York: Cambridge University Press, 2014.

———. "The Literal Sense of the Books of Samuel and Kings: From Andrew of St Victor to Nicholas of Lyra." In Krey and L. Smith, *Nicholas of Lyra*, 59–81.

Vincent of Lérins. *A Commonitory*. In *NPNF²*, vol. 11.

Walton, John H. *Genesis 1 as Ancient Cosmology*. Winona Lake, IN: Eisenbrauns, 2011.

———. *The Lost World of Genesis One: Ancient Cosmology and the Origins Debate*. Downers Grove, IL: IVP Academic, 2009.

Wansbrough, Henry. *The Use and Abuse of the Bible: A Brief History of Biblical Interpretation*. New York: T&T Clark, 2010.

Webster, John. *Holy Scripture: A Dogmatic Sketch*. Current Issues in Theology. Cambridge: Cambridge University Press, 2003.

Wells, David F. *Above All Earthly Pow'rs: Christ in a Postmodern World*. Grand Rapids: Eerdmans, 2005.

Wengert, Timothy J. *Reading the Bible with Martin Luther: An Introductory Guide*. Grand Rapids: Baker Academic, 2013.

Wevers, John William. "The Interpretative Character and Significance of the Septuagint Version." In Saebø, *Hebrew Bible/Old Testament*, 84–107.

Whitford, David M. "Yielding to the Prejudices of His Times: Erasmus and the Comma Johanneum." *Church History and Religious Culture* 95, no. 1 (2015): 19–40.

Wilken, Robert Louis, ed. The Church's Bible. Grand Rapids: Eerdmans, 2003–.

———. *The Spirit of Early Christian Thought: Seeking the Face of God*. New Haven: Yale University Press, 2003.

Williams, Rowan. *Arius: Heresy and Tradition*. Rev. ed. Grand Rapids: Eerdmans, 2002.

Witherington, Ben, III. *Paul's Letter to the Romans: A Socio-rhetorical Commentary*. Grand Rapids: Eerdmans, 2004.

Witt, Ronald G. "The Humanist Movement." In *Handbook of European History, 1400–1600: Late Middle Ages, Renaissance, and Reformation*, edited by Thomas A. Brady Jr., Heiko A. Oberman, and James D. Tracy, 2:93–125. Grand Rapids: Eerdmans, 1996.

Yarchin, William, ed. *History of Biblical Interpretation: A Reader*. 2004. Reprint, Grand Rapids: Baker Academic, 2011.

Young, Davis A., and Ralph F. Stearley. *The Bible, Rocks, and Time: Geological Evidence for the Age of the Earth*. Downers Grove, IL: InterVarsity, 2008.

Young, Frances M. "Alexandrian and Antiochene Exegesis." In Hauser and Watson, *A History of Biblical Interpretation*, 1:334–54.

———. *Biblical Exegesis and the Formation of Christian Culture*. Grand Rapids: Baker Academic, 2002.

Zaharopoulos, Dimitri Z. *Theodore of Mopsuestia on the Bible: A Study of His Old Testament Exegesis*. Mahwah, NJ: Paulist Press, 1989.

Zinn, Grover A., Jr. "Exegesis and Spirituality in the Writings of Gregory the Great." In *Gregory the Great: A Symposium*, edited by John C. Cavadini, 168–80. Notre Dame, IN: University of Notre Dame Press, 1995.

Scripture Index

Name Index

Subject Index